SONGS TO MAKE YOU SMILE

nkaya

TOKYOPOP®

HAMBURG // LONDON // LOS ANGELES // TOKYO

Songs to Make You Smile
Created by Natsuki Takaya

Translation - Alethea & Athena Nibley
English Adaptation - Paul Morrissey
Copy Editor - Daniella Orihuela-Gruber
Retouch and Lettering - Star Print Brokers
Production Artist - Rui Kyo
Graphic Designer - Louis Csontos

Editor - Cindy Suzuki
Print Production Manager - Lucas Rivera
Managing Editor - Vy Nguyen
Senior Designer - Louis Csontos
Art Director - Al-Insan Lashley
Director of Sales and Manufacturing - Allyson De Simone
Associate Publisher - Marco F. Pavia
President and C.O.O. - John Parker
C.E.O. and Chief Creative Officer - Stu Levy

A  Manga

TOKYOPOP and  are trademarks or registered trademarks of TOKYOPOP Inc.

TOKYOPOP Inc.
5900 Wilshire Blvd. Suite 2000
Los Angeles, CA 90036

E-mail: info@TOKYOPOP.com
Come visit us online at www.TOKYOPOP.com

ISBN: 978-1-4278-1797-6

First TOKYOPOP printing: May 2010
10 9 8 7 6 5 4 3 2 1
Printed in the USA

SONGS TO MAKE YOU SMILE

NATSUKI TAKAYA

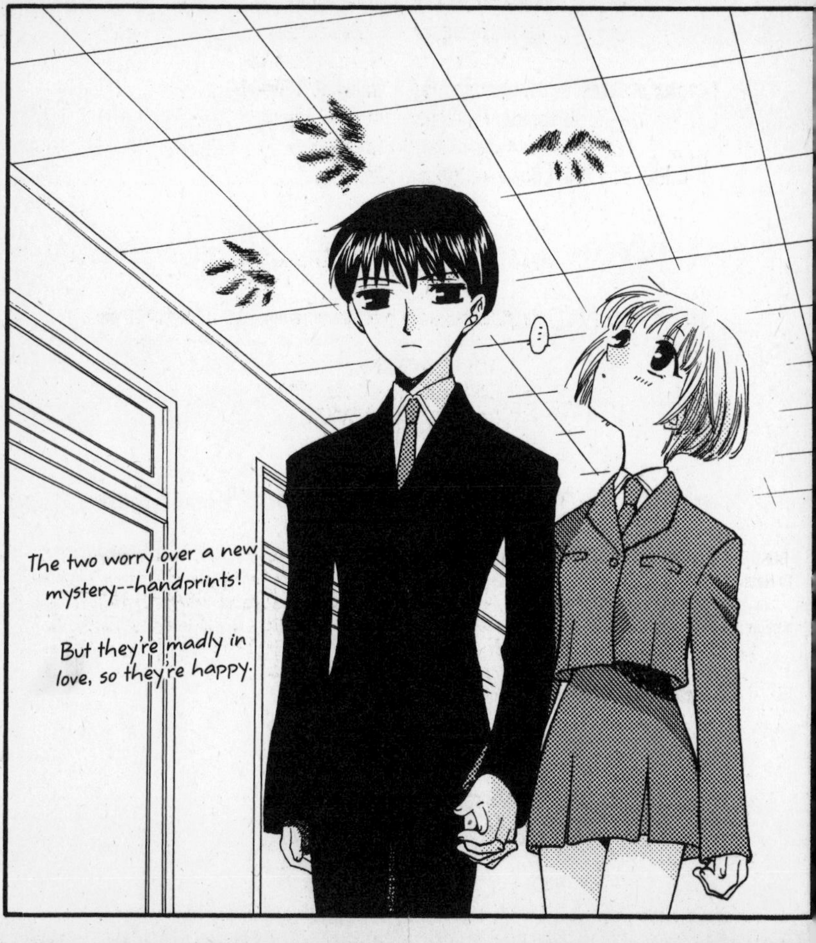
...
The two worry over a new mystery--handprints!
But they're madly in love, so they're happy.

CONTENTS

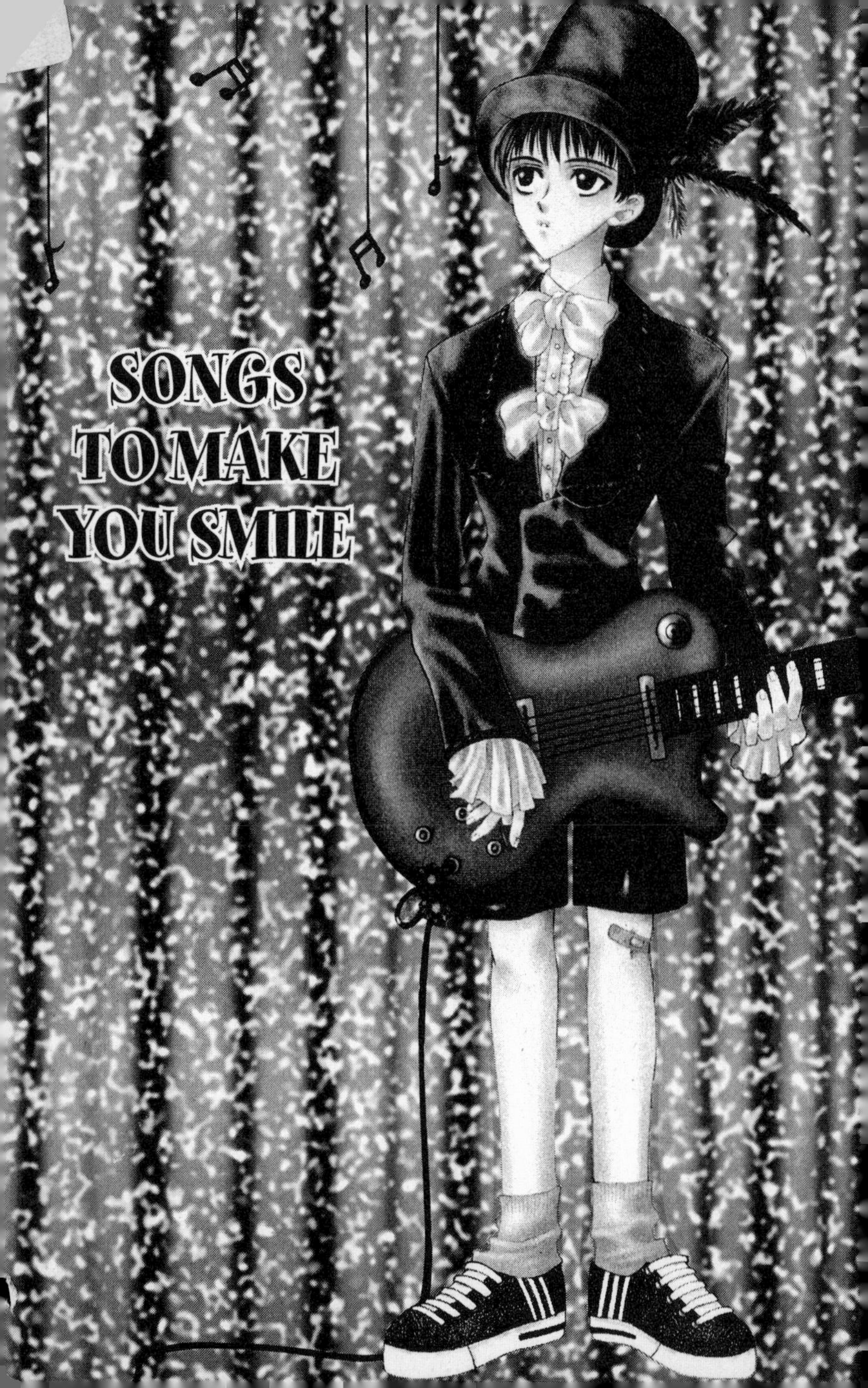
SONGS
TO MAKE
YOU SMILE

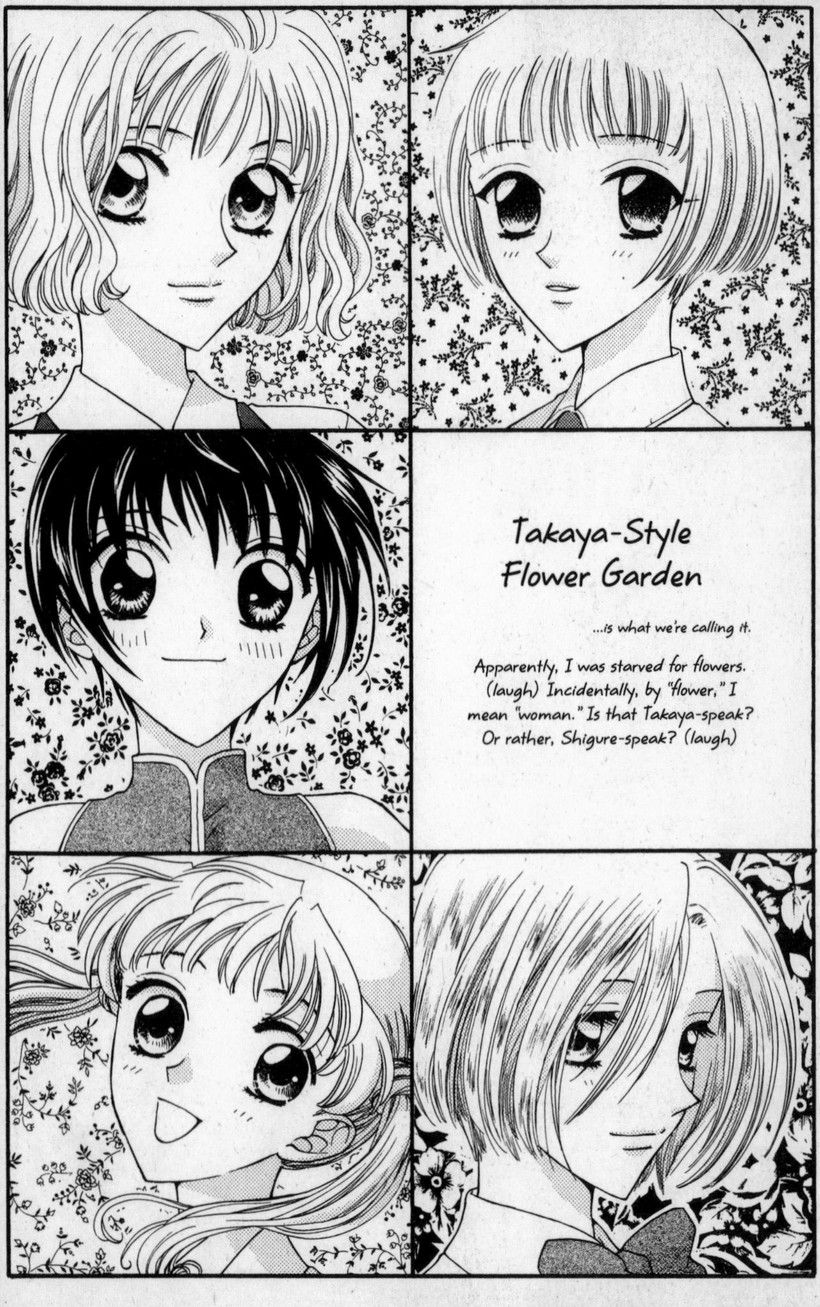
Takaya-Style
Flower Garden
...is what we're calling it.
Apparently, I was starved for flowers. (laugh) Incidentally, by "flower," I mean "woman." Is that Takaya-speak? Or rather, Shigure-speak? (laugh)

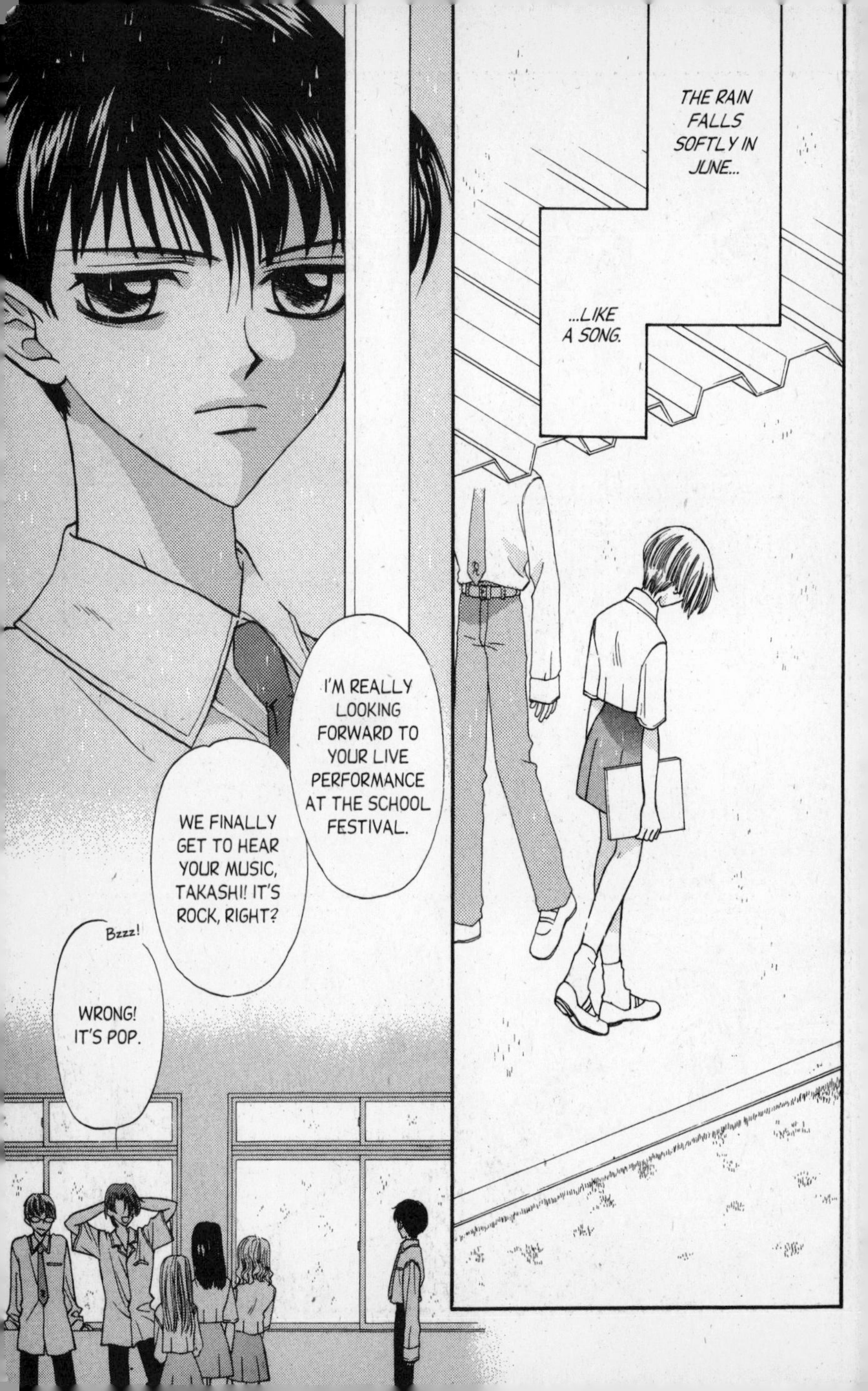
THE RAIN FALLS SOFTLY IN JUNE...
...LIKE A SONG.
I'M REALLY LOOKING FORWARD TO YOUR LIVE PERFORMANCE AT THE SCHOOL FESTIVAL.
WE FINALLY GET TO HEAR YOUR MUSIC, TAKASHI! IT'S ROCK, RIGHT?
Bzzz!
WRONG! IT'S POP.

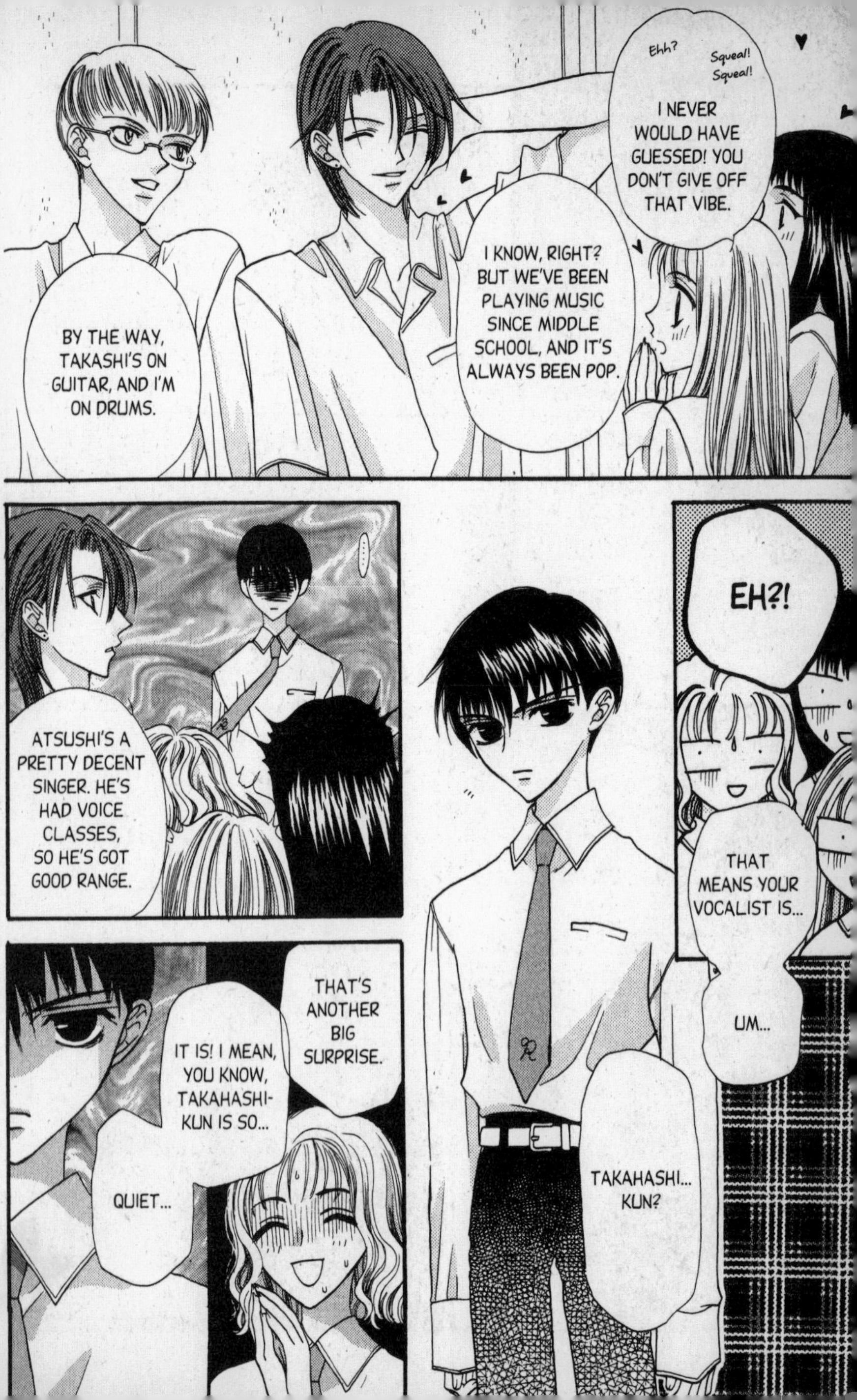
Ehh?
Squeal! Squeal!
I NEVER WOULD HAVE GUESSED! YOU DON'T GIVE OFF THAT VIBE.
I KNOW, RIGHT? BUT WE'VE BEEN PLAYING MUSIC SINCE MIDDLE SCHOOL, AND IT'S ALWAYS BEEN POP.
BY THE WAY, TAKASHI'S ON GUITAR, AND I'M ON DRUMS.
EH?!
THAT MEANS YOUR VOCALIST IS...
UM...
TAKAHASHI... KUN?
ATSUSHI'S A PRETTY DECENT SINGER. HE'S HAD VOICE CLASSES, SO HE'S GOT GOOD RANGE.
THAT'S ANOTHER BIG SURPRISE.
IT IS! I MEAN, YOU KNOW, TAKAHASHI-KUN IS SO...
QUIET...

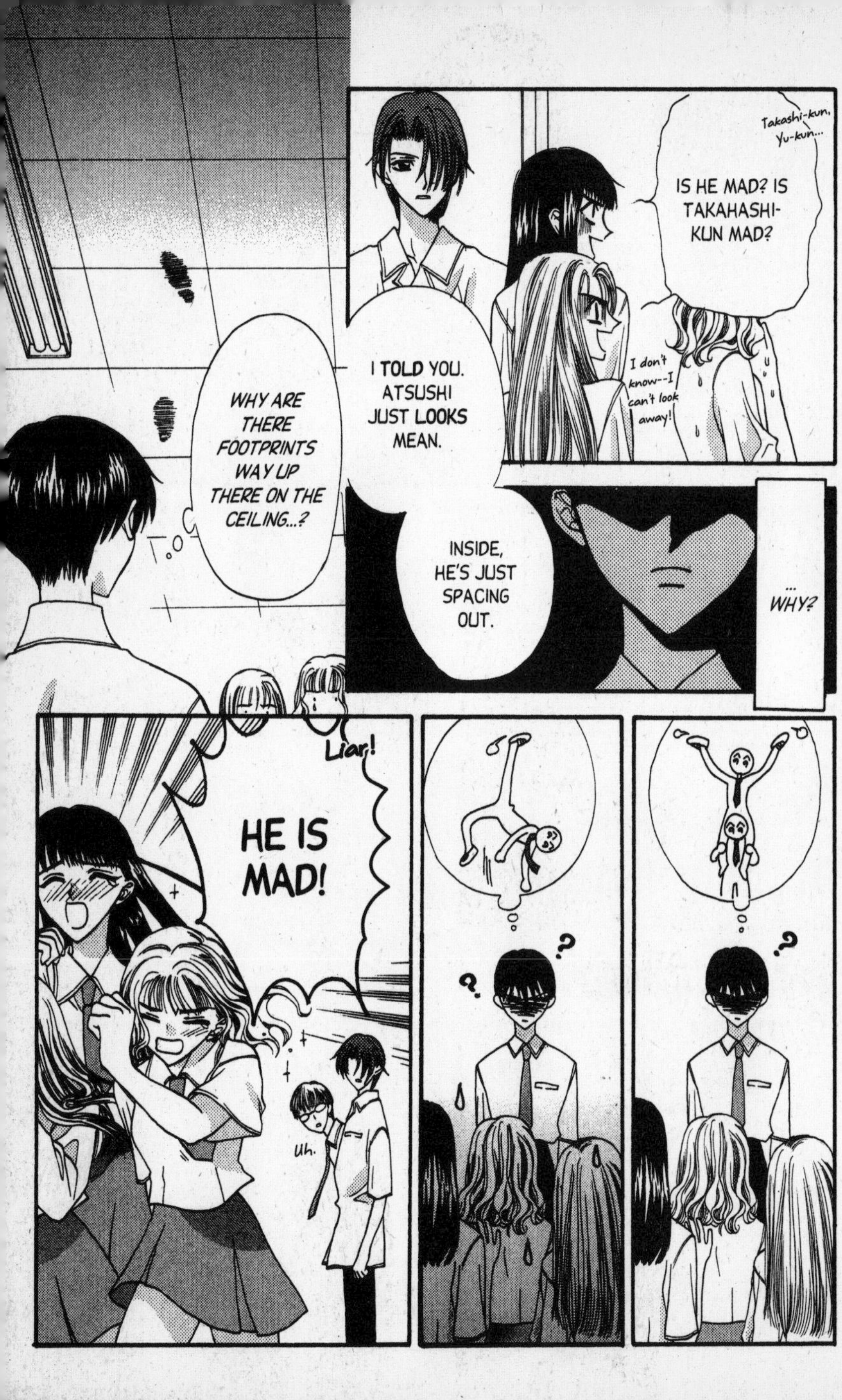

Takashi-kun, Yu-kun...
IS HE MAD? IS TAKAHASHI-KUN MAD?
I don't know--I can't look away!
I TOLD YOU. ATSUSHI JUST LOOKS MEAN.
INSIDE, HE'S JUST SPACING OUT.
...WHY?
WHY ARE THERE FOOTPRINTS WAY UP THERE ON THE CEILING...?
Liar!
HE IS MAD!
Uh.

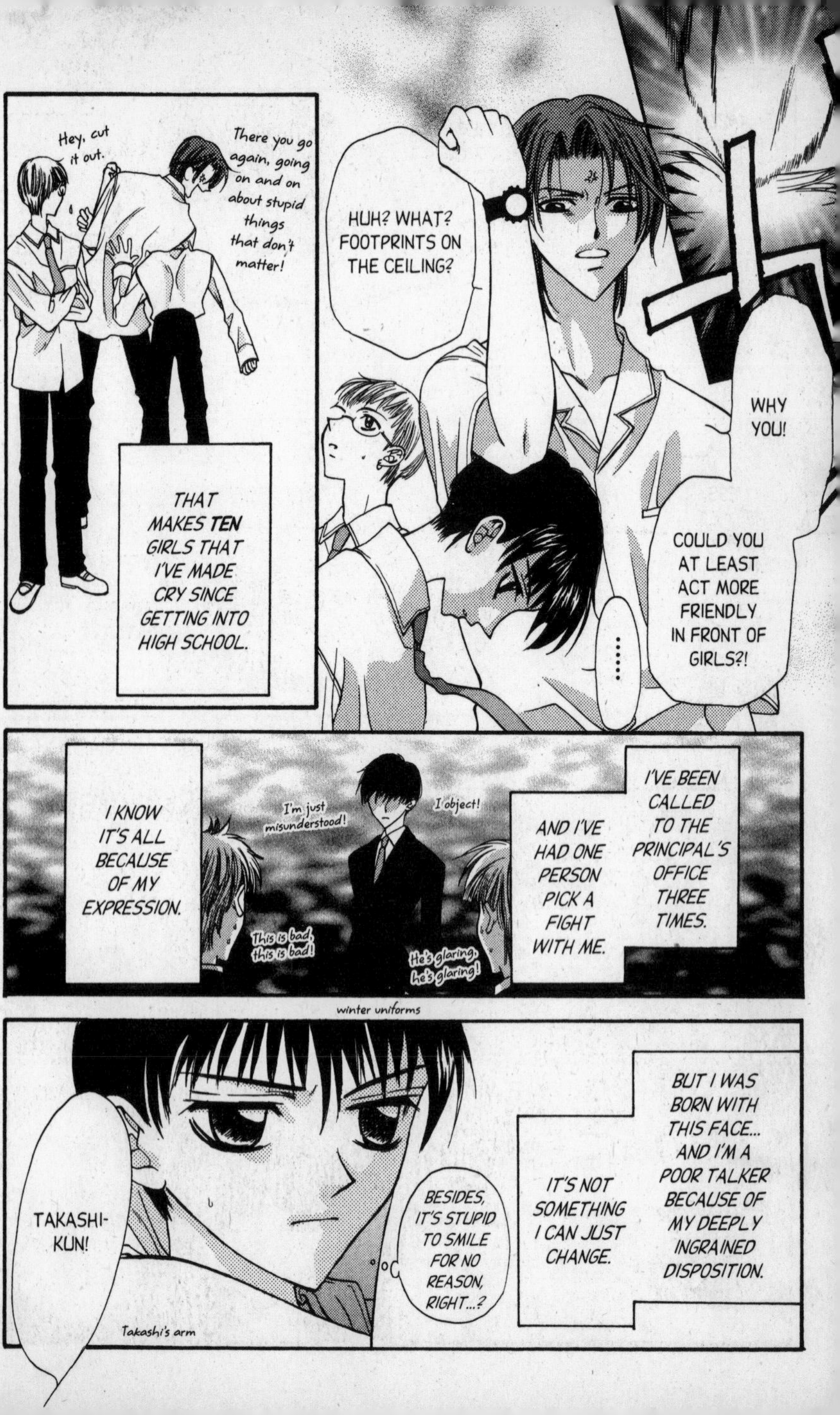
WHY YOU!
HUH? WHAT? FOOTPRINTS ON THE CEILING?
COULD YOU AT LEAST ACT MORE FRIENDLY IN FRONT OF GIRLS?!
......
There you go again, going on and on about stupid things that don't matter!
Hey, cut it out.
THAT MAKES **TEN** GIRLS THAT I'VE MADE CRY SINCE GETTING INTO HIGH SCHOOL.
I'VE BEEN CALLED TO THE PRINCIPAL'S OFFICE THREE TIMES.
AND I'VE HAD ONE PERSON PICK A FIGHT WITH ME.
I object!
He's glaring, he's glaring!
I'm just misunderstood!
This is bad, this is bad!
I KNOW IT'S ALL BECAUSE OF MY EXPRESSION.
winter uniforms
BUT I WAS BORN WITH THIS FACE... AND I'M A POOR TALKER BECAUSE OF MY DEEPLY INGRAINED DISPOSITION.
IT'S NOT SOMETHING I CAN JUST CHANGE.
BESIDES, IT'S STUPID TO SMILE FOR NO REASON, RIGHT...?
TAKASHI-KUN!
Takashi's arm

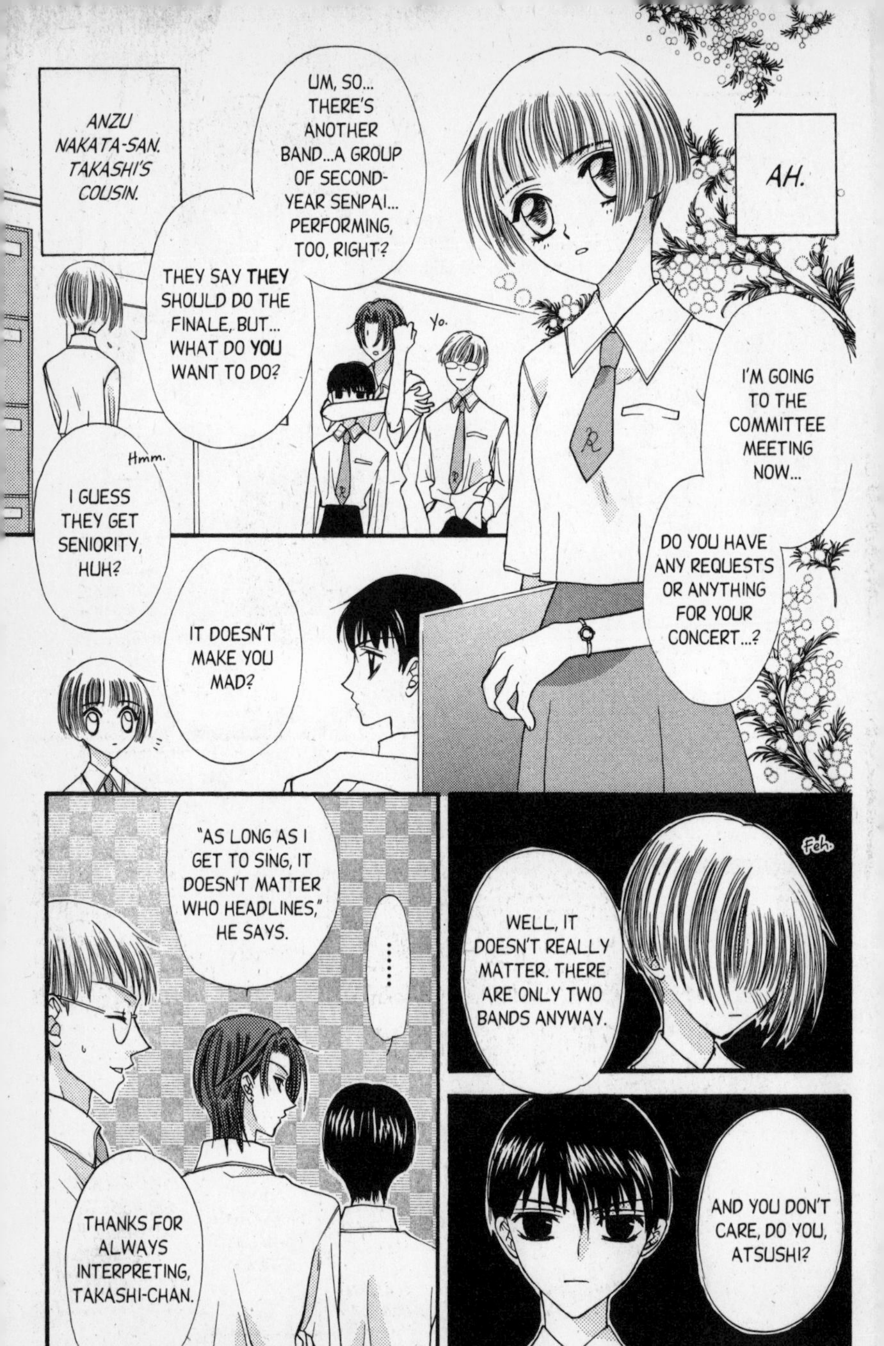
AH.
I'M GOING TO THE COMMITTEE MEETING NOW...
DO YOU HAVE ANY REQUESTS OR ANYTHING FOR YOUR CONCERT...?
ANZU NAKATA-SAN. TAKASHI'S COUSIN.
UM, SO... THERE'S ANOTHER BAND...A GROUP OF SECOND-YEAR SENPAI... PERFORMING, TOO, RIGHT?
THEY SAY **THEY** SHOULD DO THE FINALE, BUT... WHAT DO **YOU** WANT TO DO?
Yo.
Hmm.
I GUESS THEY GET SENIORITY, HUH?
IT DOESN'T MAKE YOU MAD?
Feh.
WELL, IT DOESN'T REALLY MATTER. THERE ARE ONLY TWO BANDS ANYWAY.
AND YOU DON'T CARE, DO YOU, ATSUSHI?
"AS LONG AS I GET TO SING, IT DOESN'T MATTER WHO HEADLINES," HE SAYS.
......
THANKS FOR ALWAYS INTERPRETING, TAKASHI-CHAN.

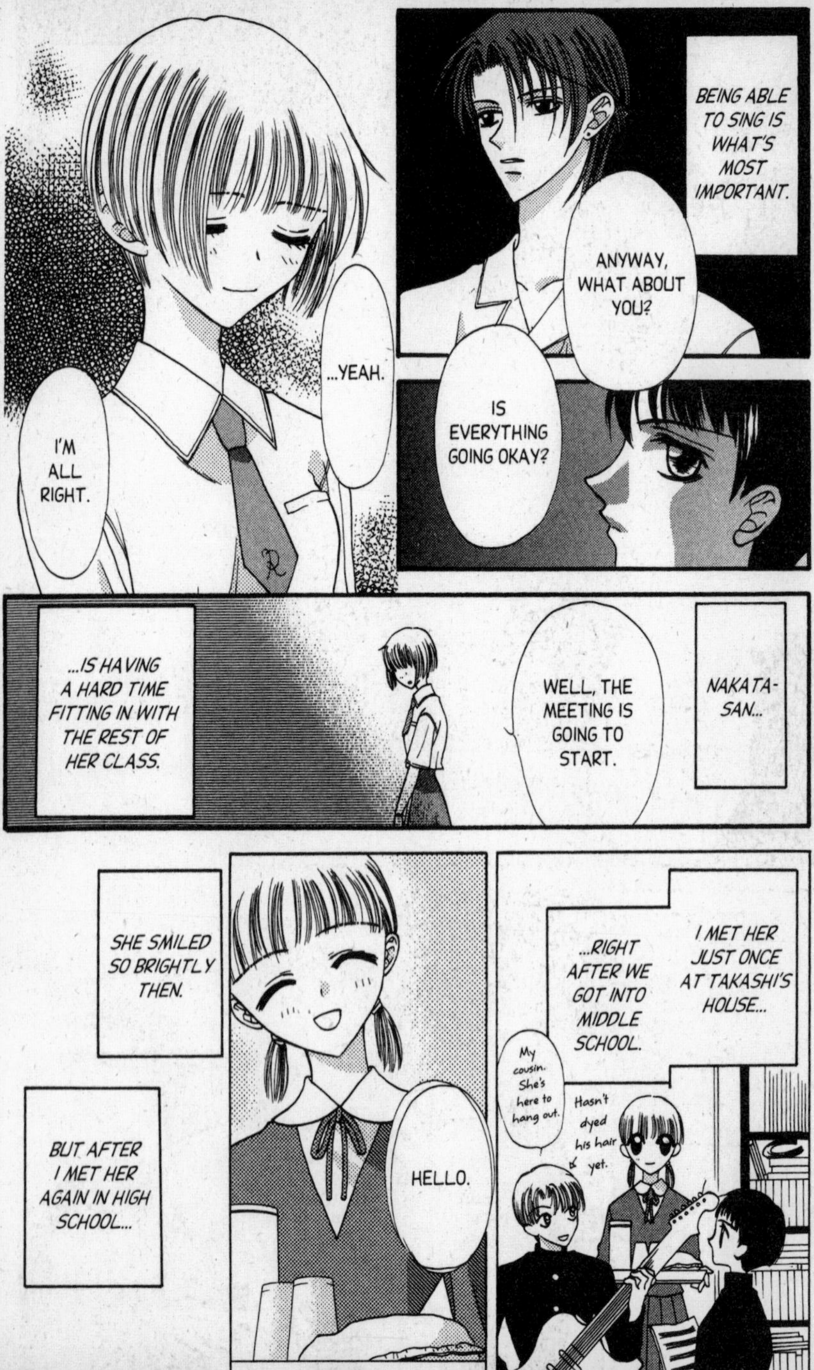
BEING ABLE TO SING IS WHAT'S MOST IMPORTANT.
ANYWAY, WHAT ABOUT YOU?
IS EVERYTHING GOING OKAY?
...YEAH.
I'M ALL RIGHT.
NAKATA-SAN...
WELL, THE MEETING IS GOING TO START.
...IS HAVING A HARD TIME FITTING IN WITH THE REST OF HER CLASS.
I MET HER JUST ONCE AT TAKASHI'S HOUSE...
...RIGHT AFTER WE GOT INTO MIDDLE SCHOOL.
My cousin. She's here to hang out.
Hasn't dyed his hair yet.
HELLO.
SHE SMILED SO BRIGHTLY THEN.
BUT AFTER I MET HER AGAIN IN HIGH SCHOOL...

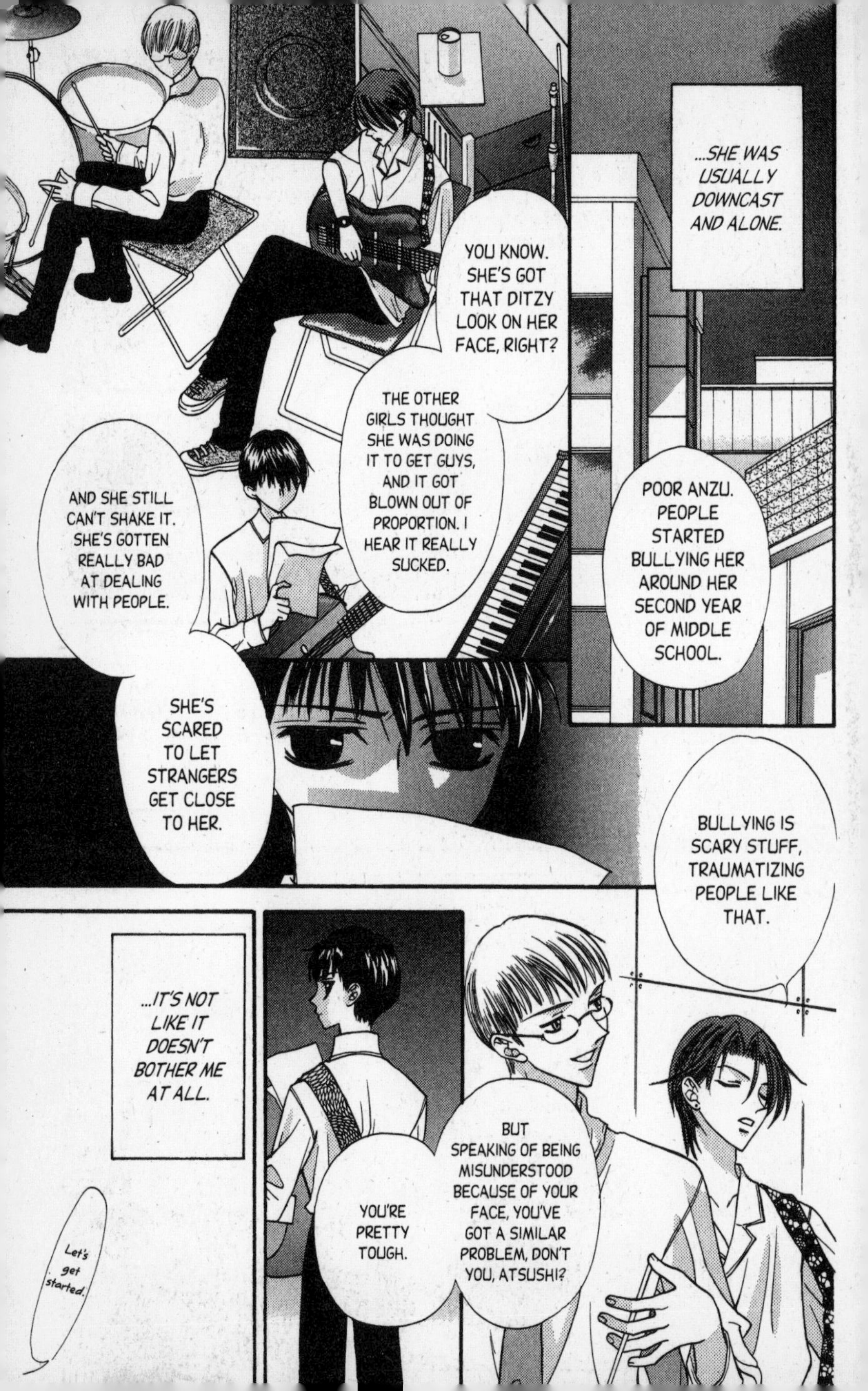
...SHE WAS USUALLY DOWNCAST AND ALONE.
POOR ANZU. PEOPLE STARTED BULLYING HER AROUND HER SECOND YEAR OF MIDDLE SCHOOL.
YOU KNOW. SHE'S GOT THAT DITZY LOOK ON HER FACE, RIGHT?
THE OTHER GIRLS THOUGHT SHE WAS DOING IT TO GET GUYS, AND IT GOT BLOWN OUT OF PROPORTION. I HEAR IT REALLY SUCKED.
AND SHE STILL CAN'T SHAKE IT. SHE'S GOTTEN REALLY BAD AT DEALING WITH PEOPLE.
BULLYING IS SCARY STUFF, TRAUMATIZING PEOPLE LIKE THAT.
SHE'S SCARED TO LET STRANGERS GET CLOSE TO HER.
BUT SPEAKING OF BEING MISUNDERSTOOD BECAUSE OF YOUR FACE, YOU'VE GOT A SIMILAR PROBLEM, DON'T YOU, ATSUSHI?
YOU'RE PRETTY TOUGH.
...IT'S NOT LIKE IT DOESN'T BOTHER ME AT ALL.
Let's get started.

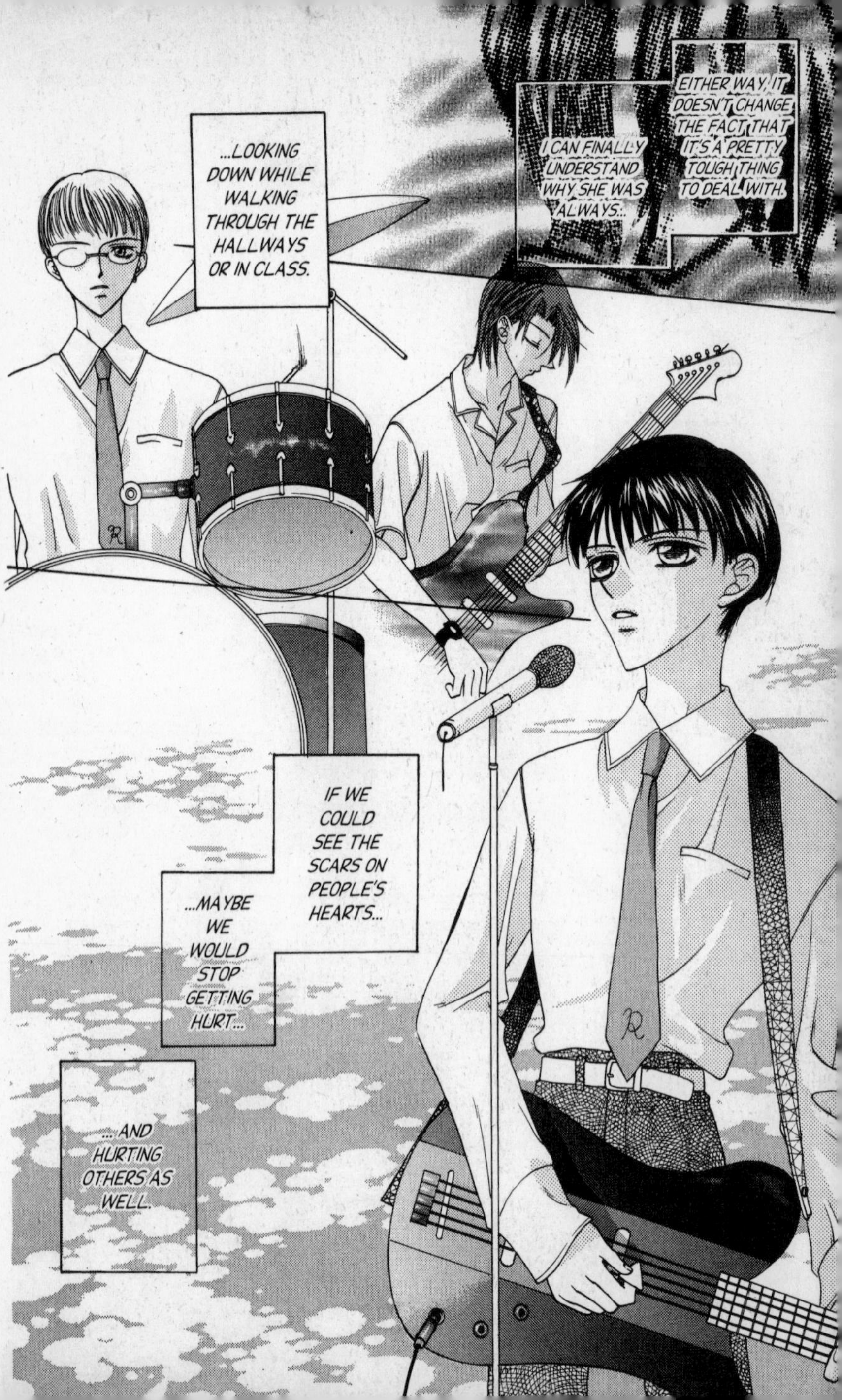
EITHER WAY, IT DOESN'T CHANGE THE FACT THAT IT'S A PRETTY TOUGH THING TO DEAL WITH.
I CAN FINALLY UNDERSTAND WHY SHE WAS ALWAYS...
...LOOKING DOWN WHILE WALKING THROUGH THE HALLWAYS OR IN CLASS.
IF WE COULD SEE THE SCARS ON PEOPLE'S HEARTS...
...MAYBE WE WOULD STOP GETTING HURT...
...AND HURTING OTHERS AS WELL.

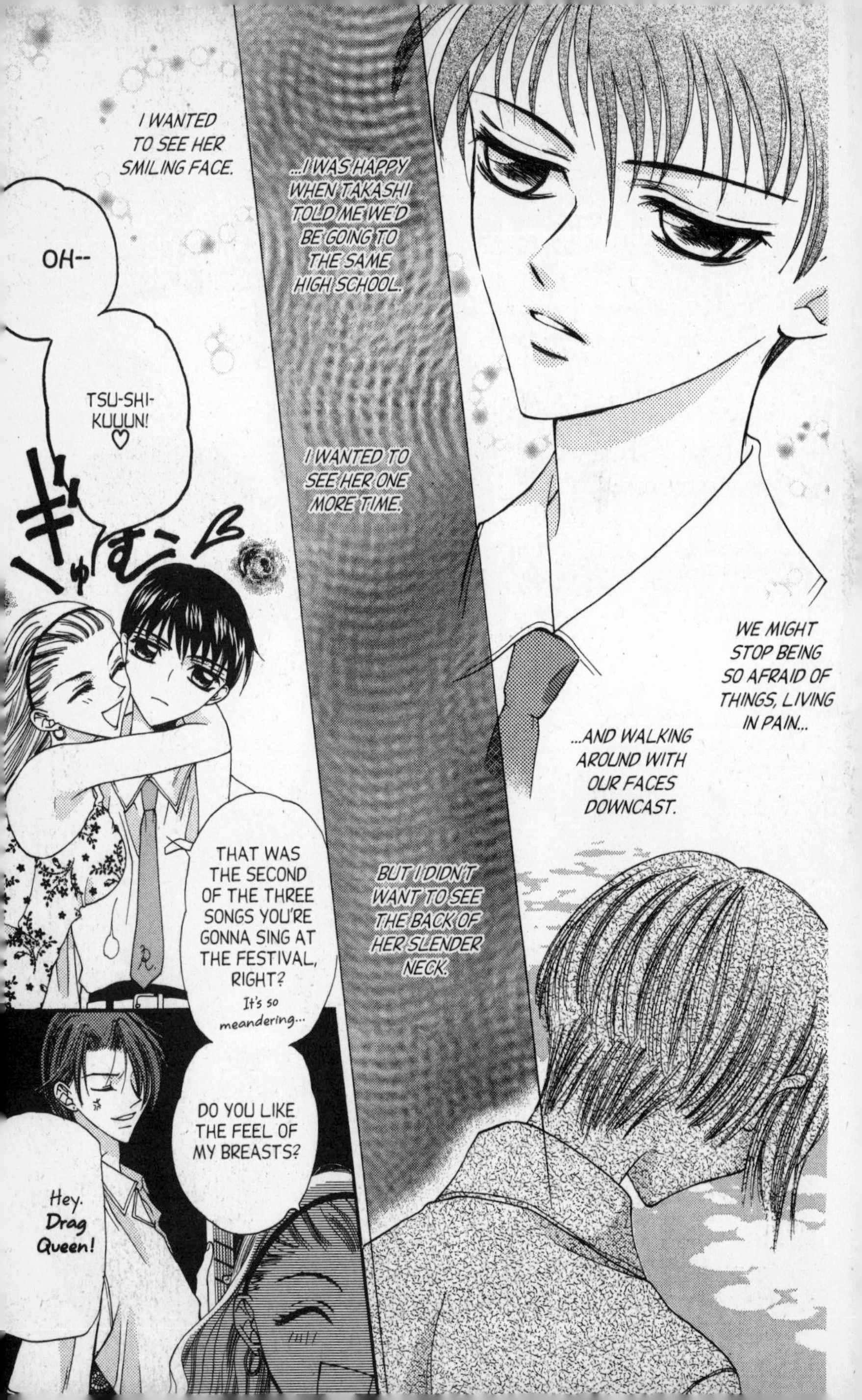
WE MIGHT STOP BEING SO AFRAID OF THINGS, LIVING IN PAIN...
...AND WALKING AROUND WITH OUR FACES DOWNCAST.
...I WAS HAPPY WHEN TAKASHI TOLD ME WE'D BE GOING TO THE SAME HIGH SCHOOL.
I WANTED TO SEE HER ONE MORE TIME.
BUT I DIDN'T WANT TO SEE THE BACK OF HER SLENDER NECK.
I WANTED TO SEE HER SMILING FACE.
OH--
TSU-SHI-KUUUN! ♡
ぎゅむっ
THAT WAS THE SECOND OF THE THREE SONGS YOU'RE GONNA SING AT THE FESTIVAL, RIGHT?
It's so meandering...
DO YOU LIKE THE FEEL OF MY BREASTS?
Hey. Drag Queen!

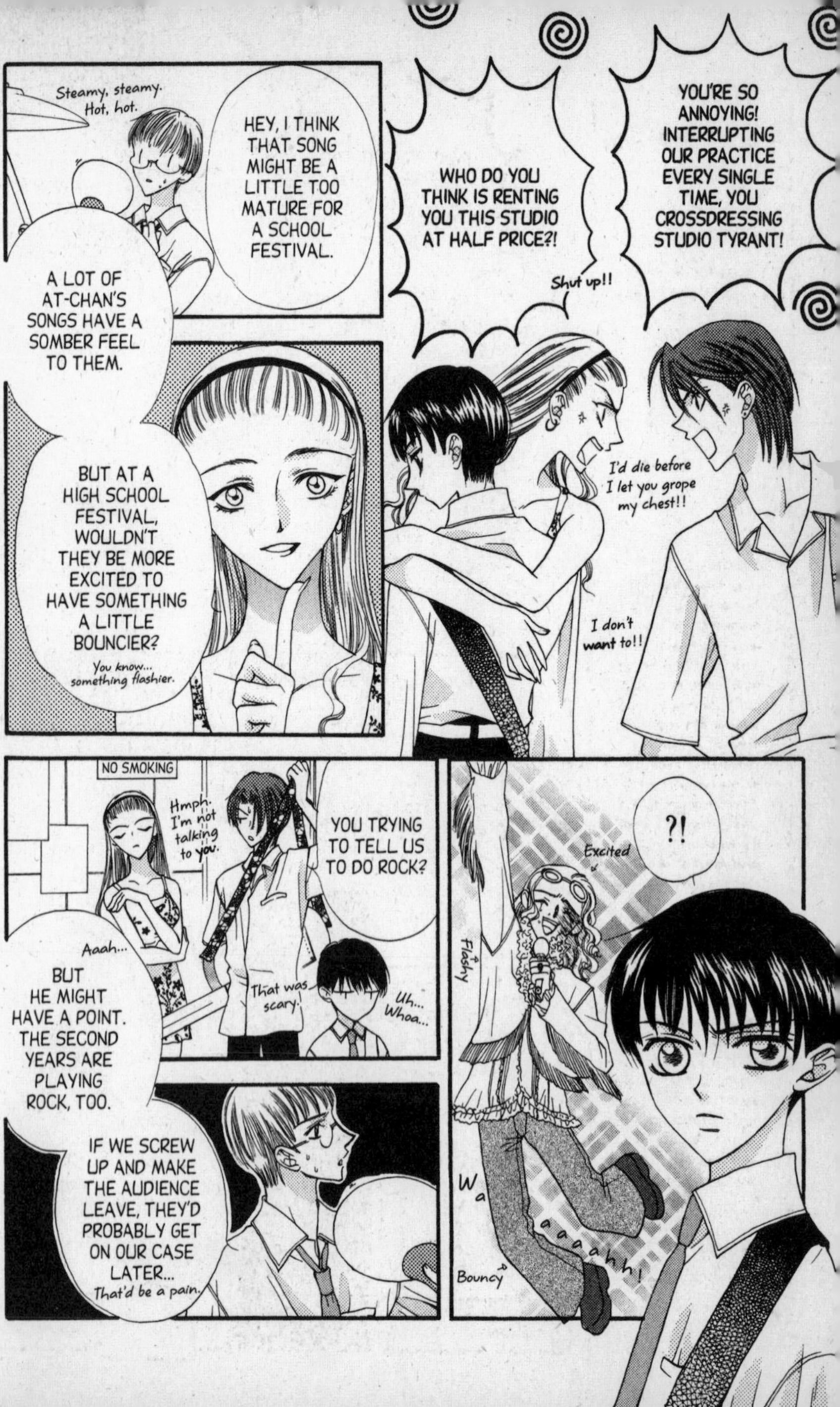
YOU'RE SO ANNOYING! INTERRUPTING OUR PRACTICE EVERY SINGLE TIME, YOU CROSSDRESSING STUDIO TYRANT!
WHO DO YOU THINK IS RENTING YOU THIS STUDIO AT HALF PRICE?!
Shut up!!
I'd die before I let you grope my chest!!
I don't want to!!
HEY, I THINK THAT SONG MIGHT BE A LITTLE TOO MATURE FOR A SCHOOL FESTIVAL.
Steamy, steamy. Hot, hot.
A LOT OF AT-CHAN'S SONGS HAVE A SOMBER FEEL TO THEM.
BUT AT A HIGH SCHOOL FESTIVAL, WOULDN'T THEY BE MORE EXCITED TO HAVE SOMETHING A LITTLE BOUNCIER?
You know... something flashier.
?!
Excited
Flashy
Waaaaaaahh!
Bouncy
NO SMOKING
YOU TRYING TO TELL US TO DO ROCK?
Hmph. I'm not talking to you.
That was scary!
Uh... Whoa...
Aaah...
BUT HE MIGHT HAVE A POINT. THE SECOND YEARS ARE PLAYING ROCK, TOO.
IF WE SCREW UP AND MAKE THE AUDIENCE LEAVE, THEY'D PROBABLY GET ON OUR CASE LATER...
That'd be a pain.

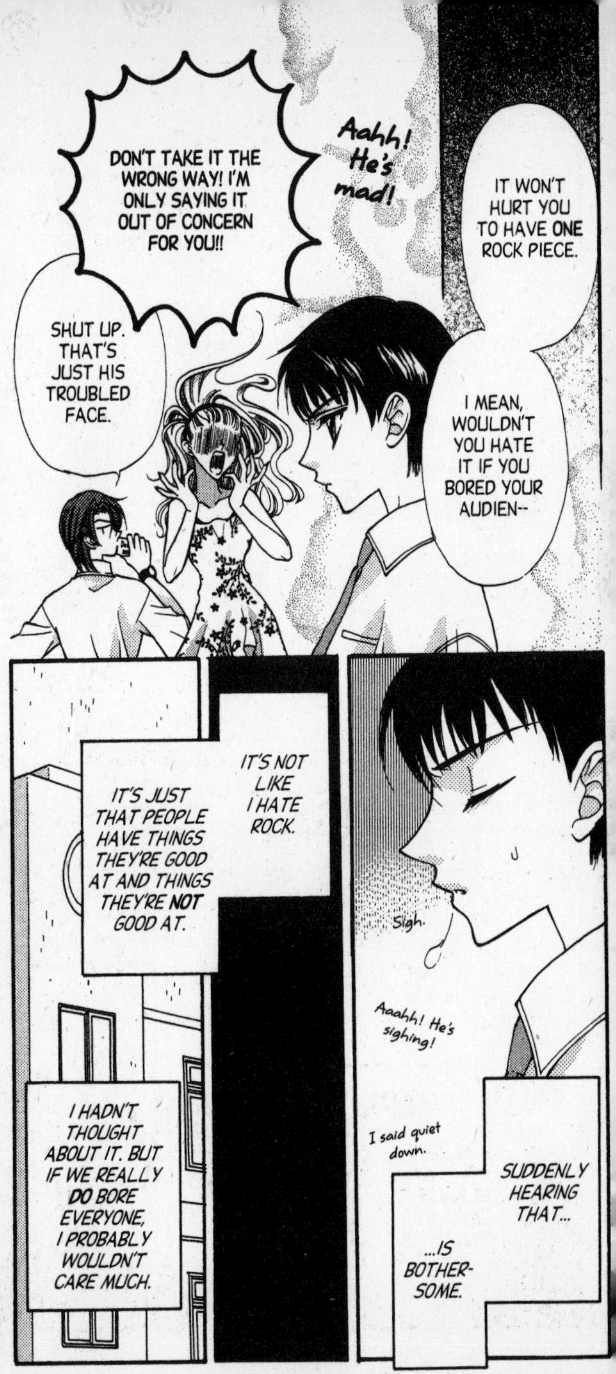
IT WON'T HURT YOU TO HAVE ONE ROCK PIECE.
I MEAN, WOULDN'T YOU HATE IT IF YOU BORED YOUR AUDIEN--
Aahh! He's mad!
DON'T TAKE IT THE WRONG WAY! I'M ONLY SAYING IT OUT OF CONCERN FOR YOU!!
SHUT UP. THAT'S JUST HIS TROUBLED FACE.
Sigh.
Aaahh! He's sighing!
I said quiet down.
SUDDENLY HEARING THAT...
...IS BOTHER-SOME.
IT'S NOT LIKE I HATE ROCK.
IT'S JUST THAT PEOPLE HAVE THINGS THEY'RE GOOD AT AND THINGS THEY'RE NOT GOOD AT.
I HADN'T THOUGHT ABOUT IT. BUT IF WE REALLY DO BORE EVERYONE, I PROBABLY WOULDN'T CARE MUCH.

Songs to Make You Smile

Part 1

Pleased to meet you and hello! I'm Takaya. This is my first short story anthology.

Oww!!

That being the case (what being the case?)... it's incredible to have works from not so long ago, and works from long, long ago put together in one volume like this. The aura of a younger (obviously) little girl doing her utmost to draw manga really comes through, and it's kind of ticklish, and kind of deeply emotional. Yes. I think about myself working so hard to draw manga back then (oh, I'm still working really hard to draw manga now, of course) and wonder what kind of face I would have made if I had been told, "This will be in a book in X years" (laugh). I'm sure I would have bawled (laugh).

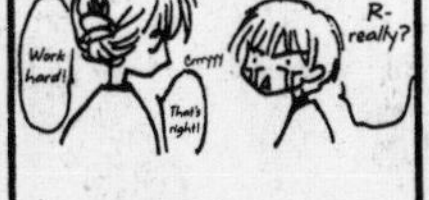
Like this?
R-really?
Work hard!
That's right!

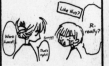

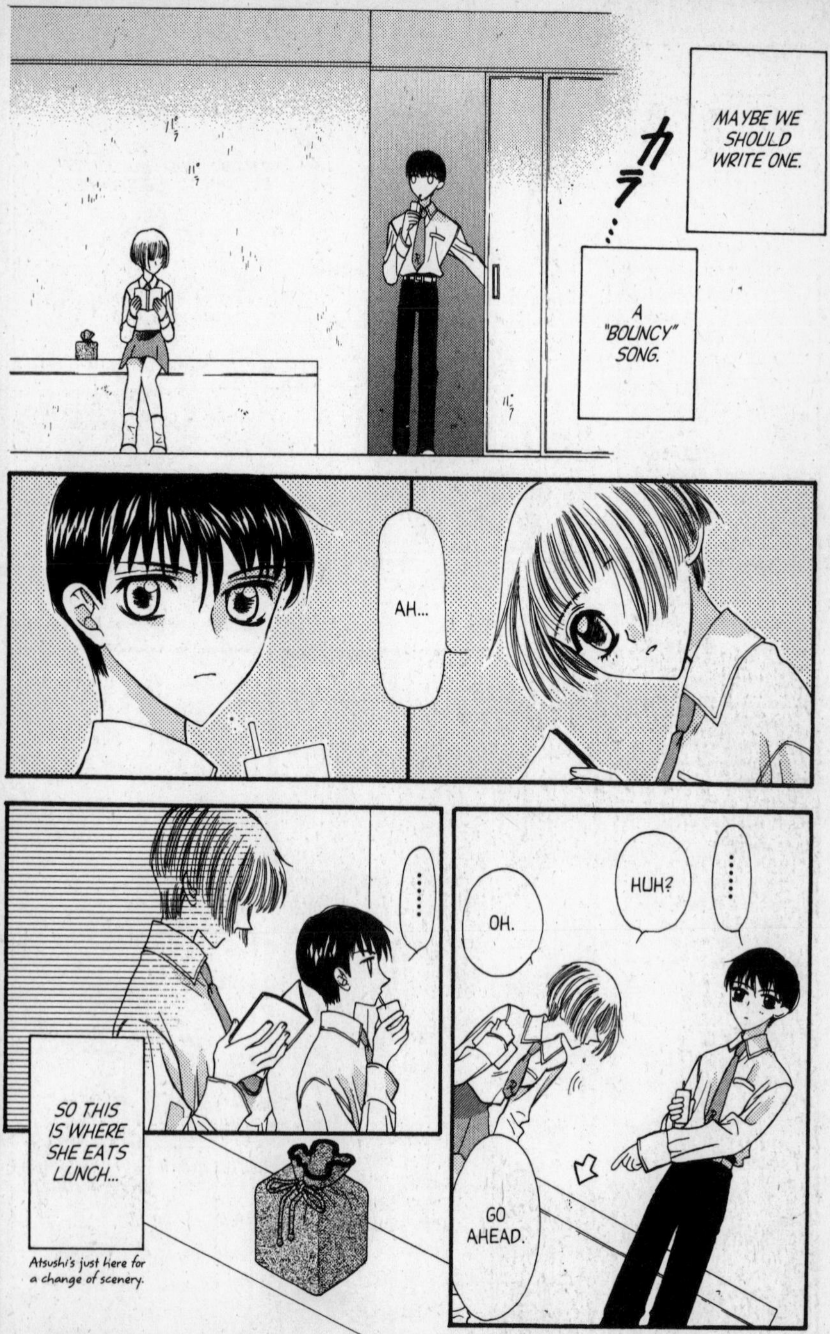
MAYBE WE SHOULD WRITE ONE.
A "BOUNCY" SONG.
カラ…
AH...
......
HUH?
OH.
GO AHEAD.
......
SO THIS IS WHERE SHE EATS LUNCH...
Atsushi's just here for a change of scenery.

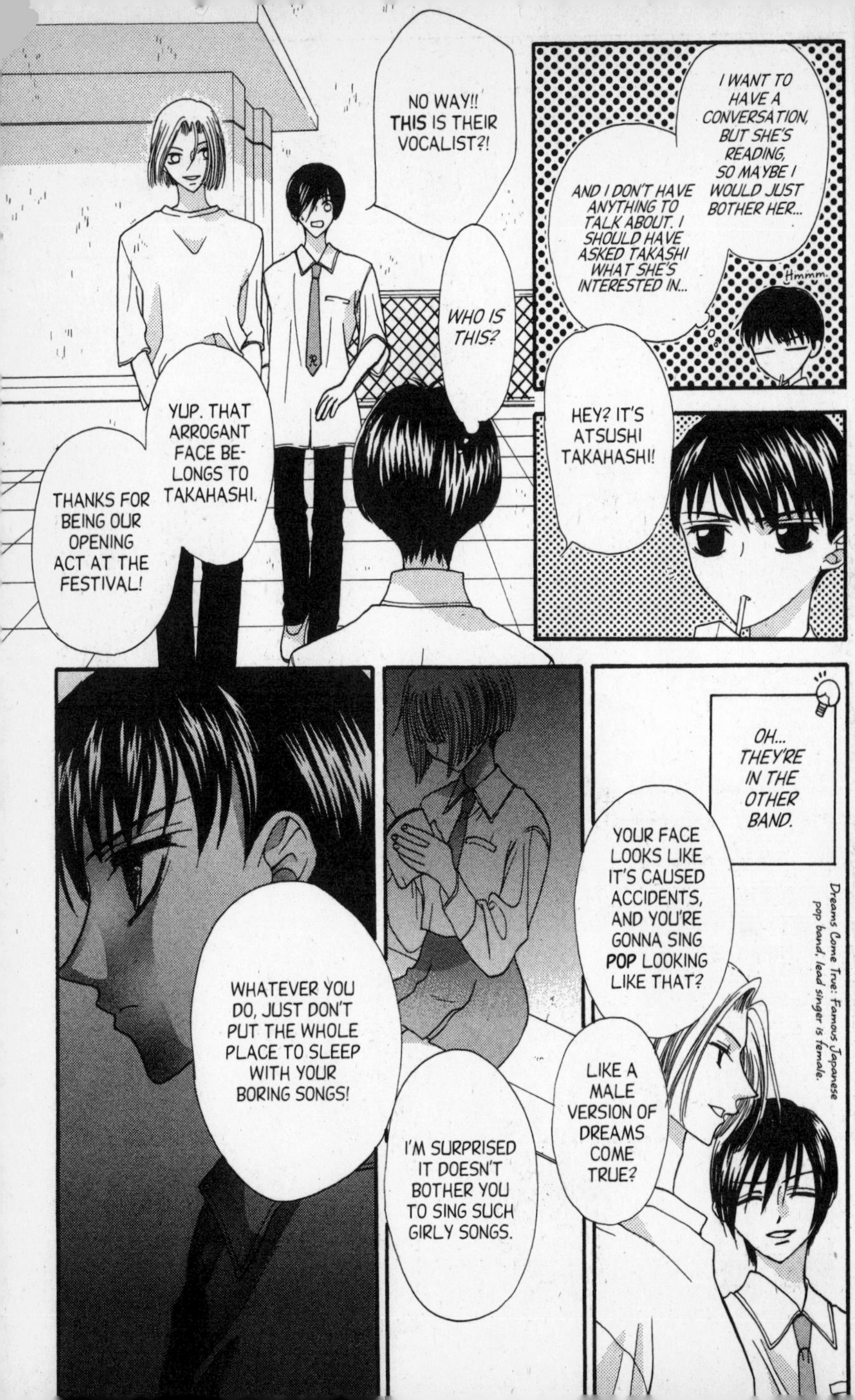
I WANT TO HAVE A CONVERSATION, BUT SHE'S READING, SO MAYBE I WOULD JUST BOTHER HER...
AND I DON'T HAVE ANYTHING TO TALK ABOUT. I SHOULD HAVE ASKED TAKASHI WHAT SHE'S INTERESTED IN...
Hmmm.
HEY? IT'S ATSUSHI TAKAHASHI!
NO WAY!! THIS IS THEIR VOCALIST?!
WHO IS THIS?
YUP. THAT ARROGANT FACE BE-LONGS TO TAKAHASHI.
THANKS FOR BEING OUR OPENING ACT AT THE FESTIVAL!
OH... THEY'RE IN THE OTHER BAND.
YOUR FACE LOOKS LIKE IT'S CAUSED ACCIDENTS, AND YOU'RE GONNA SING POP LOOKING LIKE THAT?
LIKE A MALE VERSION OF DREAMS COME TRUE?
I'M SURPRISED IT DOESN'T BOTHER YOU TO SING SUCH GIRLY SONGS.
WHATEVER YOU DO, JUST DON'T PUT THE WHOLE PLACE TO SLEEP WITH YOUR BORING SONGS!

Dreams Come True: Famous Japanese pop band, lead singer is female.

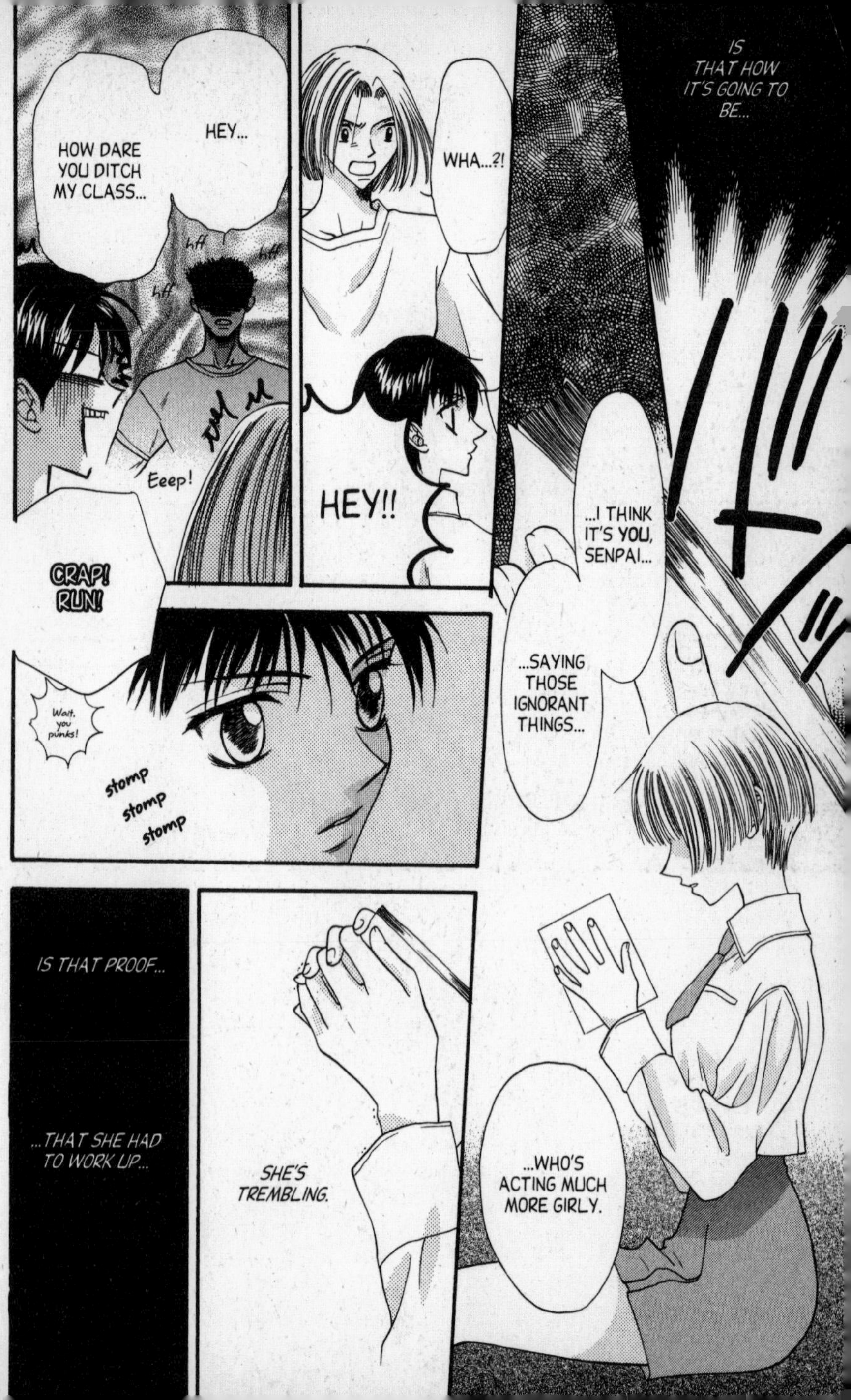
IS THAT HOW IT'S GOING TO BE...
...I THINK IT'S YOU, SENPAI...
...SAYING THOSE IGNORANT THINGS...
...WHO'S ACTING MUCH MORE GIRLY.
WHA...?!
HEY!!
HEY...
HOW DARE YOU DITCH MY CLASS...
hff
hff
hff
Eeep!
CRAP! RUN!
Wait, you punks!
stomp
stomp
stomp
SHE'S TREMBLING.
IS THAT PROOF...
...THAT SHE HAD TO WORK UP...

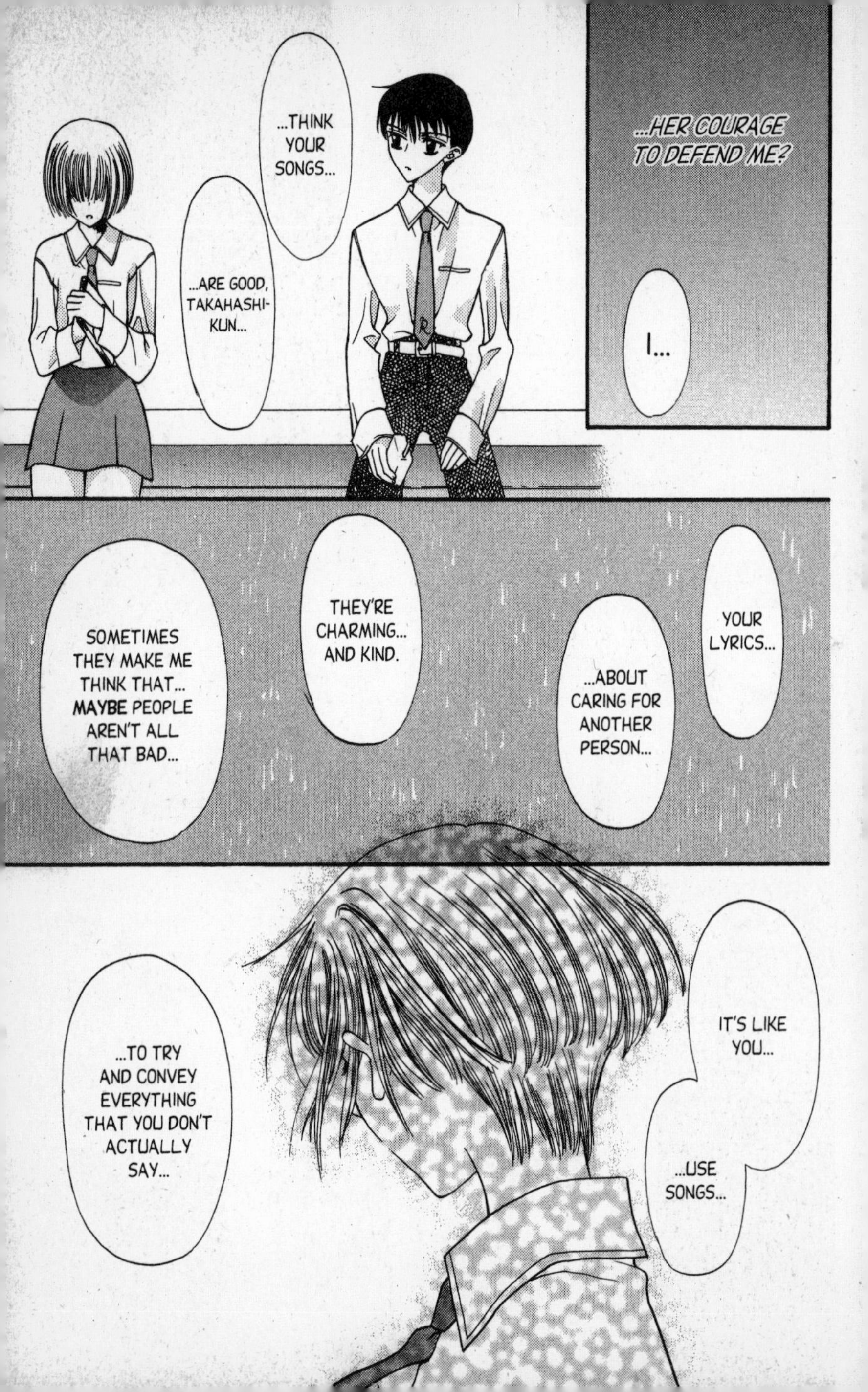

...HER COURAGE TO DEFEND ME?
I...
...THINK YOUR SONGS...
...ARE GOOD, TAKAHASHI-KUN...
YOUR LYRICS...
...ABOUT CARING FOR ANOTHER PERSON...
THEY'RE CHARMING... AND KIND.
SOMETIMES THEY MAKE ME THINK THAT... **MAYBE** PEOPLE AREN'T ALL THAT BAD...
IT'S LIKE YOU...
...USE SONGS...
...TO TRY AND CONVEY EVERYTHING THAT YOU DON'T ACTUALLY SAY...

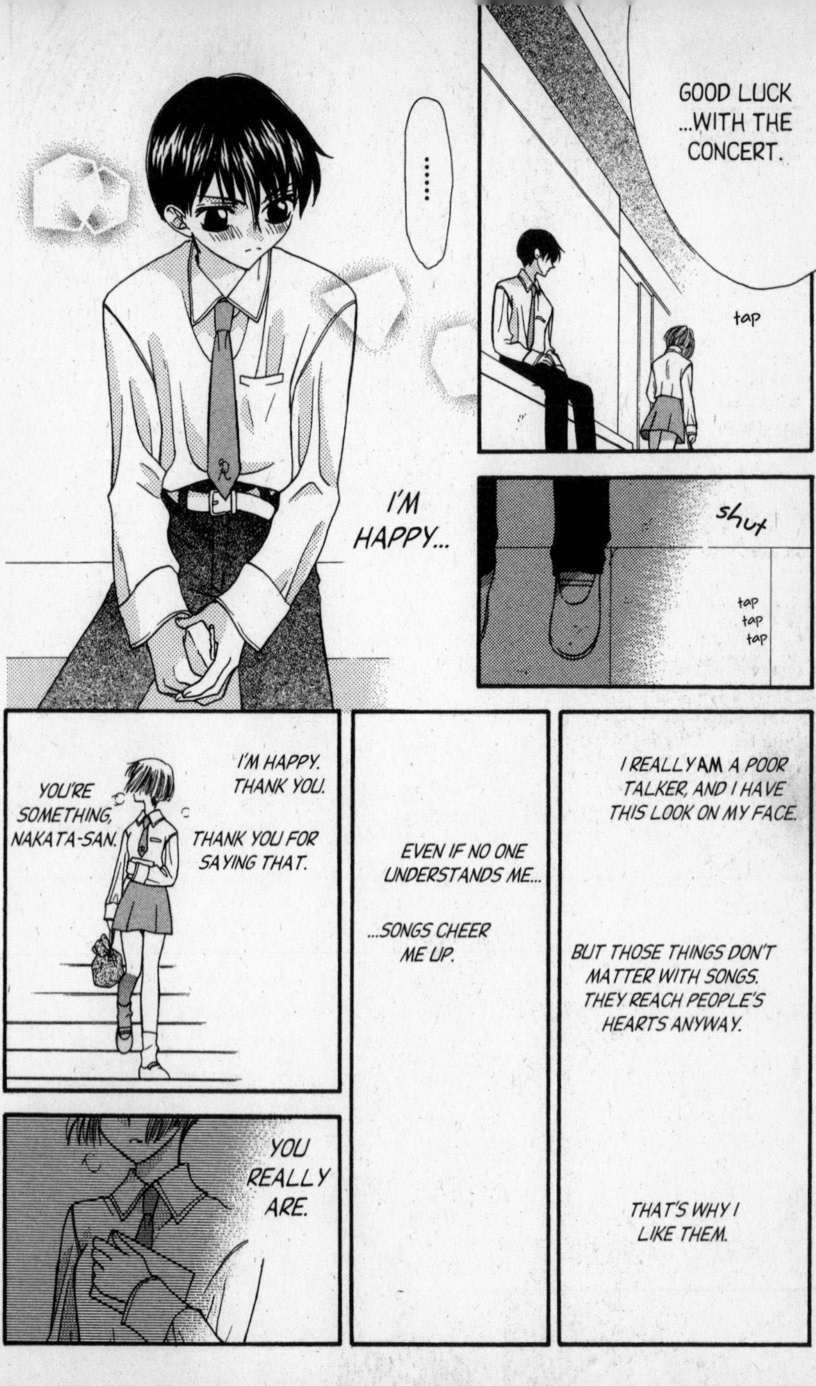
GOOD LUCK ...WITH THE CONCERT.
tap
shut
tap tap tap
......
I'M HAPPY...
I REALLY AM A POOR TALKER, AND I HAVE THIS LOOK ON MY FACE.
BUT THOSE THINGS DON'T MATTER WITH SONGS. THEY REACH PEOPLE'S HEARTS ANYWAY.
THAT'S WHY I LIKE THEM.
EVEN IF NO ONE UNDERSTANDS ME...
...SONGS CHEER ME UP.
I'M HAPPY. THANK YOU.
YOU'RE SOMETHING, NAKATA-SAN.
THANK YOU FOR SAYING THAT.
YOU REALLY ARE.

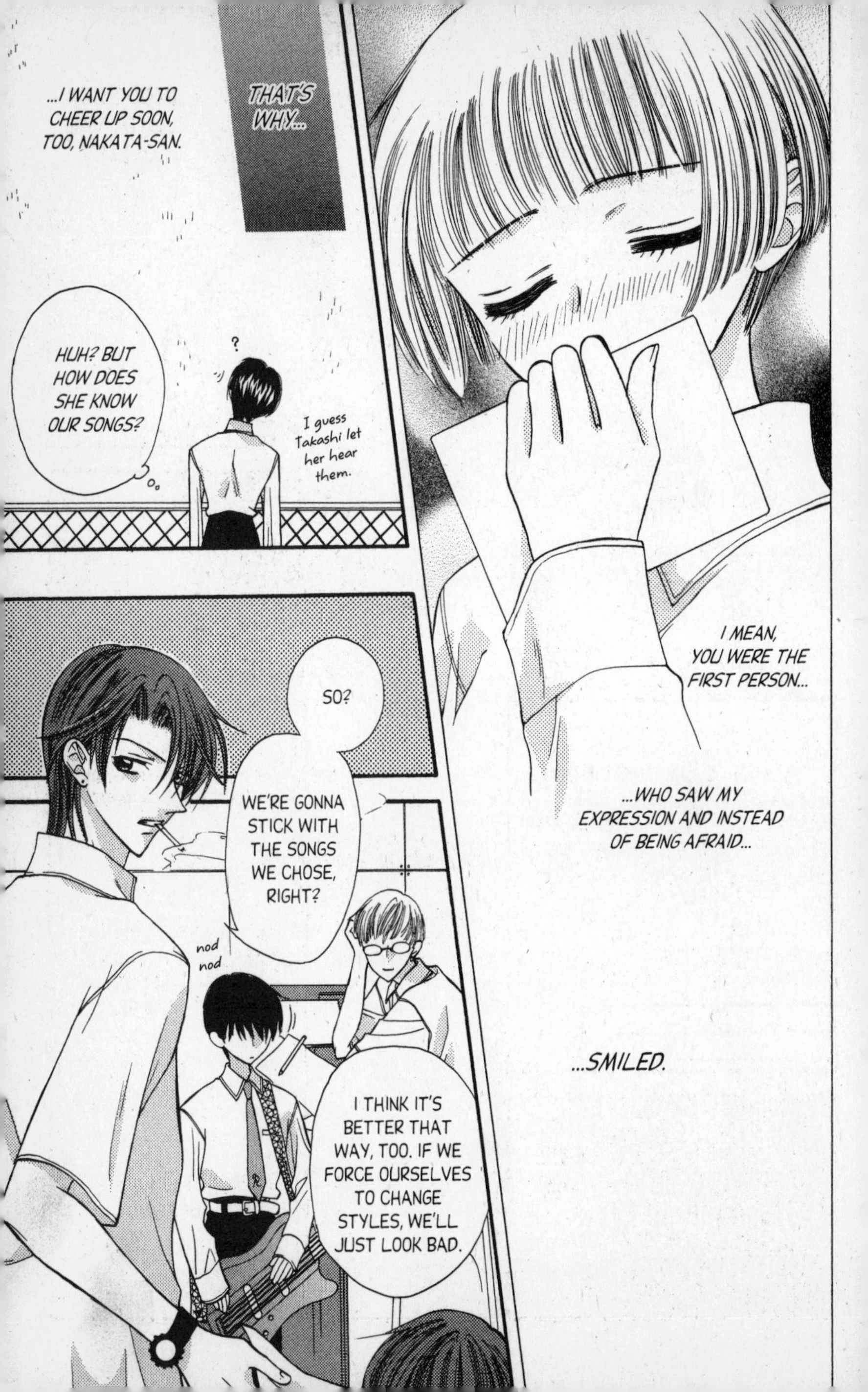
I MEAN, YOU WERE THE FIRST PERSON...
...WHO SAW MY EXPRESSION AND INSTEAD OF BEING AFRAID...
...SMILED.
THAT'S WHY...
...I WANT YOU TO CHEER UP SOON, TOO, NAKATA-SAN.
?
HUH? BUT HOW DOES SHE KNOW OUR SONGS?
I guess Takashi let her hear them.
SO?
WE'RE GONNA STICK WITH THE SONGS WE CHOSE, RIGHT?
nod nod
I THINK IT'S BETTER THAT WAY, TOO. IF WE FORCE OURSELVES TO CHANGE STYLES, WE'LL JUST LOOK BAD.

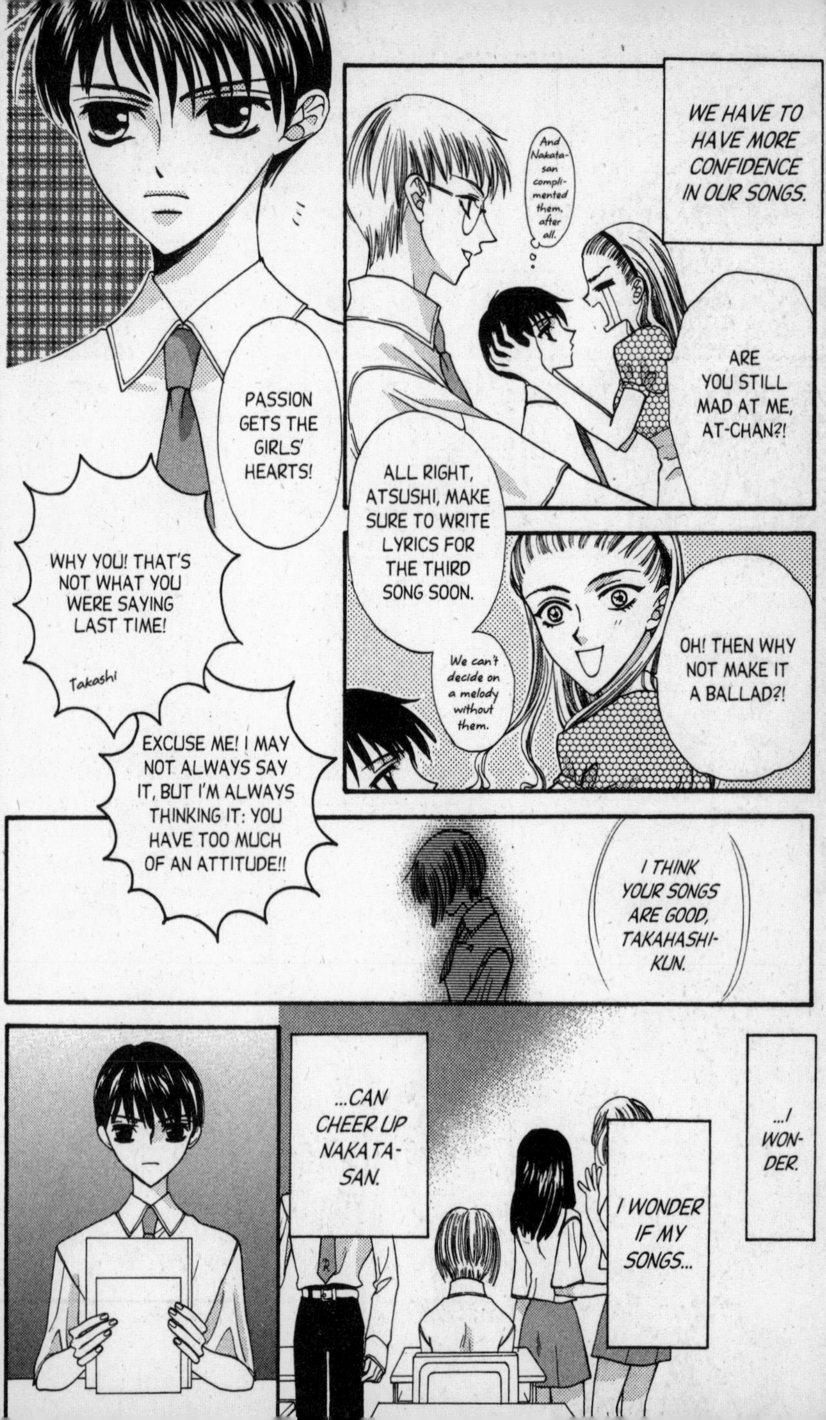
WE HAVE TO HAVE MORE CONFIDENCE IN OUR SONGS.
And Nakata-san complimented them, after all.
ARE YOU STILL MAD AT ME, AT-CHAN?!
ALL RIGHT, ATSUSHI, MAKE SURE TO WRITE LYRICS FOR THE THIRD SONG SOON.
We can't decide on a melody without them.
OH! THEN WHY NOT MAKE IT A BALLAD?!
PASSION GETS THE GIRLS' HEARTS!
WHY YOU! THAT'S NOT WHAT YOU WERE SAYING LAST TIME!
Takashi
EXCUSE ME! I MAY NOT ALWAYS SAY IT, BUT I'M ALWAYS THINKING IT: YOU HAVE TOO MUCH OF AN ATTITUDE!!
I THINK YOUR SONGS ARE GOOD, TAKAHASHI-KUN.
...I WONDER.
I WONDER IF MY SONGS...
...CAN CHEER UP NAKATA-SAN.

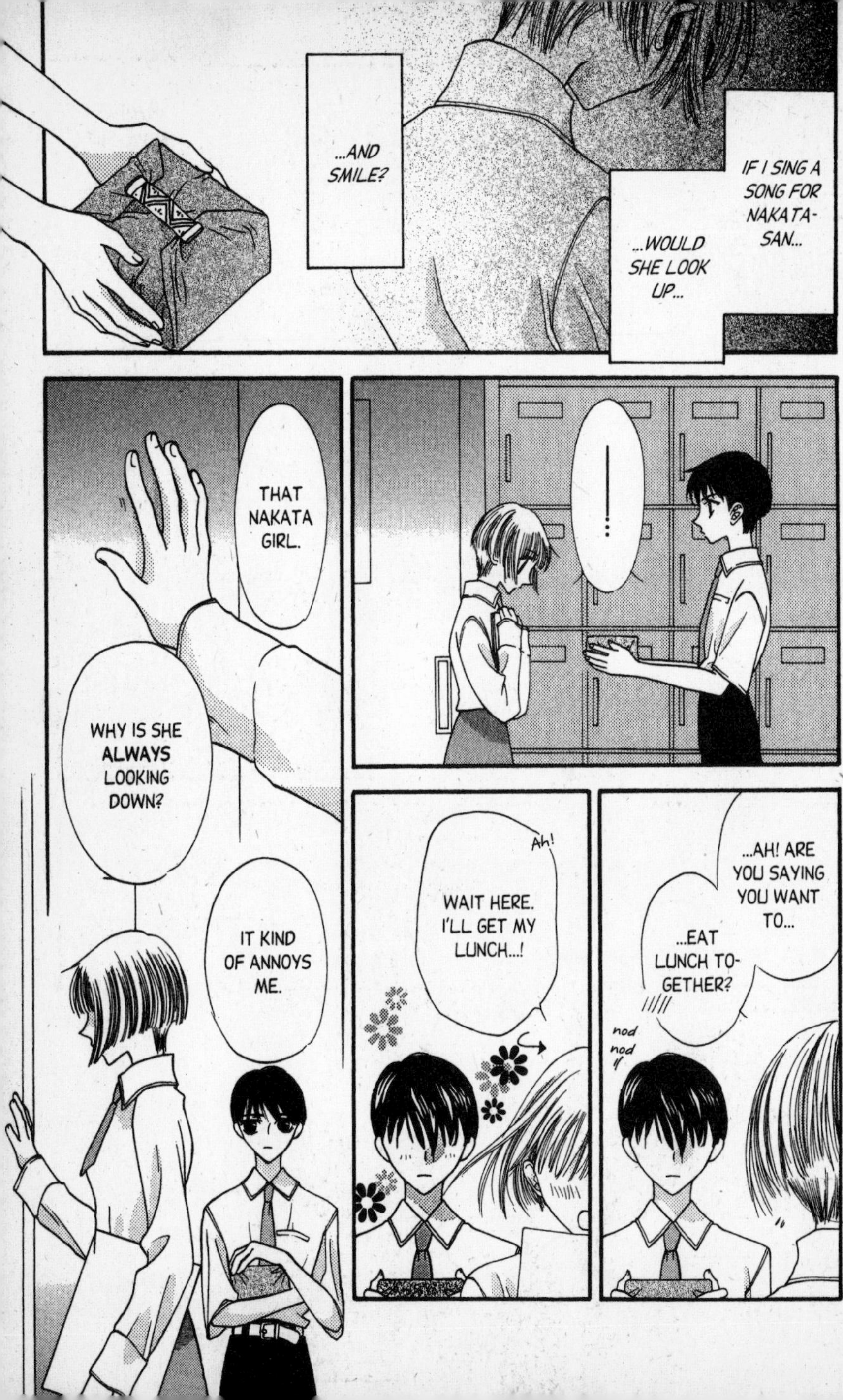
IF I SING A SONG FOR NAKATA-SAN...
...WOULD SHE LOOK UP...
...AND SMILE?
!......
...AH! ARE YOU SAYING YOU WANT TO...
...EAT LUNCH TO-GETHER?
nod nod
Ah!
WAIT HERE. I'LL GET MY LUNCH...!
THAT NAKATA GIRL.
WHY IS SHE **ALWAYS** LOOKING DOWN?
IT KIND OF ANNOYS ME.

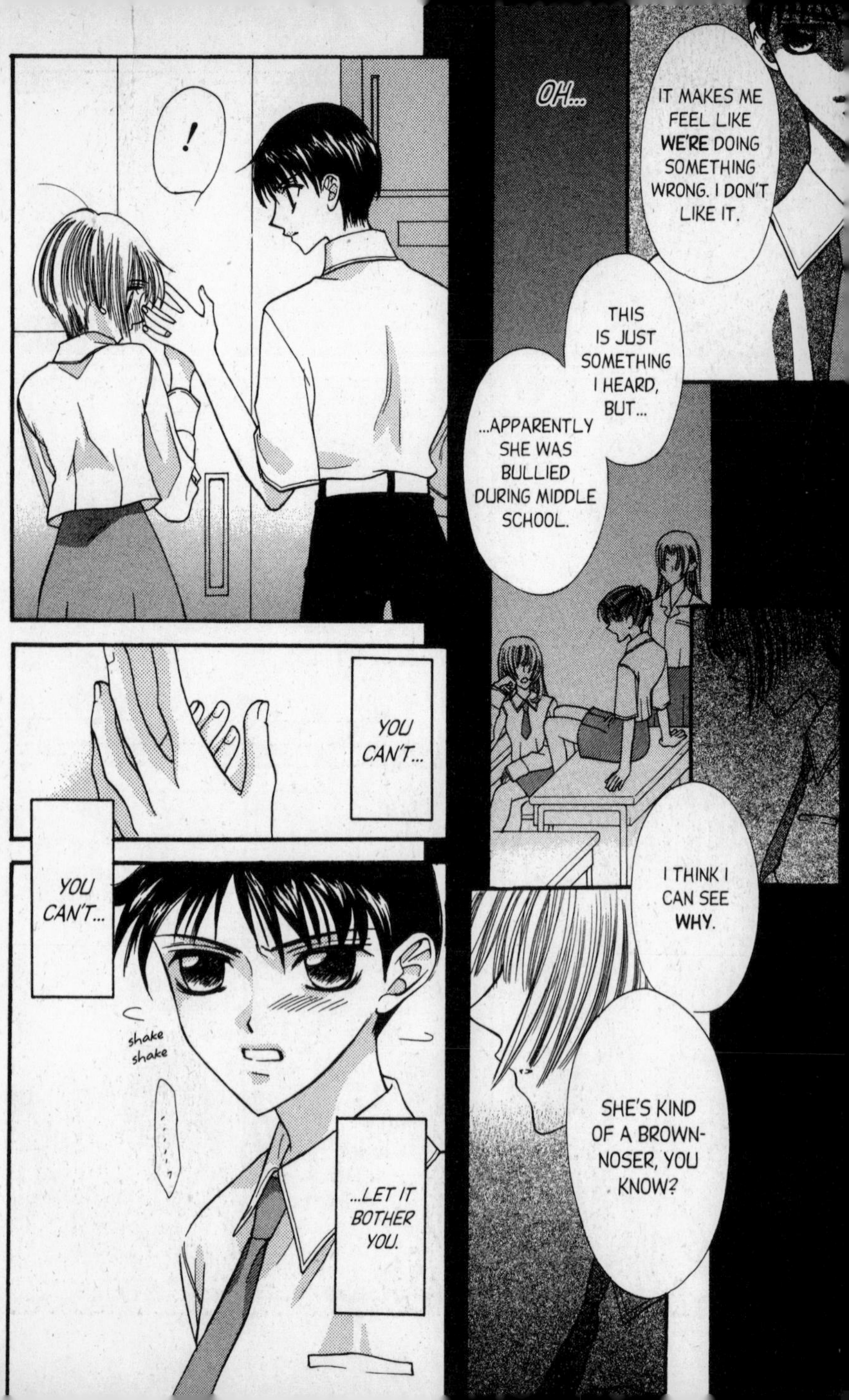
IT MAKES ME FEEL LIKE WE'RE DOING SOMETHING WRONG. I DON'T LIKE IT.
OH...
THIS IS JUST SOMETHING I HEARD, BUT...
...APPARENTLY SHE WAS BULLIED DURING MIDDLE SCHOOL.
I THINK I CAN SEE WHY.
SHE'S KIND OF A BROWN-NOSER, YOU KNOW?
!
YOU CAN'T...
YOU CAN'T...
shake shake
...LET IT BOTHER YOU.

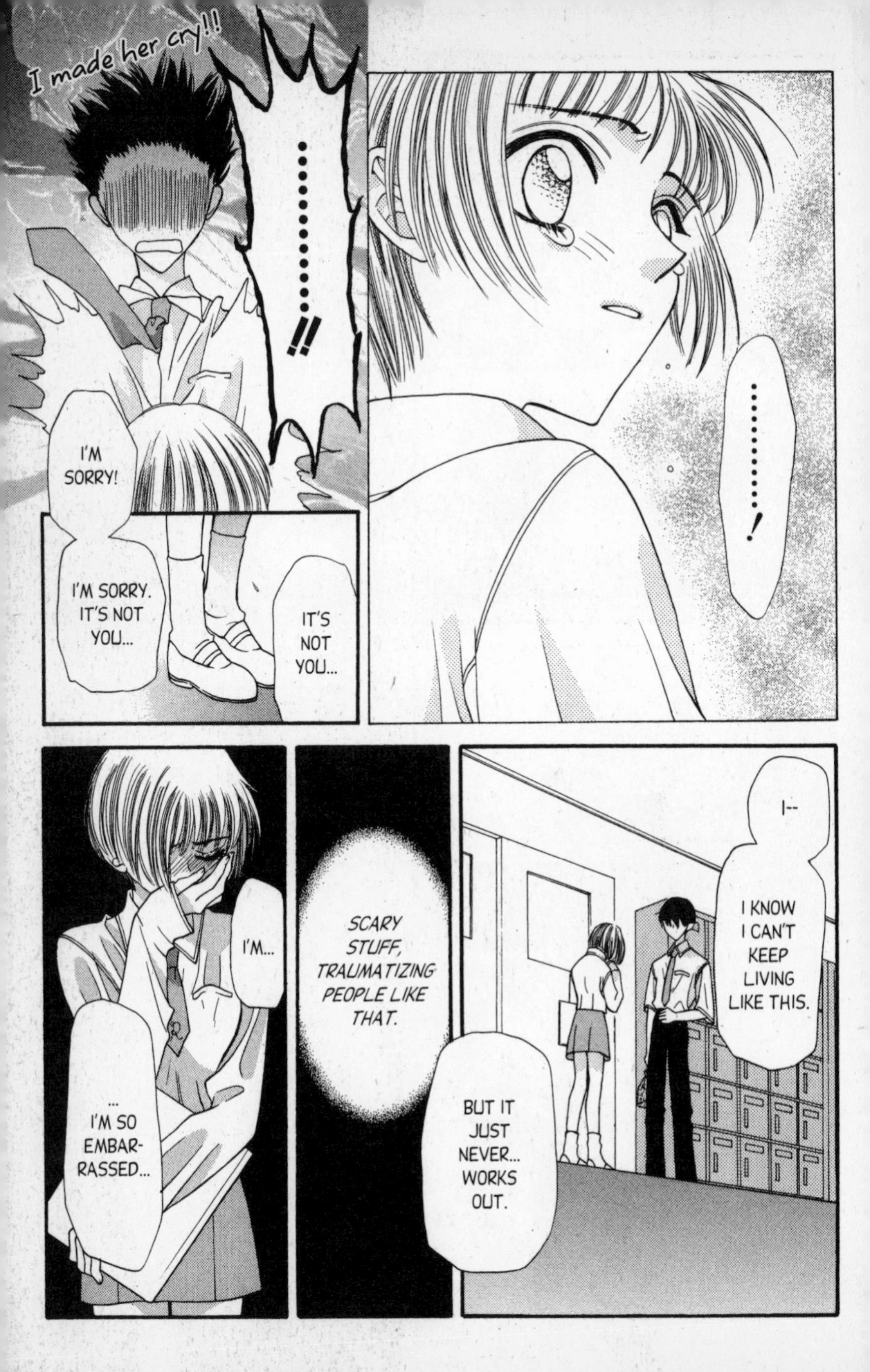
……!
I made her cry!!
……!!
I'M SORRY!
I'M SORRY. IT'S NOT YOU...
IT'S NOT YOU...
I--
I KNOW I CAN'T KEEP LIVING LIKE THIS.
BUT IT JUST NEVER... WORKS OUT.
SCARY STUFF, TRAUMATIZING PEOPLE LIKE THAT.
I'M...
... I'M SO EMBARRASSED...

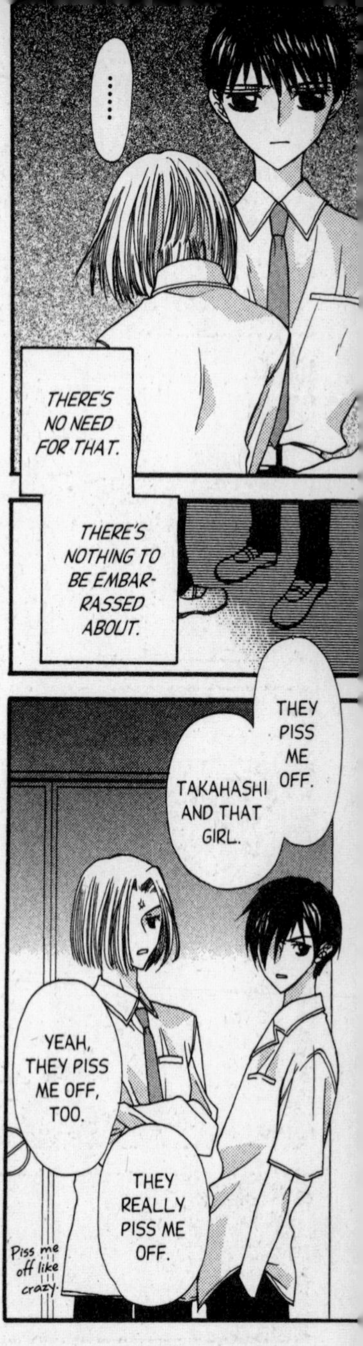
......
THERE'S NO NEED FOR THAT.
THERE'S NOTHING TO BE EMBAR-RASSED ABOUT.
THEY PISS ME OFF.
TAKAHASHI AND THAT GIRL.
YEAH, THEY PISS ME OFF, TOO.
THEY REALLY PISS ME OFF.
Piss me off like crazy.

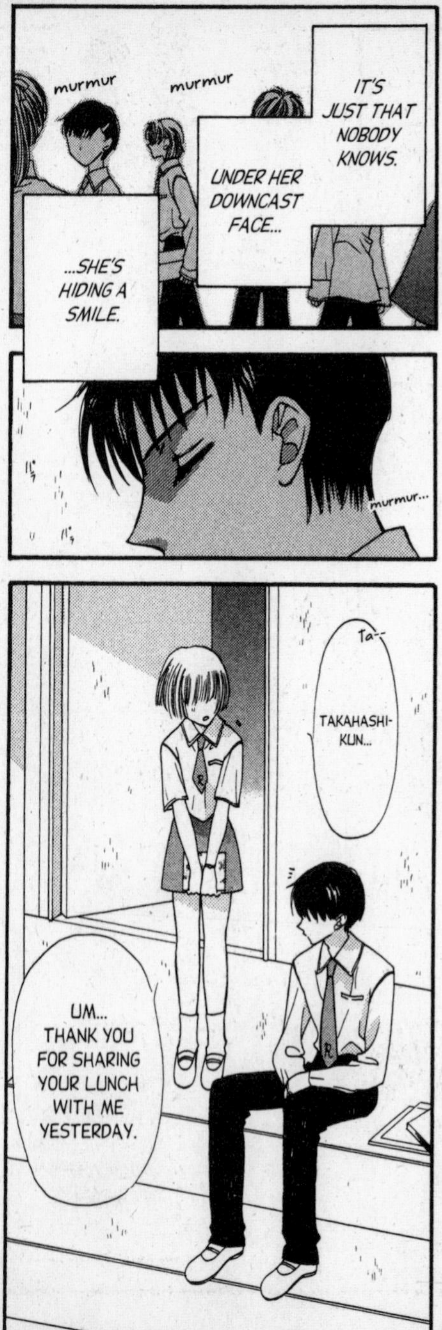
IT'S JUST THAT NOBODY KNOWS.
murmur
UNDER HER DOWNCAST FACE...
murmur
...SHE'S HIDING A SMILE.
murmur...
Ta--
TAKAHASHI-KUN...
UM... THANK YOU FOR SHARING YOUR LUNCH WITH ME YESTERDAY.

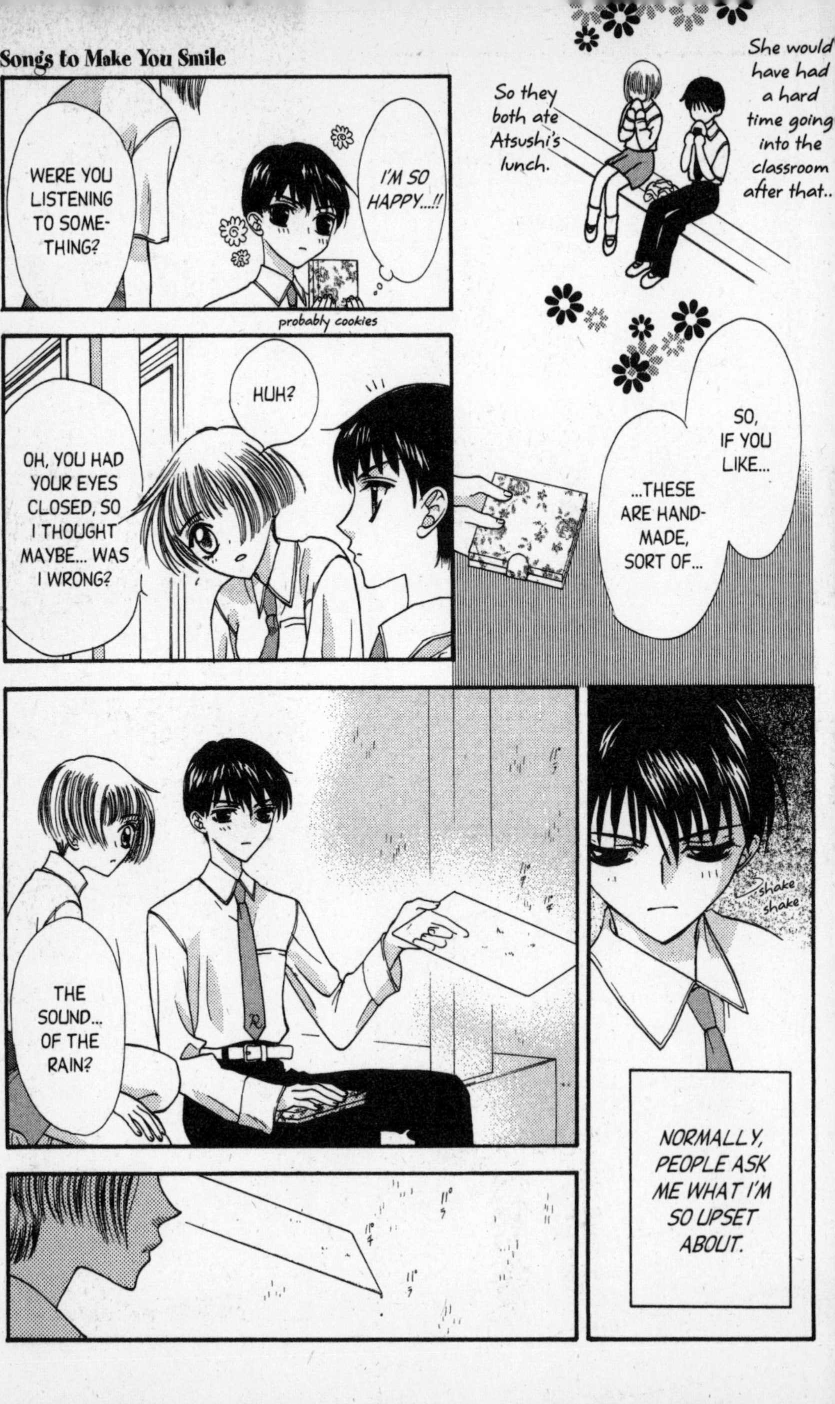
She would have had a hard time going into the classroom after that..
So they both ate Atsushi's lunch.
I'M SO HAPPY...!!
WERE YOU LISTENING TO SOME-THING?
probably cookies
SO, IF YOU LIKE...
...THESE ARE HAND-MADE, SORT OF...
HUH?
OH, YOU HAD YOUR EYES CLOSED, SO I THOUGHT MAYBE... WAS I WRONG?
shake shake
NORMALLY, PEOPLE ASK ME WHAT I'M SO UPSET ABOUT.
THE SOUND... OF THE RAIN?

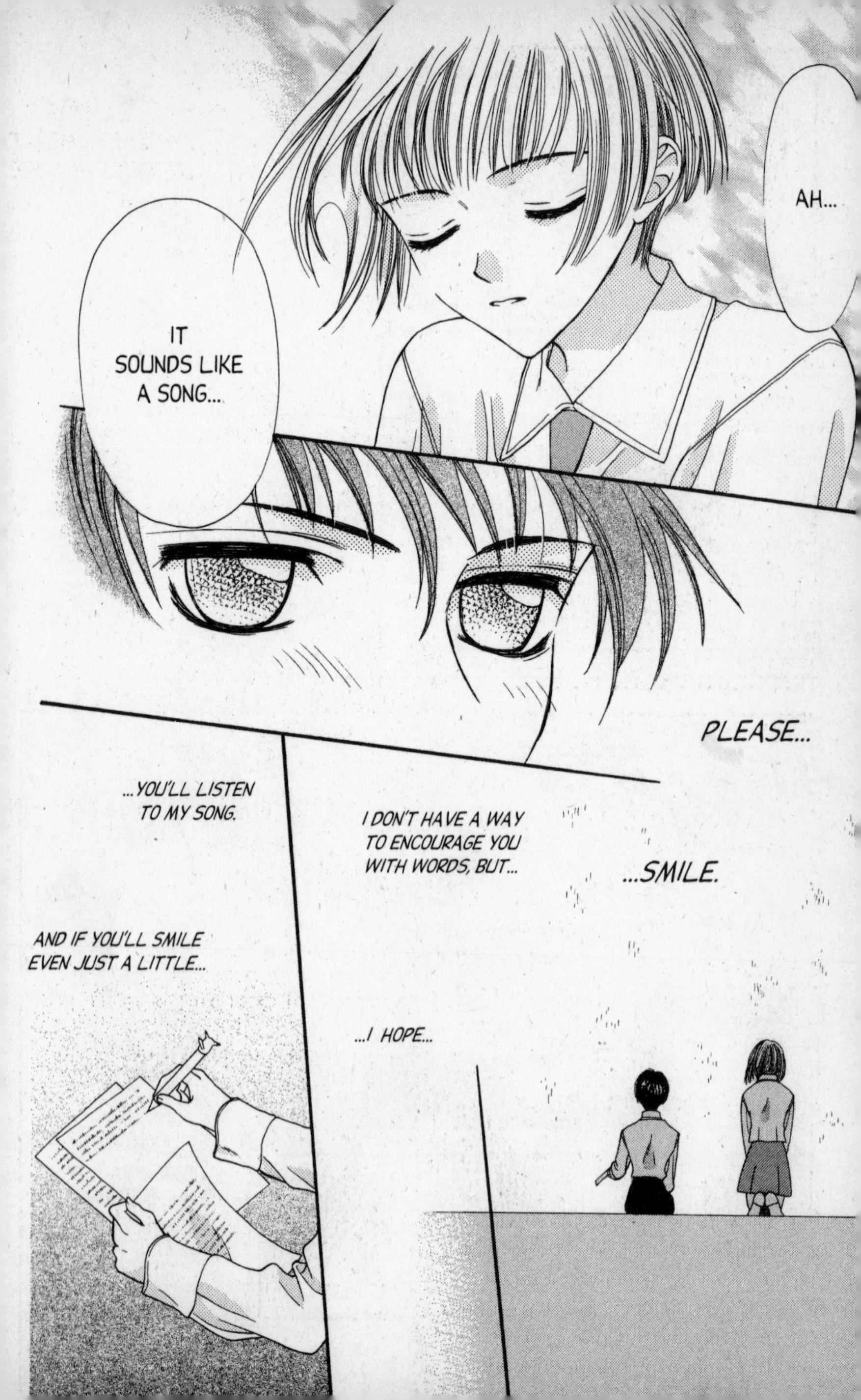
AH...
IT SOUNDS LIKE A SONG...
PLEASE...
...SMILE.
I DON'T HAVE A WAY TO ENCOURAGE YOU WITH WORDS, BUT...
...I HOPE...
...YOU'LL LISTEN TO MY SONG.
AND IF YOU'LL SMILE EVEN JUST A LITTLE...

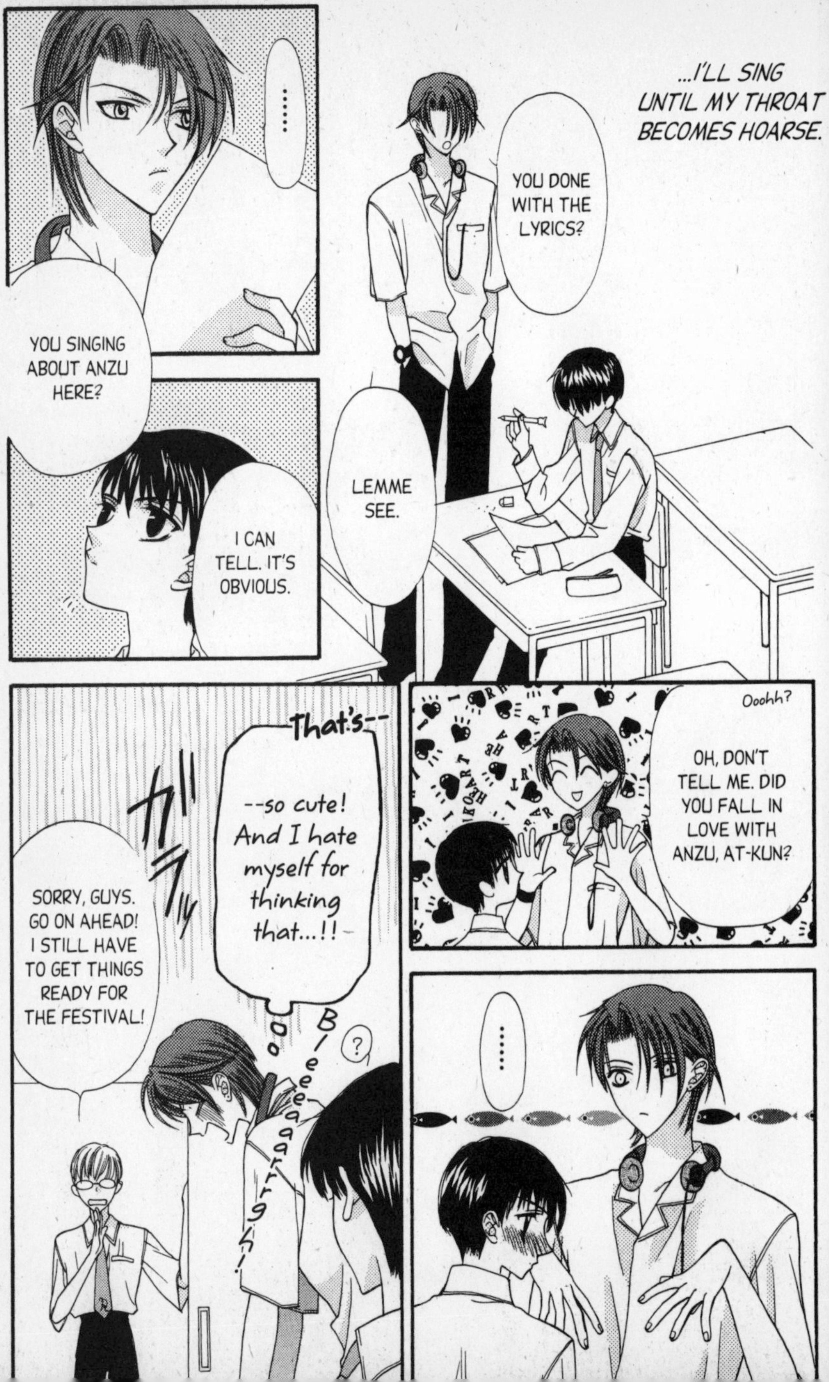
...I'LL SING UNTIL MY THROAT BECOMES HOARSE.
YOU DONE WITH THE LYRICS?
LEMME SEE.
......
YOU SINGING ABOUT ANZU HERE?
I CAN TELL. IT'S OBVIOUS.
Ooohh?
OH, DON'T TELL ME. DID YOU FALL IN LOVE WITH ANZU, AT-KUN?
......
That's--
--so cute! And I hate myself for thinking that...!!
Bleeeeaaarrrgh!
?
SORRY, GUYS. GO ON AHEAD! I STILL HAVE TO GET THINGS READY FOR THE FESTIVAL!

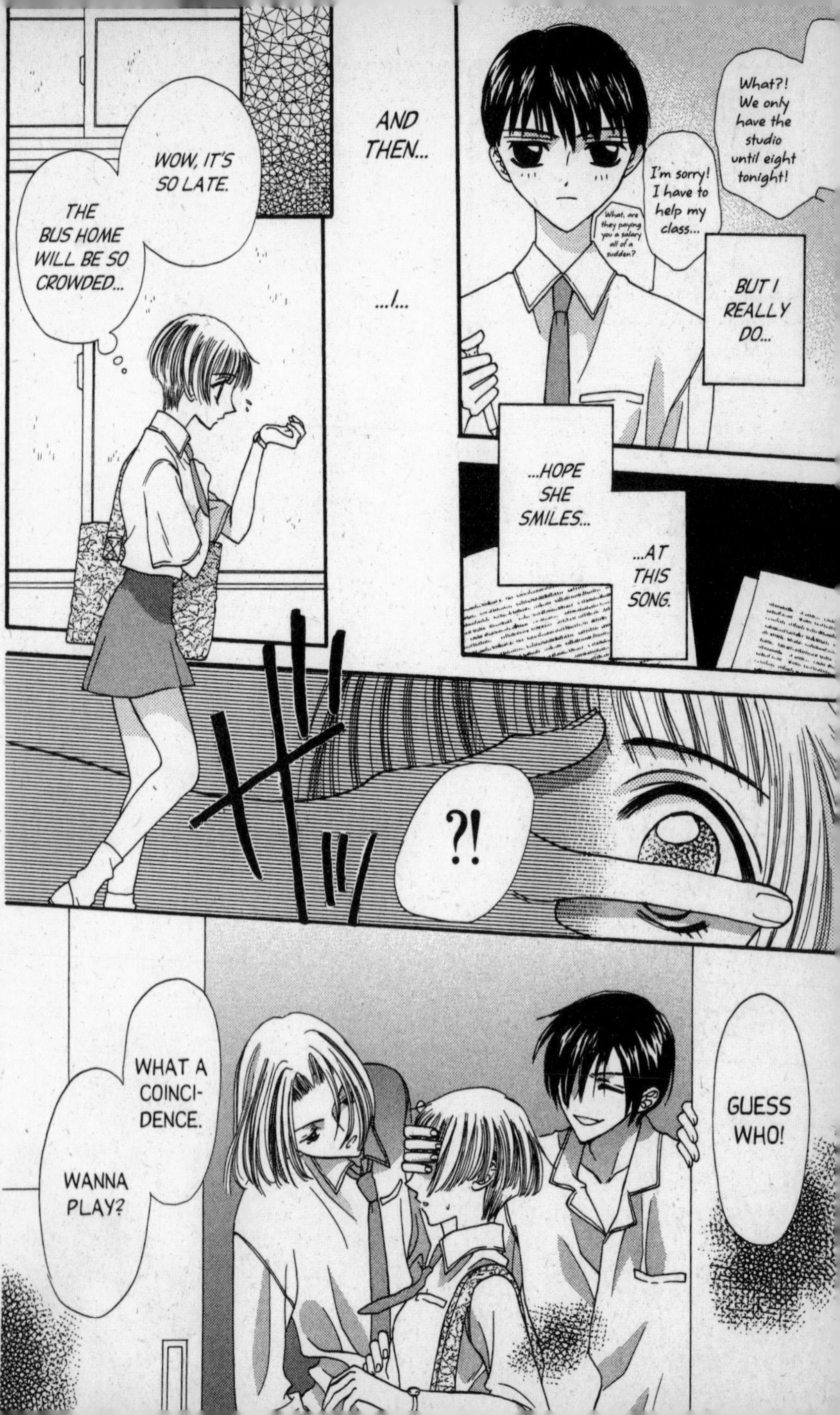
What?! We only have the studio until eight tonight!
I'm sorry! I have to help my class...
What, are they paying you a salary all of a sudden?
BUT I REALLY DO...
...HOPE SHE SMILES...
...AT THIS SONG.
WOW, IT'S SO LATE.
THE BUS HOME WILL BE SO CROWDED...
AND THEN...
...I...
?!
GUESS WHO!
WHAT A COINCIDENCE.
WANNA PLAY?

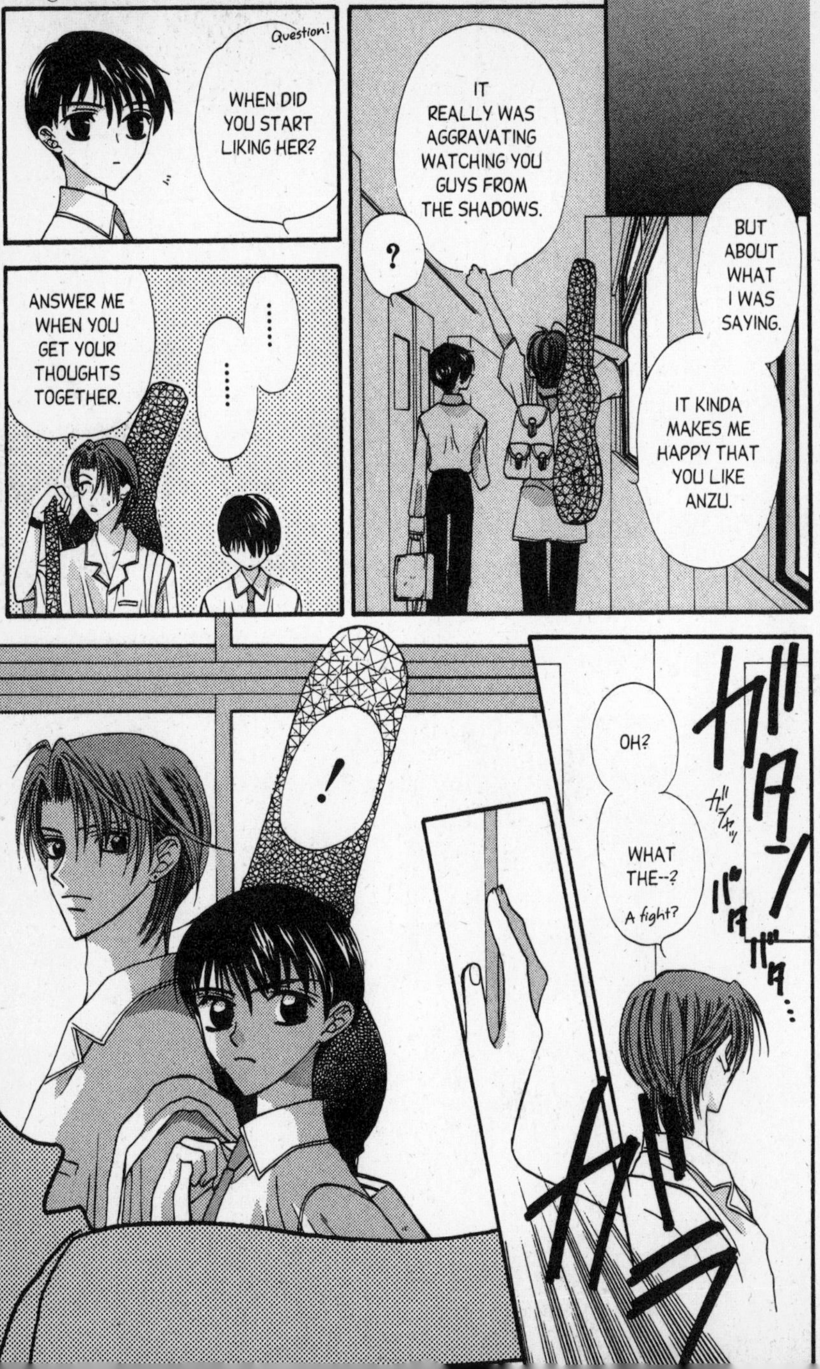
IT REALLY WAS AGGRAVATING WATCHING YOU GUYS FROM THE SHADOWS.
?
BUT ABOUT WHAT I WAS SAYING.
IT KINDA MAKES ME HAPPY THAT YOU LIKE ANZU.
Question!
WHEN DID YOU START LIKING HER?
......
......
ANSWER ME WHEN YOU GET YOUR THOUGHTS TOGETHER.
ガタン
OH?
WHAT THE--?
A fight?
バタバタ…
ガラ
!

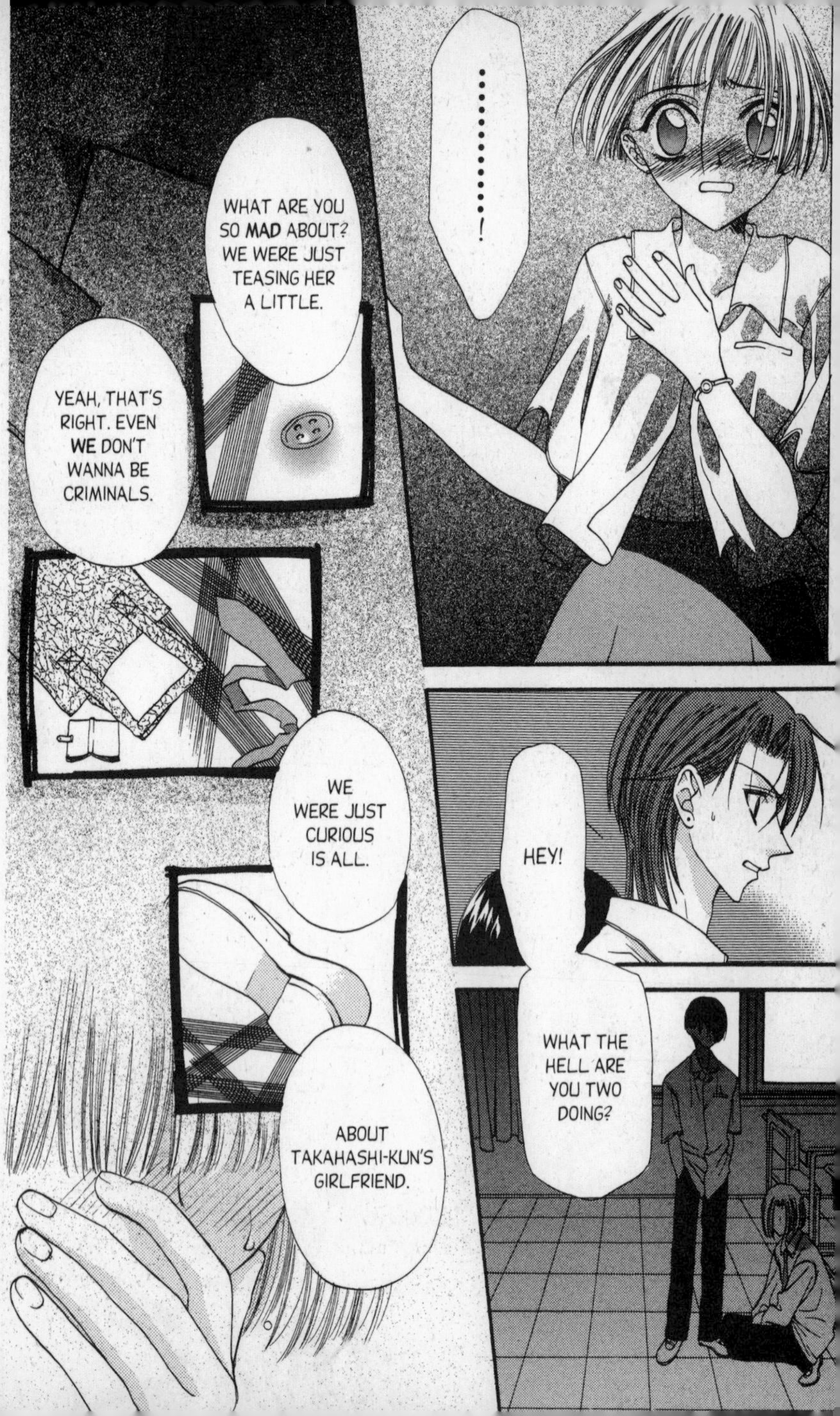

......!
HEY!
WHAT THE HELL ARE YOU TWO DOING?
WHAT ARE YOU SO **MAD** ABOUT? WE WERE JUST TEASING HER A LITTLE.
YEAH, THAT'S RIGHT. EVEN **WE** DON'T WANNA BE CRIMINALS.
WE WERE JUST CURIOUS IS ALL.
ABOUT TAKAHASHI-KUN'S GIRLFRIEND.

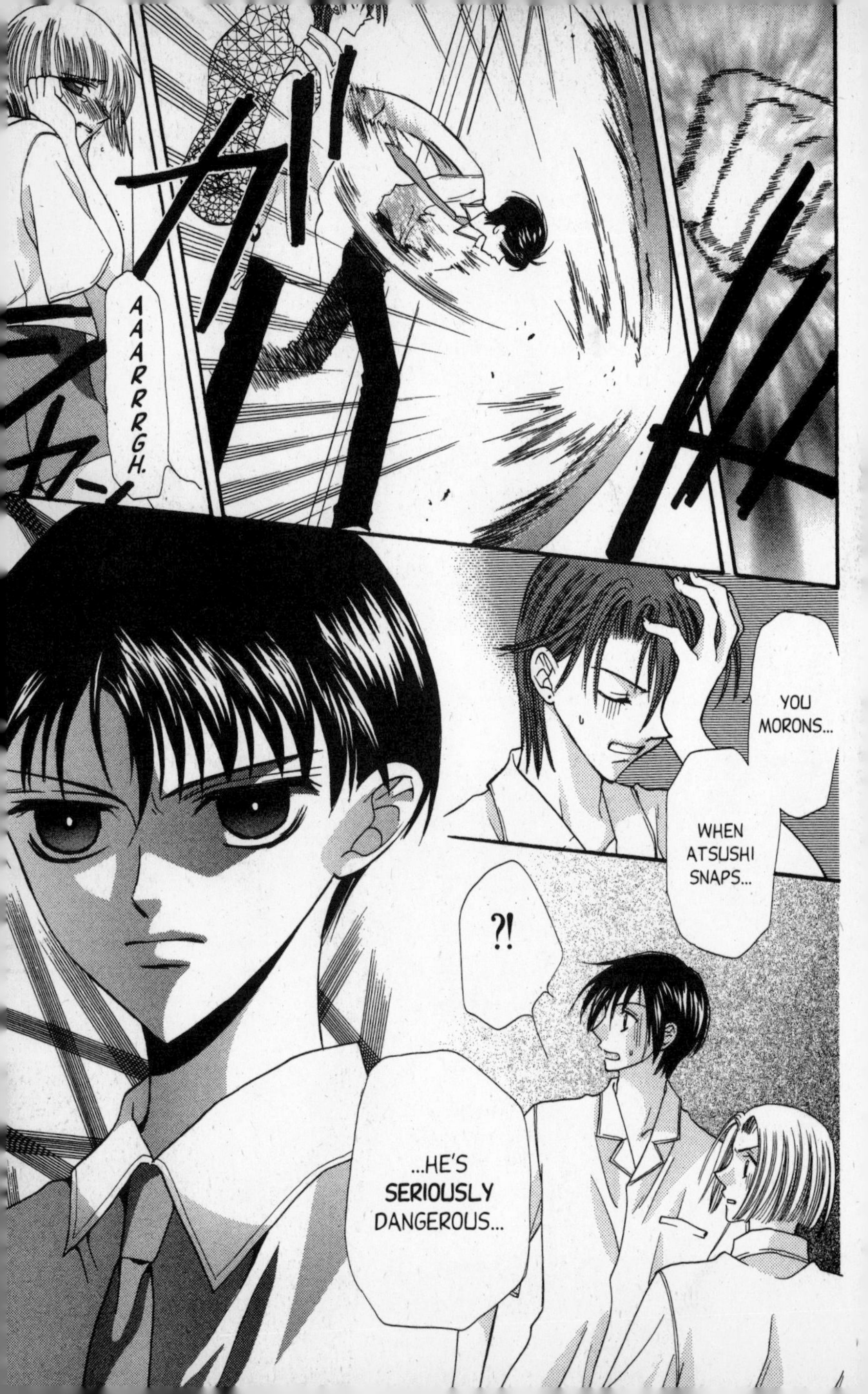
AAAARRRGH.
YOU MORONS...
WHEN ATSUSHI SNAPS...
?!
...HE'S **SERIOUSLY** DANGEROUS...

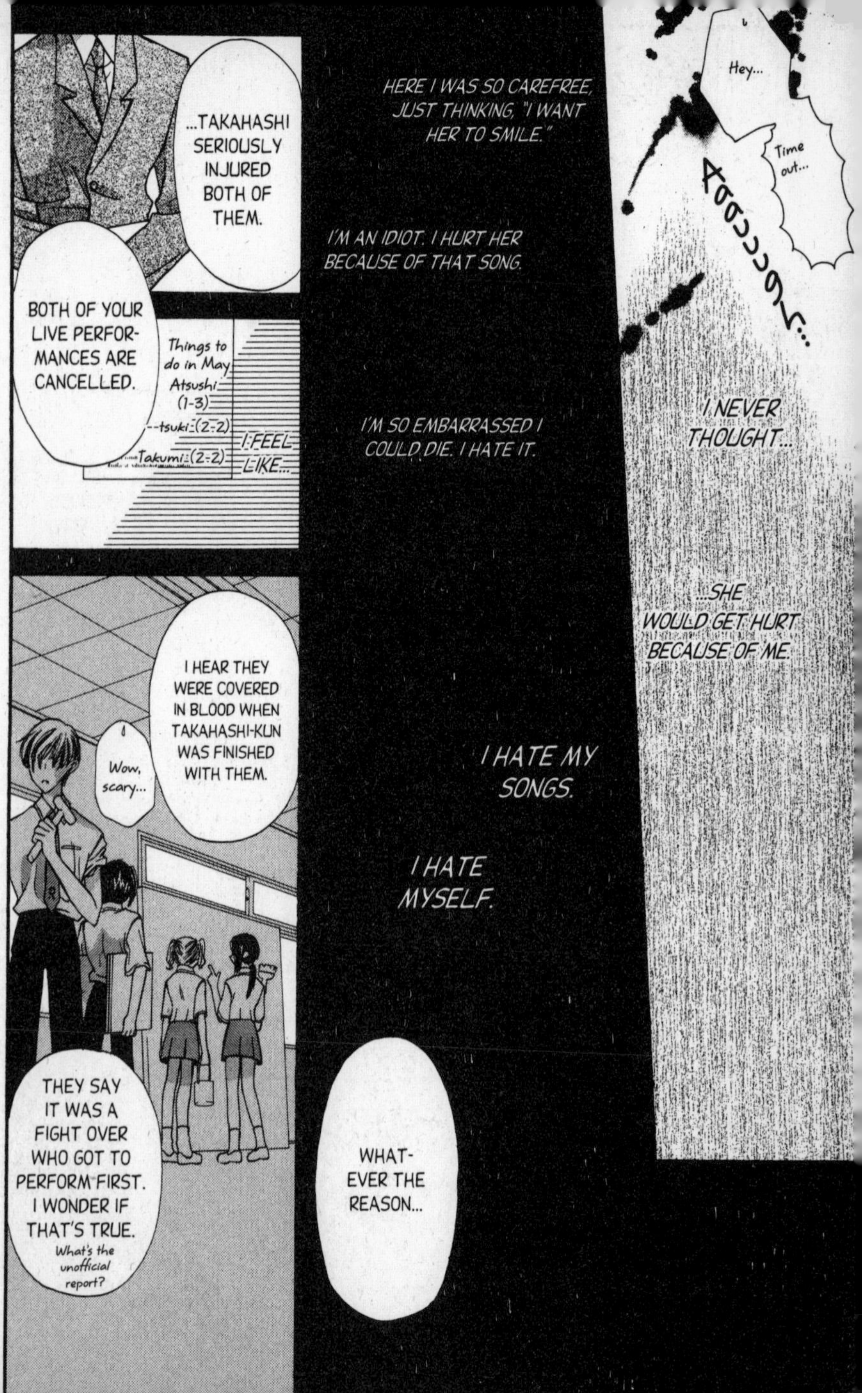
Hey...
Time out...
I NEVER THOUGHT...
...SHE WOULD GET HURT BECAUSE OF ME.
HERE I WAS SO CAREFREE, JUST THINKING, "I WANT HER TO SMILE."
I'M AN IDIOT. I HURT HER BECAUSE OF THAT SONG.
I'M SO EMBARRASSED I COULD DIE. I HATE IT.
I HATE MY SONGS.
I HATE MYSELF.
WHAT-EVER THE REASON...
...TAKAHASHI SERIOUSLY INJURED BOTH OF THEM.
BOTH OF YOUR LIVE PERFOR-MANCES ARE CANCELLED.
Things to do in May
Atsushi (1-3)
--tsuki (2-2)
Takumi (2-2)
I FEEL LIKE...
I HEAR THEY WERE COVERED IN BLOOD WHEN TAKAHASHI-KUN WAS FINISHED WITH THEM.
Wow, scary...
THEY SAY IT WAS A FIGHT OVER WHO GOT TO PERFORM FIRST. I WONDER IF THAT'S TRUE.
What's the unofficial report?

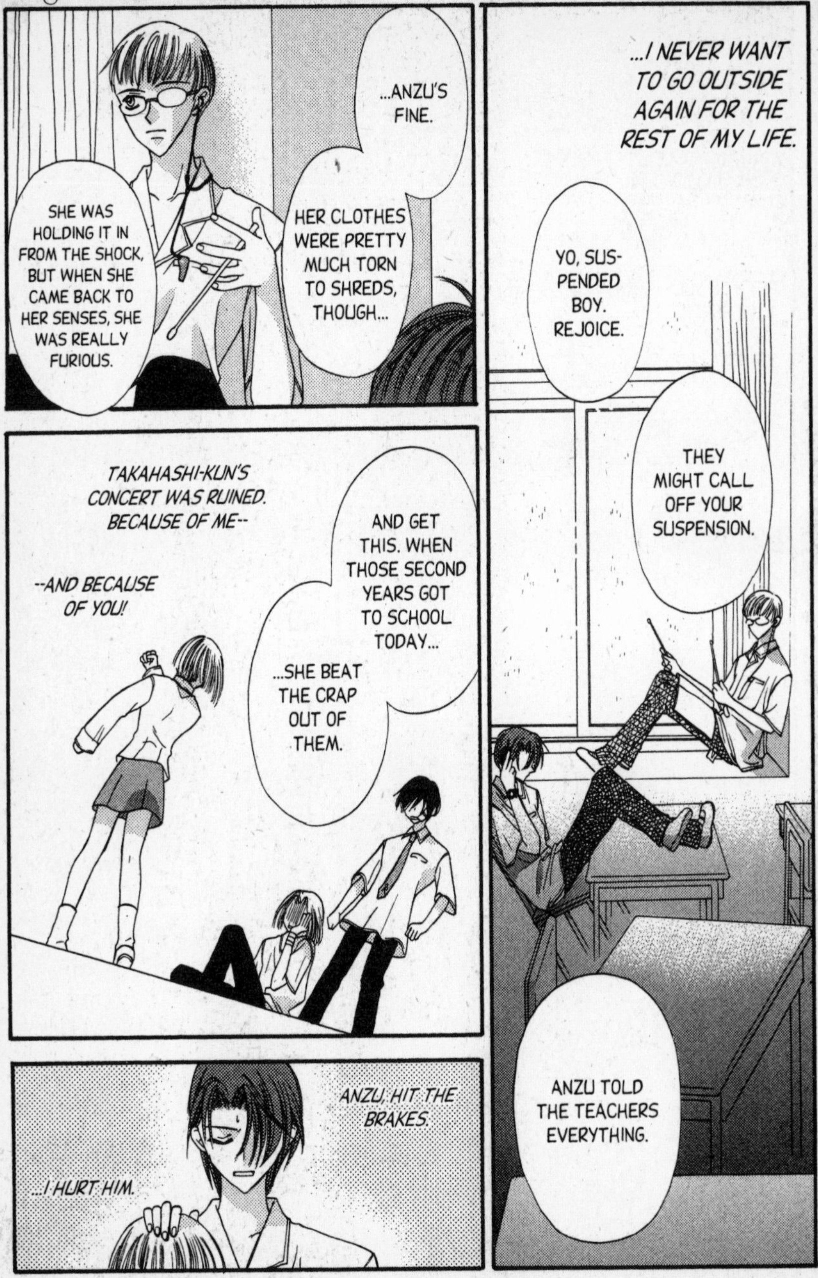
...I NEVER WANT TO GO OUTSIDE AGAIN FOR THE REST OF MY LIFE.
YO, SUS-PENDED BOY. REJOICE.
THEY MIGHT CALL OFF YOUR SUSPENSION.
ANZU TOLD THE TEACHERS EVERYTHING.
...ANZU'S FINE.
HER CLOTHES WERE PRETTY MUCH TORN TO SHREDS, THOUGH...
SHE WAS HOLDING IT IN FROM THE SHOCK, BUT WHEN SHE CAME BACK TO HER SENSES, SHE WAS REALLY FURIOUS.
AND GET THIS. WHEN THOSE SECOND YEARS GOT TO SCHOOL TODAY...
...SHE BEAT THE CRAP OUT OF THEM.
TAKAHASHI-KUN'S CONCERT WAS RUINED. BECAUSE OF ME--
--AND BECAUSE OF YOU!
ANZU, HIT THE BRAKES.
...I HURT HIM.

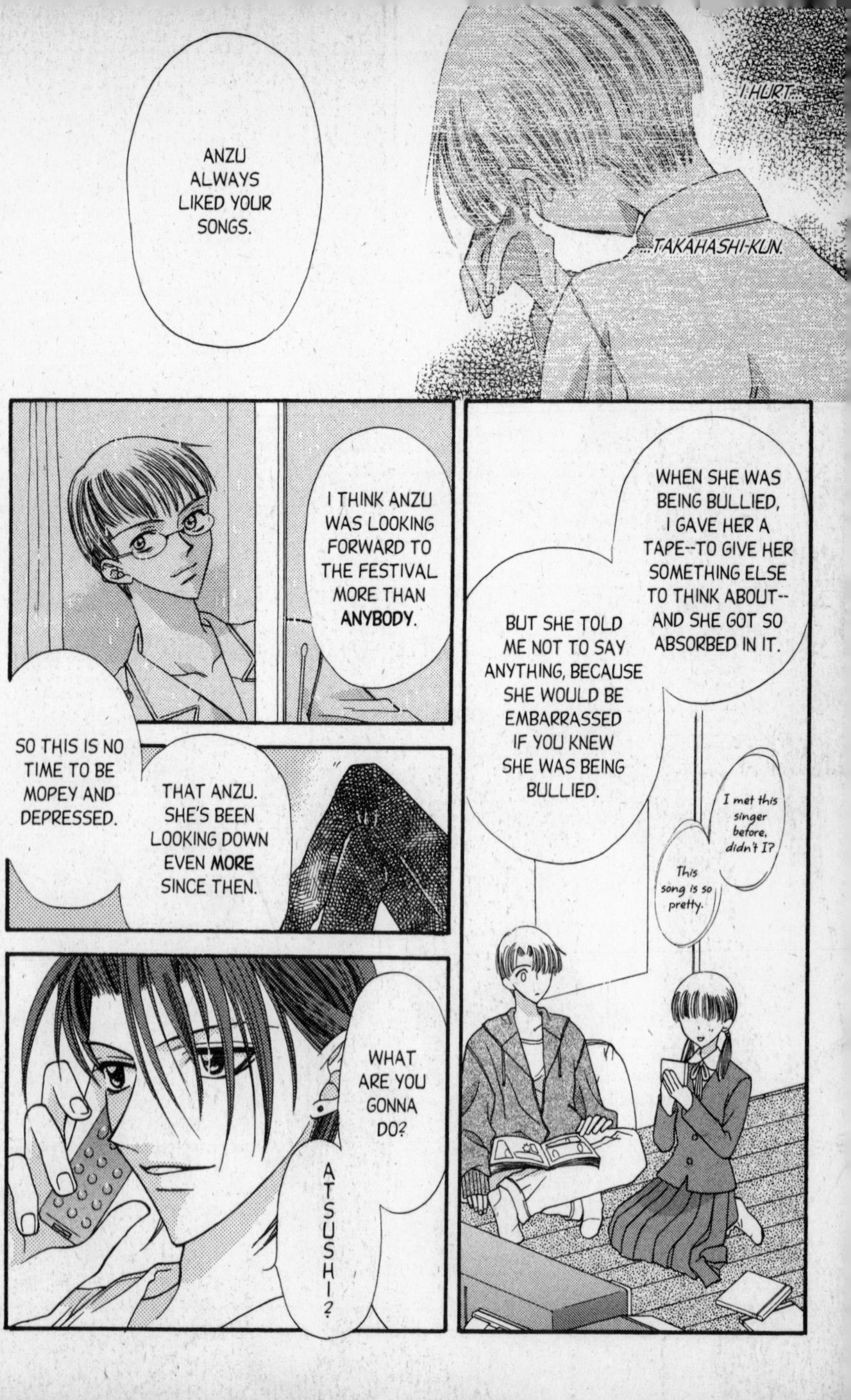
I HURT...
...TAKAHASHI-KUN.
ANZU ALWAYS LIKED YOUR SONGS.
WHEN SHE WAS BEING BULLIED, I GAVE HER A TAPE--TO GIVE HER SOMETHING ELSE TO THINK ABOUT--AND SHE GOT SO ABSORBED IN IT.
BUT SHE TOLD ME NOT TO SAY ANYTHING, BECAUSE SHE WOULD BE EMBARRASSED IF YOU KNEW SHE WAS BEING BULLIED.
I met this singer before, didn't I?
This song is so pretty.
I THINK ANZU WAS LOOKING FORWARD TO THE FESTIVAL MORE THAN **ANYBODY**.
THAT ANZU. SHE'S BEEN LOOKING DOWN EVEN **MORE** SINCE THEN.
SO THIS IS NO TIME TO BE MOPEY AND DEPRESSED.
WHAT ARE YOU GONNA DO?
ATSUSHI?

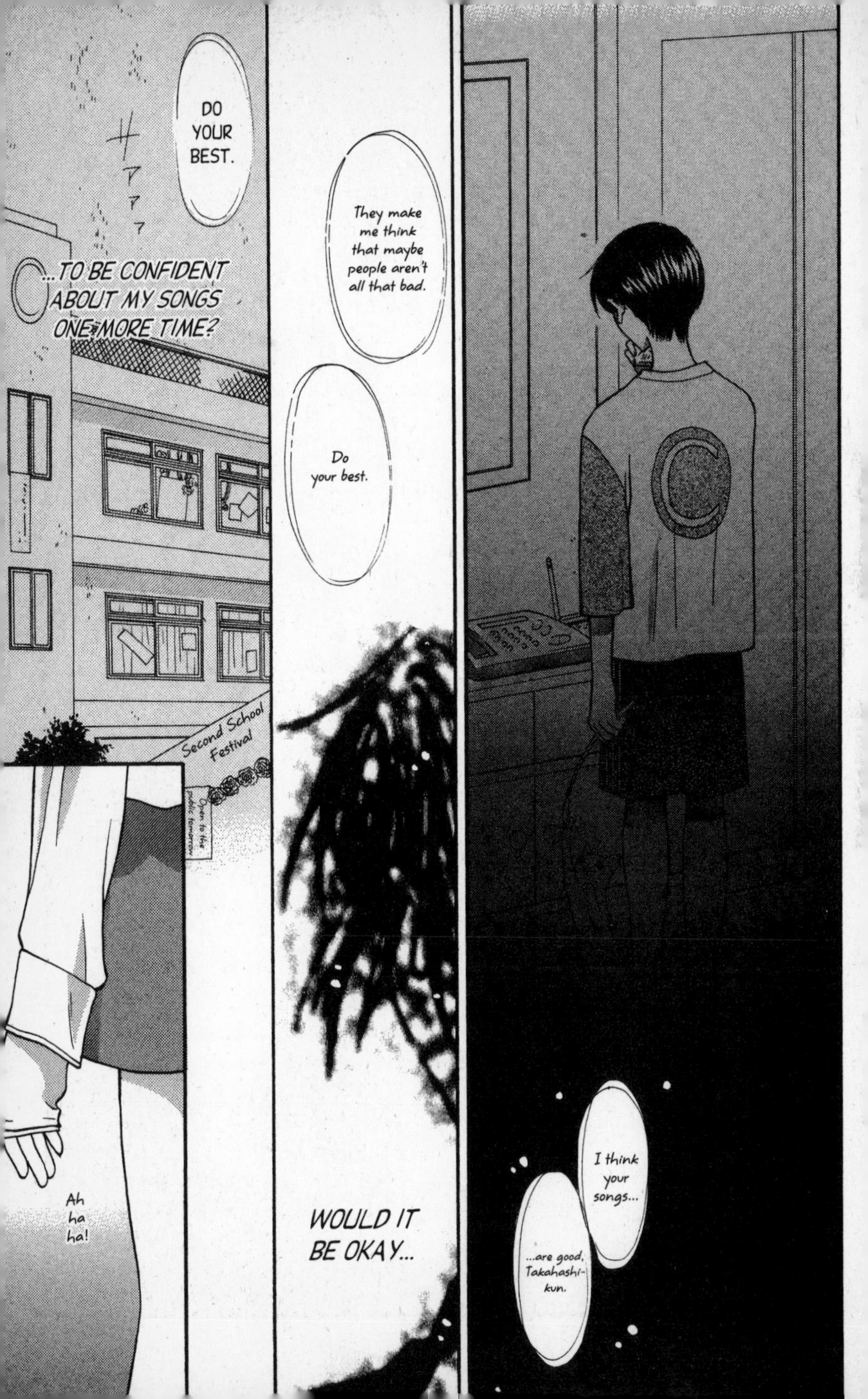
I think your songs...
...are good, Takahashi-kun.
They make me think that maybe people aren't all that bad.
Do your best.
WOULD IT BE OKAY...
DO YOUR BEST.
...TO BE CONFIDENT ABOUT MY SONGS ONE MORE TIME?
Second School Festival
Open to the public tomorrow
Ah ha ha!

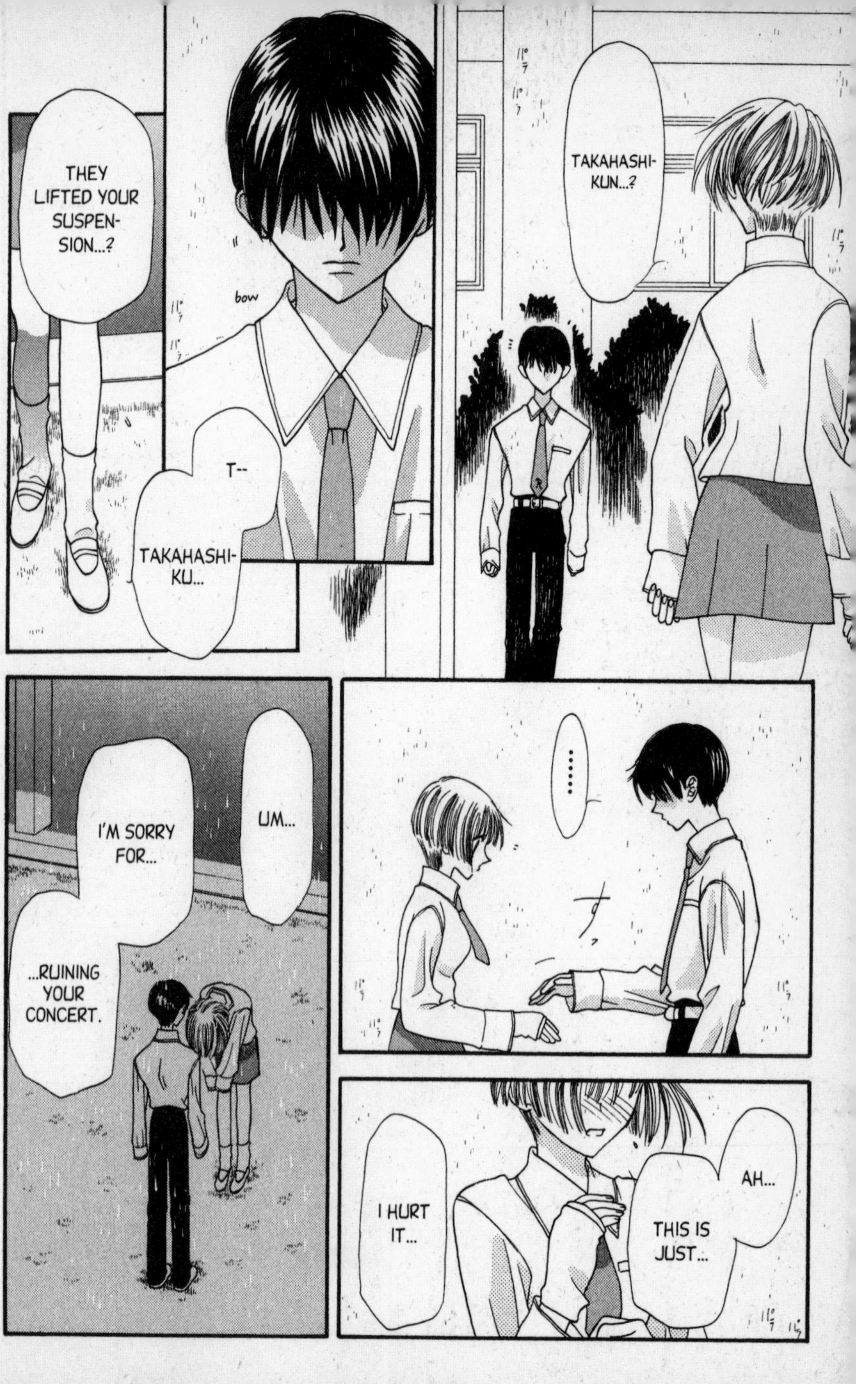
TAKAHASHI-KUN...?
bow
T--
TAKAHASHI-KU...
THEY LIFTED YOUR SUSPENSION...?
......
AH...
THIS IS JUST...
I HURT IT...
UM...
I'M SORRY FOR...
...RUINING YOUR CONCERT.

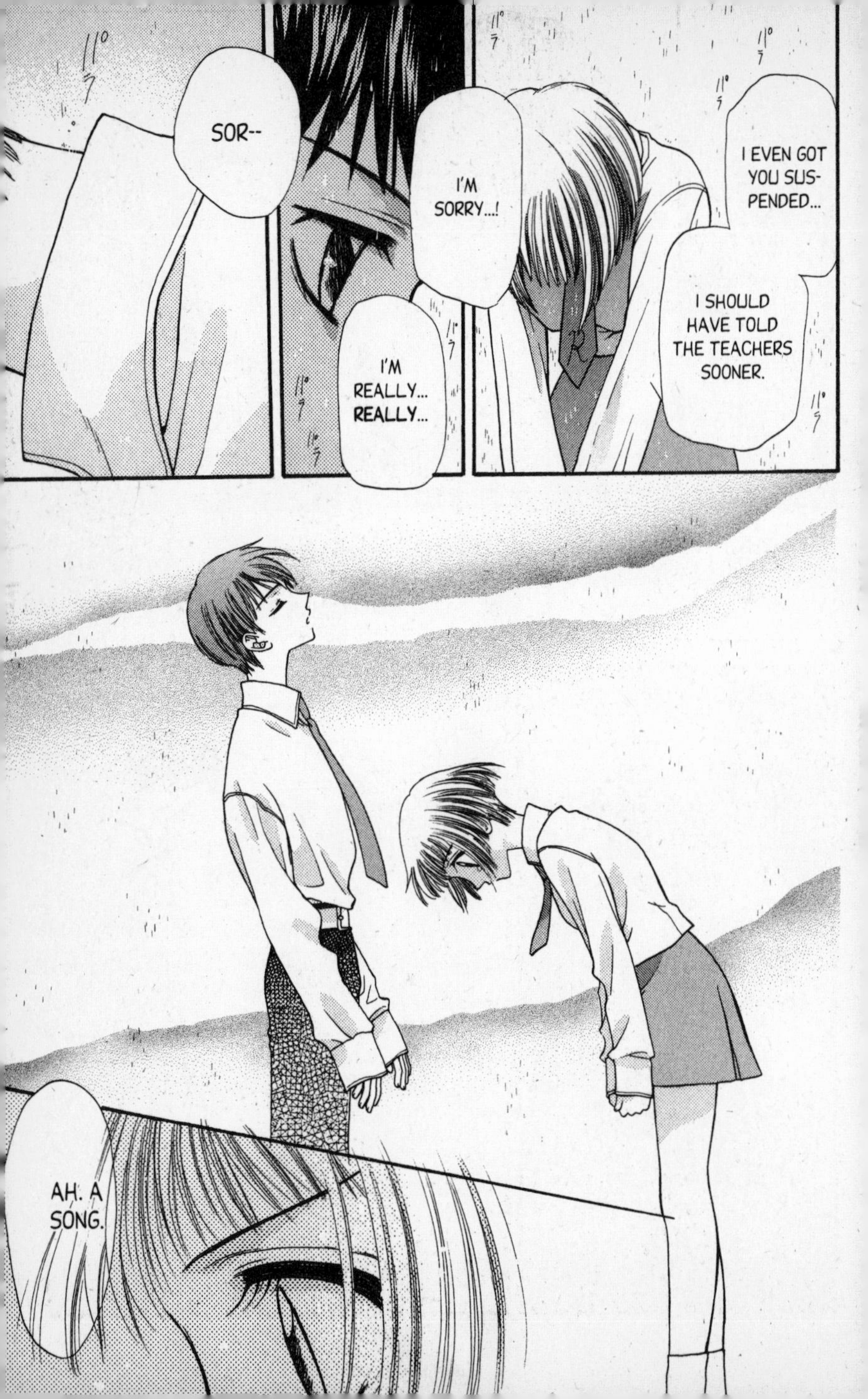
I EVEN GOT YOU SUSPENDED...
I SHOULD HAVE TOLD THE TEACHERS SOONER.
I'M SORRY...!
I'M REALLY... REALLY...
SOR--
AH. A SONG.

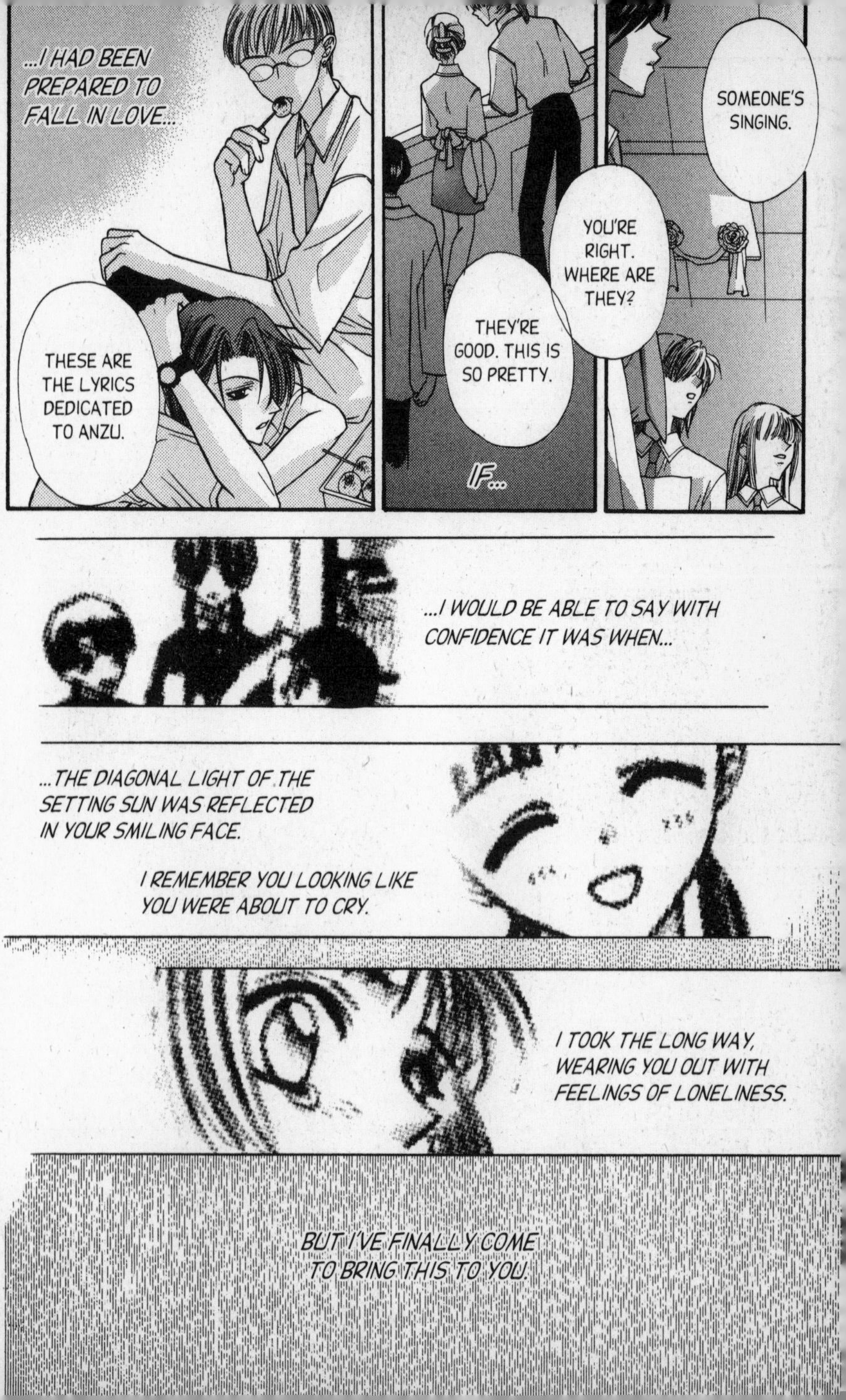
SOMEONE'S SINGING.
YOU'RE RIGHT. WHERE ARE THEY?
THEY'RE GOOD. THIS IS SO PRETTY.
IF...
...I HAD BEEN PREPARED TO FALL IN LOVE...
THESE ARE THE LYRICS DEDICATED TO ANZU.
...I WOULD BE ABLE TO SAY WITH CONFIDENCE IT WAS WHEN...
...THE DIAGONAL LIGHT OF THE SETTING SUN WAS REFLECTED IN YOUR SMILING FACE.
I REMEMBER YOU LOOKING LIKE YOU WERE ABOUT TO CRY.
I TOOK THE LONG WAY, WEARING YOU OUT WITH FEELINGS OF LONELINESS.
BUT I'VE FINALLY COME TO BRING THIS TO YOU.

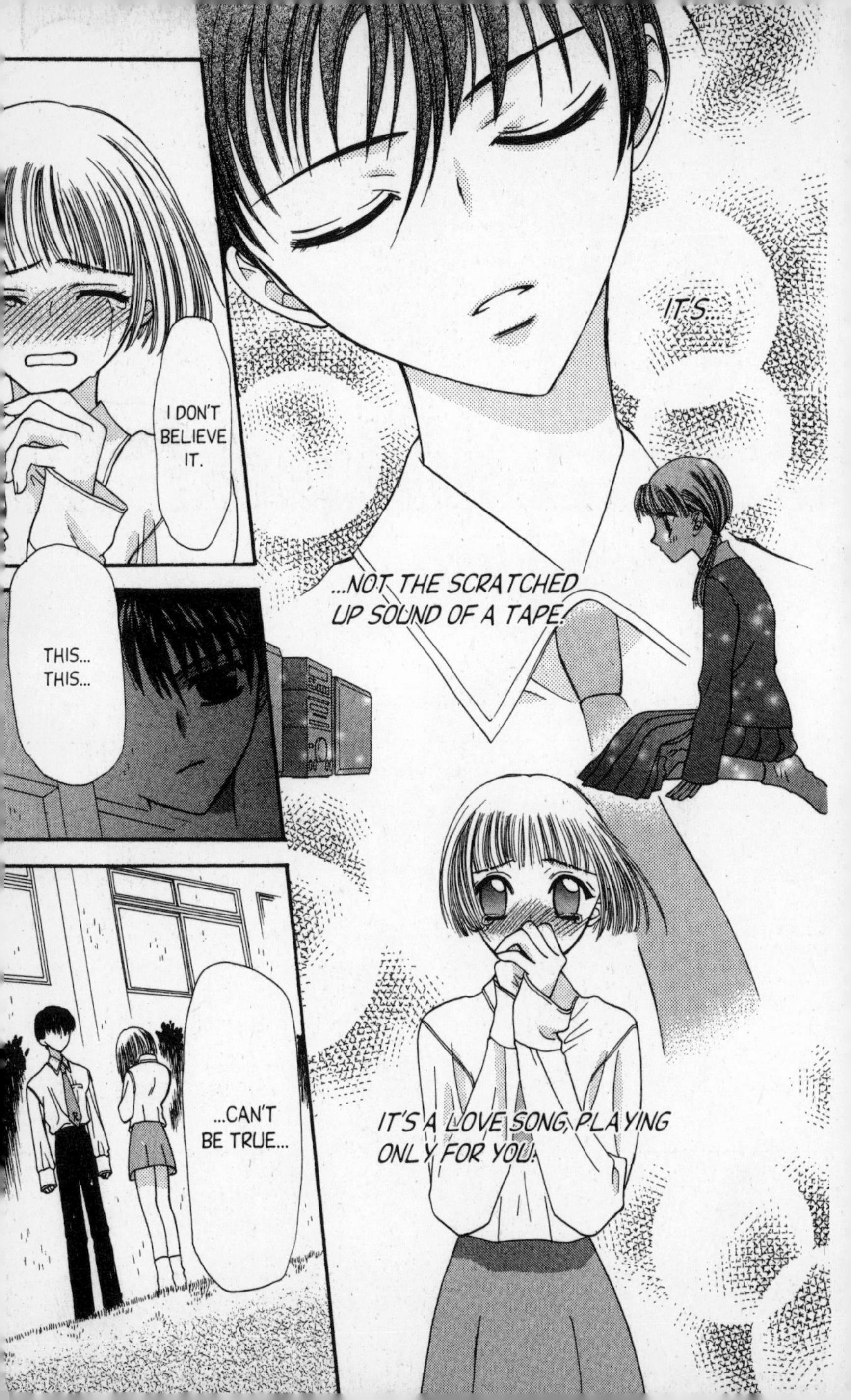
IT'S...
...NOT THE SCRATCHED UP SOUND OF A TAPE.
IT'S A LOVE SONG, PLAYING ONLY FOR YOU.
I DON'T BELIEVE IT.
THIS... THIS...
...CAN'T BE TRUE...

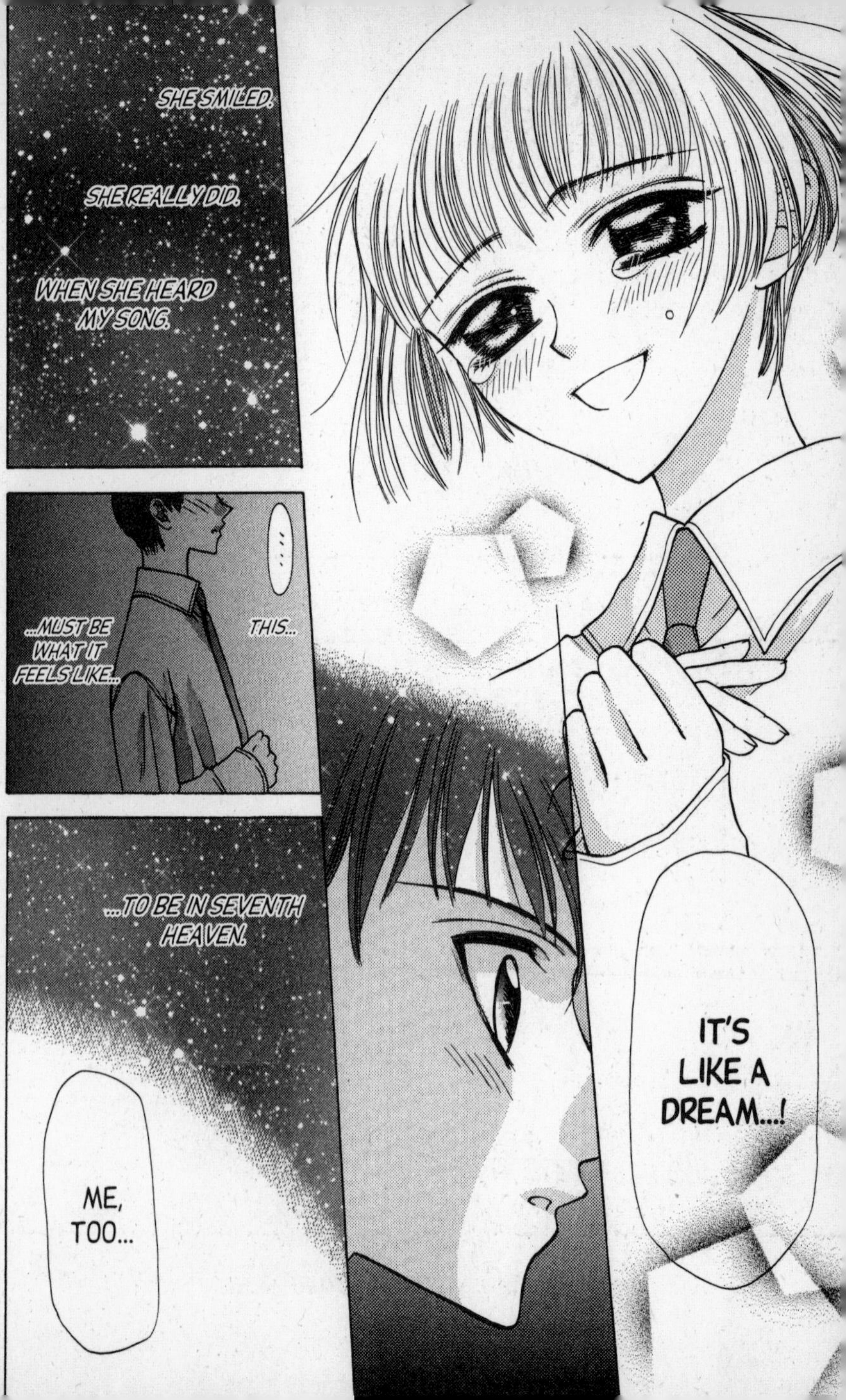
IT'S LIKE A DREAM...!
SHE SMILED.
SHE REALLY DID.
WHEN SHE HEARD MY SONG.
...
THIS...
...MUST BE WHAT IT FEELS LIKE...
...TO BE IN SEVENTH HEAVEN.
ME, TOO...

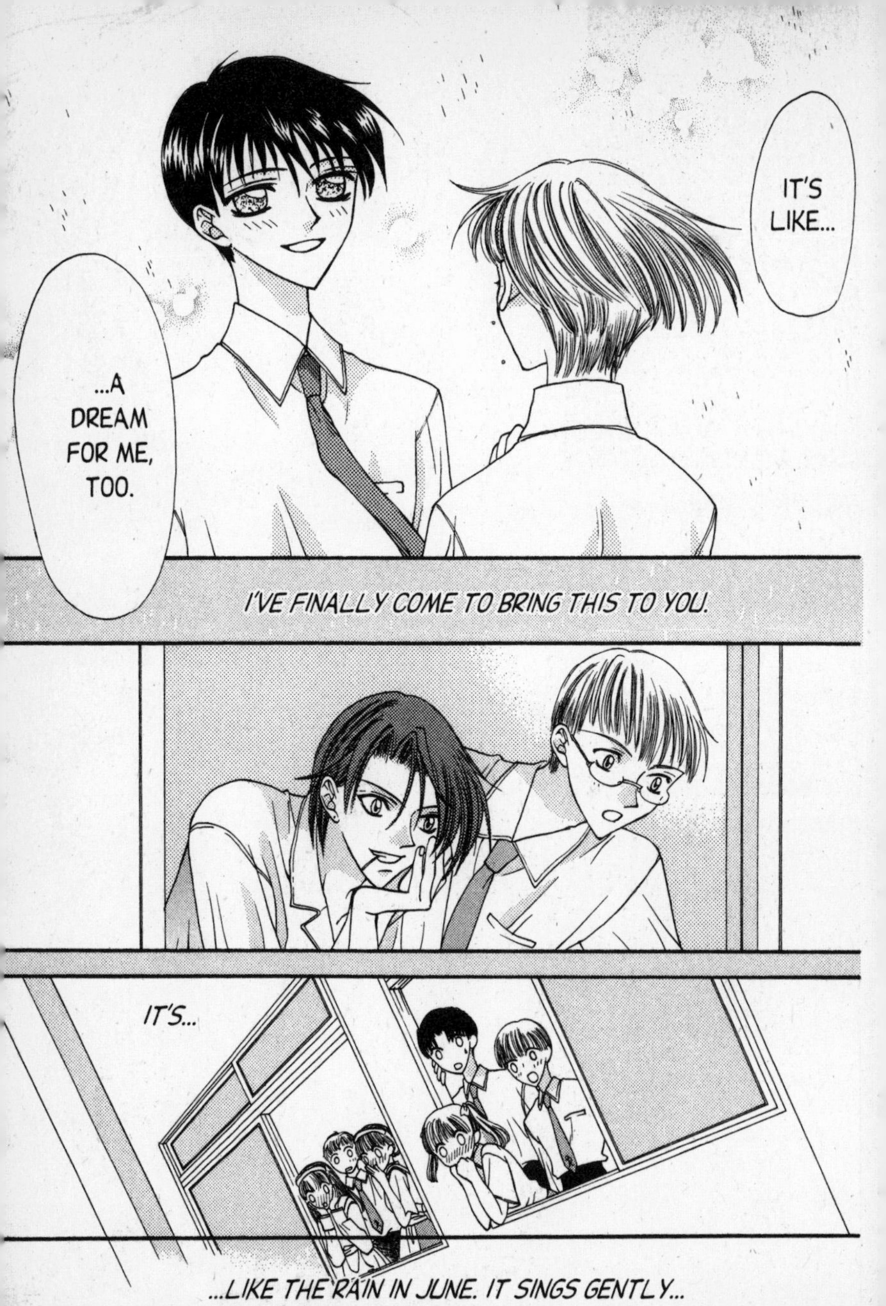
IT'S LIKE...
...A DREAM FOR ME, TOO.
I'VE FINALLY COME TO BRING THIS TO YOU.
IT'S...
...LIKE THE RAIN IN JUNE. IT SINGS GENTLY...

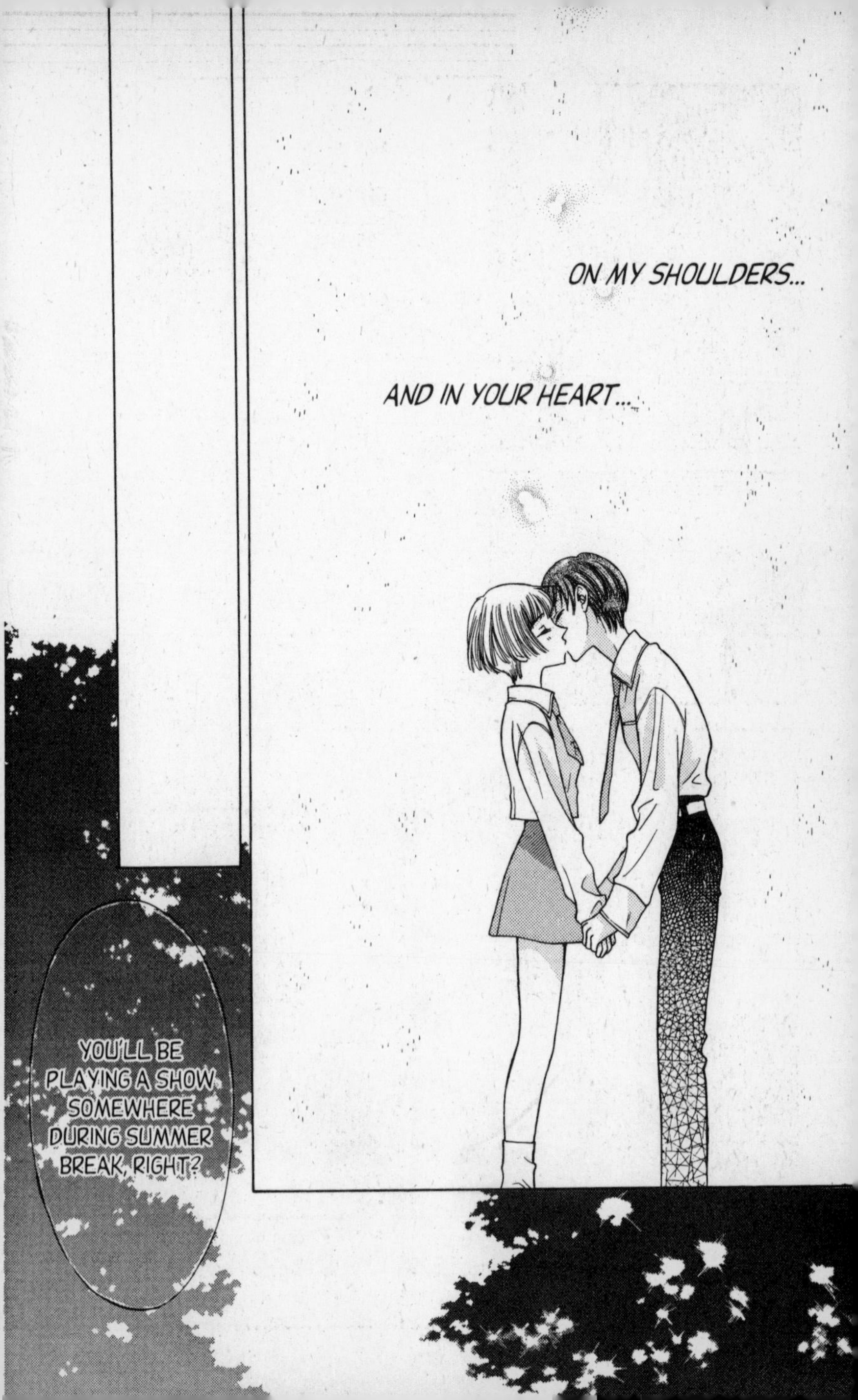
ON MY SHOULDERS...
AND IN YOUR HEART...
YOU'LL BE PLAYING A SHOW SOMEWHERE DURING SUMMER BREAK, RIGHT?

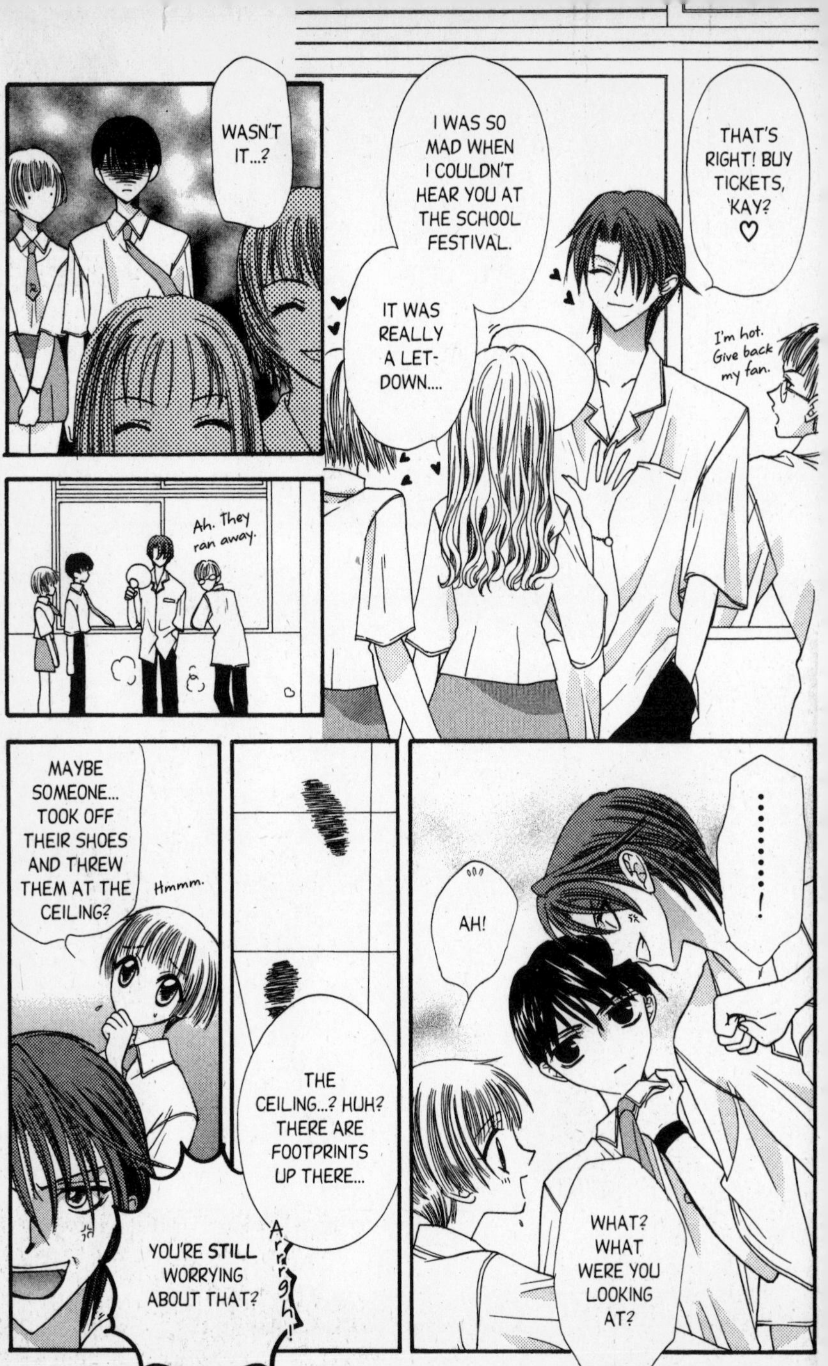
THAT'S RIGHT! BUY TICKETS, 'KAY? ♡
I WAS SO MAD WHEN I COULDN'T HEAR YOU AT THE SCHOOL FESTIVAL.
IT WAS REALLY A LET-DOWN....
I'm hot. Give back my fan.
WASN'T IT...?
Ah. They ran away.
........!
AH!
WHAT? WHAT WERE YOU LOOKING AT?
THE CEILING...? HUH? THERE ARE FOOTPRINTS UP THERE...
MAYBE SOMEONE... TOOK OFF THEIR SHOES AND THREW THEM AT THE CEILING?
Hmmm.
YOU'RE STILL WORRYING ABOUT THAT?
Arrrgh!

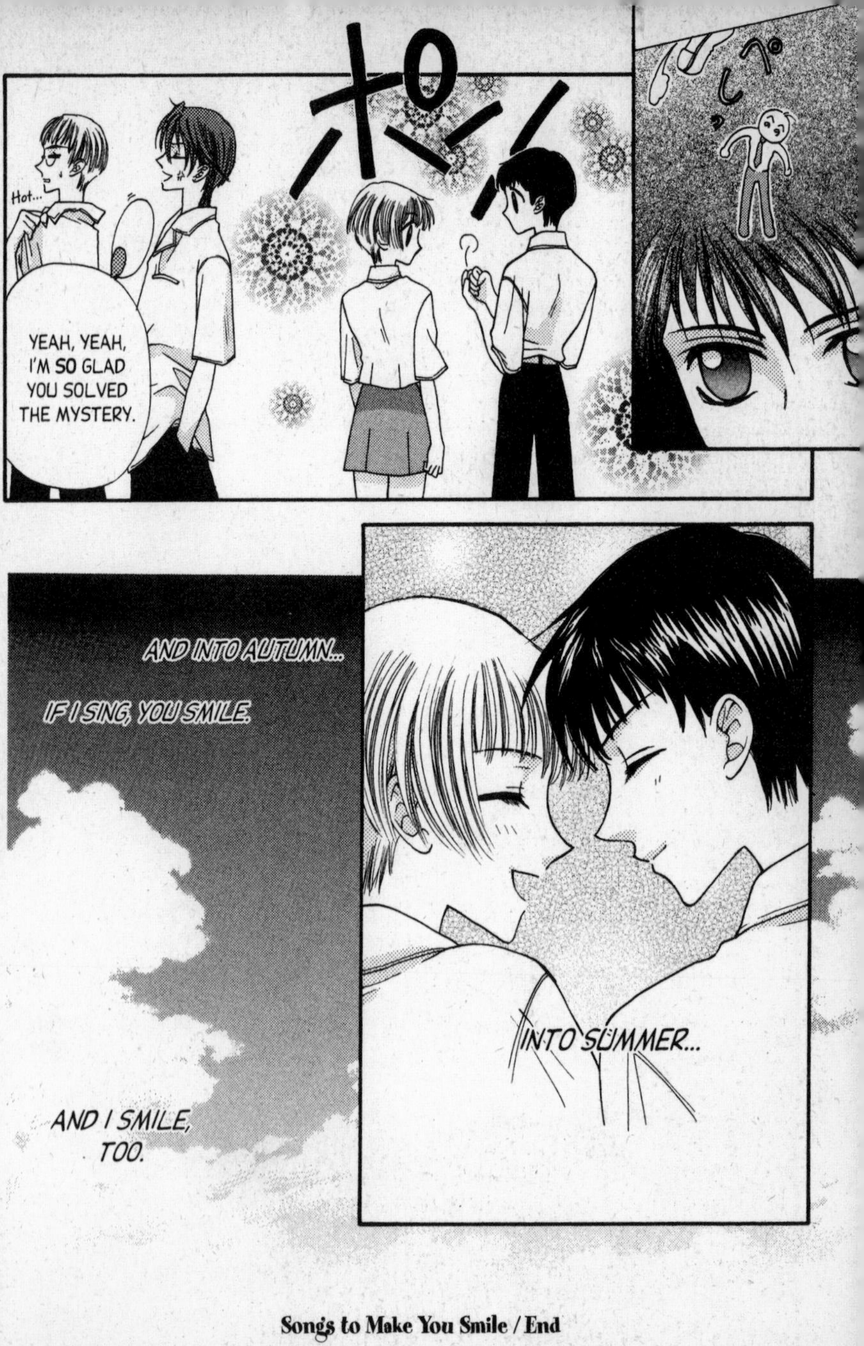
ぺしっ
ポン
Hot...
YEAH, YEAH, I'M SO GLAD YOU SOLVED THE MYSTERY.
INTO SUMMER...
AND INTO AUTUMN...
IF I SING, YOU SMILE.
AND I SMILE, TOO.

Songs to Make You Smile / End

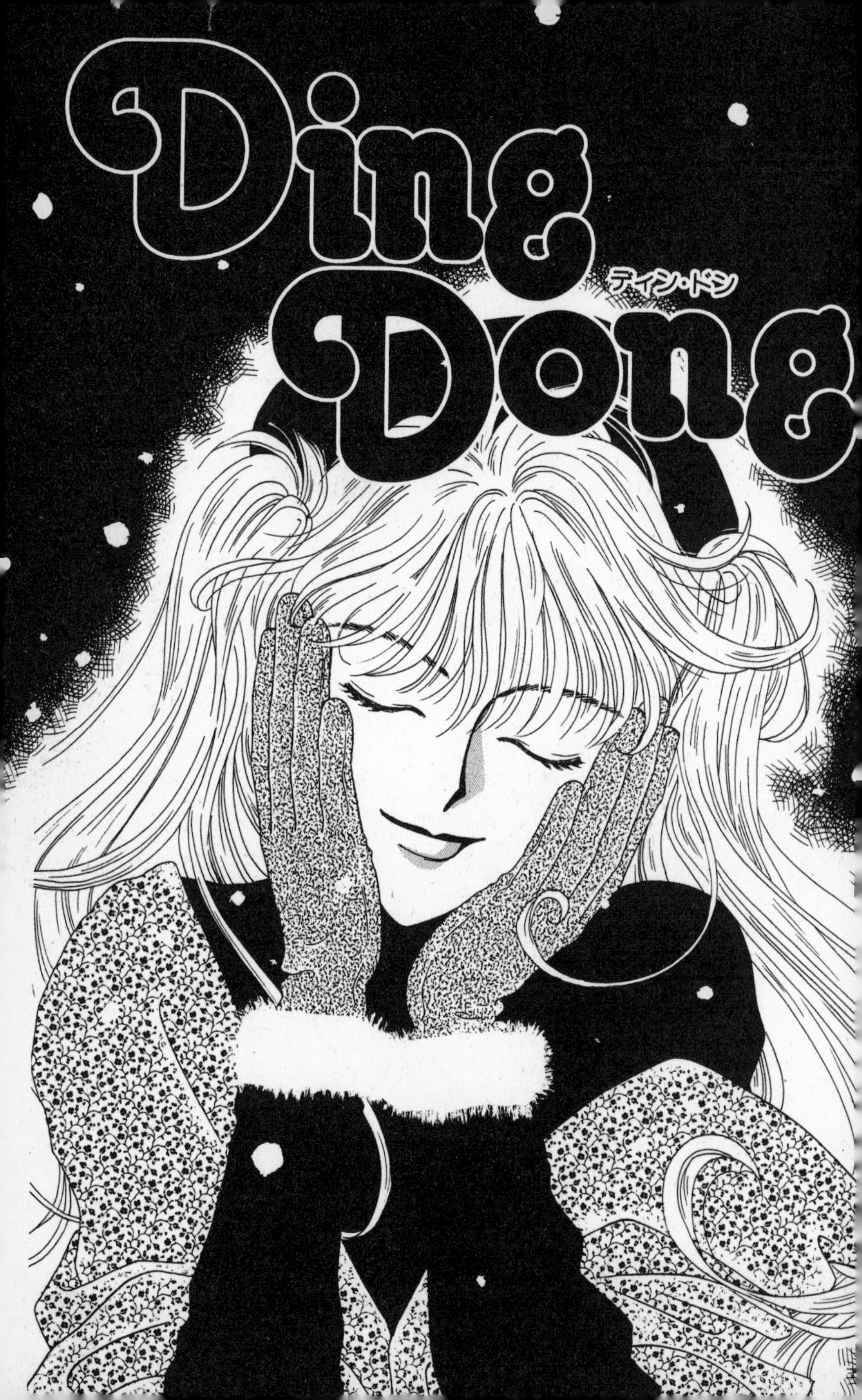
Ding Dong
ティン・ドン

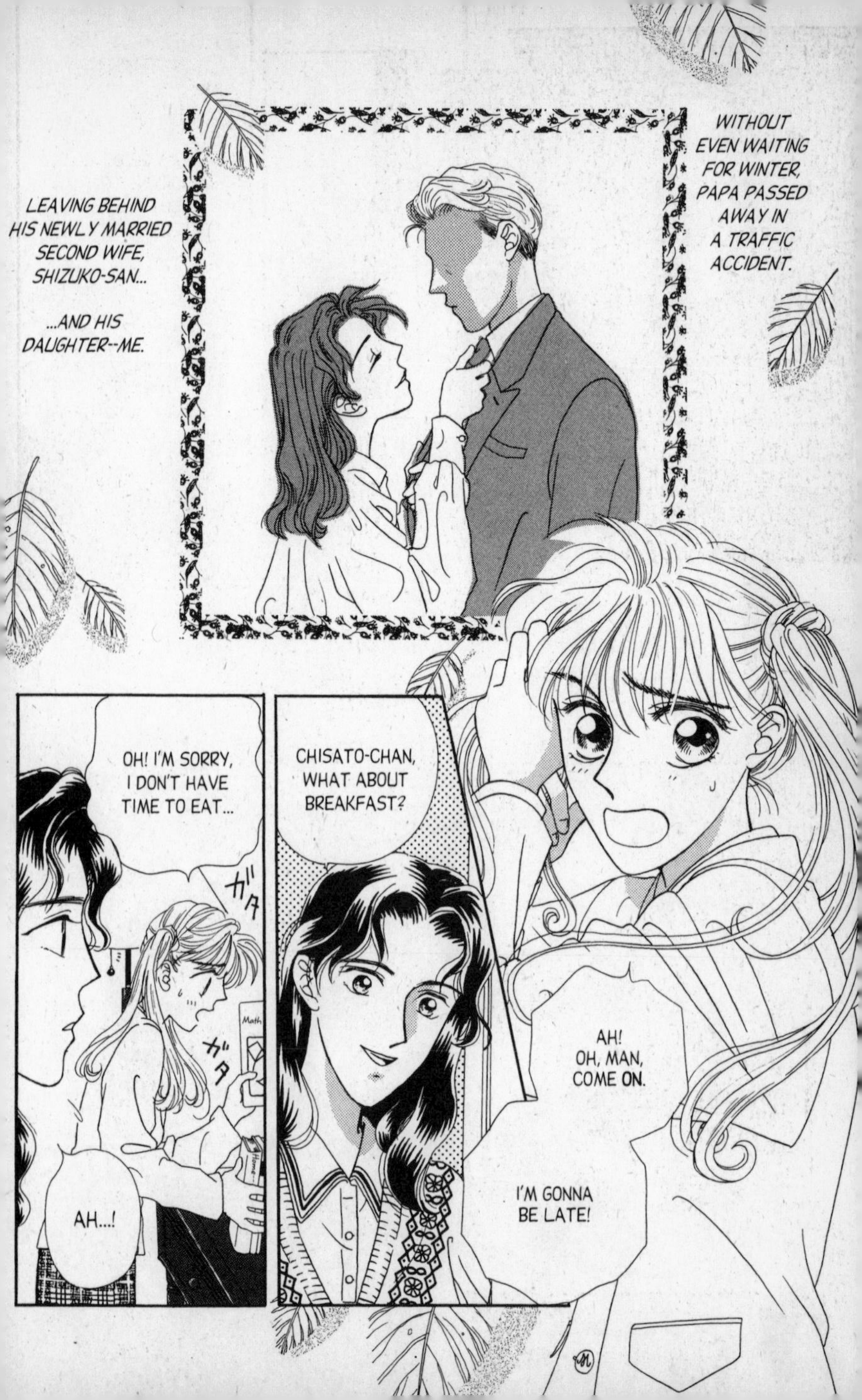
WITHOUT EVEN WAITING FOR WINTER, PAPA PASSED AWAY IN A TRAFFIC ACCIDENT.
LEAVING BEHIND HIS NEWLY MARRIED SECOND WIFE, SHIZUKO-SAN...
...AND HIS DAUGHTER--ME.
AH! OH, MAN, COME ON.
I'M GONNA BE LATE!
CHISATO-CHAN, WHAT ABOUT BREAKFAST?
OH! I'M SORRY, I DON'T HAVE TIME TO EAT...
ガタ
ガタ
AH...!

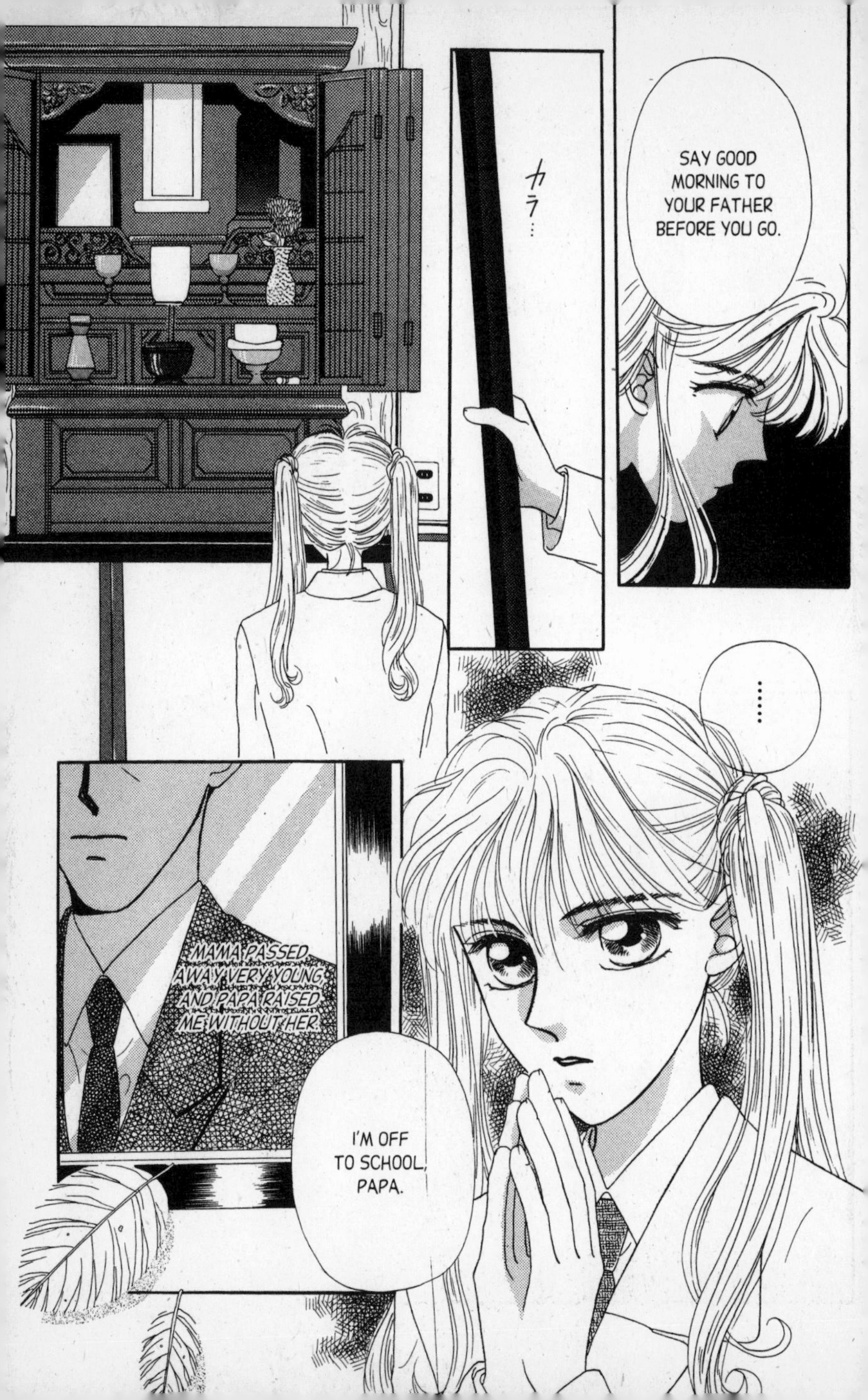

SAY GOOD MORNING TO YOUR FATHER BEFORE YOU GO.
カラ…
……
MAMA PASSED AWAY VERY YOUNG, AND PAPA RAISED ME WITHOUT HER.
I'M OFF TO SCHOOL, PAPA.

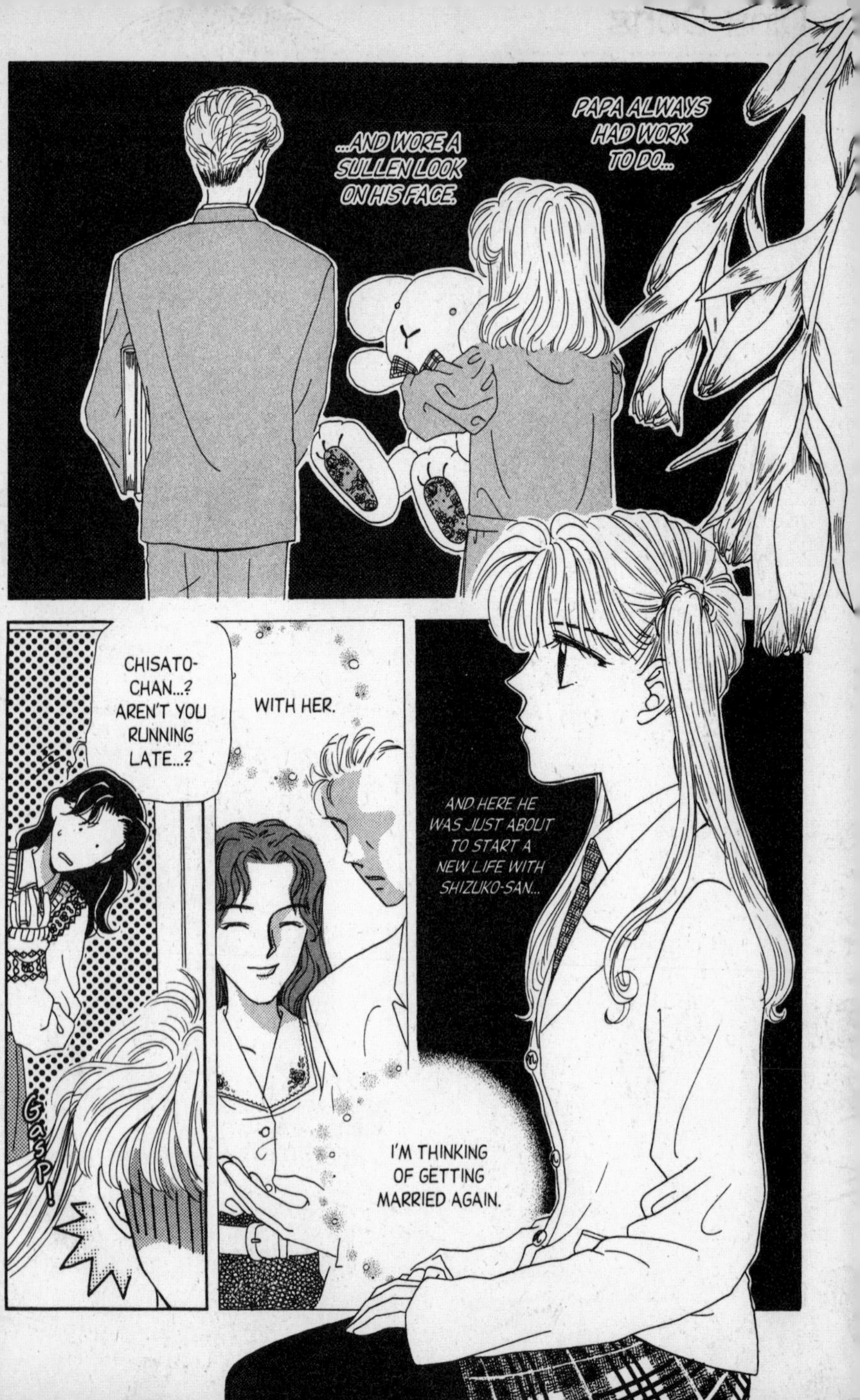
PAPA ALWAYS HAD WORK TO DO...
...AND WORE A SULLEN LOOK ON HIS FACE.
AND HERE HE WAS JUST ABOUT TO START A NEW LIFE WITH SHIZUKO-SAN...
I'M THINKING OF GETTING MARRIED AGAIN.
WITH HER.
CHISATO-CHAN...? AREN'T YOU RUNNING LATE...?
GASP!

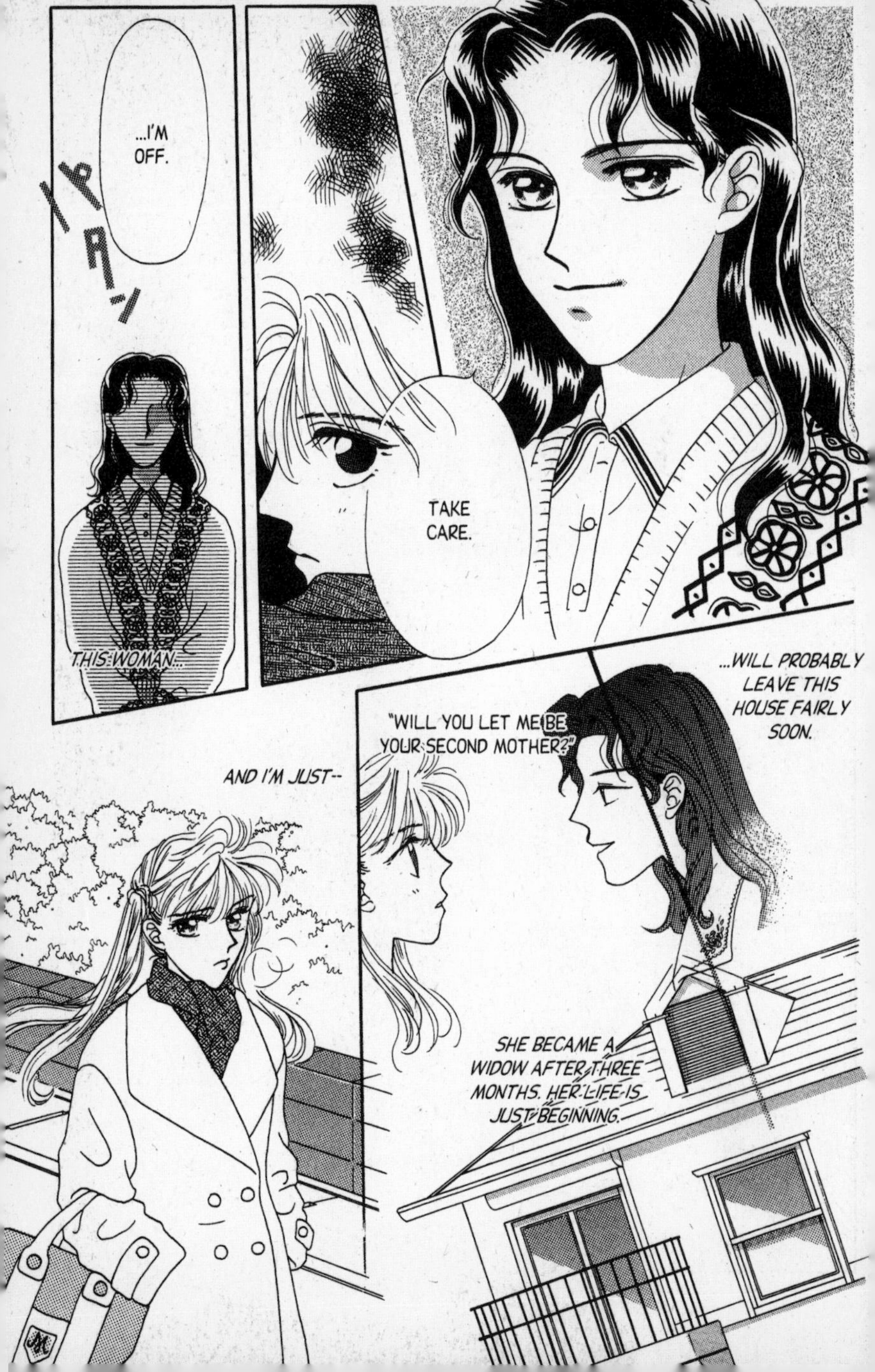
TAKE CARE.
...I'M OFF.
THIS WOMAN...
...WILL PROBABLY LEAVE THIS HOUSE FAIRLY SOON.
"WILL YOU LET ME BE YOUR SECOND MOTHER?"
SHE BECAME A WIDOW AFTER THREE MONTHS. HER LIFE IS JUST BEGINNING.
AND I'M JUST--

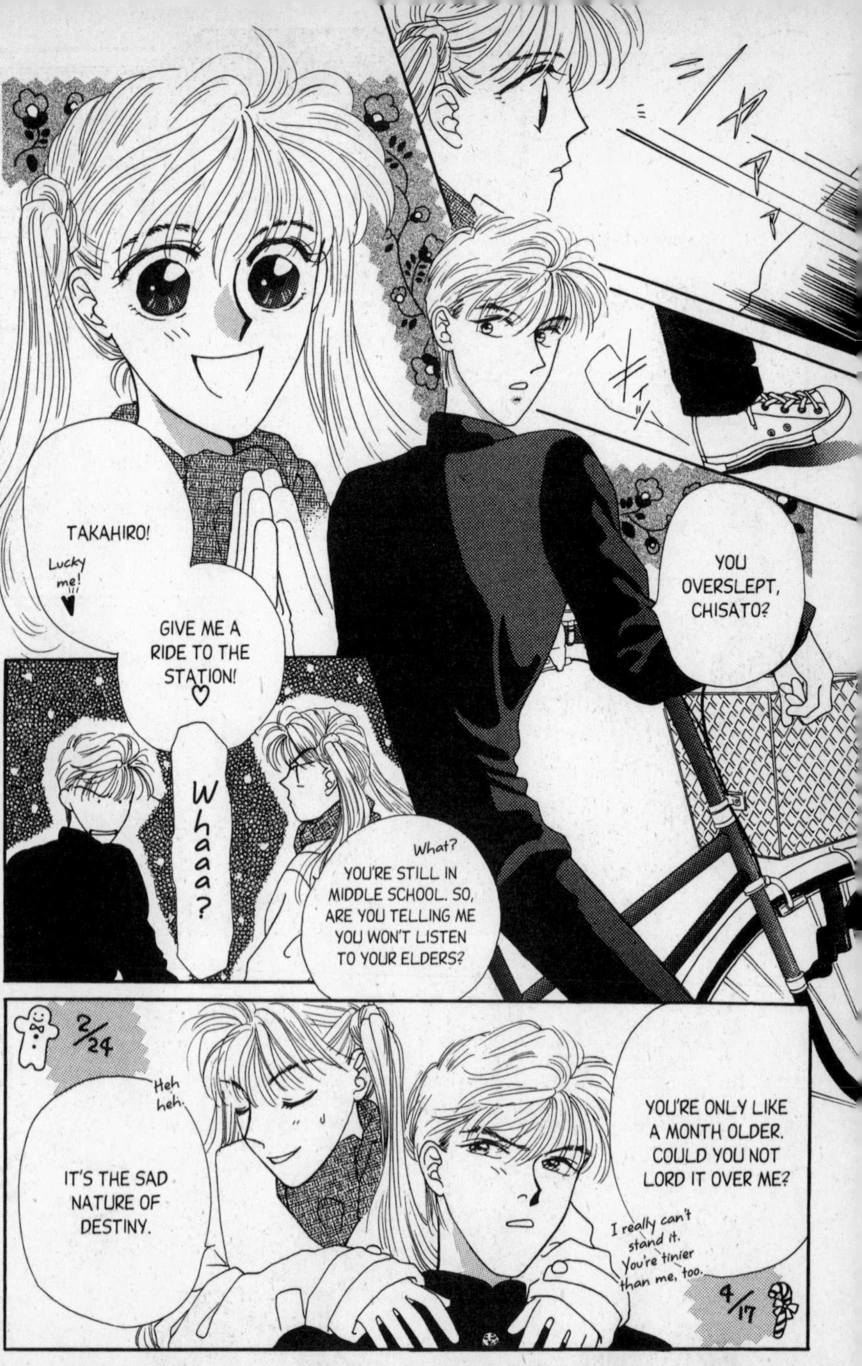
YOU OVERSLEPT, CHISATO?
TAKAHIRO!
Lucky me!
GIVE ME A RIDE TO THE STATION!
Whaaa?
What?
YOU'RE STILL IN MIDDLE SCHOOL. SO, ARE YOU TELLING ME YOU WON'T LISTEN TO YOUR ELDERS?
YOU'RE ONLY LIKE A MONTH OLDER. COULD YOU NOT LORD IT OVER ME?
I really can't stand it. You're tinier than me, too.
4/17
2/24
Heh heh.
IT'S THE SAD NATURE OF DESTINY.

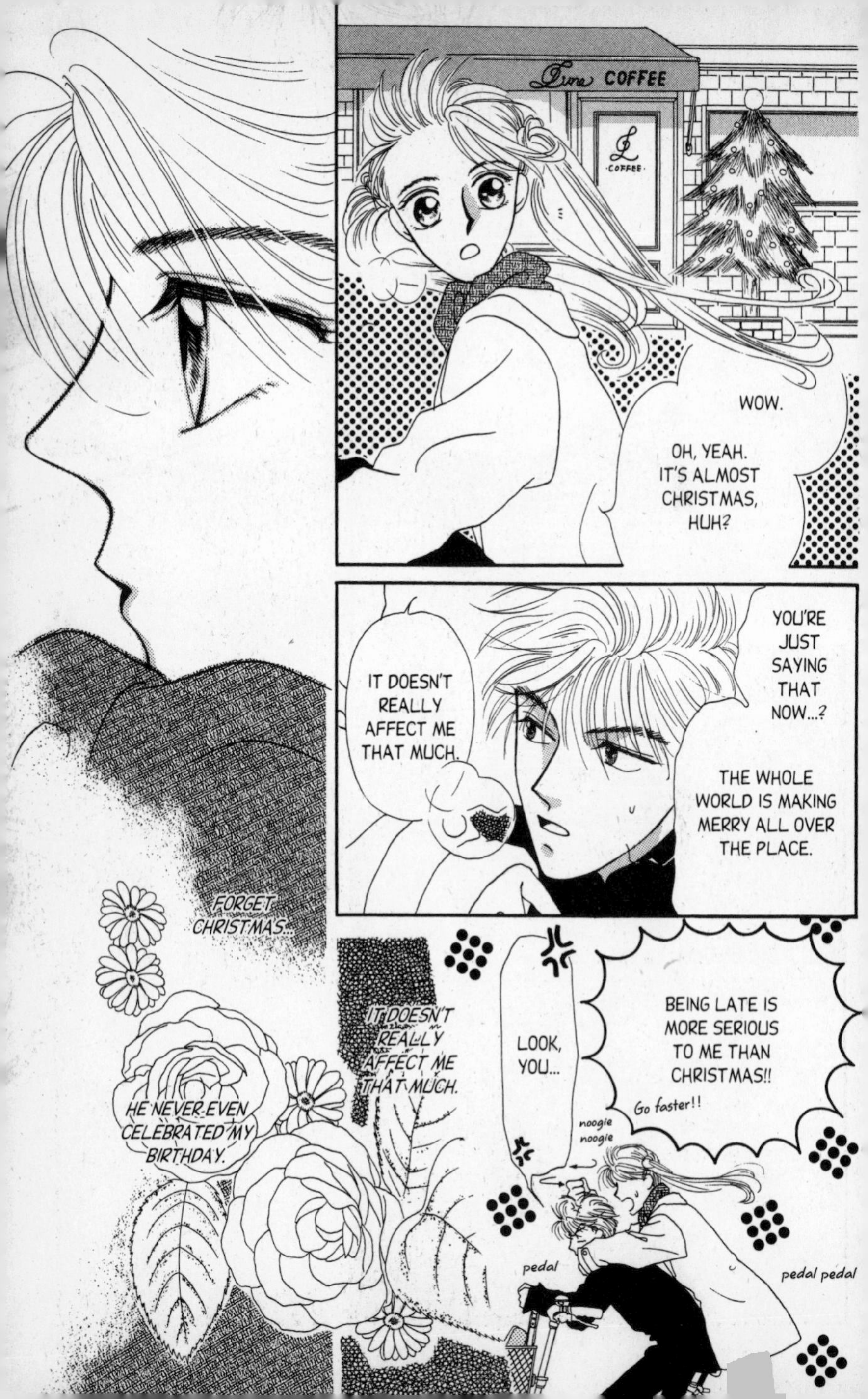
L COFFEE
WOW.
OH, YEAH. IT'S ALMOST CHRISTMAS, HUH?
YOU'RE JUST SAYING THAT NOW...?
THE WHOLE WORLD IS MAKING MERRY ALL OVER THE PLACE.
IT DOESN'T REALLY AFFECT ME THAT MUCH.
BEING LATE IS MORE SERIOUS TO ME THAN CHRISTMAS!!
Go faster!!
LOOK, YOU...
noogie noogie
pedal pedal
pedal
FORGET CHRISTMAS...
IT DOESN'T REALLY AFFECT ME THAT MUCH.
HE NEVER EVEN CELEBRATED MY BIRTHDAY.

I GOT PRESENTS FROM MY GRANDPARENTS EVERY YEAR.

BUT...

...THE ONE PERSON I WANTED A GIFT FROM THE MOST NEVER GAVE ME A SINGLE PRESENT.

NOT ONCE.

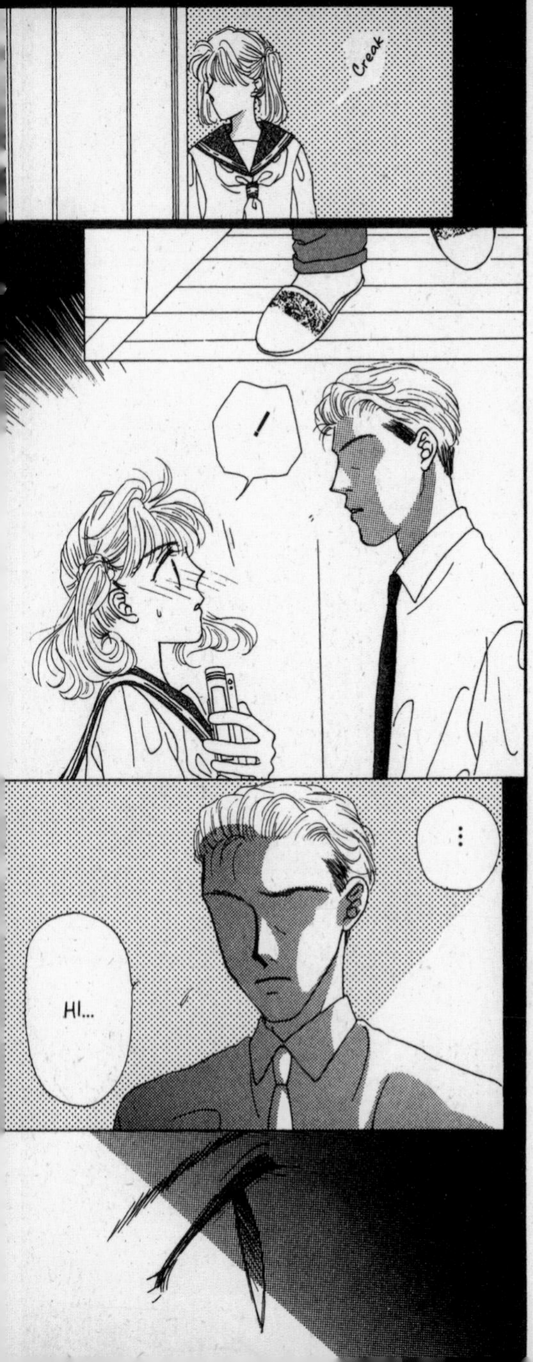
Creak
!
...
HI...

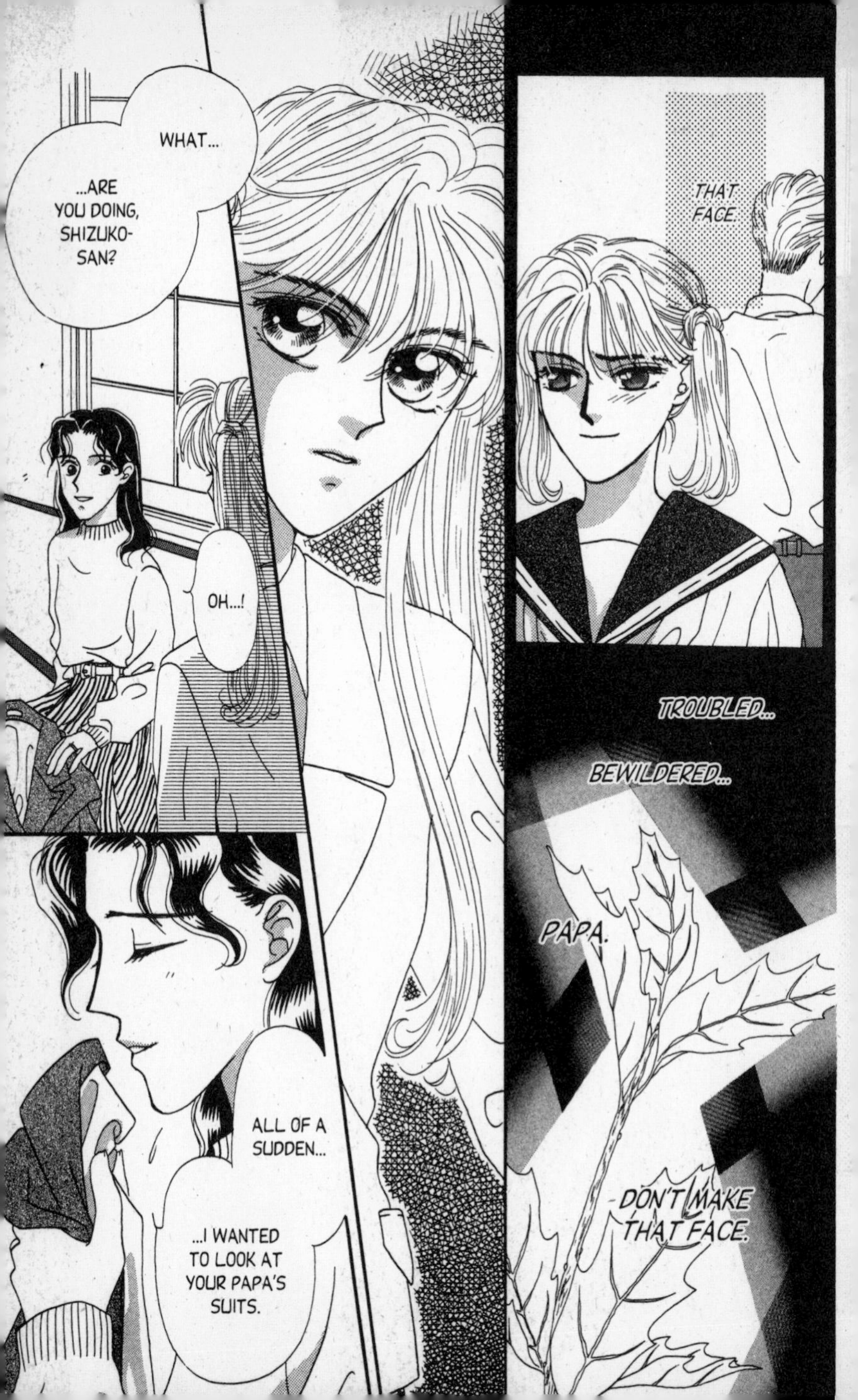
THAT FACE.
TROUBLED...
BEWILDERED...
PAPA.
DON'T MAKE THAT FACE.
WHAT...
...ARE YOU DOING, SHIZUKO-SAN?
OH...!
ALL OF A SUDDEN...
...I WANTED TO LOOK AT YOUR PAPA'S SUITS.

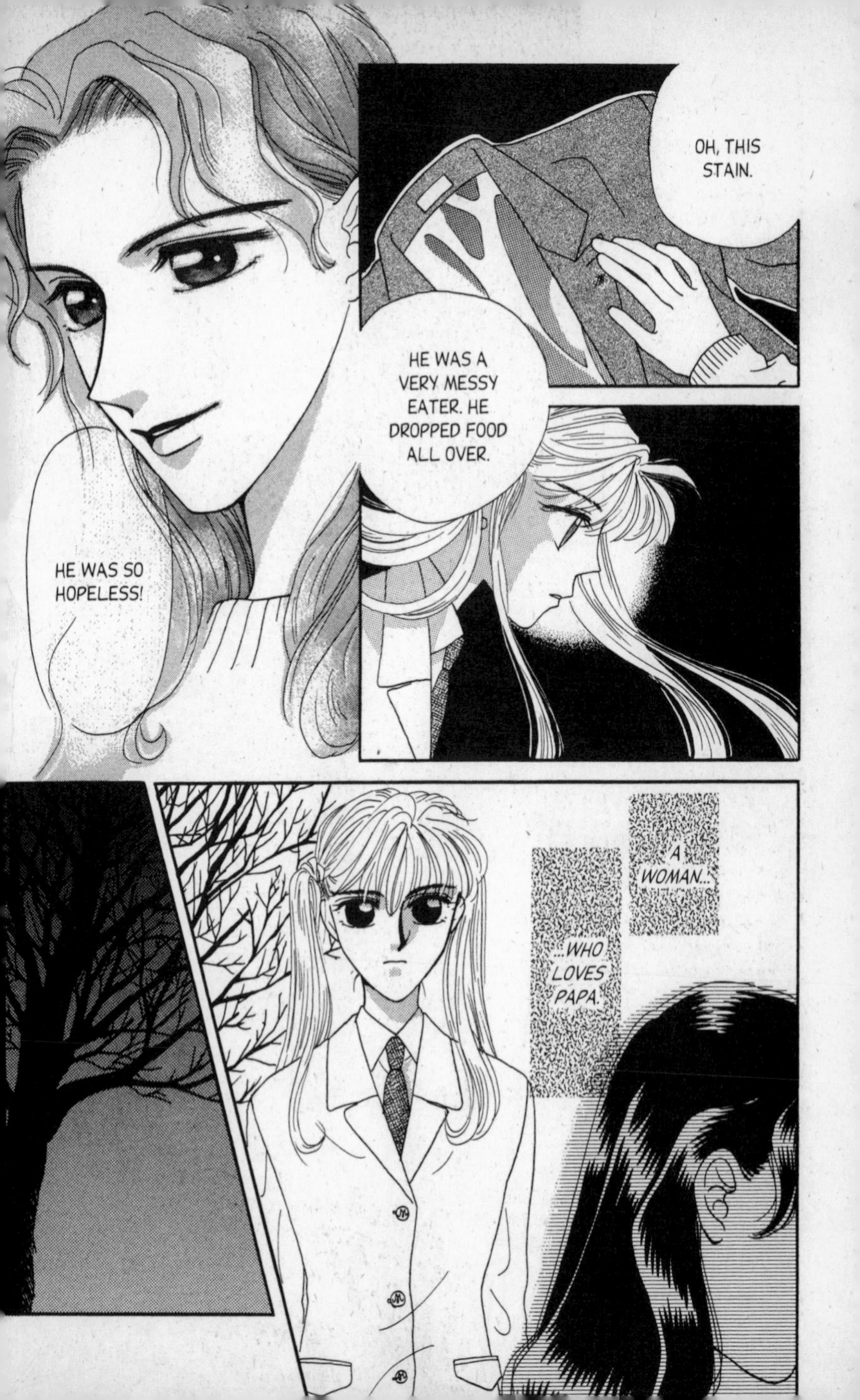
OH, THIS STAIN.
HE WAS A VERY MESSY EATER. HE DROPPED FOOD ALL OVER.
HE WAS SO HOPELESS!
A WOMAN...
...WHO LOVES PAPA.

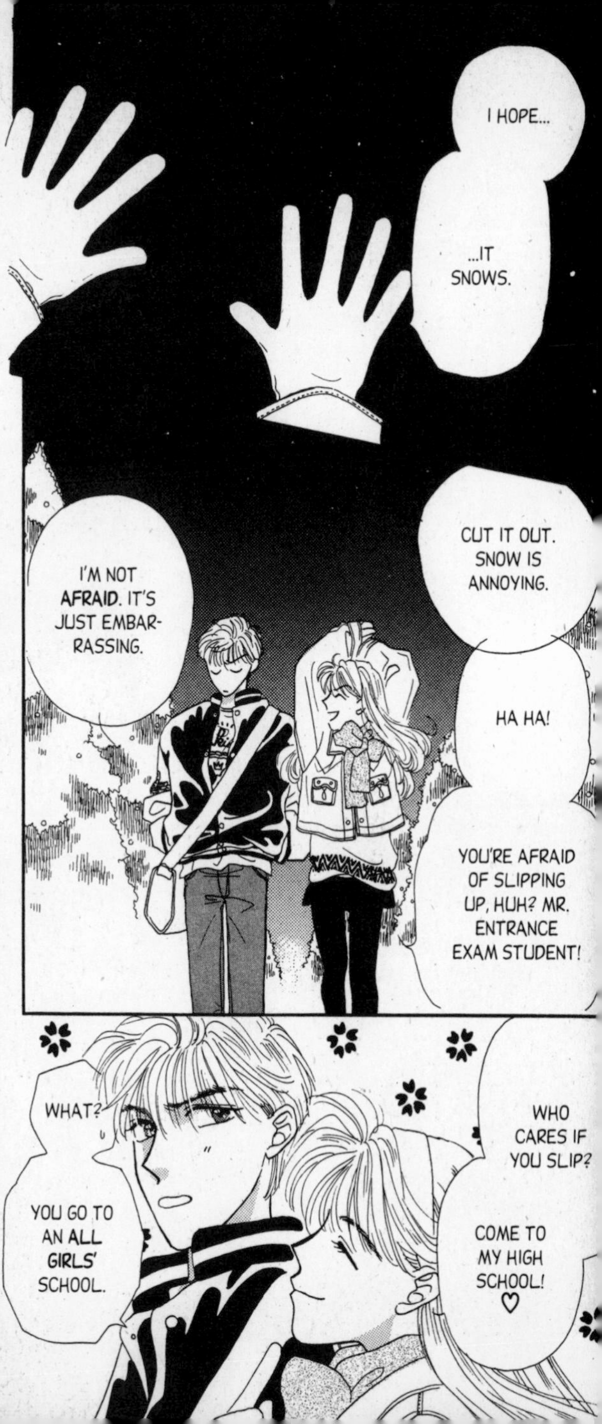
I HOPE...
...IT SNOWS.
CUT IT OUT. SNOW IS ANNOYING.
HA HA!
YOU'RE AFRAID OF SLIPPING UP, HUH? MR. ENTRANCE EXAM STUDENT!
I'M NOT AFRAID. IT'S JUST EMBARRASSING.
WHO CARES IF YOU SLIP?
COME TO MY HIGH SCHOOL! ♡
WHAT?
YOU GO TO AN ALL GIRLS' SCHOOL.

Part 2

Somehow, except for "Princess Dark Black" and "Songs to Make You Smle" all these stories are so nostalgic I don't know what to say (laugh). When I did "Princess Dark Black" times were so tough. I had a 104-degree fever and I thought I was done for. So whenever I look at that story, all the pain would come back, and I was like, "Nooo!" But when the CD came out, that changed (laugh). A complete 180 (laugh). It was like, "Thanks, Princess Dark Black! Bravo!!" ~

"Songs to Make You Smle" gave me a little trouble--it turned out completely different from the original rough draft. I wrote it after Tsubasa, so I had comments like, "So you can draw stories like this, too..." Thinking about it now, "Songs to Make You Smle" is the pop version, and "Voice" is the classical version. I like that! ~

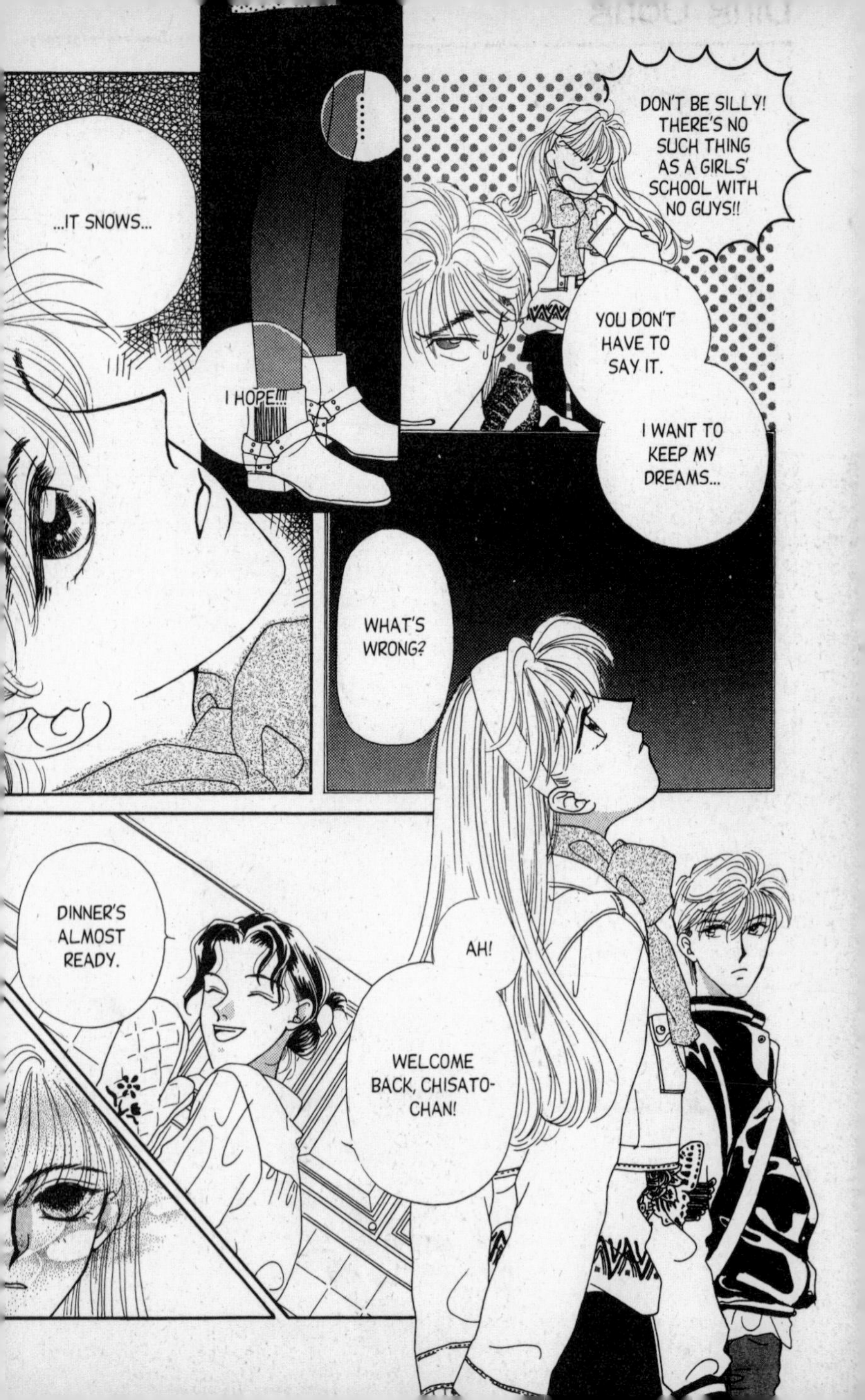
DON'T BE SILLY! THERE'S NO SUCH THING AS A GIRLS' SCHOOL WITH NO GUYS!!
YOU DON'T HAVE TO SAY IT.
I WANT TO KEEP MY DREAMS...
I HOPE!!!
WHAT'S WRONG?
...IT SNOWS...
AH!
WELCOME BACK, CHISATO-CHAN!
DINNER'S ALMOST READY.

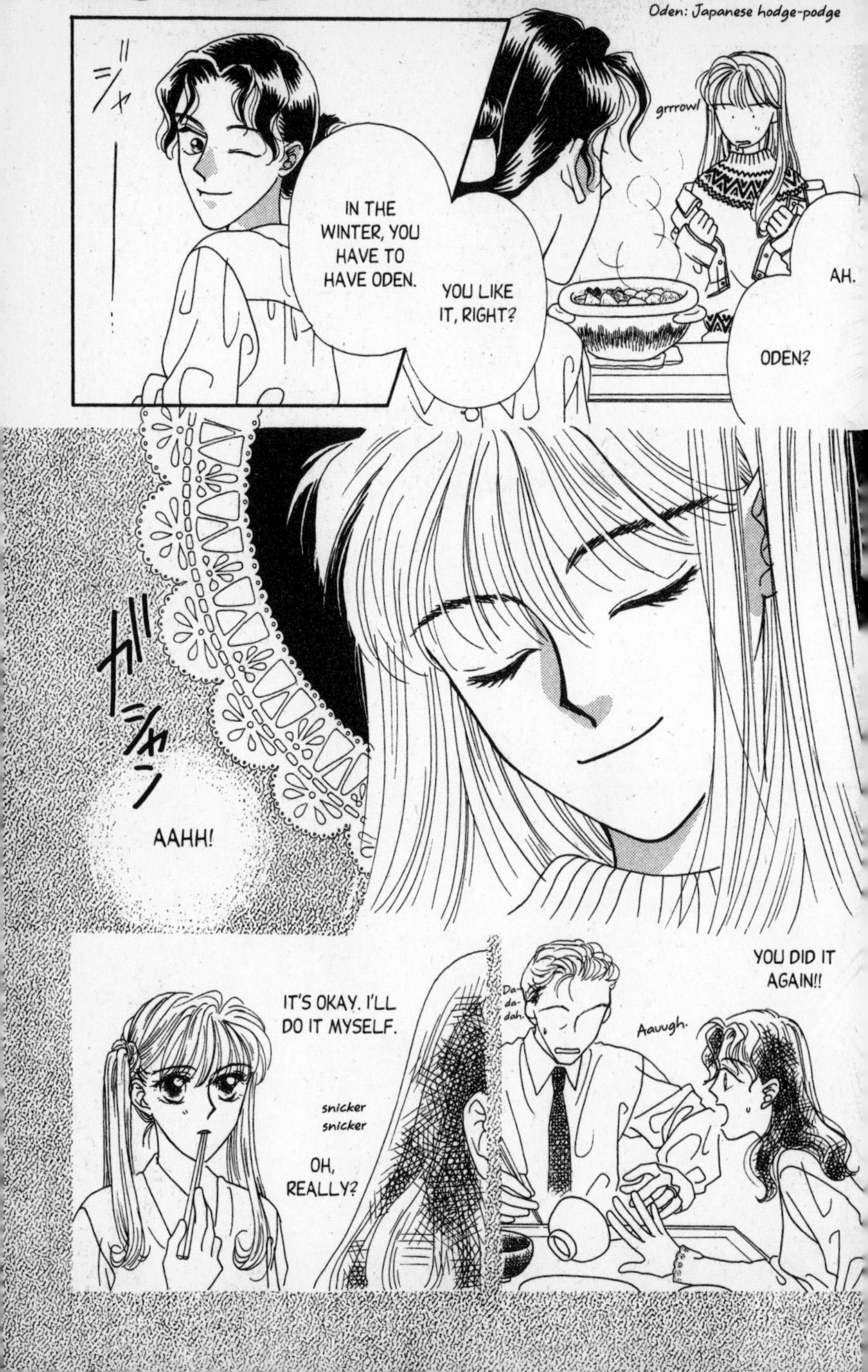
Oden: Japanese hodge-podge
grrrowl
AH.
ODEN?
ジャ
IN THE WINTER, YOU HAVE TO HAVE ODEN.
YOU LIKE IT, RIGHT?
ガシャン
AAHH!
YOU DID IT AGAIN!!
Aauugh.
Da-da-dah.
IT'S OKAY. I'LL DO IT MYSELF.
snicker snicker
OH, REALLY?

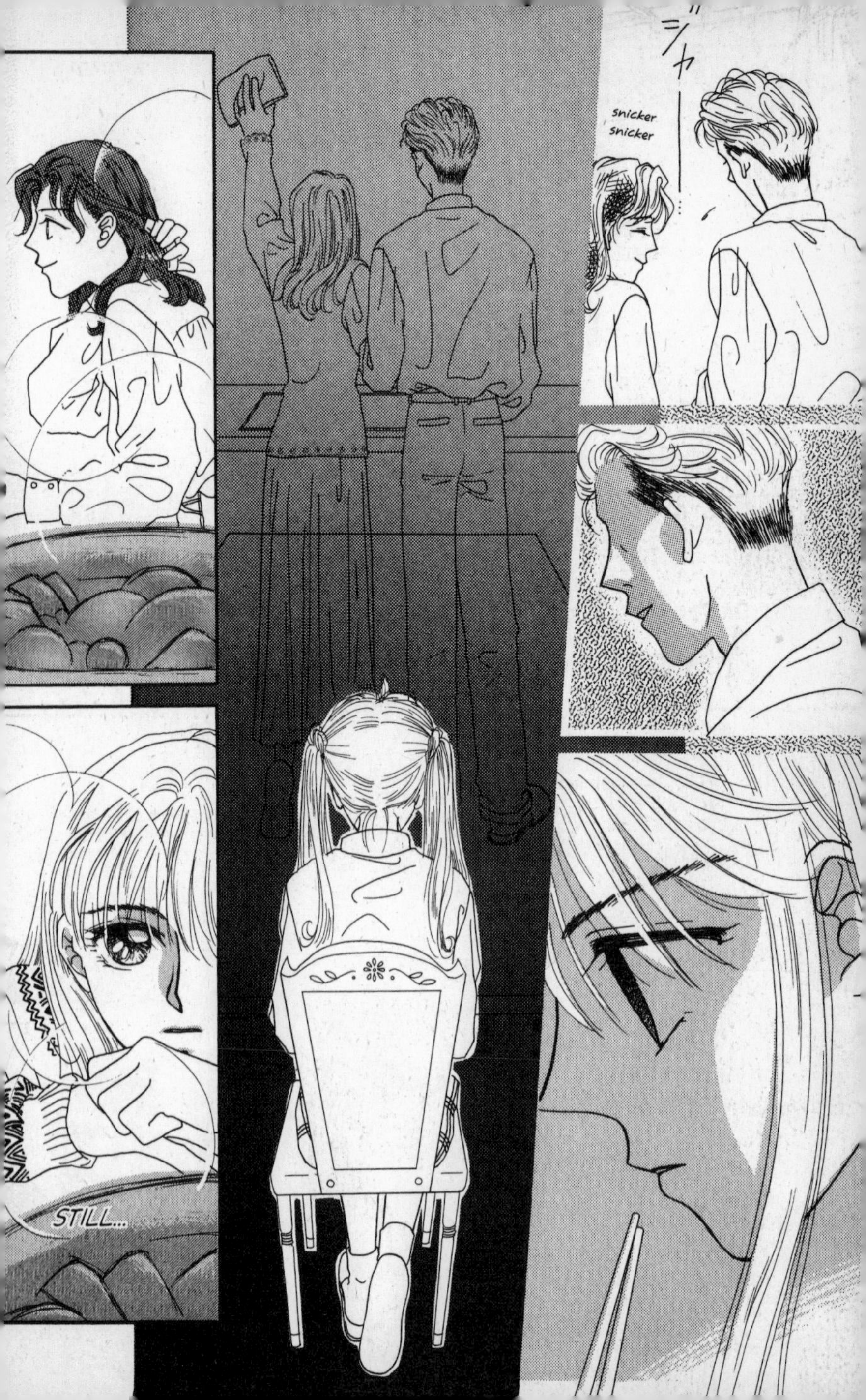
ジャー
snicker
snicker
STILL...

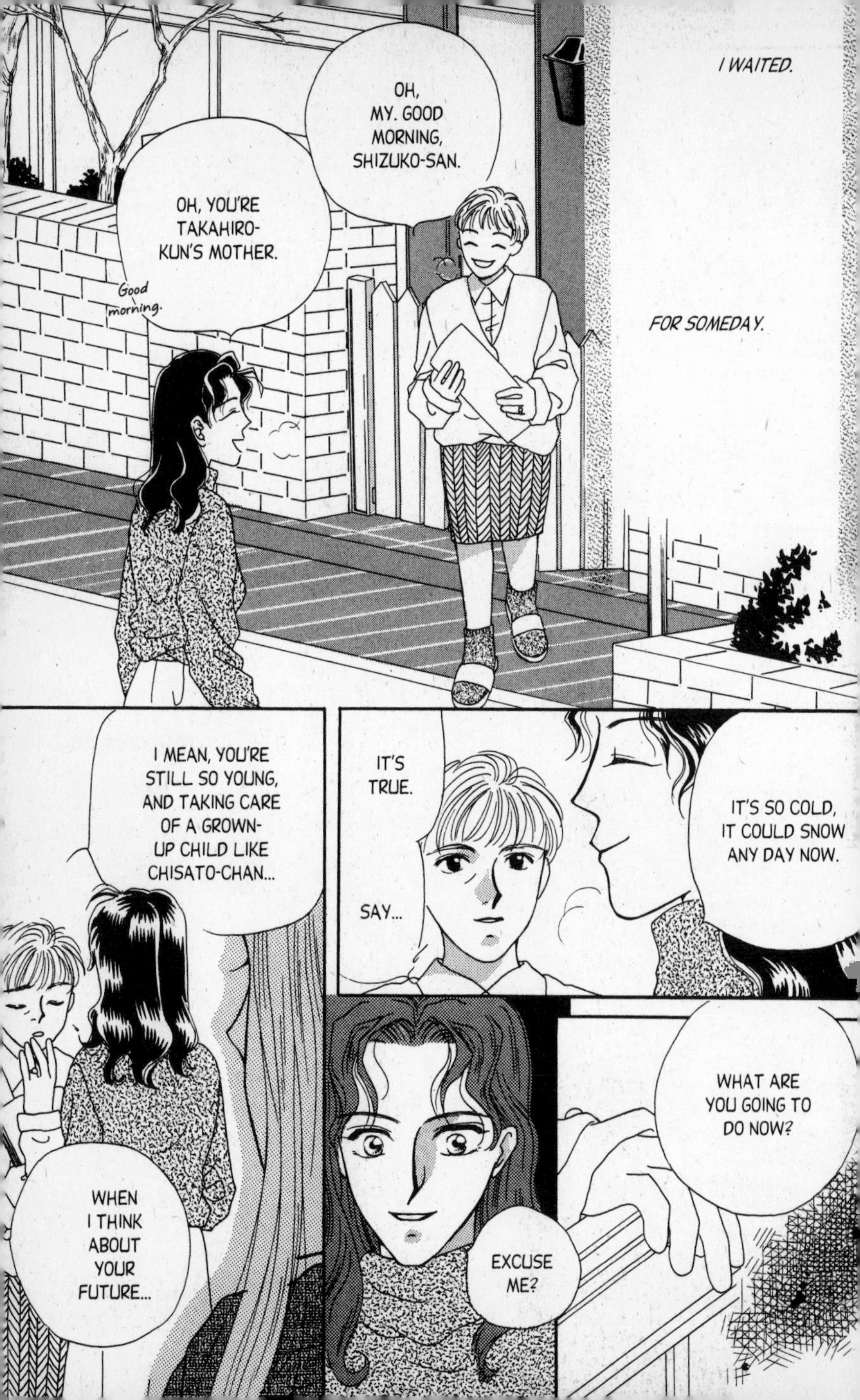
I WAITED.
FOR SOMEDAY.
OH, MY. GOOD MORNING, SHIZUKO-SAN.
OH, YOU'RE TAKAHIRO-KUN'S MOTHER.
Good morning.
IT'S SO COLD, IT COULD SNOW ANY DAY NOW.
IT'S TRUE.
SAY...
WHAT ARE YOU GOING TO DO NOW?
EXCUSE ME?
I MEAN, YOU'RE STILL SO YOUNG, AND TAKING CARE OF A GROWN-UP CHILD LIKE CHISATO-CHAN...
WHEN I THINK ABOUT YOUR FUTURE...

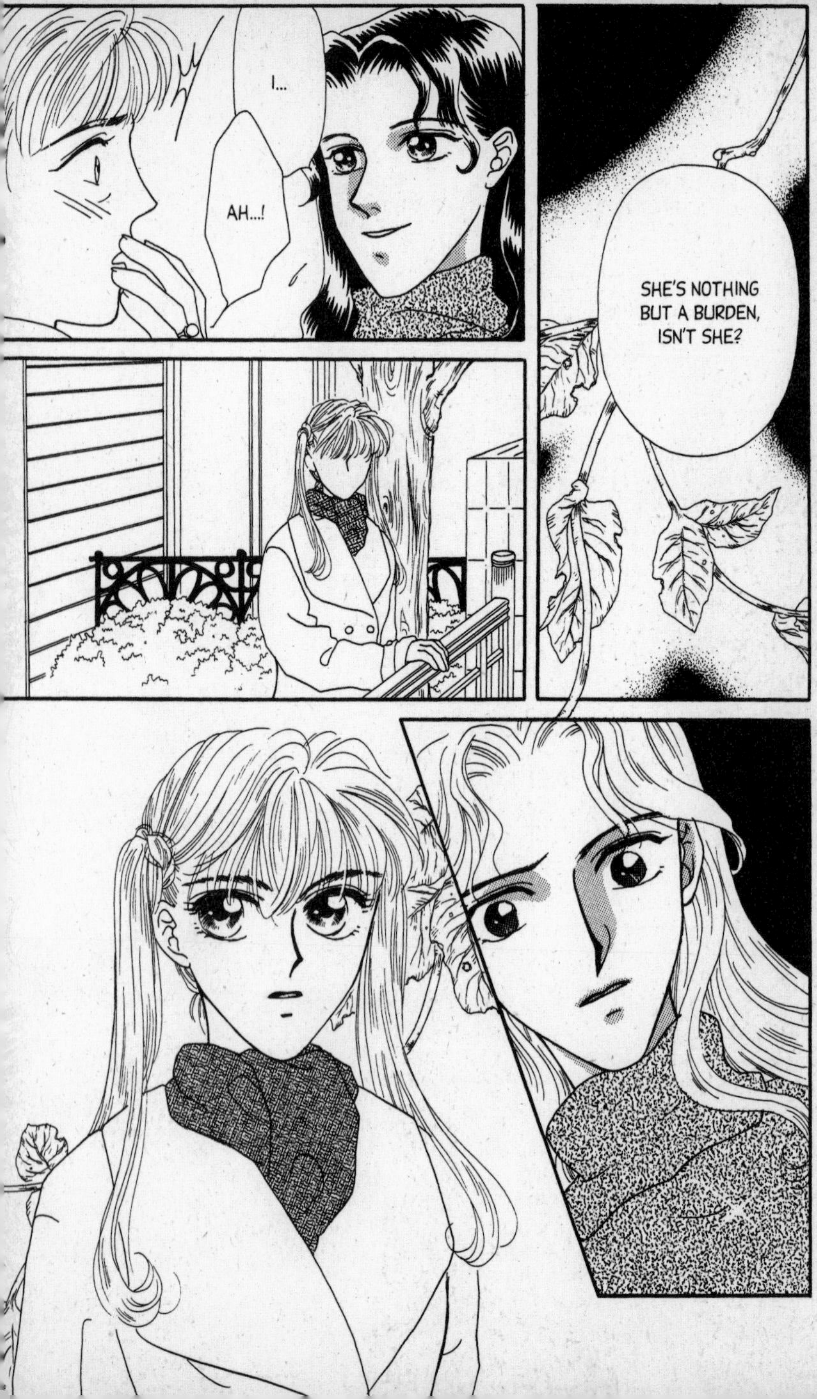
SHE'S NOTHING BUT A BURDEN, ISN'T SHE?
I...
AH...!

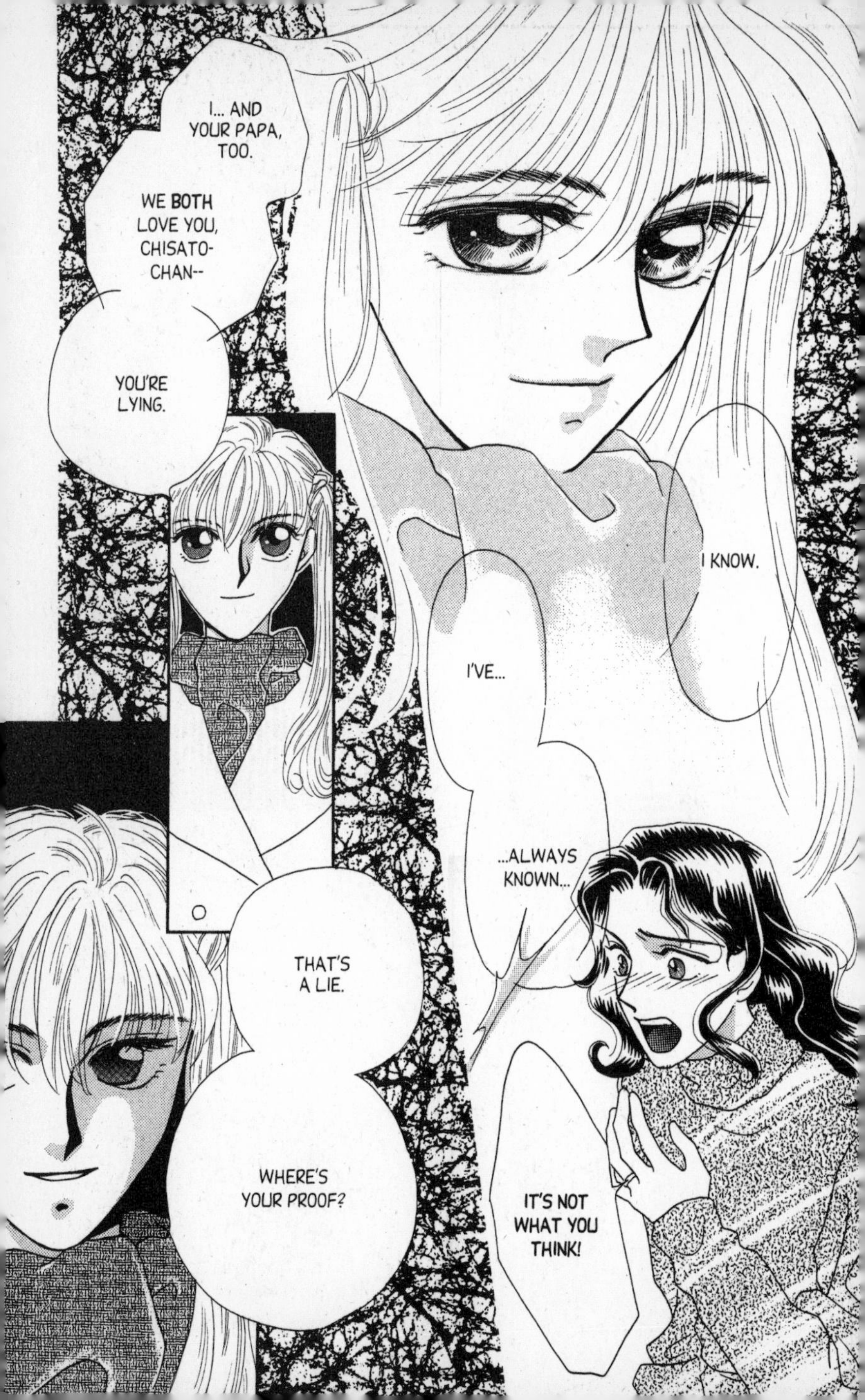

I... AND YOUR PAPA, TOO.
WE BOTH LOVE YOU, CHISATO-CHAN--
YOU'RE LYING.
I KNOW.
I'VE...
...ALWAYS KNOWN...
IT'S NOT WHAT YOU THINK!
THAT'S A LIE.
WHERE'S YOUR PROOF?

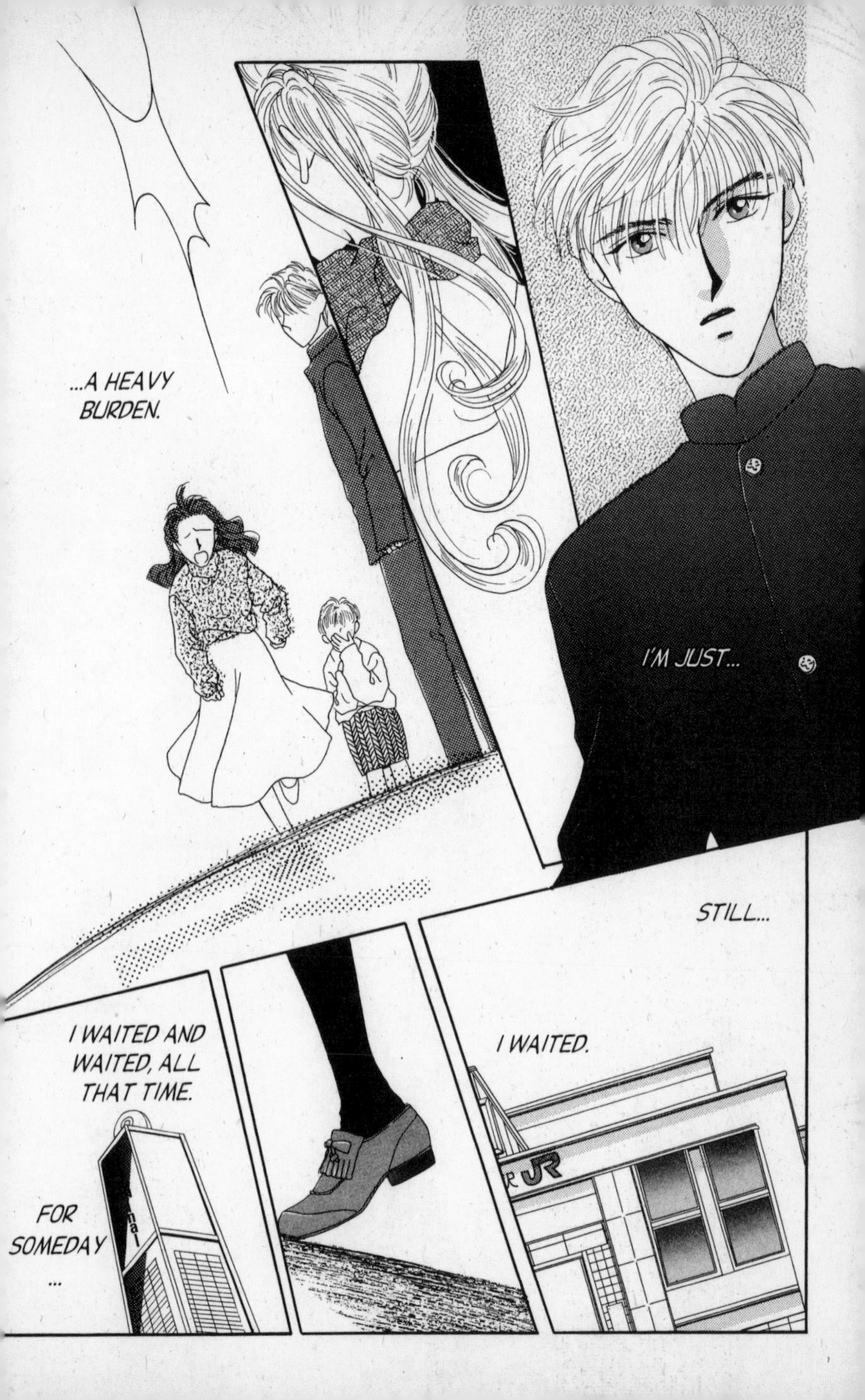
I'M JUST...
...A HEAVY BURDEN.
STILL...
I WAITED.
JR
I WAITED AND WAITED, ALL THAT TIME.
FOR SOMEDAY ...

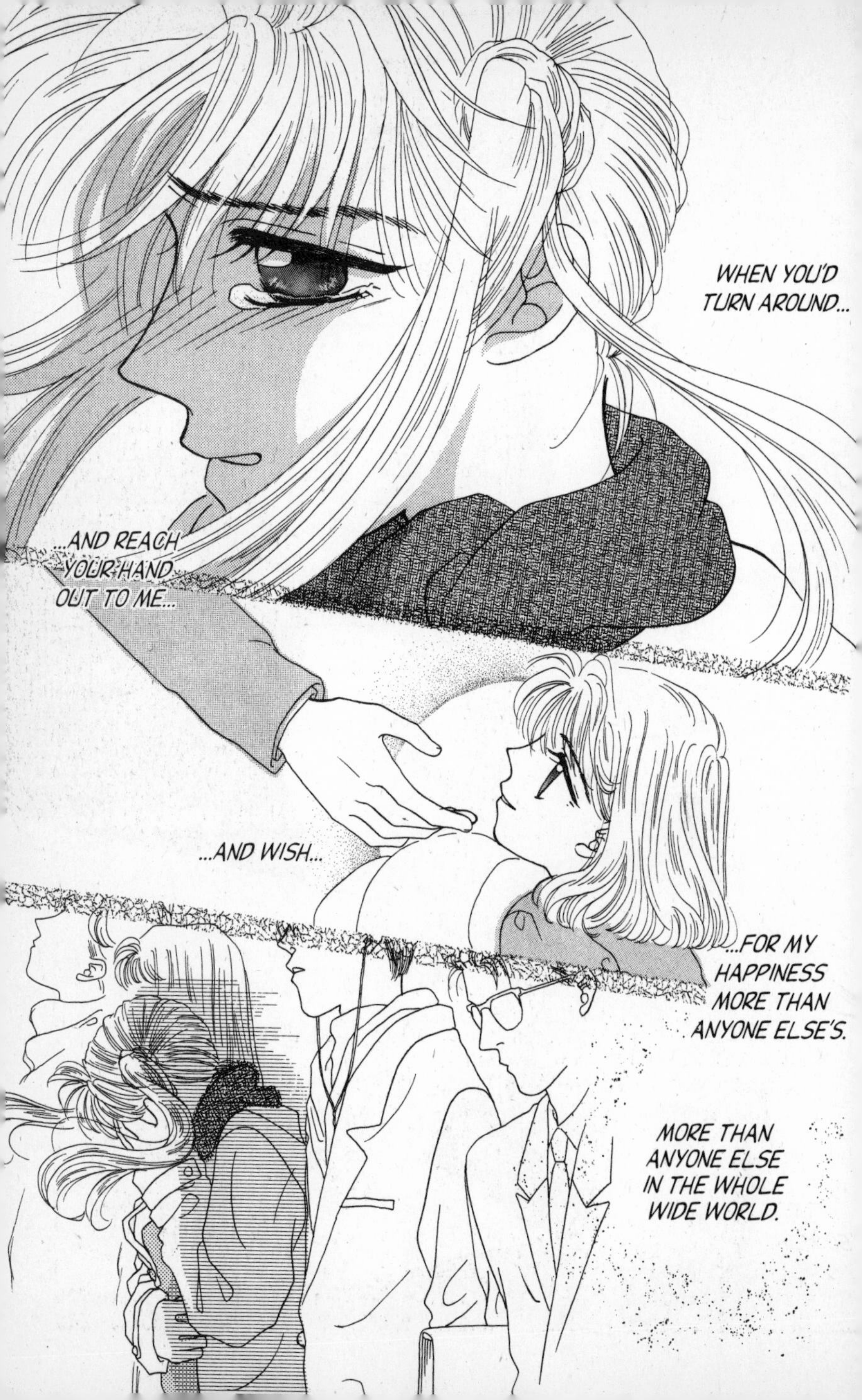
WHEN YOU'D TURN AROUND...
...AND REACH YOUR HAND OUT TO ME...
...AND WISH...
...FOR MY HAPPINESS MORE THAN ANYONE ELSE'S.
MORE THAN ANYONE ELSE IN THE WHOLE WIDE WORLD.

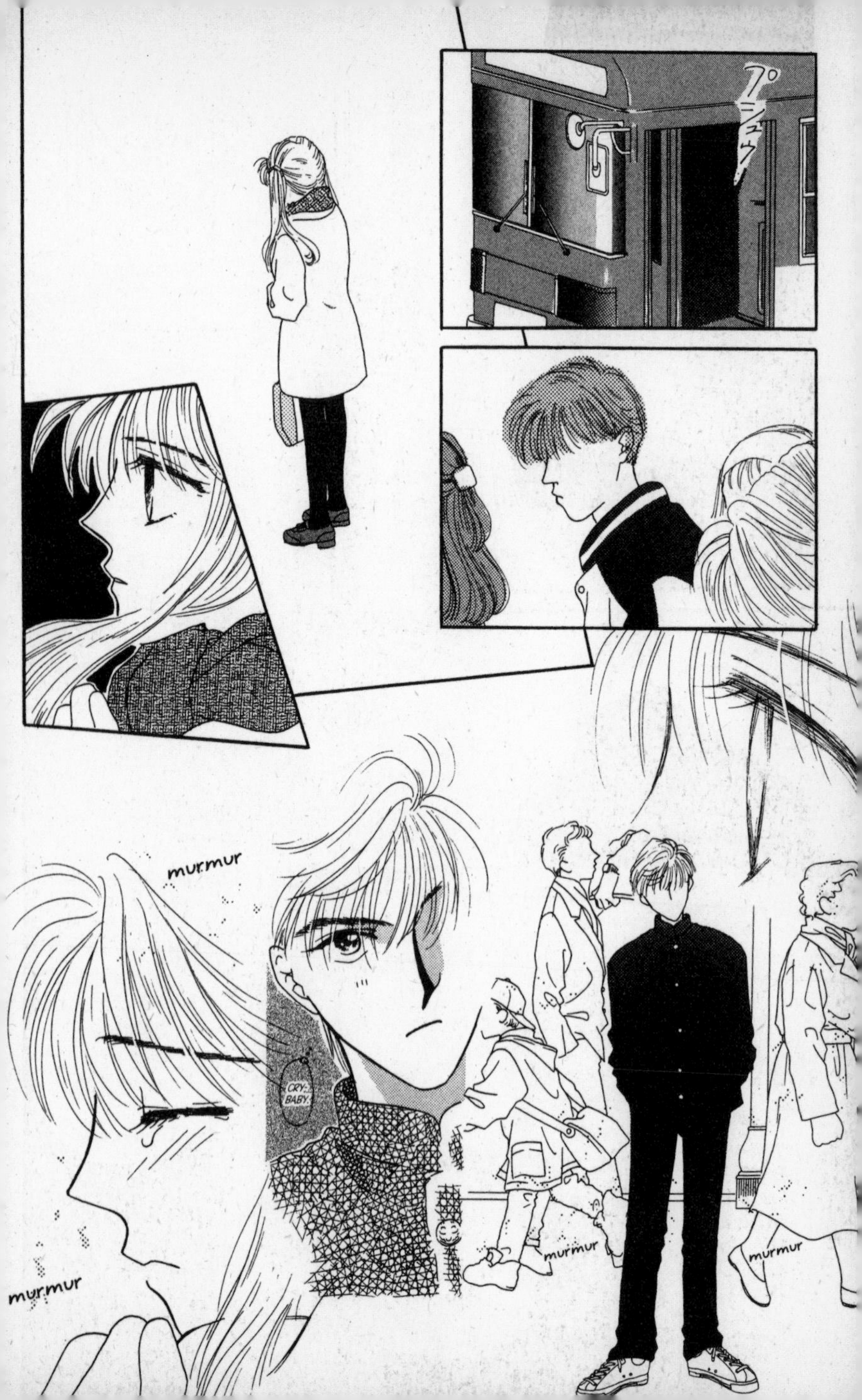
プシュウ
murmur
murmur
CRY-BABY.
murmur
murmur

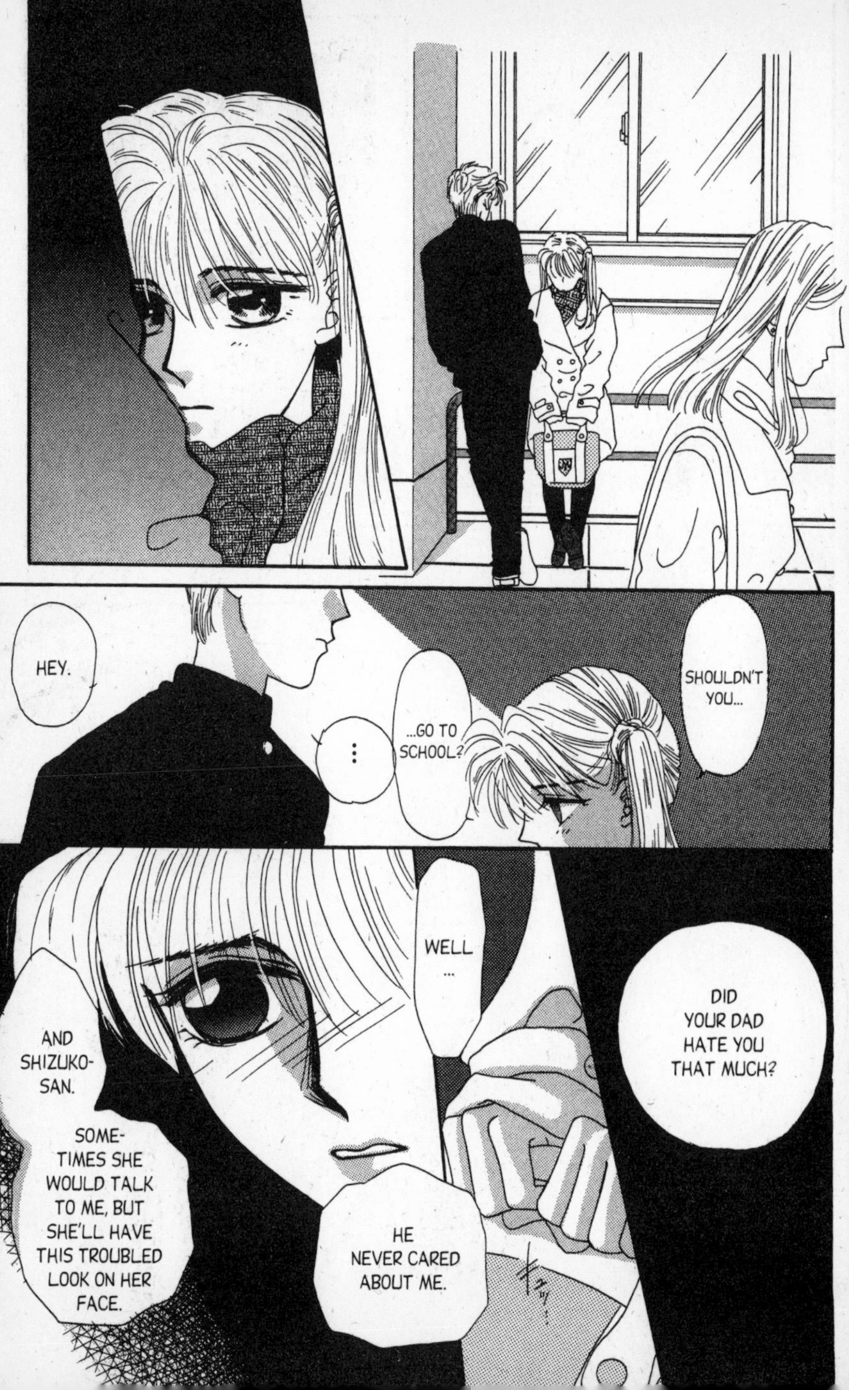
SHOULDN'T YOU...
...GO TO SCHOOL?
...
HEY.
DID YOUR DAD HATE YOU THAT MUCH?
WELL ...
HE NEVER CARED ABOUT ME.
AND SHIZUKO-SAN.
SOME-TIMES SHE WOULD TALK TO ME, BUT SHE'LL HAVE THIS TROUBLED LOOK ON HER FACE.

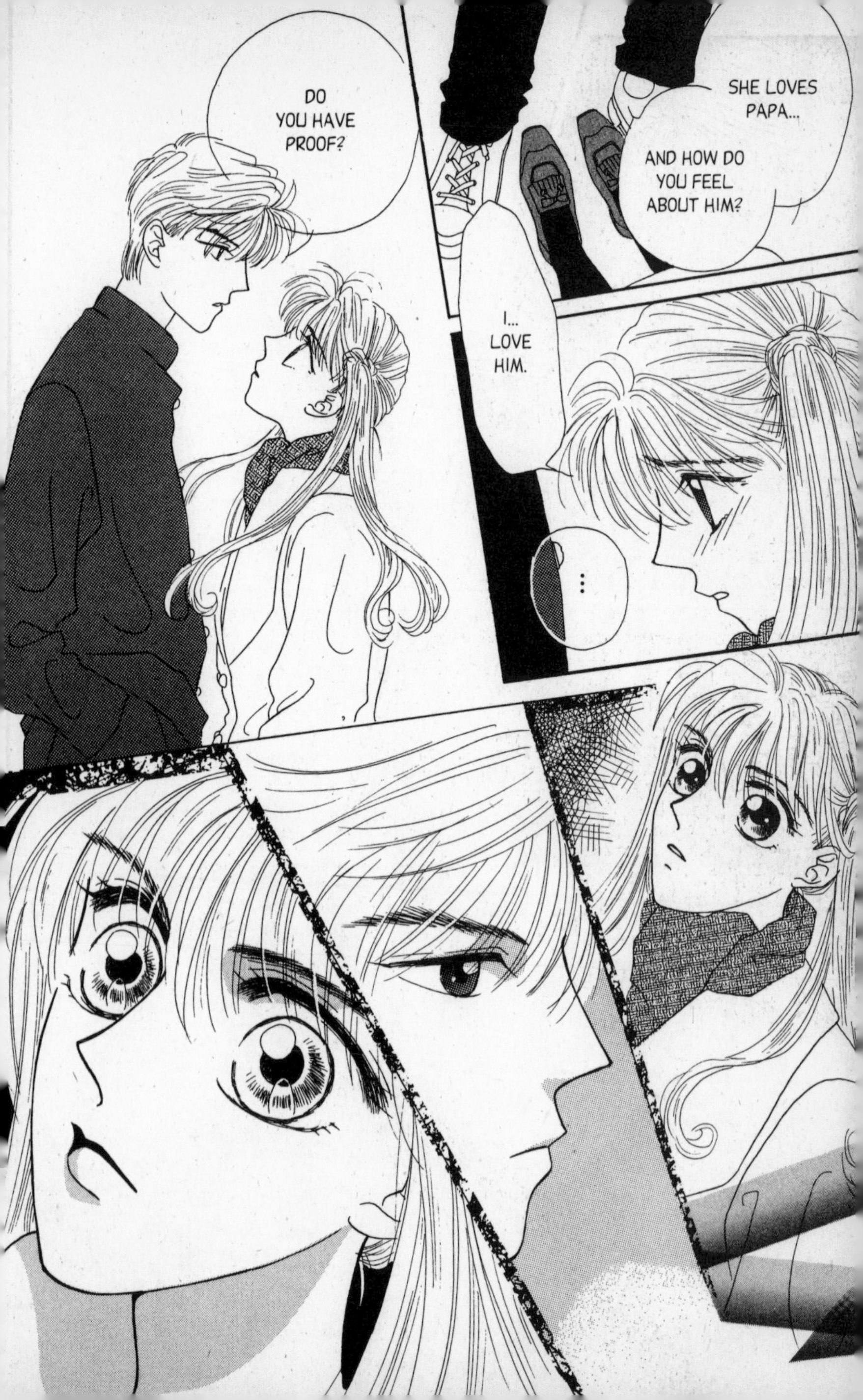
SHE LOVES PAPA...
AND HOW DO YOU FEEL ABOUT HIM?
I... LOVE HIM.
...
DO YOU HAVE PROOF?

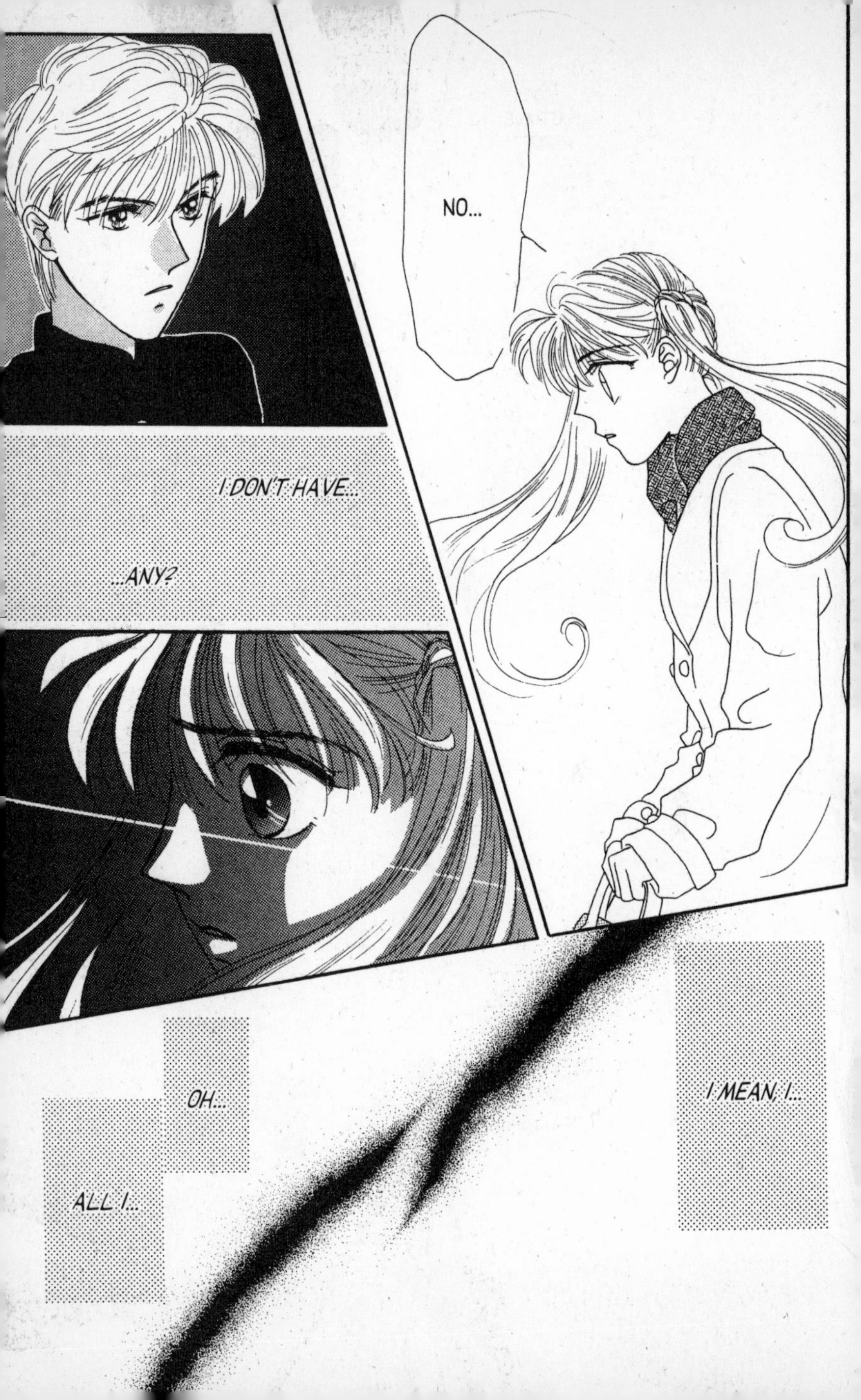
NO...
I DON'T HAVE...
...ANY?
I MEAN I...
OH...
ALL I...

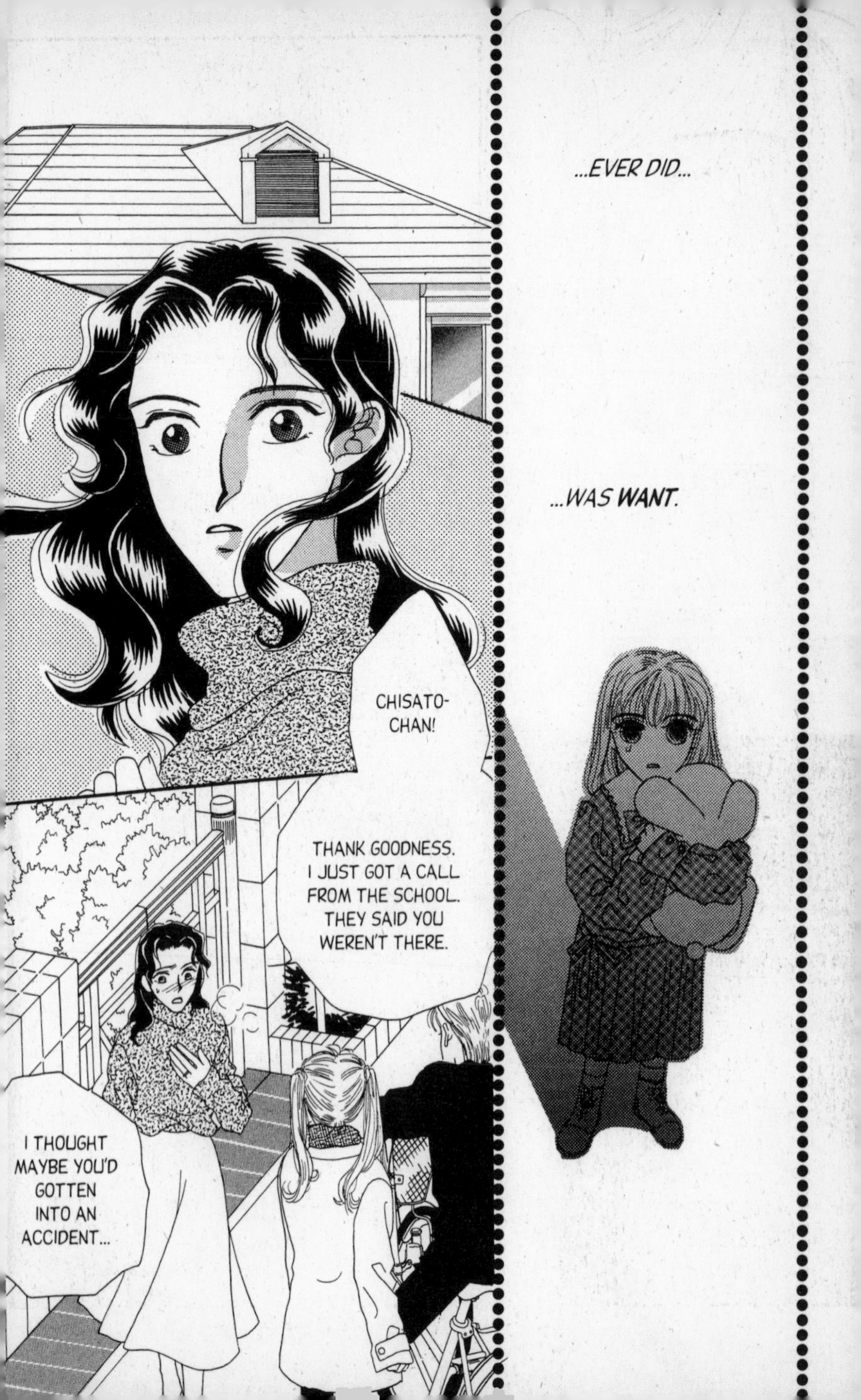
...EVER DID...
...WAS WANT.
CHISATO-CHAN!
THANK GOODNESS. I JUST GOT A CALL FROM THE SCHOOL. THEY SAID YOU WEREN'T THERE.
I THOUGHT MAYBE YOU'D GOTTEN INTO AN ACCIDENT...

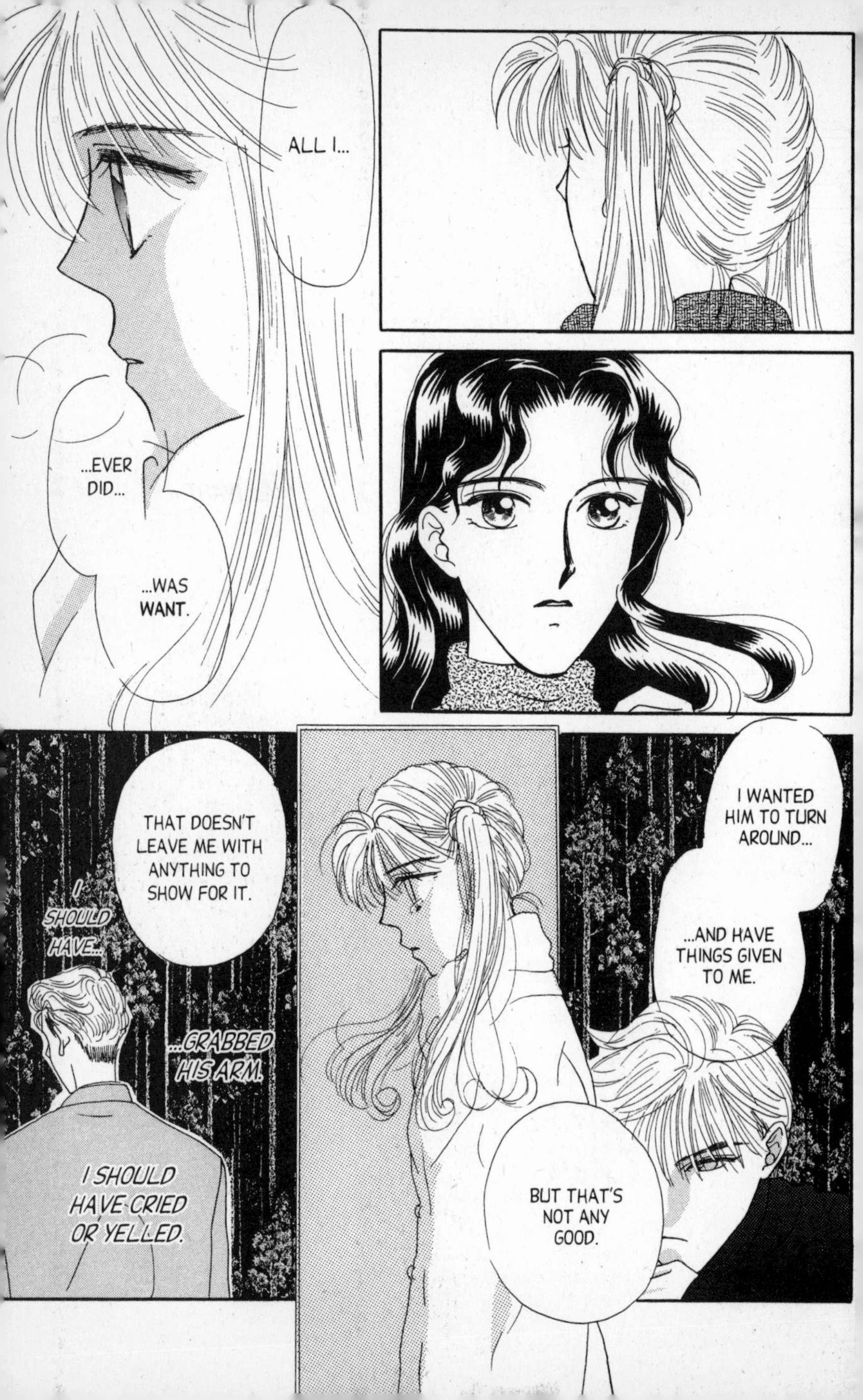
ALL I...
...EVER DID...
...WAS WANT.
I WANTED HIM TO TURN AROUND...
...AND HAVE THINGS GIVEN TO ME.
BUT THAT'S NOT ANY GOOD.
THAT DOESN'T LEAVE ME WITH ANYTHING TO SHOW FOR IT.
I SHOULD HAVE...
...GRABBED HIS ARM.
I SHOULD HAVE CRIED OR YELLED.

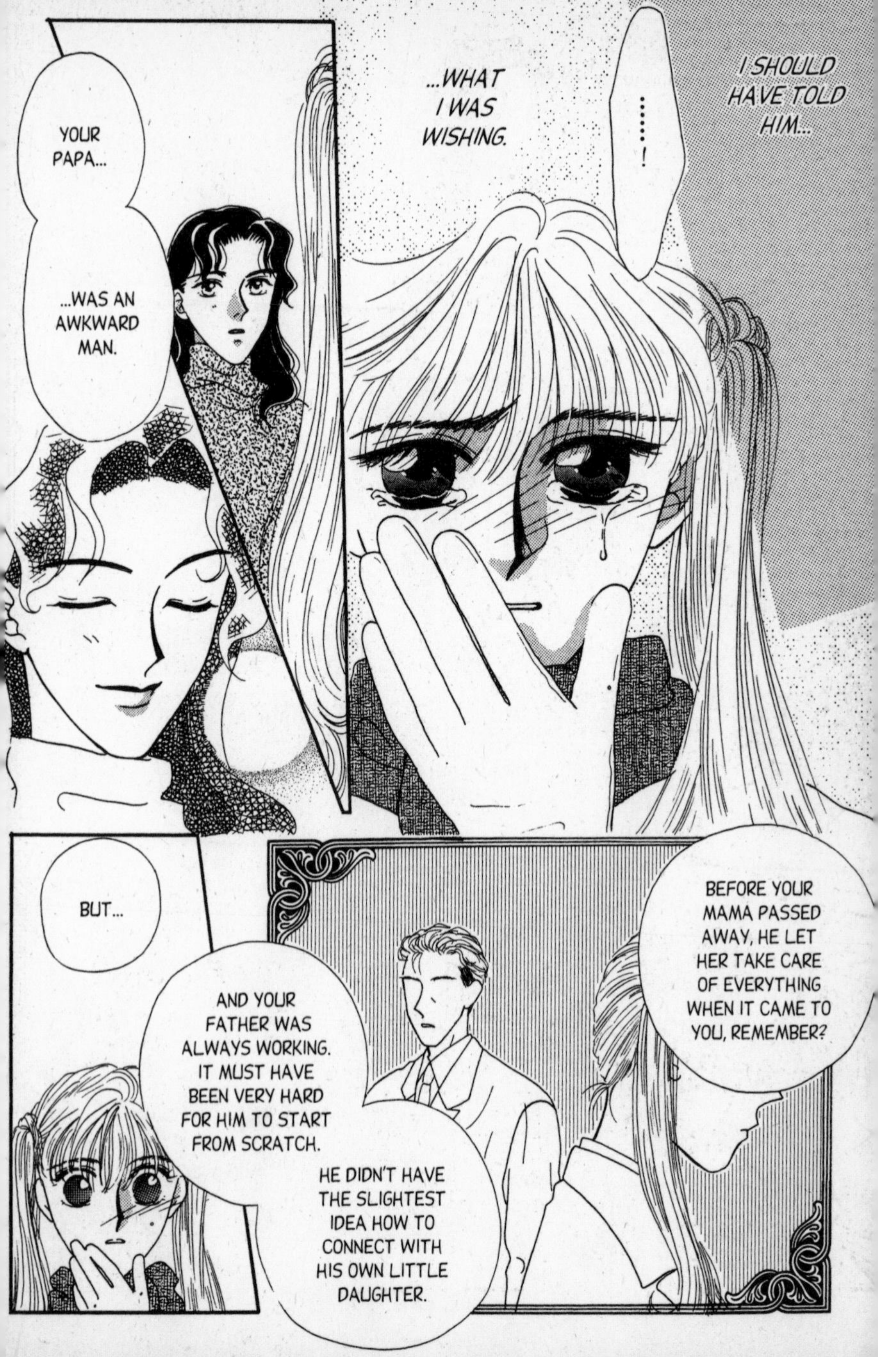
I SHOULD HAVE TOLD HIM...
......!
...WHAT I WAS WISHING.
YOUR PAPA...
...WAS AN AWKWARD MAN.
BEFORE YOUR MAMA PASSED AWAY, HE LET HER TAKE CARE OF EVERYTHING WHEN IT CAME TO YOU, REMEMBER?
BUT...
AND YOUR FATHER WAS ALWAYS WORKING. IT MUST HAVE BEEN VERY HARD FOR HIM TO START FROM SCRATCH.
HE DIDN'T HAVE THE SLIGHTEST IDEA HOW TO CONNECT WITH HIS OWN LITTLE DAUGHTER.

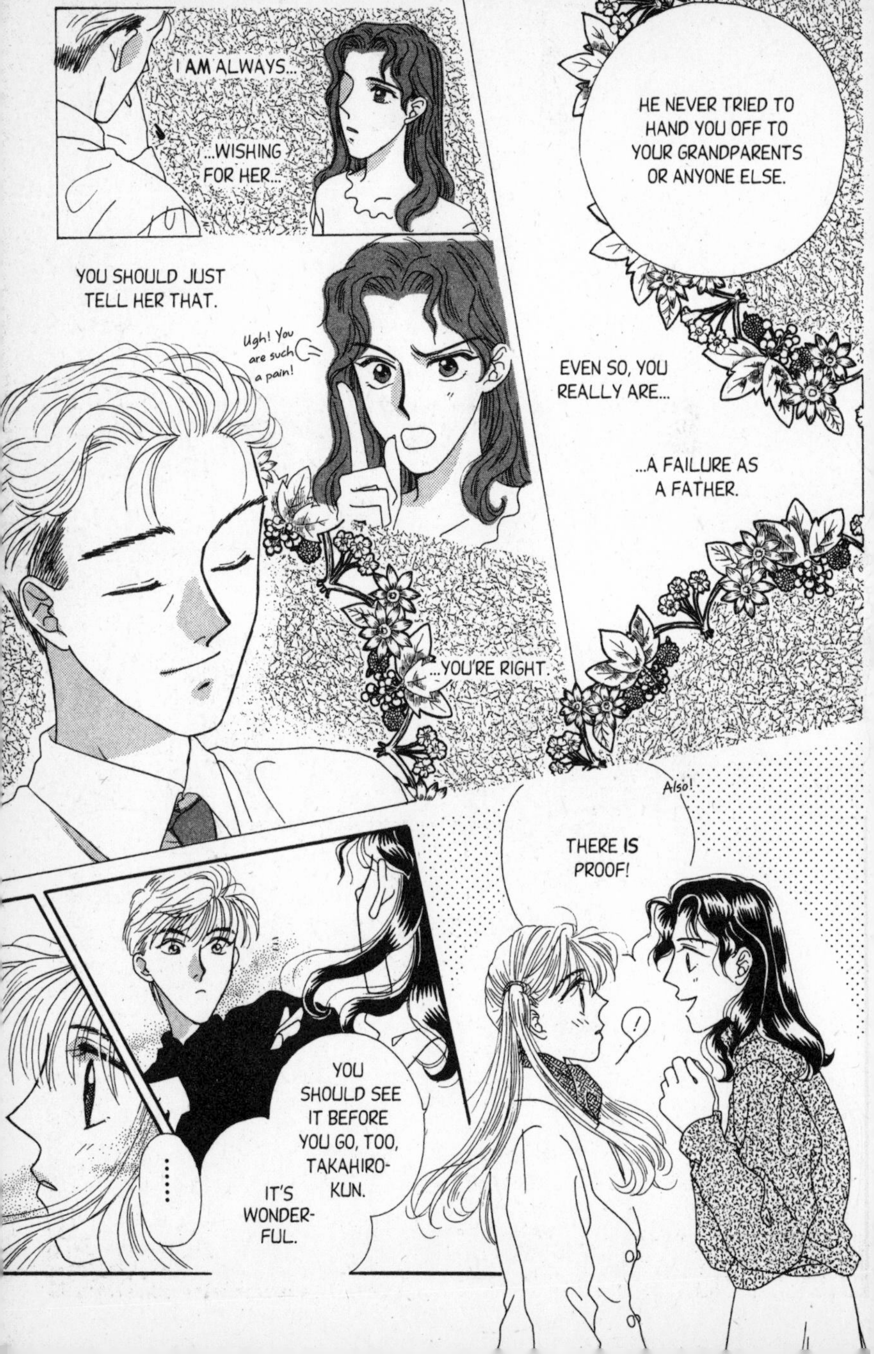
HE NEVER TRIED TO HAND YOU OFF TO YOUR GRANDPARENTS OR ANYONE ELSE.
EVEN SO, YOU REALLY ARE...
...A FAILURE AS A FATHER.
I AM ALWAYS...
...WISHING FOR HER...
YOU SHOULD JUST TELL HER THAT.
Ugh! You are such a pain!
...YOU'RE RIGHT.
Also!
THERE IS PROOF!
!
YOU SHOULD SEE IT BEFORE YOU GO, TOO, TAKAHIRO-KUN.
IT'S WONDER-FUL.
......

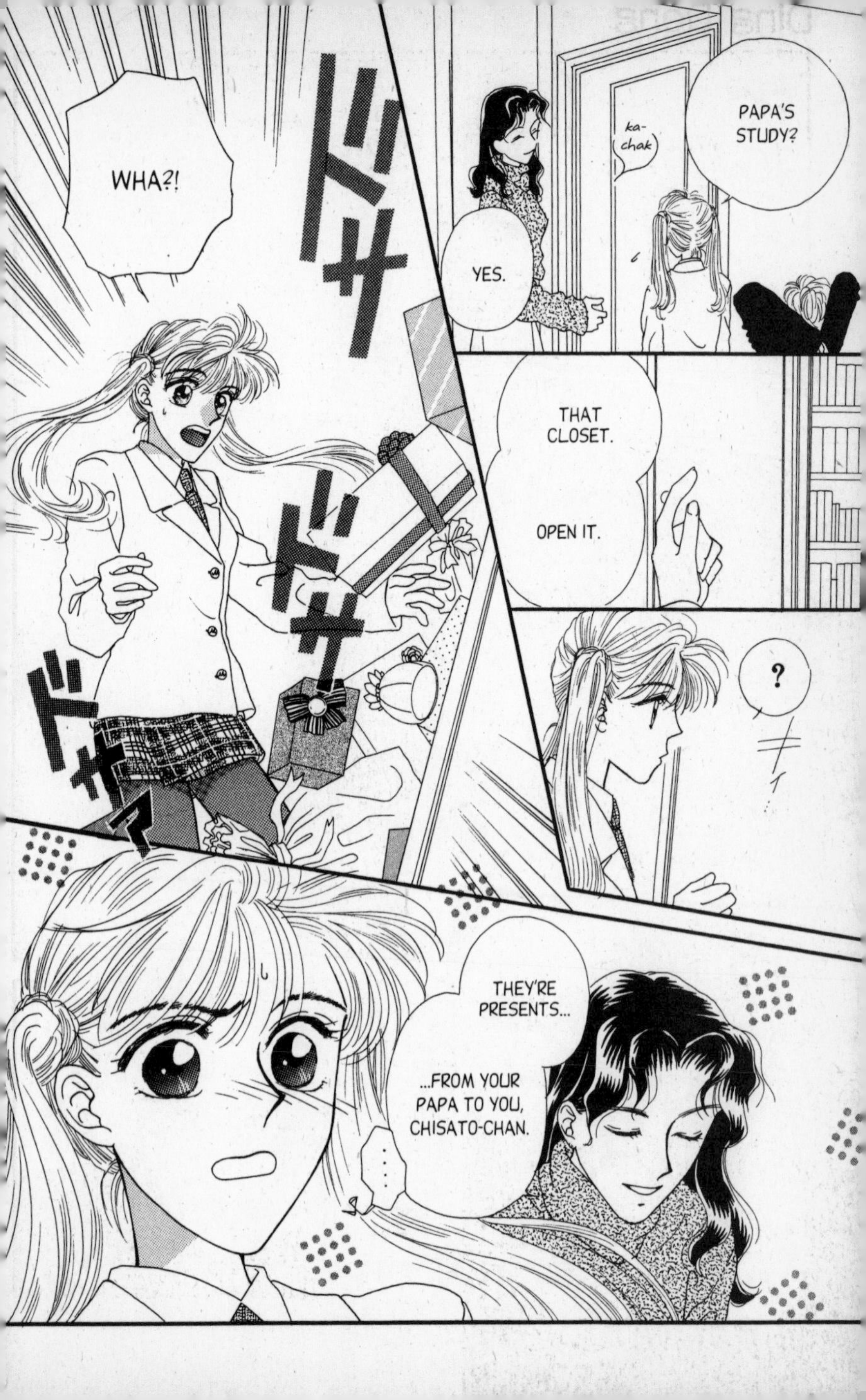
PAPA'S STUDY?
ka-chak
YES.
THAT CLOSET.
OPEN IT.
?
WHA?!
ドサ
ドサ
ドシャア
THEY'RE PRESENTS...
...FROM YOUR PAPA TO YOU, CHISATO-CHAN.
...

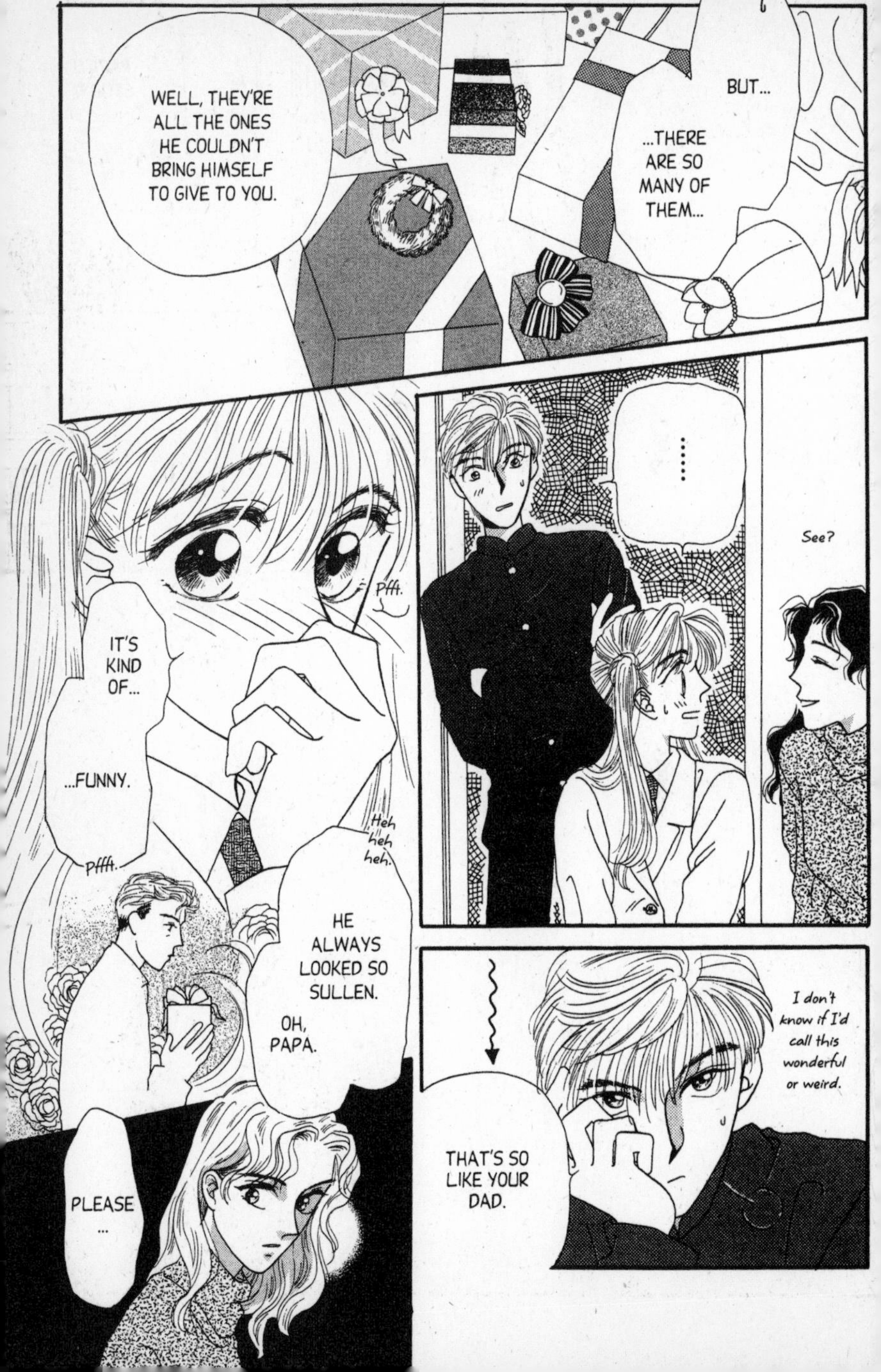
BUT...
...THERE ARE SO MANY OF THEM...
WELL, THEY'RE ALL THE ONES HE COULDN'T BRING HIMSELF TO GIVE TO YOU.
See?
......
I don't know if I'd call this wonderful or weird.
THAT'S SO LIKE YOUR DAD.
Pfft.
IT'S KIND OF...
...FUNNY.
Pfft.
Heh heh heh.
HE ALWAYS LOOKED SO SULLEN.
OH, PAPA.
PLEASE ...

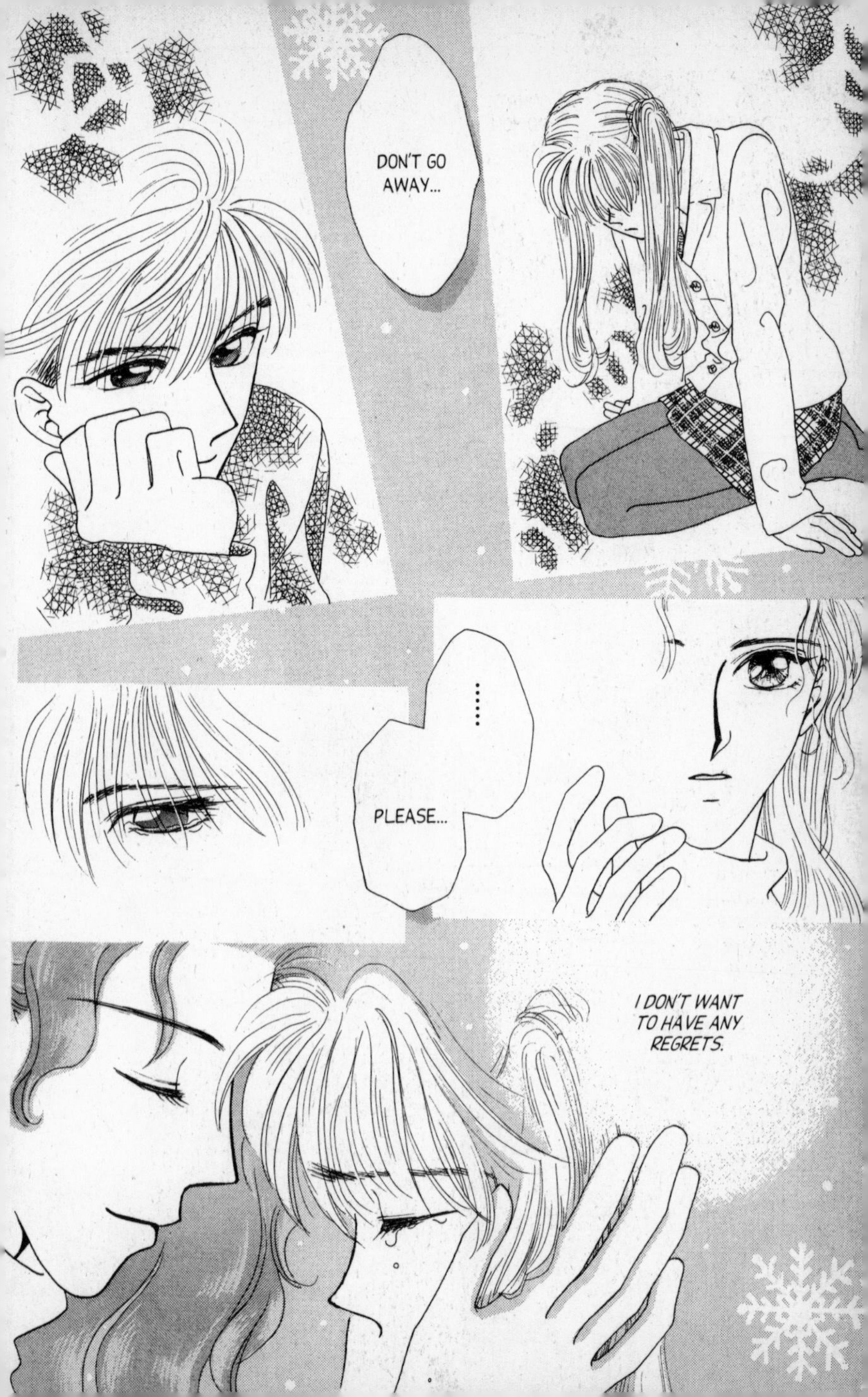
DON'T GO AWAY...
......
PLEASE...
I DON'T WANT TO HAVE ANY REGRETS.

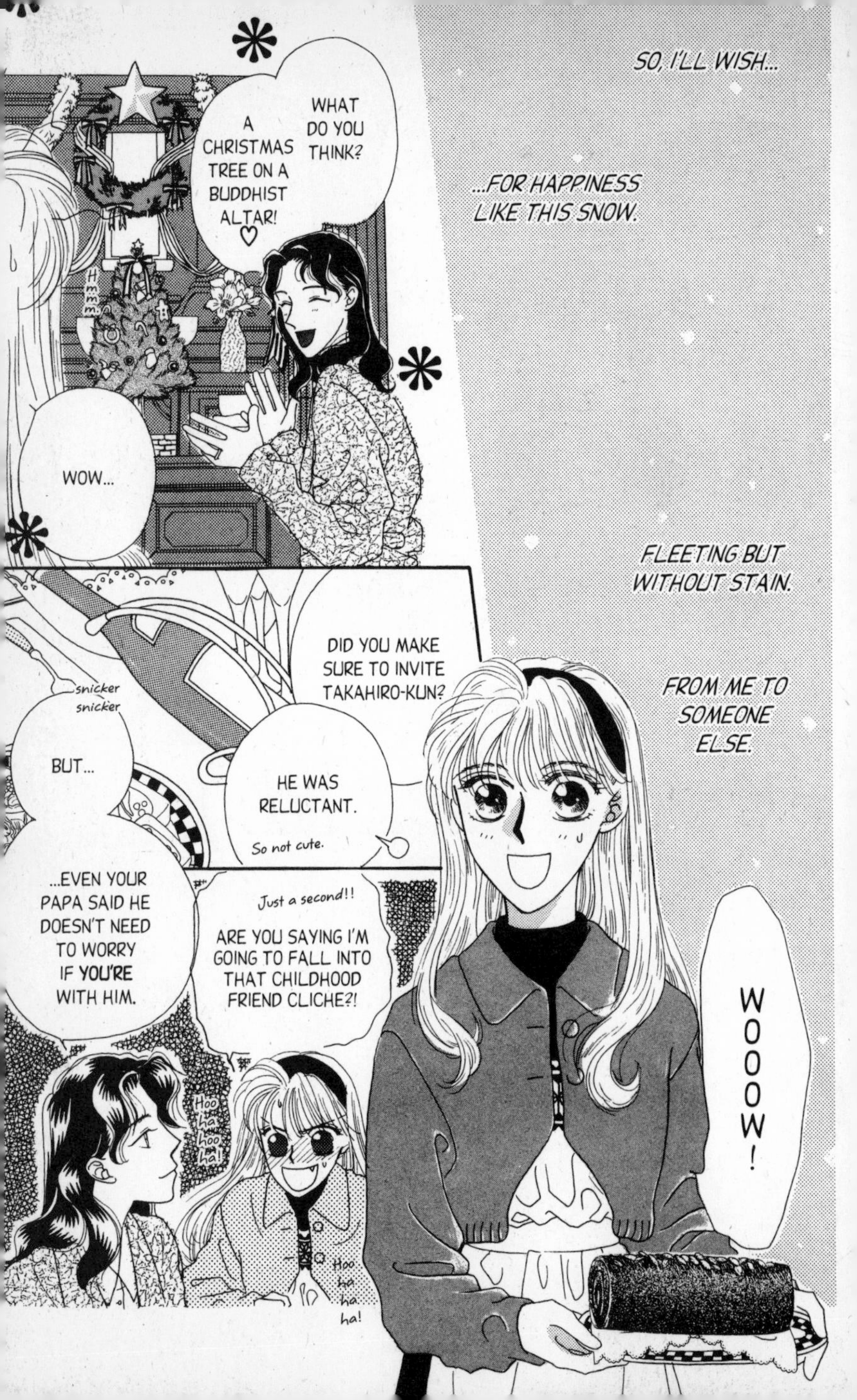
SO, I'LL WISH...
...FOR HAPPINESS LIKE THIS SNOW.
FLEETING BUT WITHOUT STAIN.
FROM ME TO SOMEONE ELSE.
WOOOW!
WHAT DO YOU THINK?
A CHRISTMAS TREE ON A BUDDHIST ALTAR! ♡
Hmmm
WOW...
DID YOU MAKE SURE TO INVITE TAKAHIRO-KUN?
HE WAS RELUCTANT.
So not cute.
snicker snicker
BUT...
...EVEN YOUR PAPA SAID HE DOESN'T NEED TO WORRY IF YOU'RE WITH HIM.
Just a second!!
ARE YOU SAYING I'M GOING TO FALL INTO THAT CHILDHOOD FRIEND CLICHE?!
Hoo ha hoo ha!
Hoo ha ha ha!

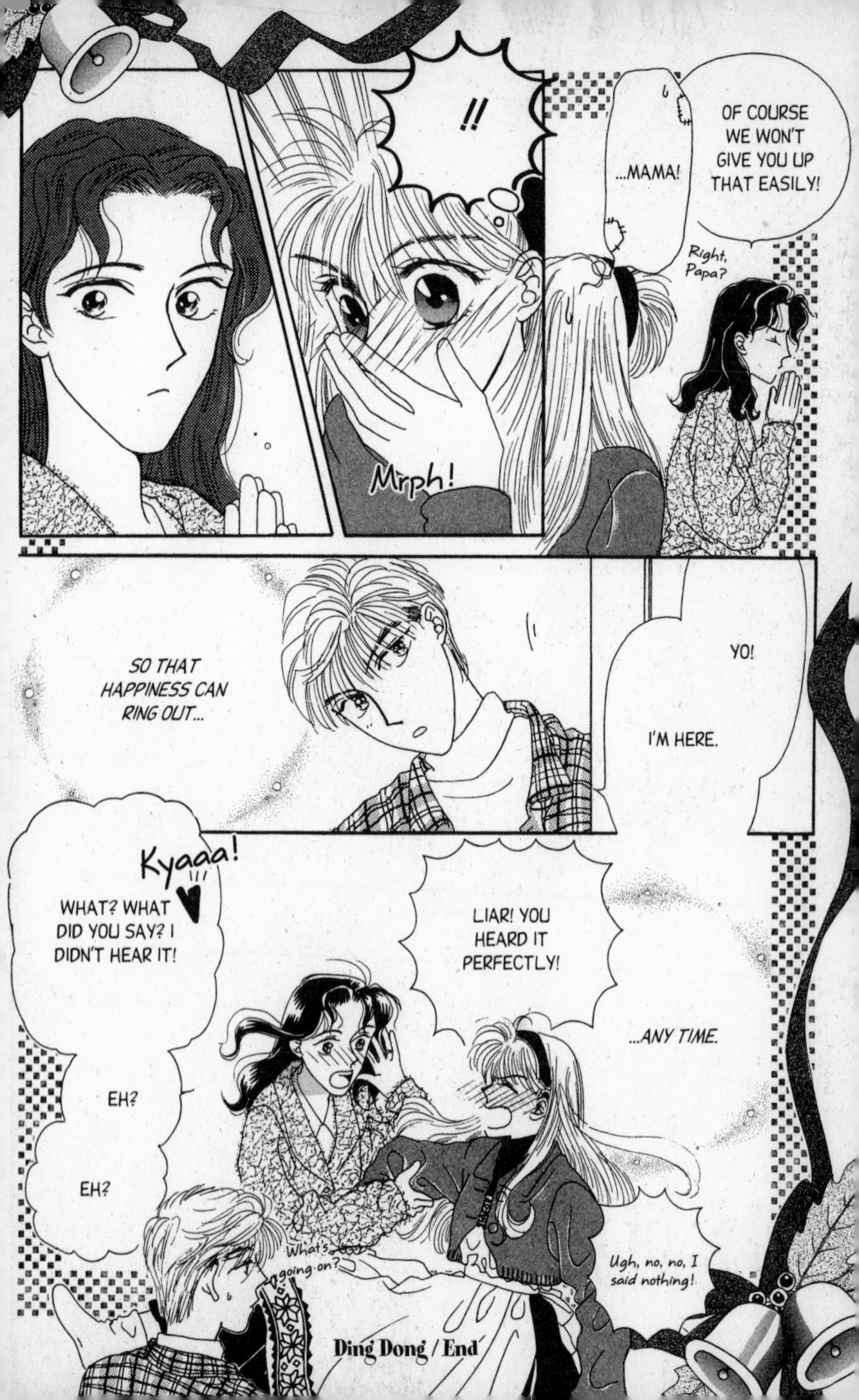
OF COURSE WE WON'T GIVE YOU UP THAT EASILY!
Right, Papa?
...MAMA!
!!
Mrph!
YO!
I'M HERE.
SO THAT HAPPINESS CAN RING OUT...
...ANY TIME.
LIAR! YOU HEARD IT PERFECTLY!
Kyaaa!
WHAT? WHAT DID YOU SAY? I DIDN'T HEAR IT!
Ugh, no, no, I said nothing!
What's going on?
EH?
EH?
Ding Dong / End

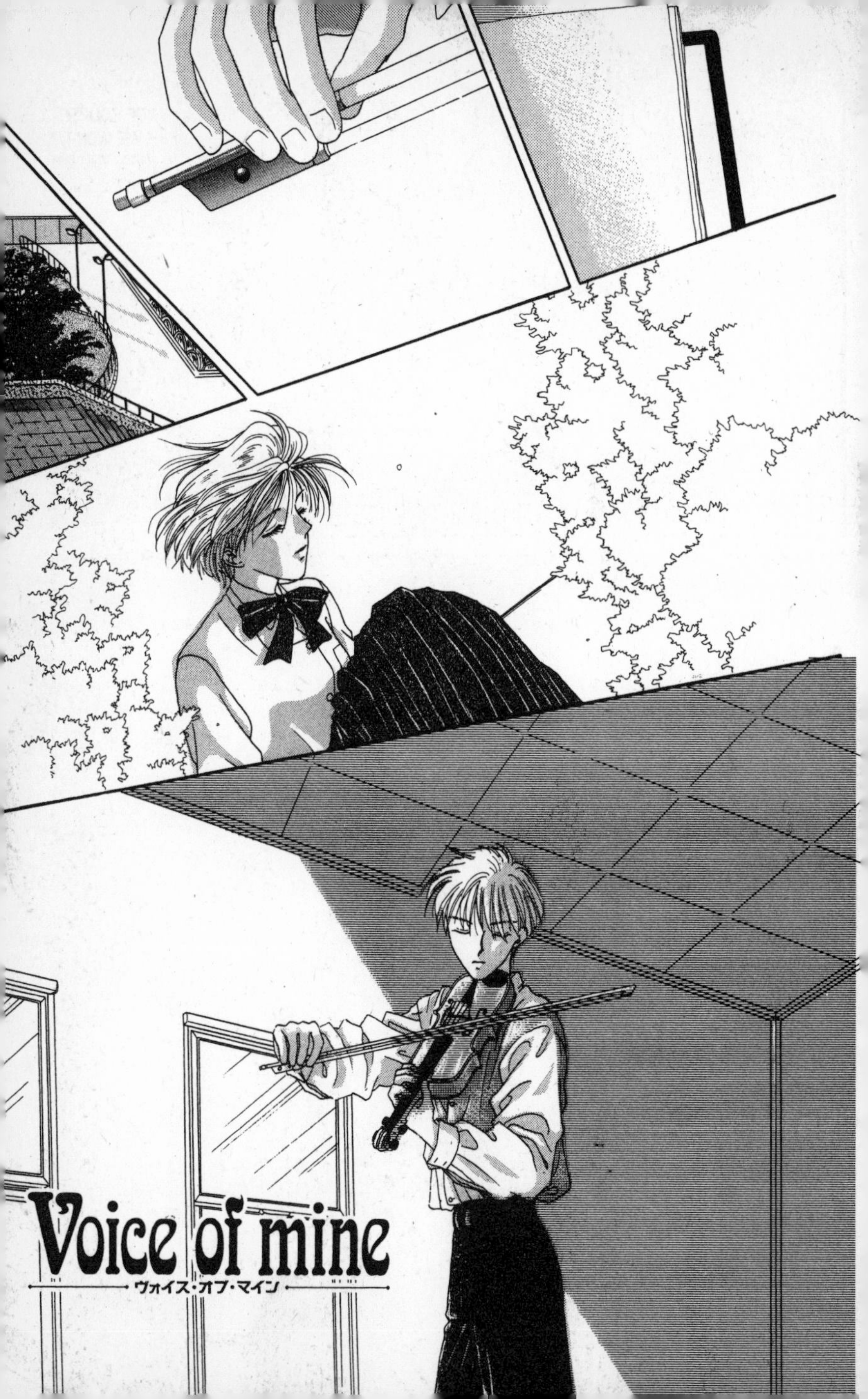
Voice of mine
ヴォイス・オブ・マイン

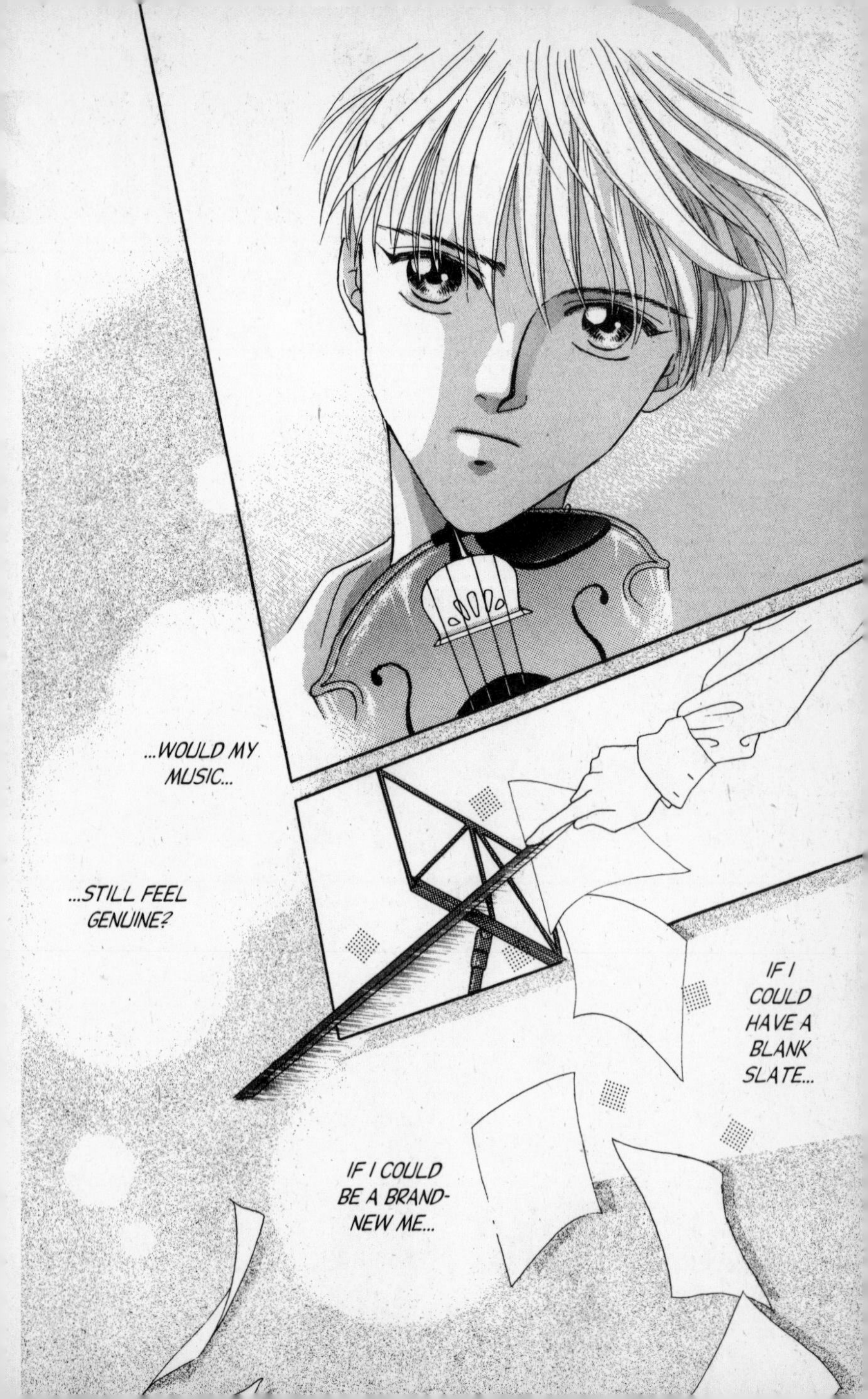
IF I COULD HAVE A BLANK SLATE...
IF I COULD BE A BRAND-NEW ME...
...WOULD MY MUSIC...
...STILL FEEL GENUINE?

Voice of mine

ヴォイス・オブ・マイン

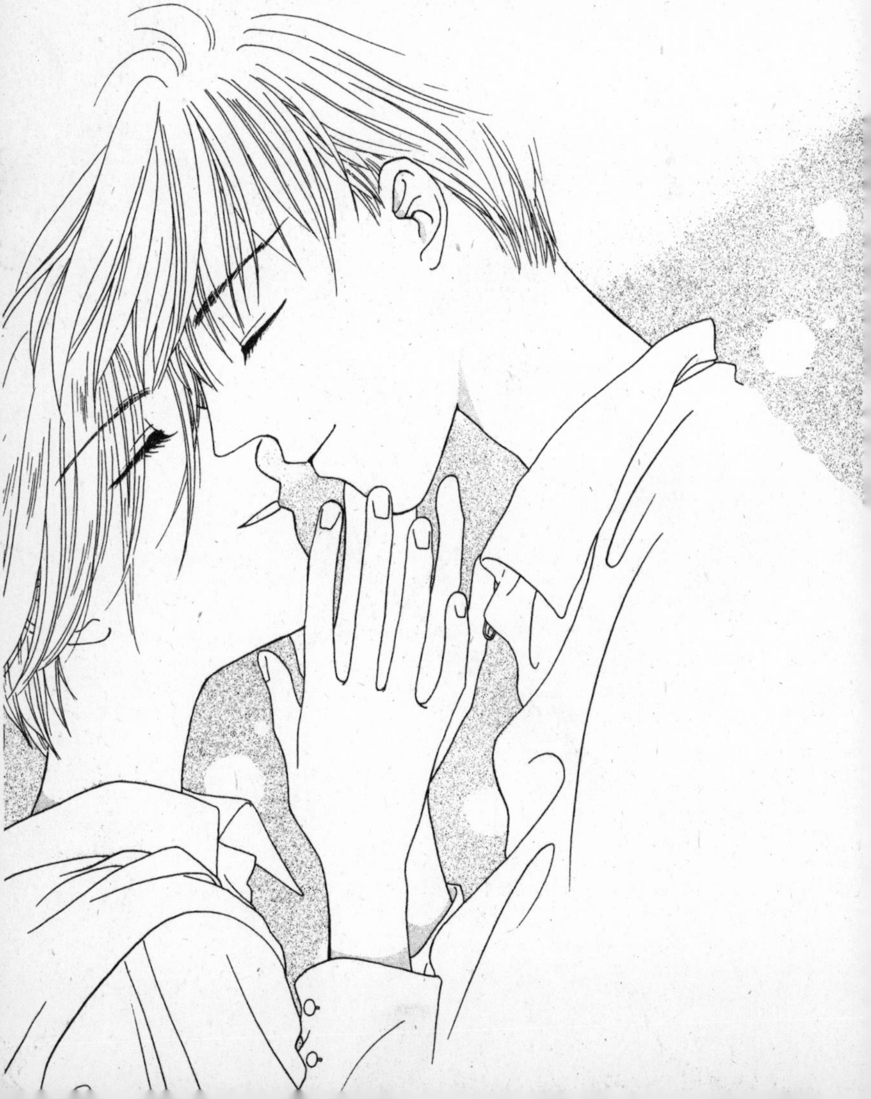

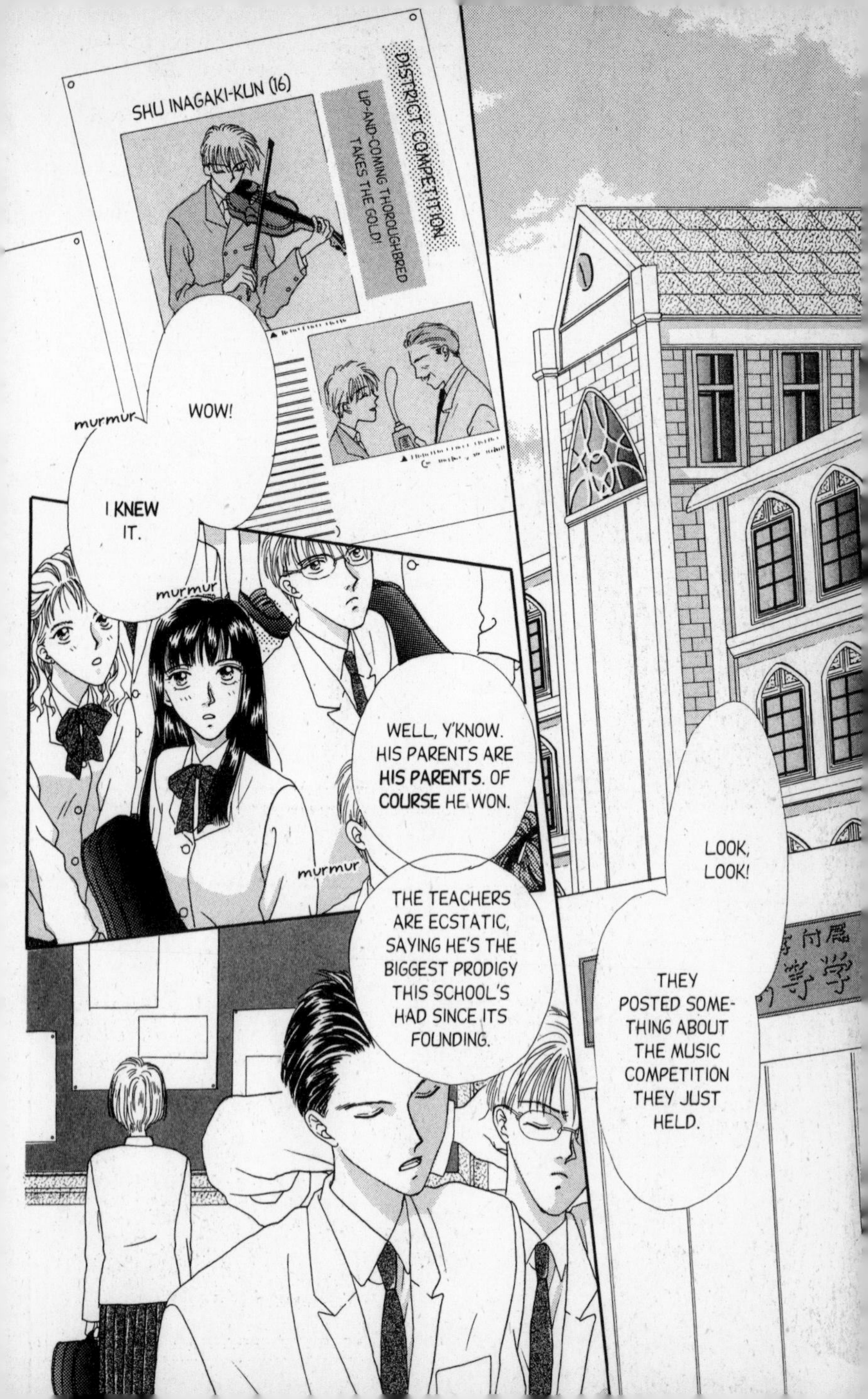
LOOK, LOOK!
THEY POSTED SOME-THING ABOUT THE MUSIC COMPETITION THEY JUST HELD.
DISTRICT COMPETITION
UP-AND-COMING THOROUGHBRED TAKES THE GOLD!
SHU INAGAKI-KUN (16)
WOW!
murmur
I KNEW IT.
murmur
WELL, Y'KNOW. HIS PARENTS ARE **HIS PARENTS**. OF **COURSE** HE WON.
murmur
THE TEACHERS ARE ECSTATIC, SAYING HE'S THE BIGGEST PRODIGY THIS SCHOOL'S HAD SINCE ITS FOUNDING.

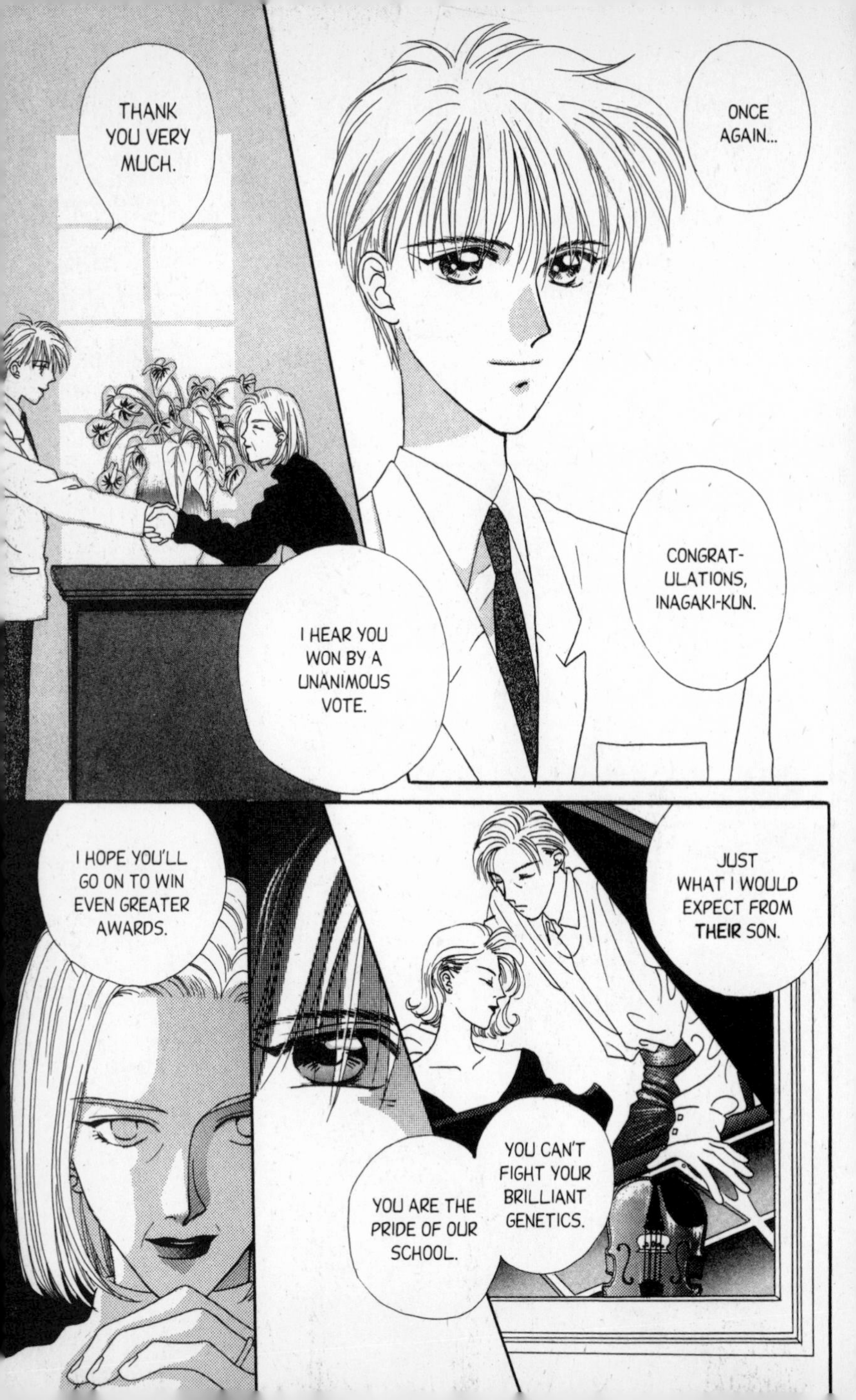
ONCE AGAIN...
CONGRAT-ULATIONS, INAGAKI-KUN.
I HEAR YOU WON BY A UNANIMOUS VOTE.
THANK YOU VERY MUCH.
JUST WHAT I WOULD EXPECT FROM **THEIR** SON.
YOU CAN'T FIGHT YOUR BRILLIANT GENETICS.
YOU ARE THE PRIDE OF OUR SCHOOL.
I HOPE YOU'LL GO ON TO WIN EVEN GREATER AWARDS.

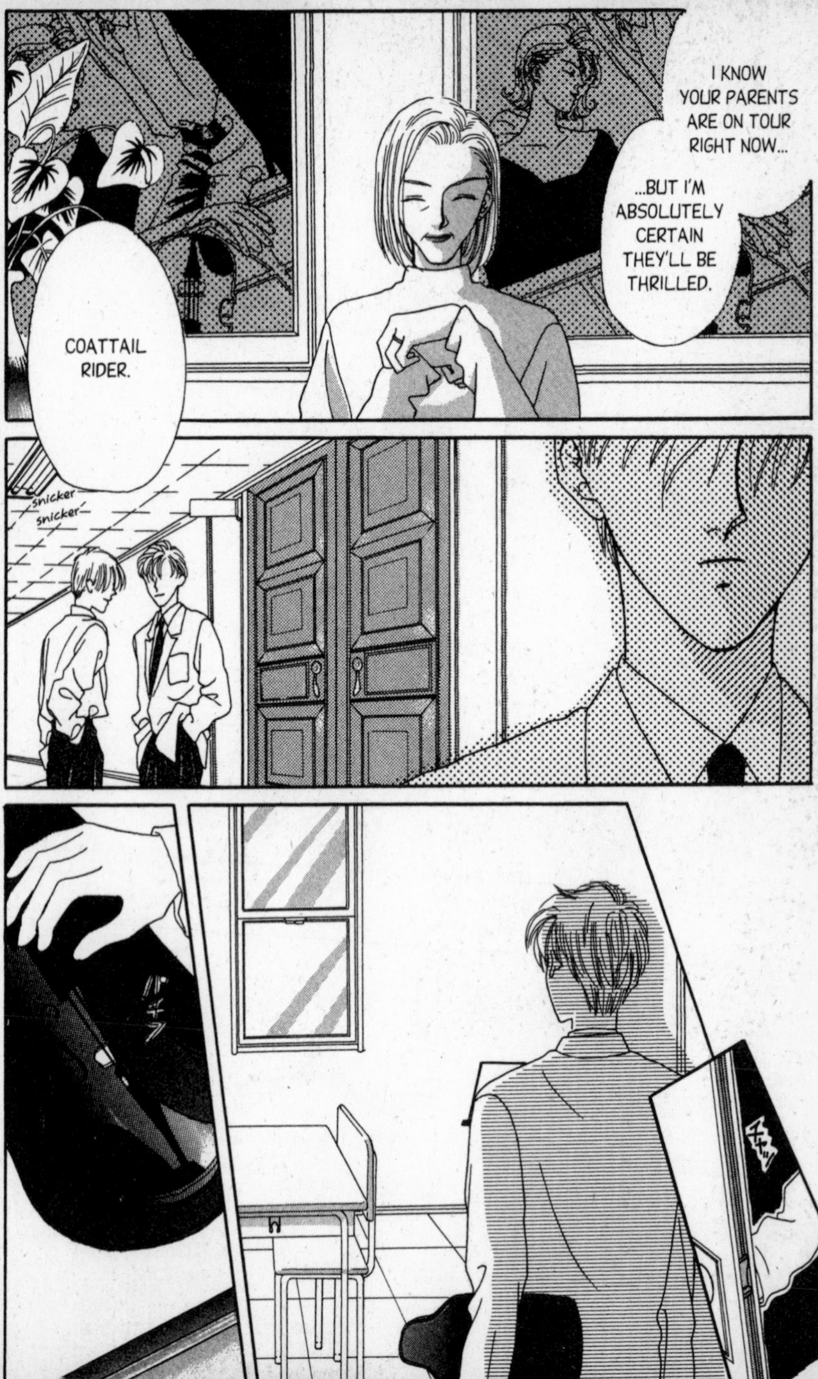
I KNOW YOUR PARENTS ARE ON TOUR RIGHT NOW...
...BUT I'M ABSOLUTELY CERTAIN THEY'LL BE THRILLED.
COATTAIL RIDER.
snicker
snicker

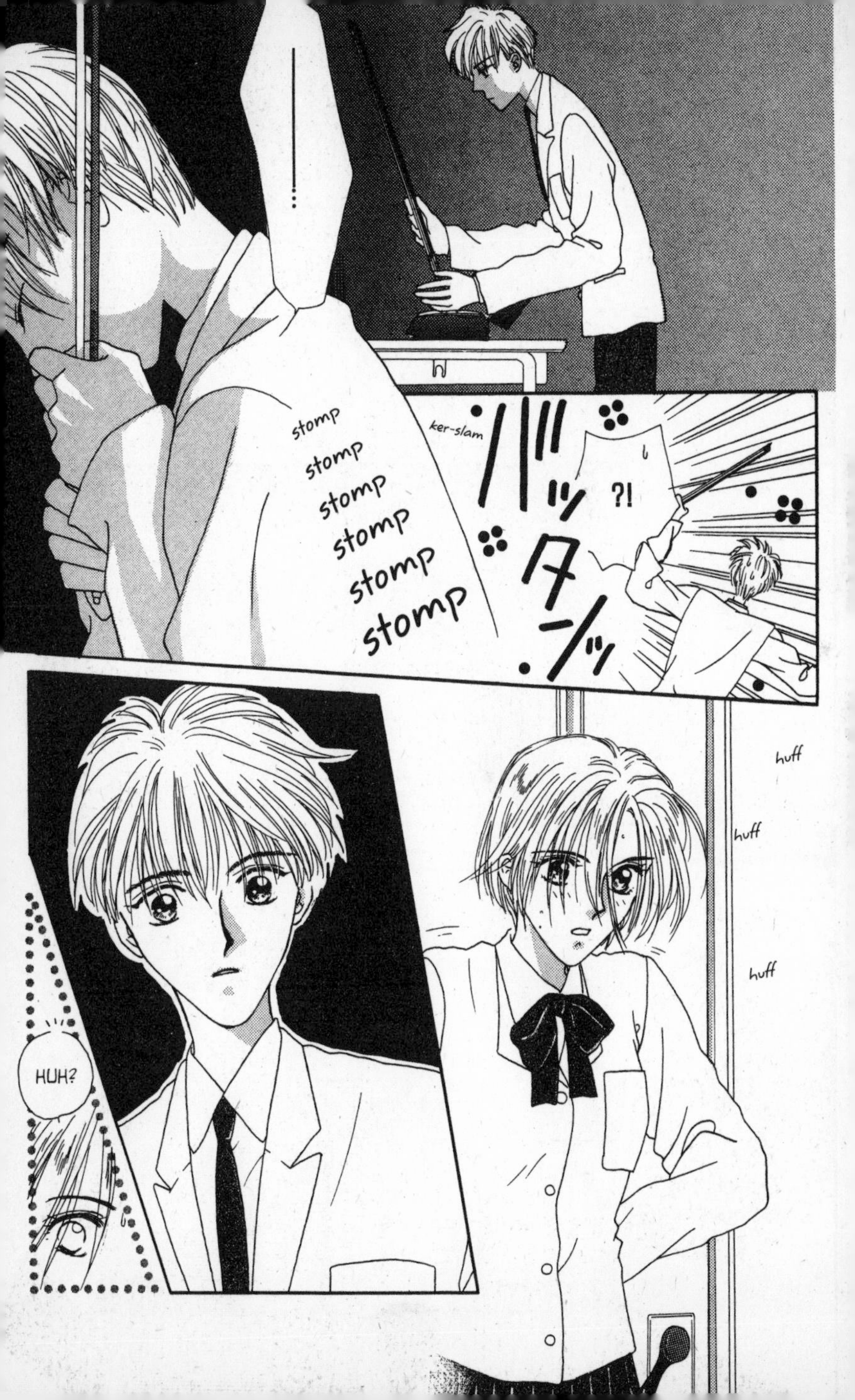
ker-slam
バッタンッ
?!
......
stomp
stomp
stomp
stomp
stomp
stomp
huff
huff
huff
HUH?

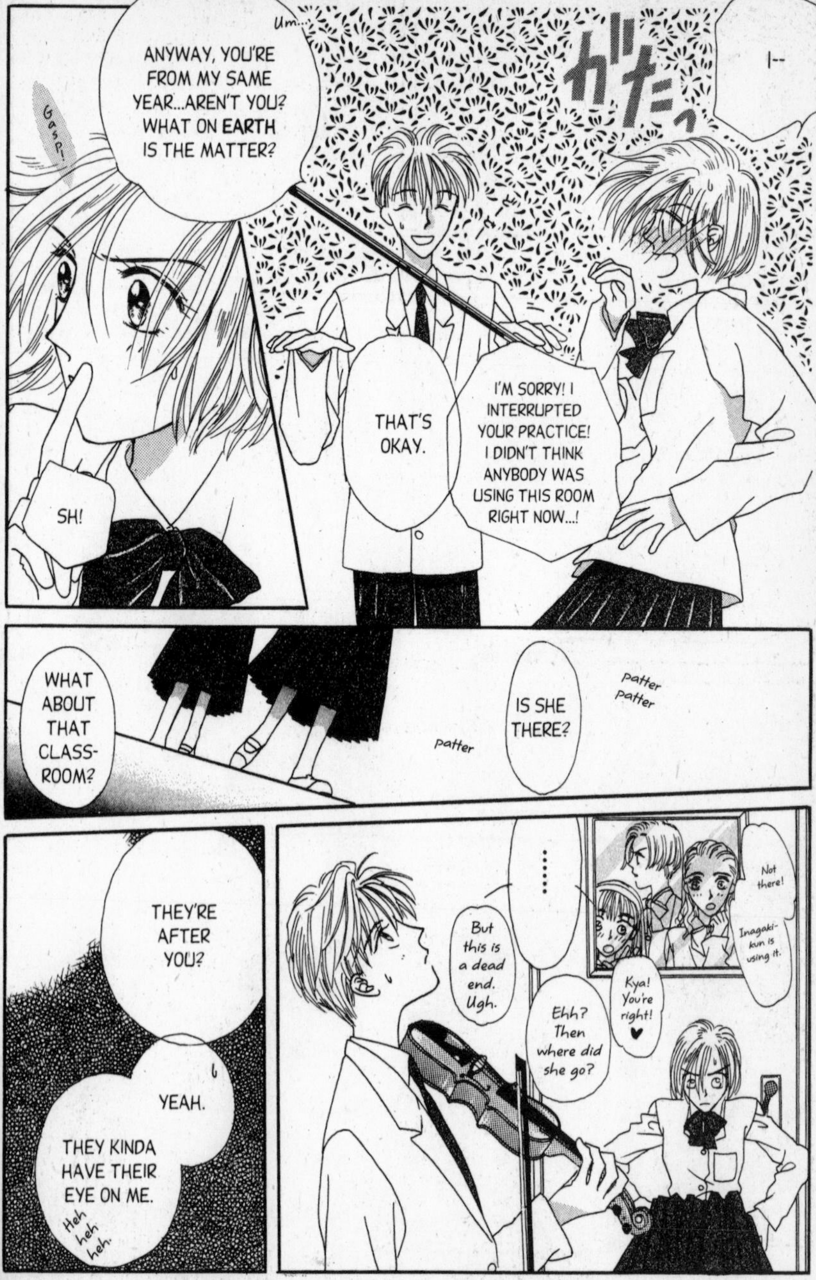
I--
ガタっ
Um...
I'M SORRY! I INTERRUPTED YOUR PRACTICE! I DIDN'T THINK ANYBODY WAS USING THIS ROOM RIGHT NOW...!
THAT'S OKAY.
ANYWAY, YOU'RE FROM MY SAME YEAR...AREN'T YOU? WHAT ON **EARTH** IS THE MATTER?
Gasp!
SH!
patter patter
IS SHE THERE?
patter
WHAT ABOUT THAT CLASSROOM?
Not there!
Inagaki-kun is using it.
Kya! You're right! ♥
......
Ehh? Then where did she go?
But this is a dead end. Ugh.
THEY'RE AFTER YOU?
YEAH.
THEY KINDA HAVE THEIR EYE ON ME.
Heh heh heh.

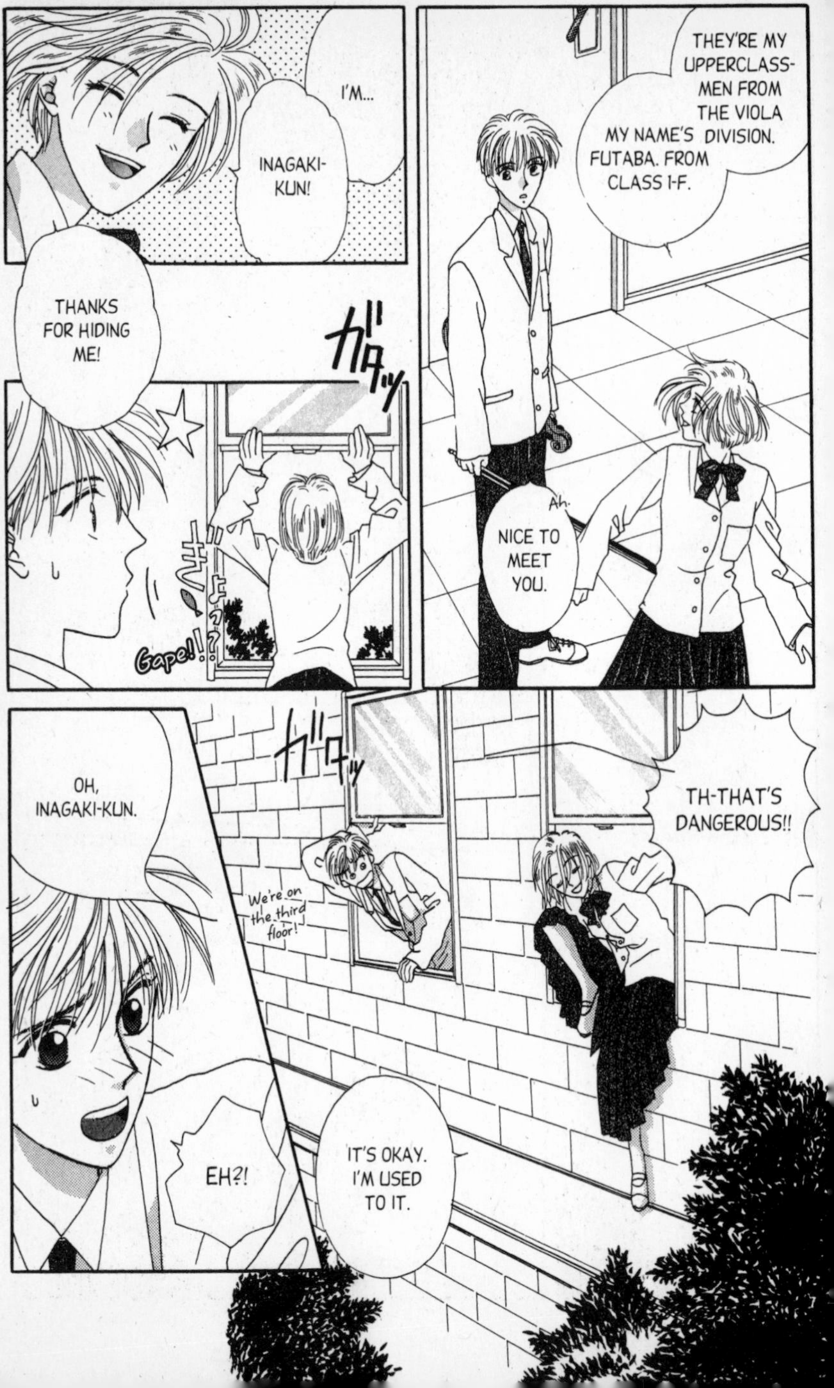
THEY'RE MY UPPERCLASSMEN FROM THE VIOLA DIVISION.
MY NAME'S FUTABA. FROM CLASS 1-F.
Ah.
NICE TO MEET YOU.
I'M...
INAGAKI-KUN!
THANKS FOR HIDING ME!
ガタッ
ぎょっ!?
Gape!!?
ガタッ
TH-THAT'S DANGEROUS!!
We're on the third floor!
IT'S OKAY. I'M USED TO IT.
OH, INAGAKI-KUN.
EH?!

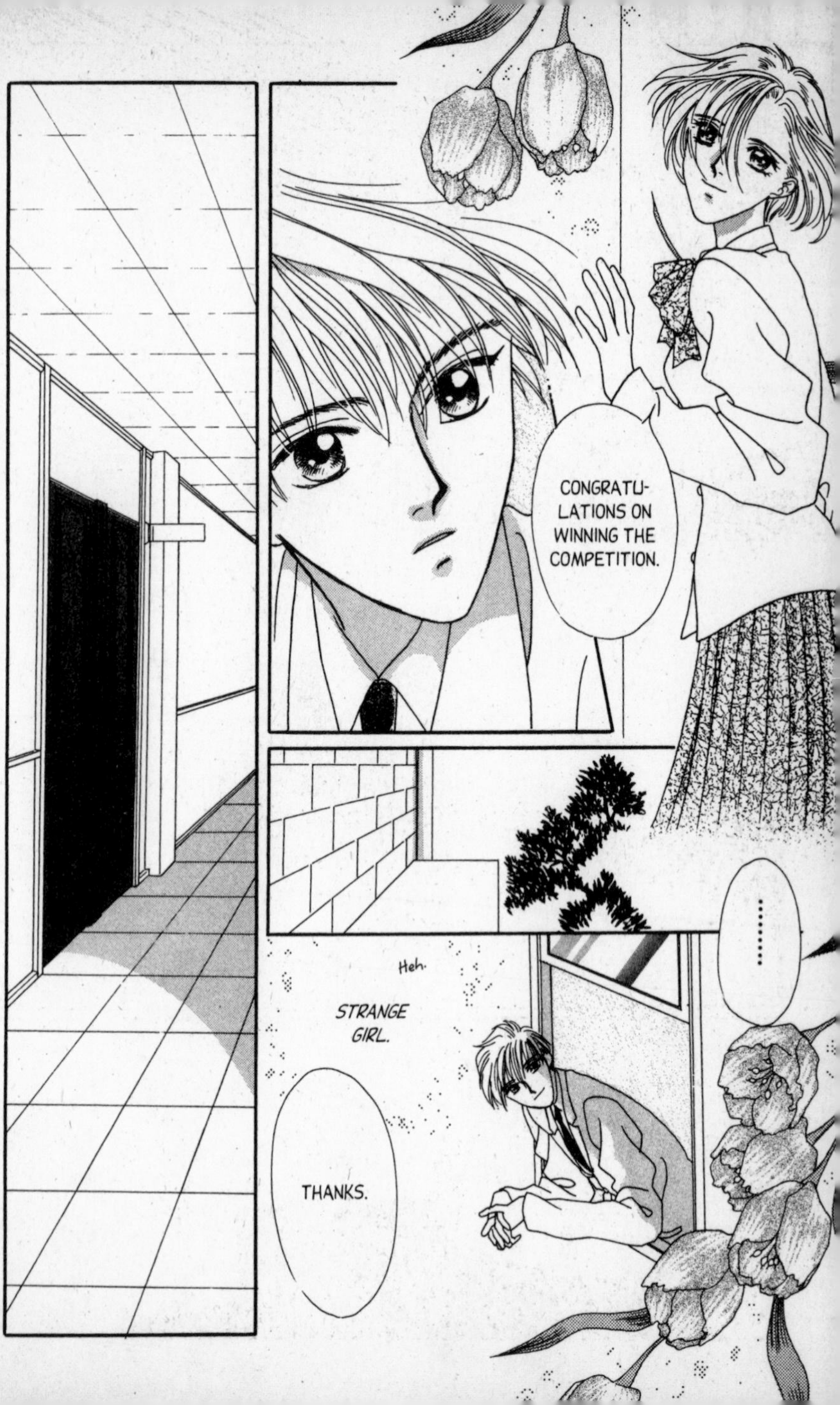
CONGRATU-LATIONS ON WINNING THE COMPETITION.
....
Heh.
STRANGE GIRL.
THANKS.

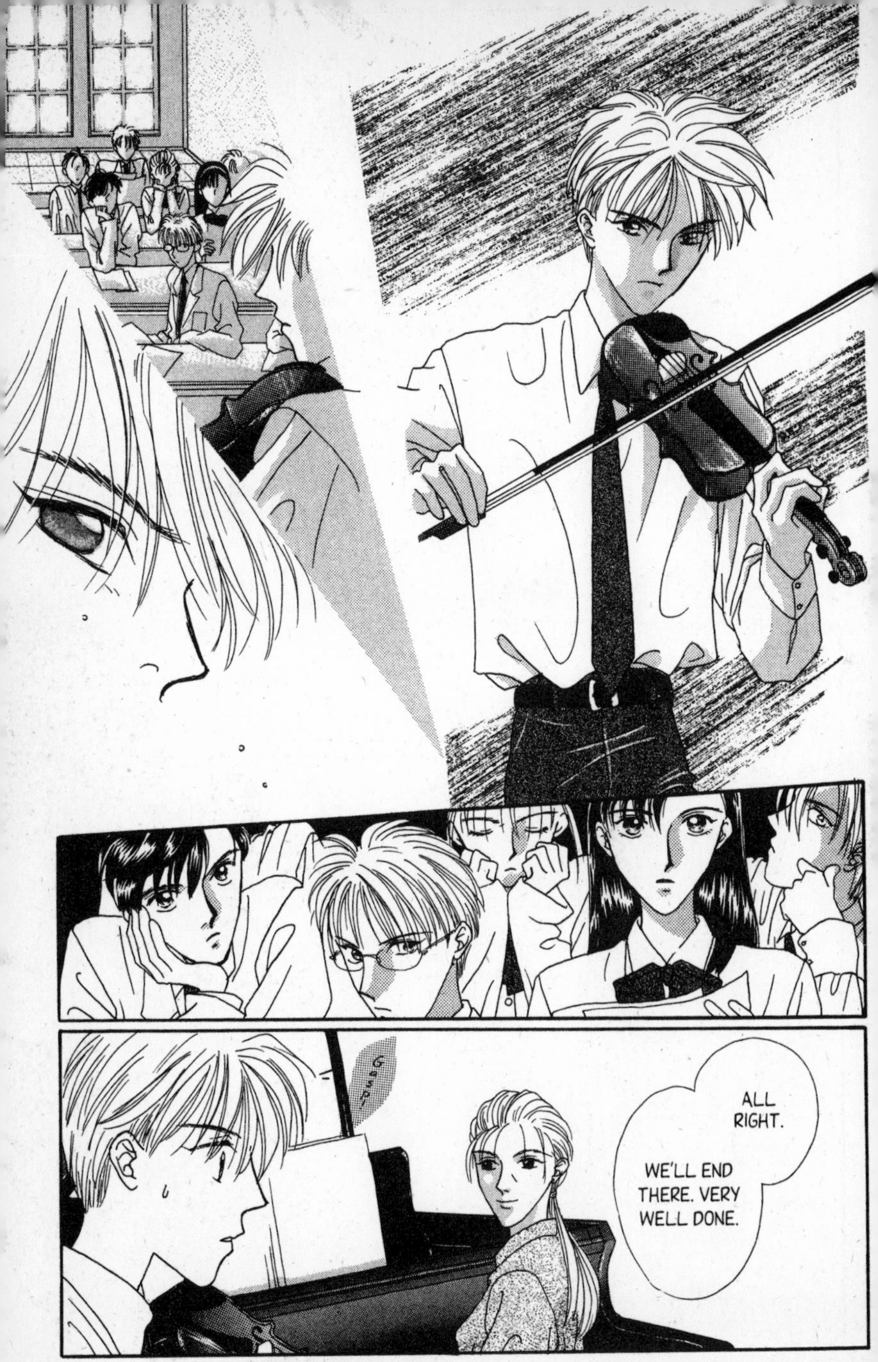
ALL RIGHT.
WE'LL END THERE. VERY WELL DONE.
Gasp!

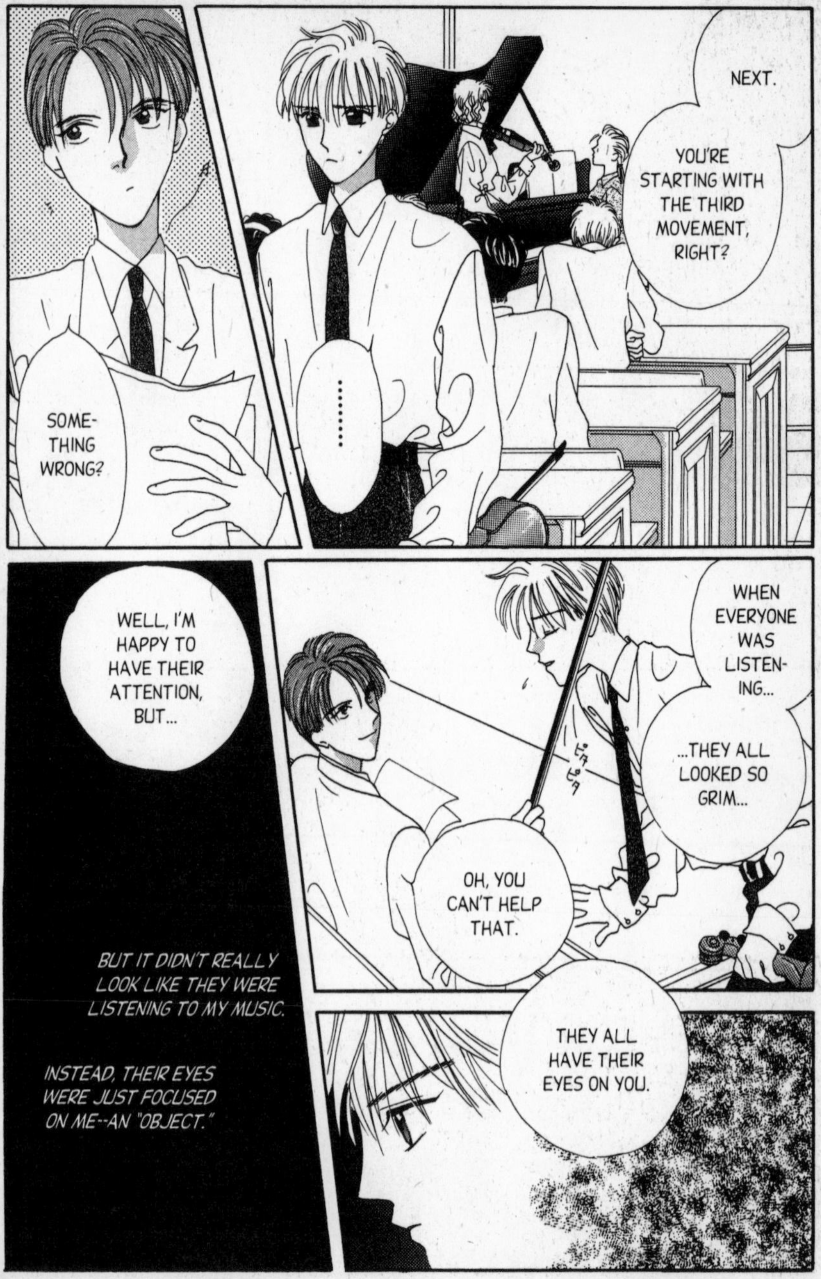
NEXT.
YOU'RE STARTING WITH THE THIRD MOVEMENT, RIGHT?
......
SOME-THING WRONG?
WHEN EVERYONE WAS LISTEN-ING...
...THEY ALL LOOKED SO GRIM...
OH, YOU CAN'T HELP THAT.
THEY ALL HAVE THEIR EYES ON YOU.
WELL, I'M HAPPY TO HAVE THEIR ATTENTION, BUT...
BUT IT DIDN'T REALLY LOOK LIKE THEY WERE LISTENING TO MY MUSIC.
INSTEAD, THEIR EYES WERE JUST FOCUSED ON ME--AN "OBJECT."

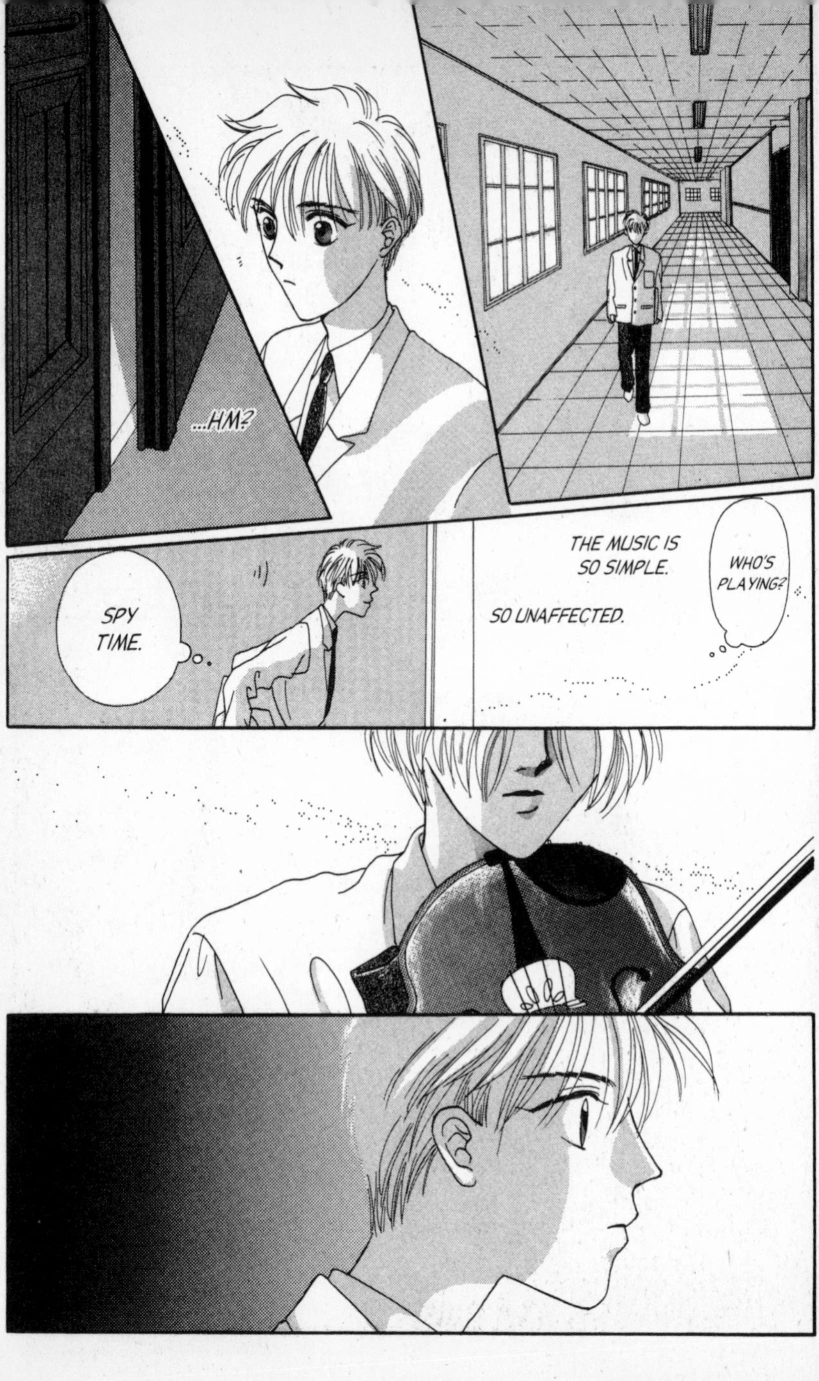
...HM?
WHO'S PLAYING?
THE MUSIC IS SO SIMPLE.
SO UNAFFECTED.
SPY TIME.

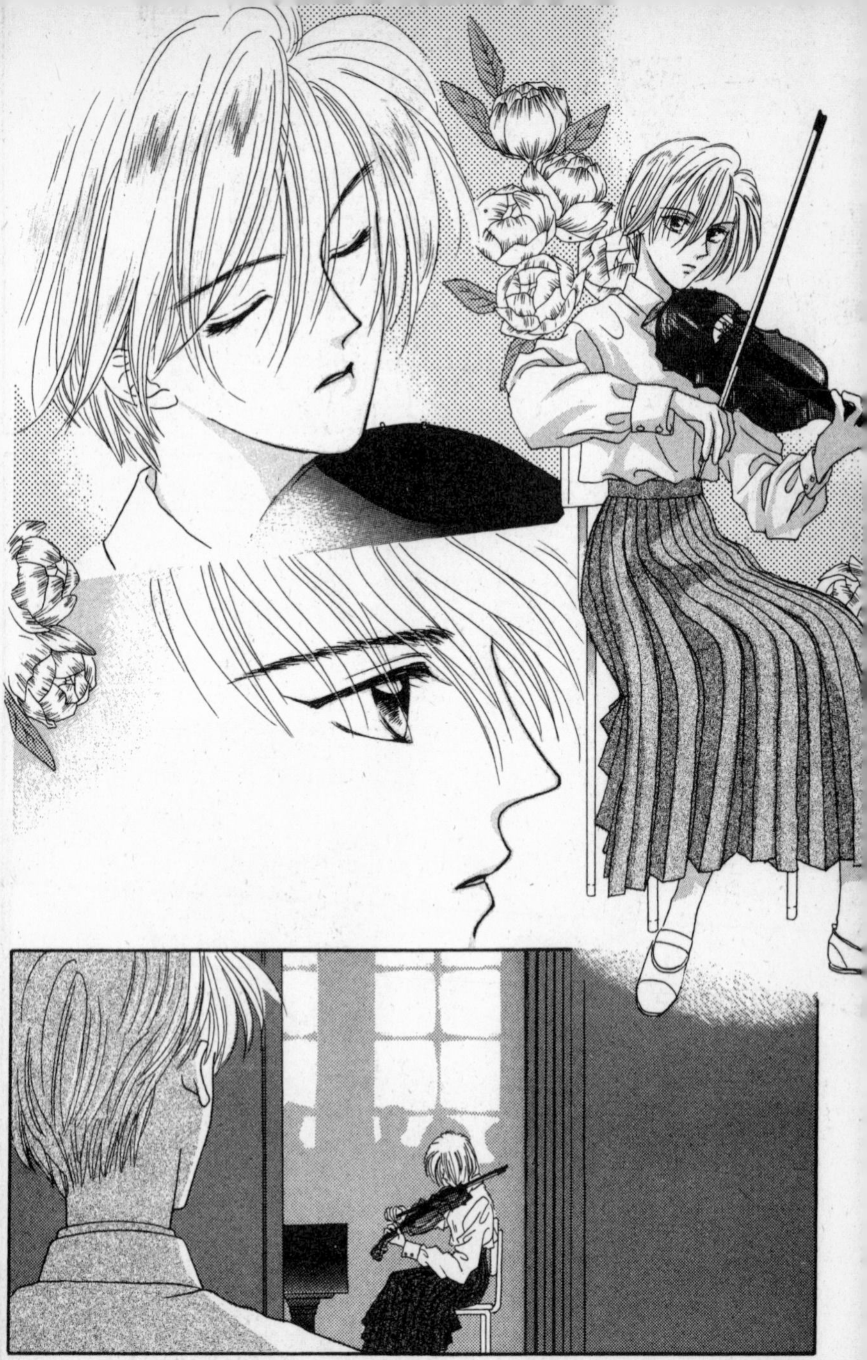

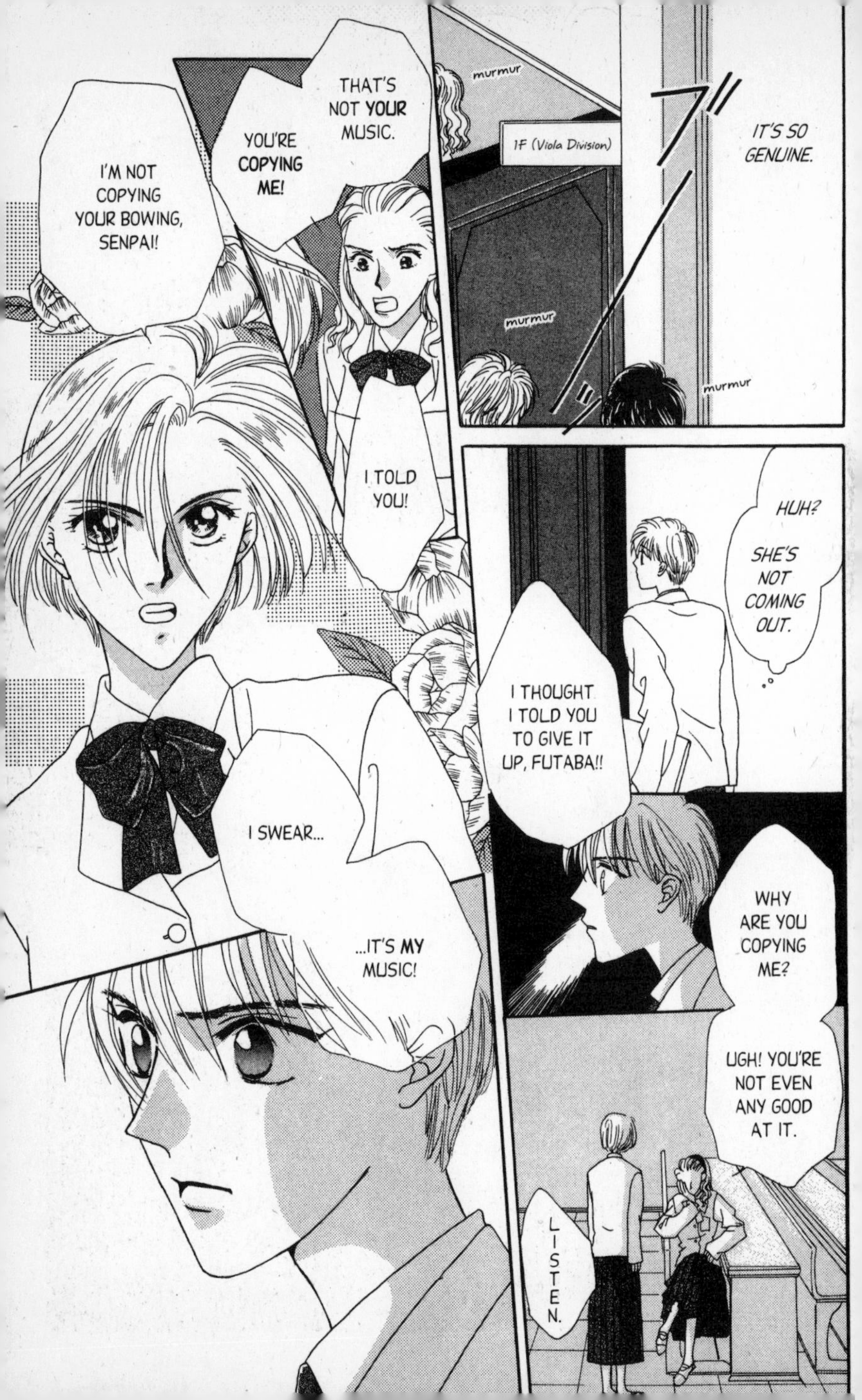

IT'S SO GENUINE.
1F (Viola Division)
murmur
murmur
murmur
HUH?
SHE'S NOT COMING OUT.
I THOUGHT I TOLD YOU TO GIVE IT UP, FUTABA!!
WHY ARE YOU COPYING ME?
UGH! YOU'RE NOT EVEN ANY GOOD AT IT.
LISTEN.
THAT'S NOT **YOUR** MUSIC.
YOU'RE **COPYING** ME!
I'M NOT COPYING YOUR BOWING, SENPAI!
I TOLD YOU!
I SWEAR...
...IT'S **MY** MUSIC!

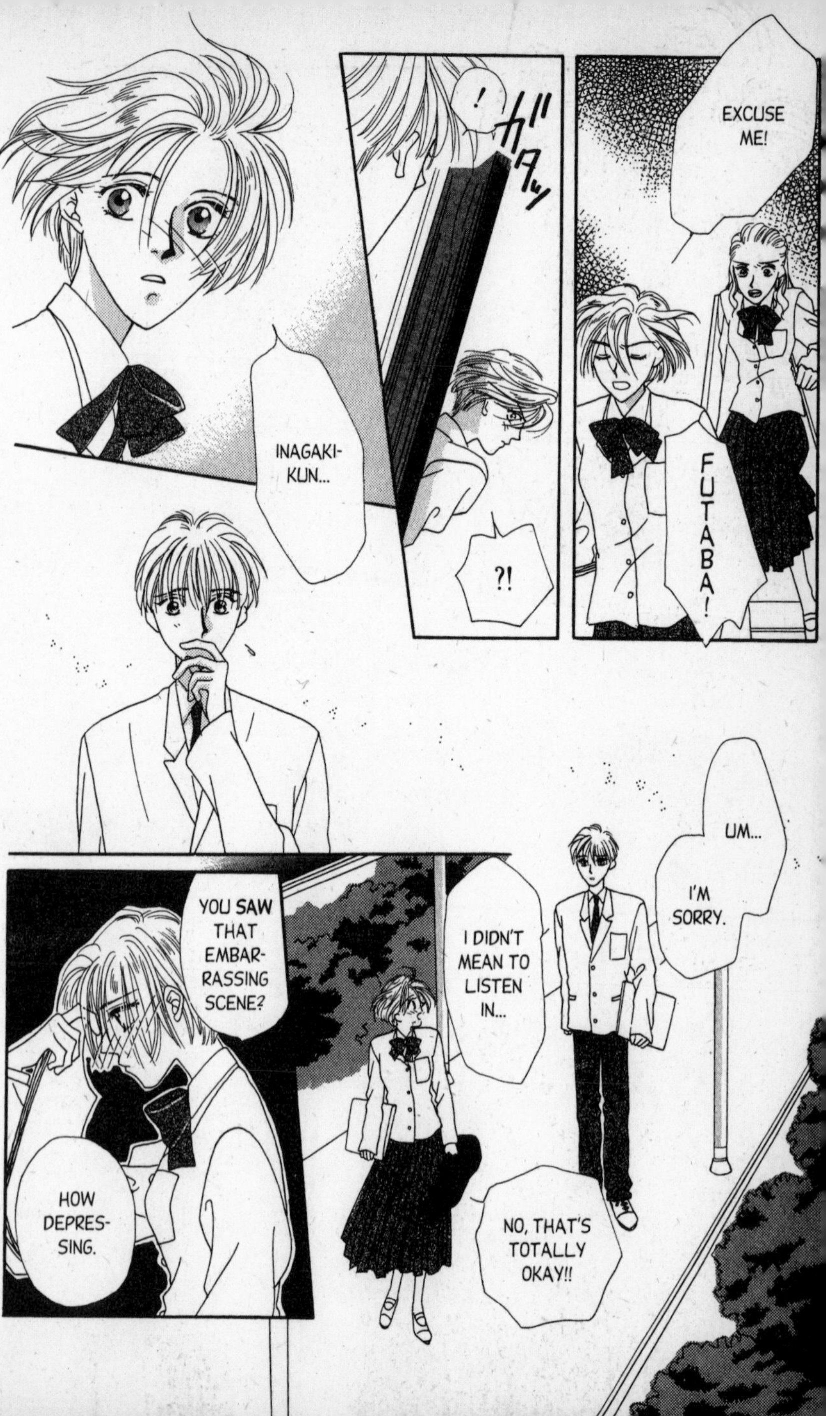
EXCUSE ME!
FUTABA!
!
ガタッ
?!
INAGAKI-KUN...
UM...
I'M SORRY.
I DIDN'T MEAN TO LISTEN IN...
NO, THAT'S TOTALLY OKAY!!
YOU SAW THAT EMBARRASSING SCENE?
HOW DEPRESSING.

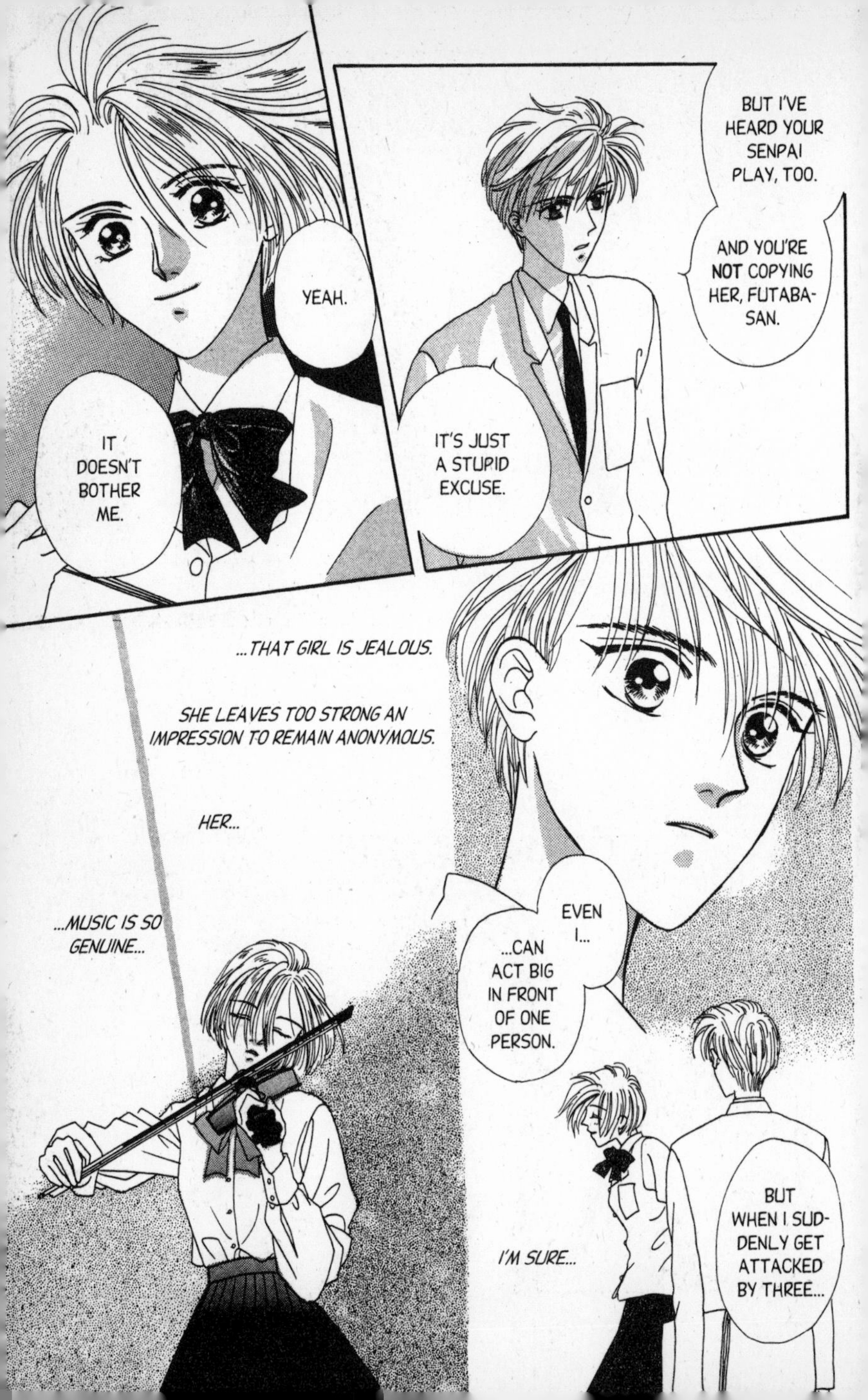
BUT I'VE HEARD YOUR SENPAI PLAY, TOO.
AND YOU'RE **NOT** COPYING HER, FUTABA-SAN.
IT'S JUST A STUPID EXCUSE.
YEAH.
IT DOESN'T BOTHER ME.
EVEN I...
...CAN ACT BIG IN FRONT OF ONE PERSON.
BUT WHEN I SUD-DENLY GET ATTACKED BY THREE...
I'M SURE...
...THAT GIRL IS JEALOUS.
SHE LEAVES TOO STRONG AN IMPRESSION TO REMAIN ANONYMOUS.
HER...
...MUSIC IS SO GENUINE...

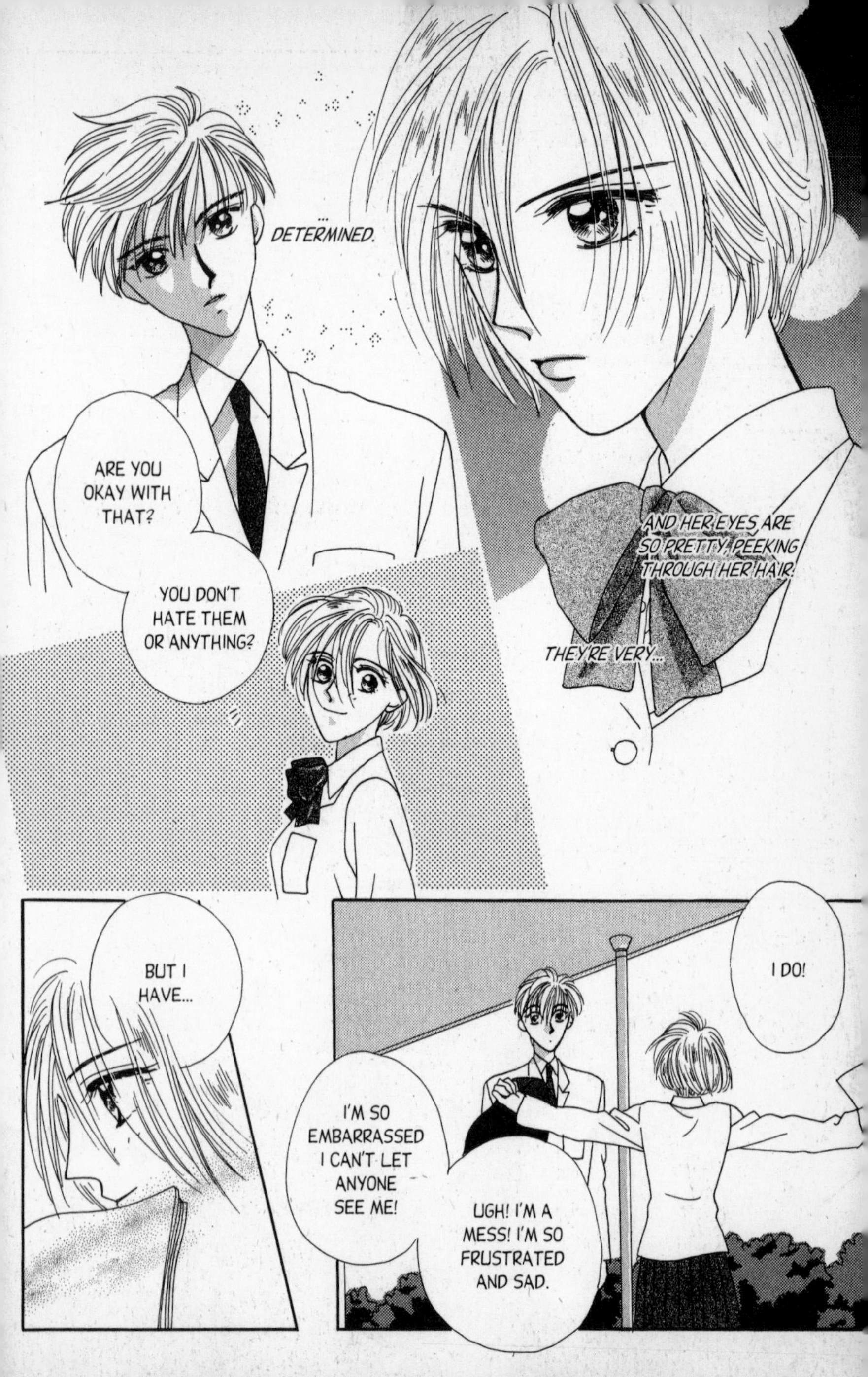
AND HER EYES ARE SO PRETTY, PEEKING THROUGH HER HAIR.
THEY'RE VERY...
...DETERMINED.
ARE YOU OKAY WITH THAT?
YOU DON'T HATE THEM OR ANYTHING?
I DO!
UGH! I'M A MESS! I'M SO FRUSTRATED AND SAD.
I'M SO EMBARRASSED I CAN'T LET ANYONE SEE ME!
BUT I HAVE...

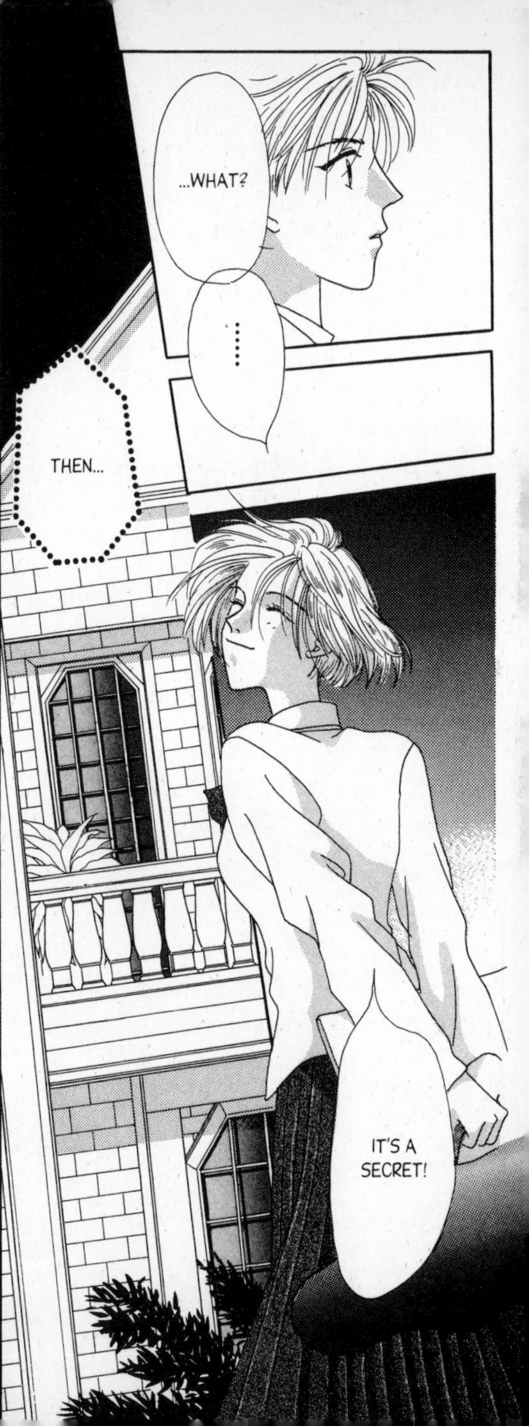
...WHAT?
......
THEN...
IT'S A SECRET!

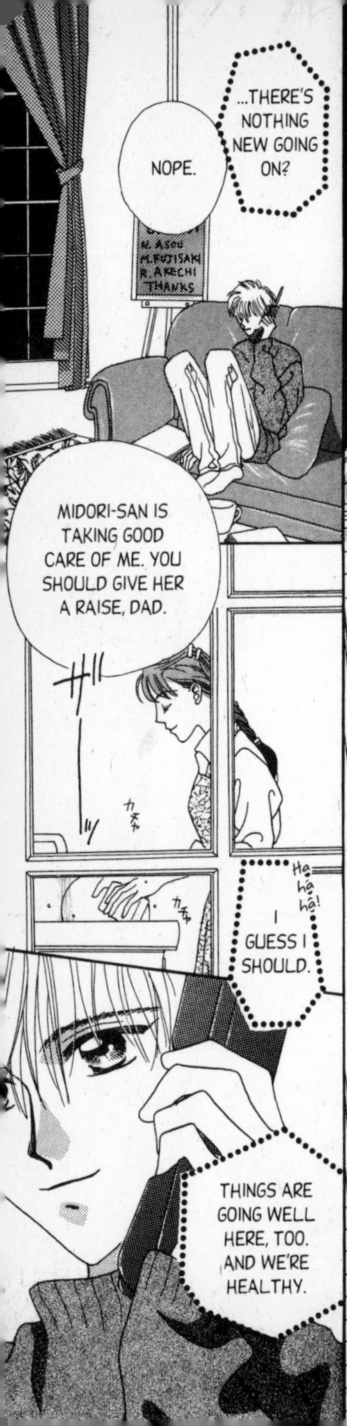
...THERE'S NOTHING NEW GOING ON?
NOPE.
N. ASOU
M. FUJISAKI
R. AKECHI
THANKS
MIDORI-SAN IS TAKING GOOD CARE OF ME. YOU SHOULD GIVE HER A RAISE, DAD.
Ha ha ha!
I GUESS I SHOULD.
THINGS ARE GOING WELL HERE, TOO. AND WE'RE HEALTHY.

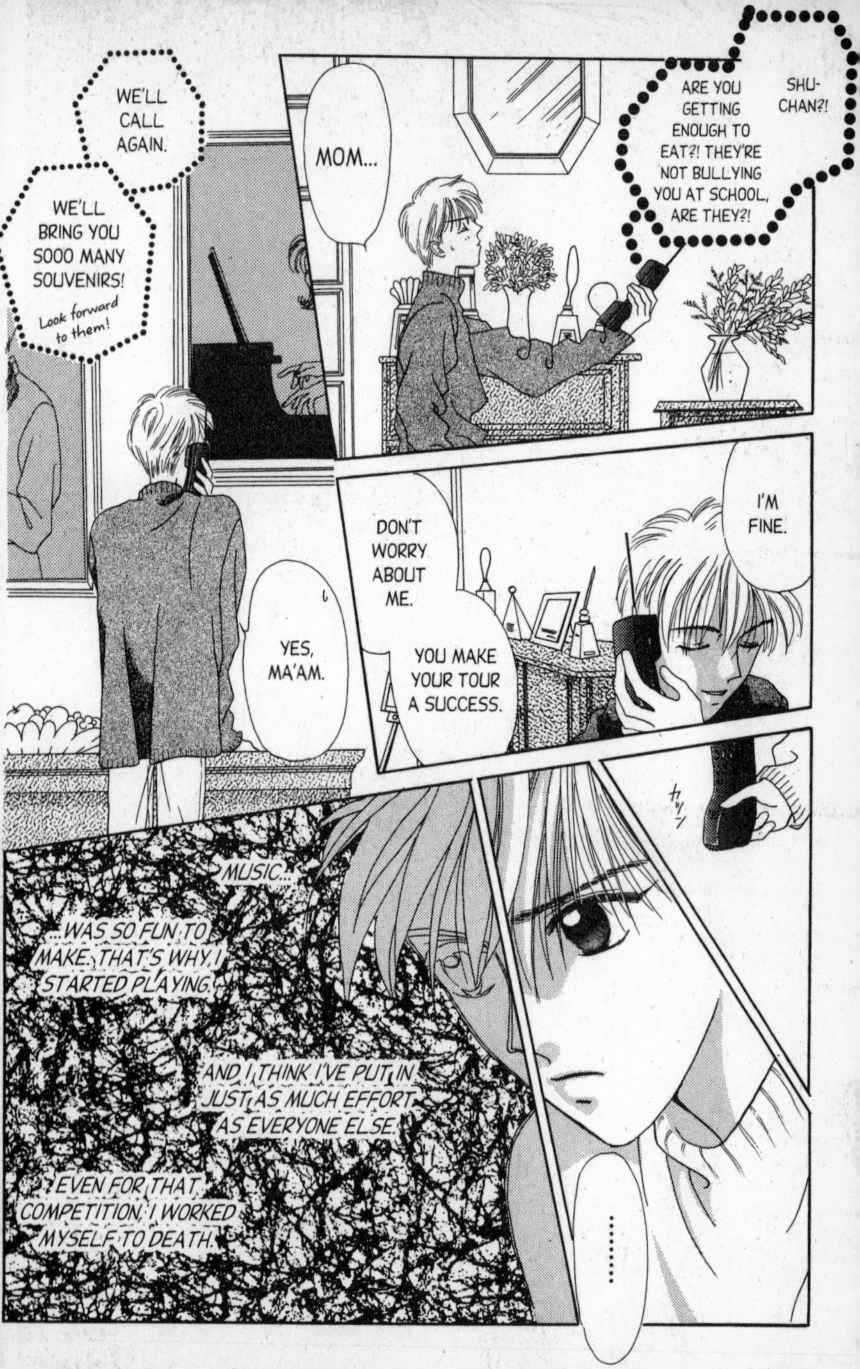

SHU-CHAN?!
ARE YOU GETTING ENOUGH TO EAT?! THEY'RE NOT BULLYING YOU AT SCHOOL, ARE THEY?!
MOM...
I'M FINE.
DON'T WORRY ABOUT ME.
YOU MAKE YOUR TOUR A SUCCESS.
WE'LL CALL AGAIN.
WE'LL BRING YOU SOOO MANY SOUVENIRS!
Look forward to them!
YES, MA'AM.
カツン
MUSIC...
...WAS SO FUN TO MAKE. THAT'S WHY I STARTED PLAYING.
AND I THINK I'VE PUT IN JUST AS MUCH EFFORT AS EVERYONE ELSE.
EVEN FOR THAT COMPETITION, I WORKED MYSELF TO DEATH.
......

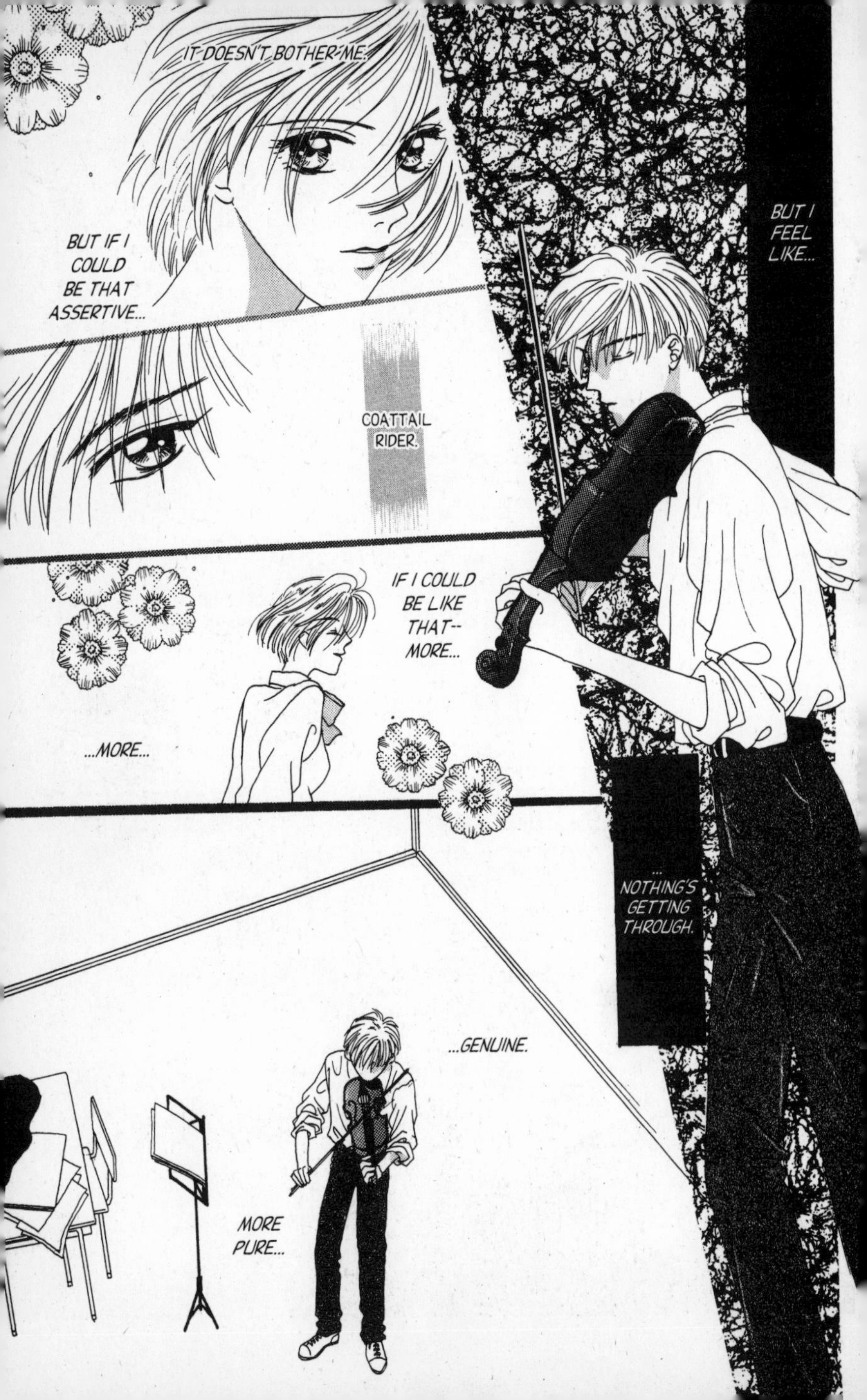

BUT I FEEL LIKE...
...NOTHING'S GETTING THROUGH.
IT DOESN'T BOTHER ME.
BUT IF I COULD BE THAT ASSERTIVE...
COATTAIL RIDER.
IF I COULD BE LIKE THAT-- MORE...
...MORE...
...GENUINE.
MORE PURE...

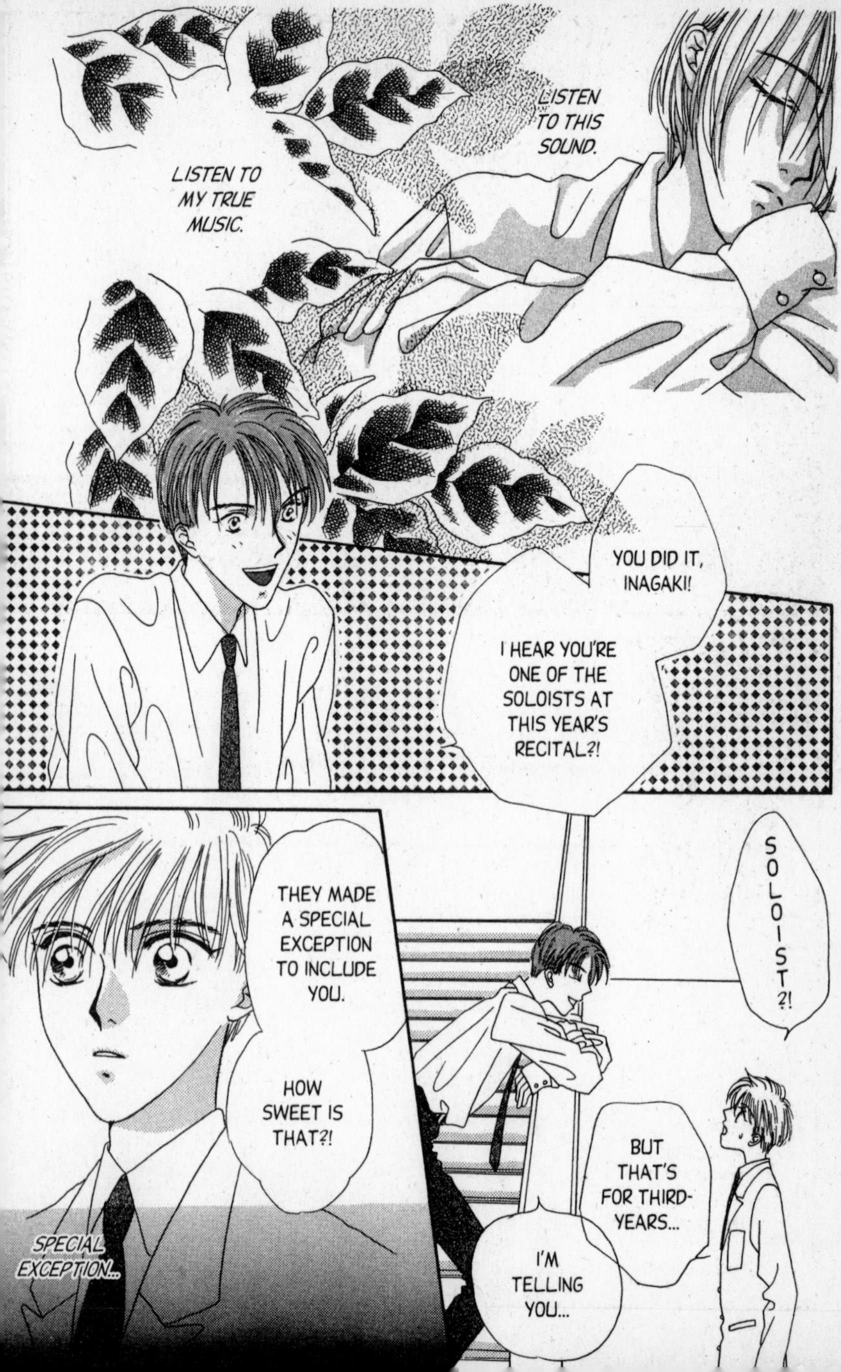
LISTEN TO THIS SOUND.
LISTEN TO MY TRUE MUSIC.
YOU DID IT, INAGAKI!
I HEAR YOU'RE ONE OF THE SOLOISTS AT THIS YEAR'S RECITAL?!
SOLOIST?!
BUT THAT'S FOR THIRD-YEARS...
I'M TELLING YOU...
THEY MADE A SPECIAL EXCEPTION TO INCLUDE YOU.
HOW SWEET IS THAT?!
SPECIAL EXCEPTION...

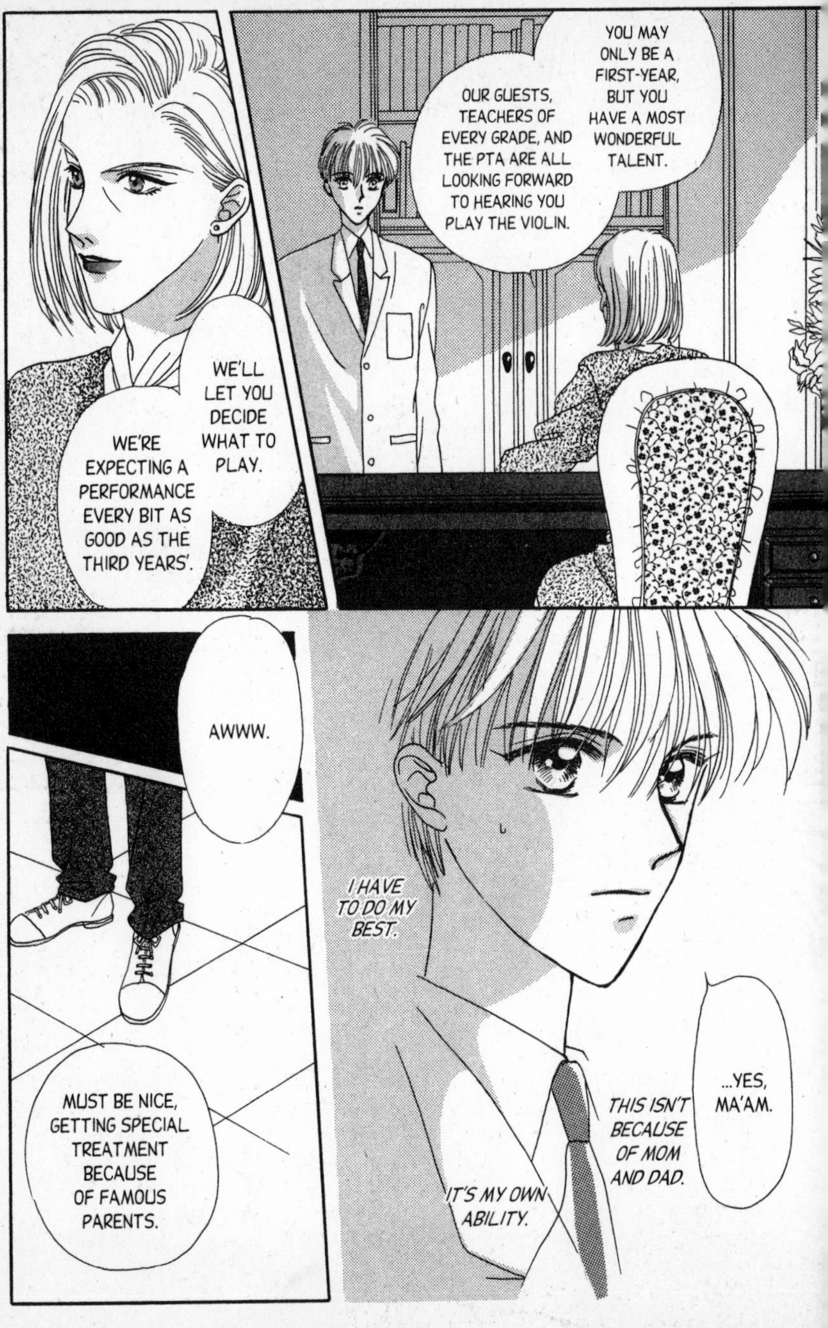
YOU MAY ONLY BE A FIRST-YEAR, BUT YOU HAVE A MOST WONDERFUL TALENT.
OUR GUESTS, TEACHERS OF EVERY GRADE, AND THE PTA ARE ALL LOOKING FORWARD TO HEARING YOU PLAY THE VIOLIN.
WE'LL LET YOU DECIDE WHAT TO PLAY.
WE'RE EXPECTING A PERFORMANCE EVERY BIT AS GOOD AS THE THIRD YEARS'.
...YES, MA'AM.
THIS ISN'T BECAUSE OF MOM AND DAD.
IT'S MY OWN ABILITY.
I HAVE TO DO MY BEST.
AWWW.
MUST BE NICE, GETTING SPECIAL TREATMENT BECAUSE OF FAMOUS PARENTS.

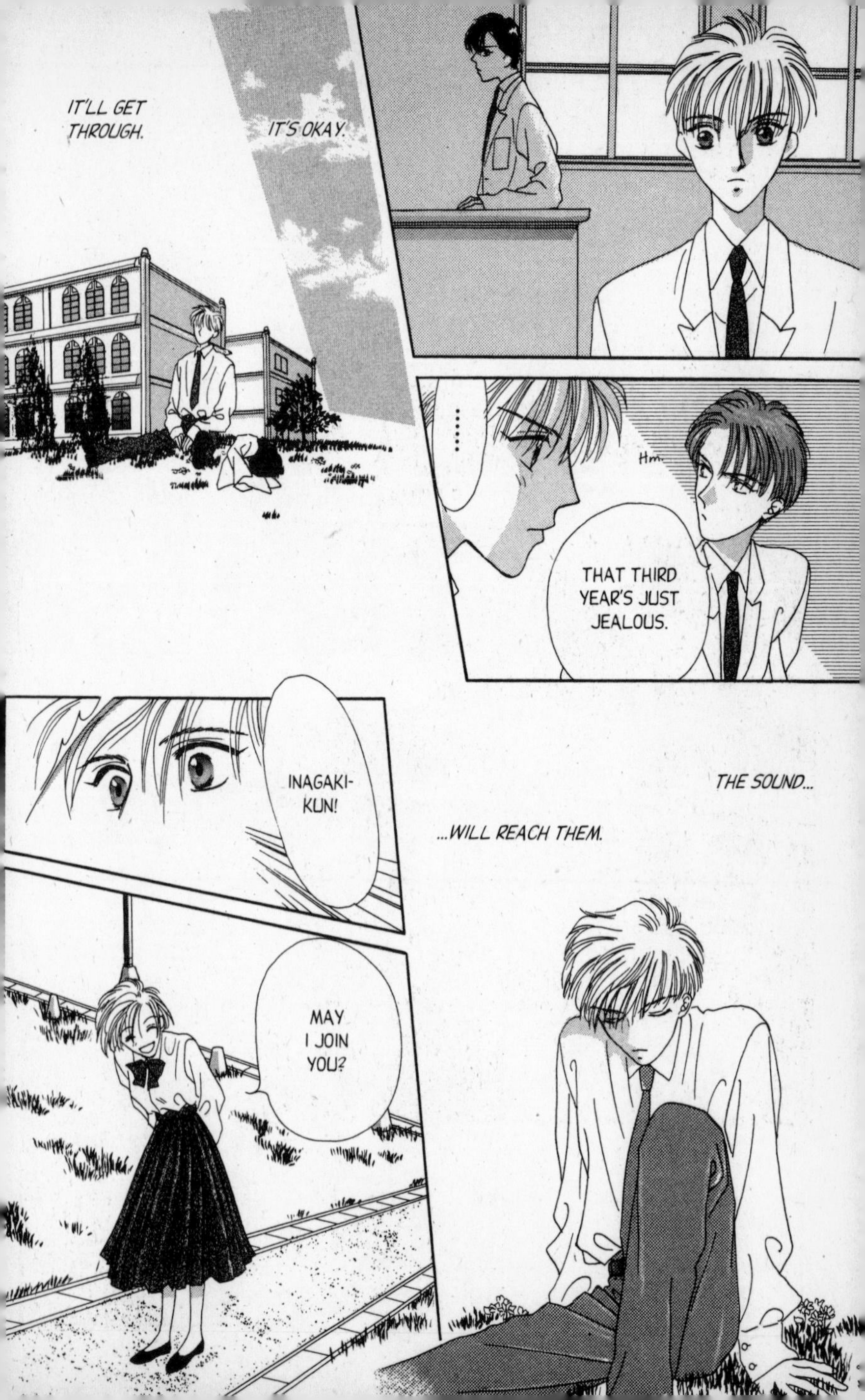
......
Hm
THAT THIRD YEAR'S JUST JEALOUS.
IT'S OKAY.
IT'LL GET THROUGH.
THE SOUND...
...WILL REACH THEM.
INAGAKI-KUN!
MAY I JOIN YOU?

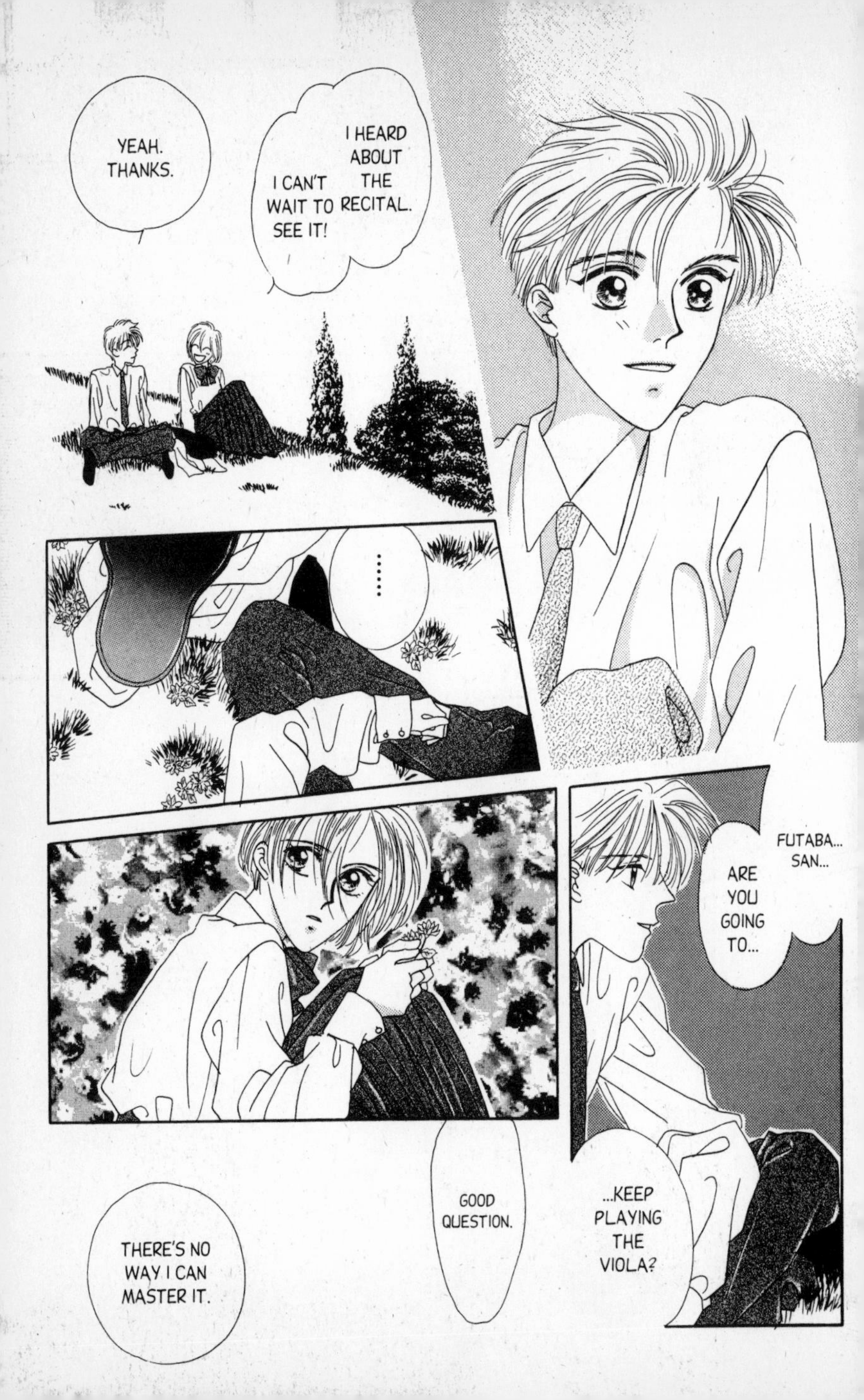
I HEARD ABOUT THE RECITAL. I CAN'T WAIT TO SEE IT!
YEAH. THANKS.
......
FUTABA... SAN...
ARE YOU GOING TO...
...KEEP PLAYING THE VIOLA?
GOOD QUESTION.
THERE'S NO WAY I CAN MASTER IT.

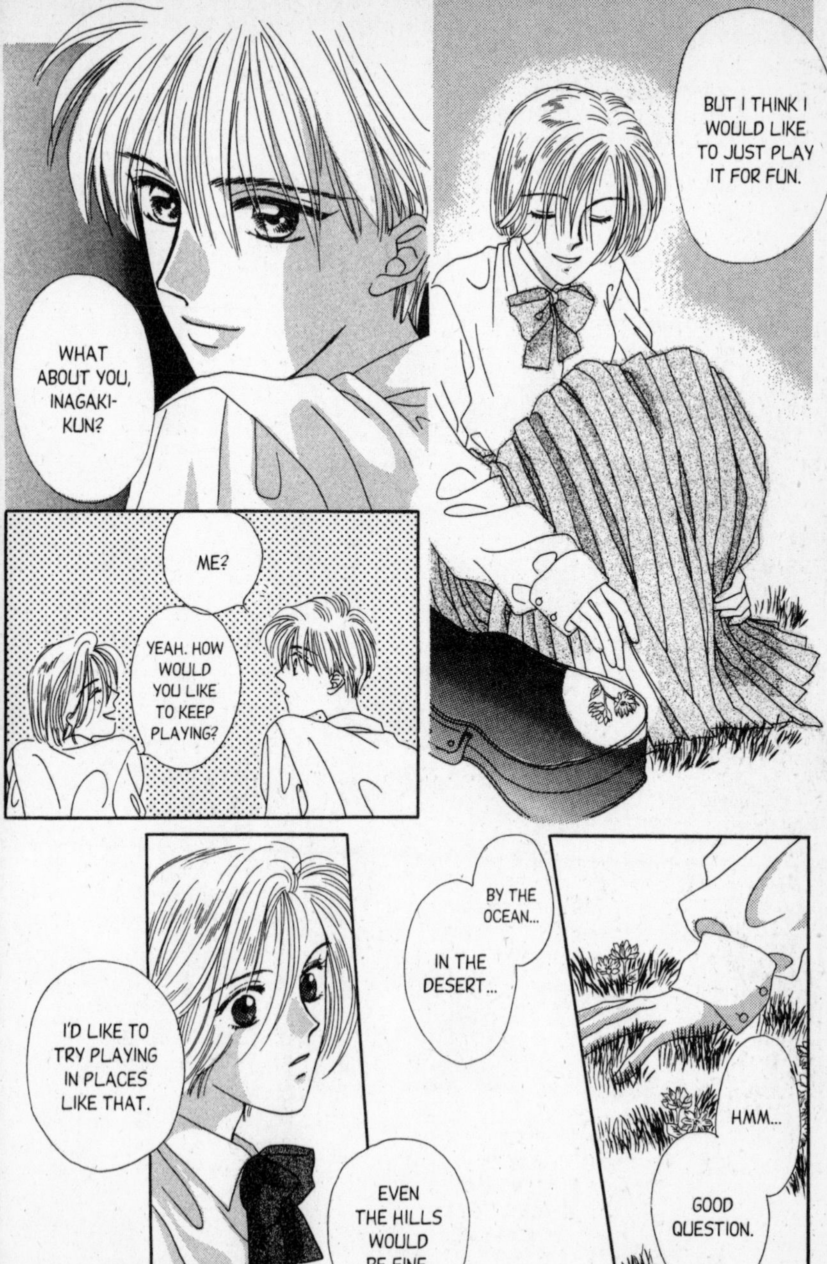

BUT I THINK I WOULD LIKE TO JUST PLAY IT FOR FUN.
WHAT ABOUT YOU, INAGAKI-KUN?
ME?
YEAH. HOW WOULD YOU LIKE TO KEEP PLAYING?
HMM...
GOOD QUESTION.
BY THE OCEAN...
IN THE DESERT...
I'D LIKE TO TRY PLAYING IN PLACES LIKE THAT.
EVEN THE HILLS WOULD BE FINE.

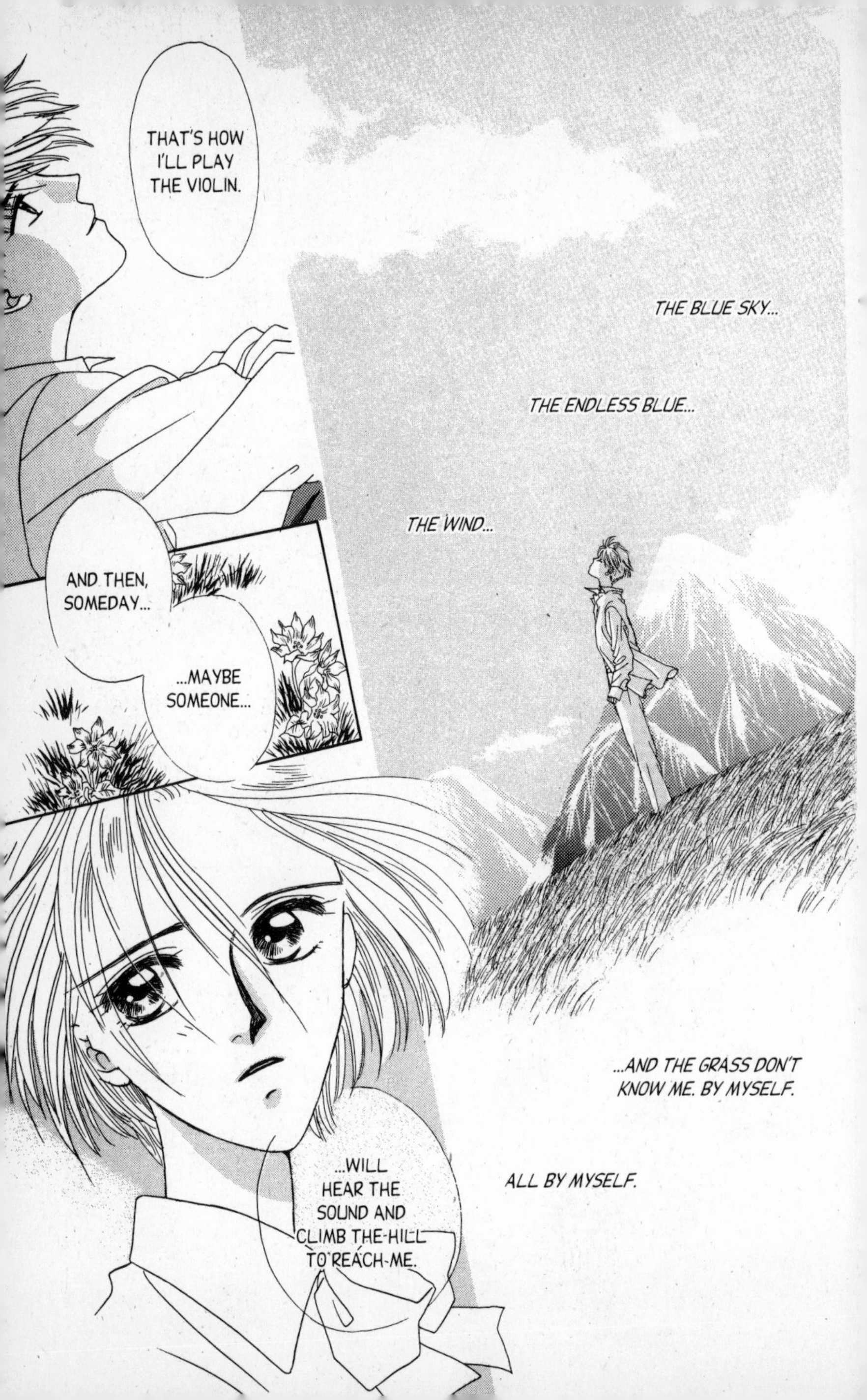
THE BLUE SKY...
THE ENDLESS BLUE...
THE WIND...
...AND THE GRASS DON'T KNOW ME. BY MYSELF.
ALL BY MYSELF.
THAT'S HOW I'LL PLAY THE VIOLIN.
AND THEN, SOMEDAY...
...MAYBE SOMEONE...
...WILL HEAR THE SOUND AND CLIMB THE HILL TO REACH ME.

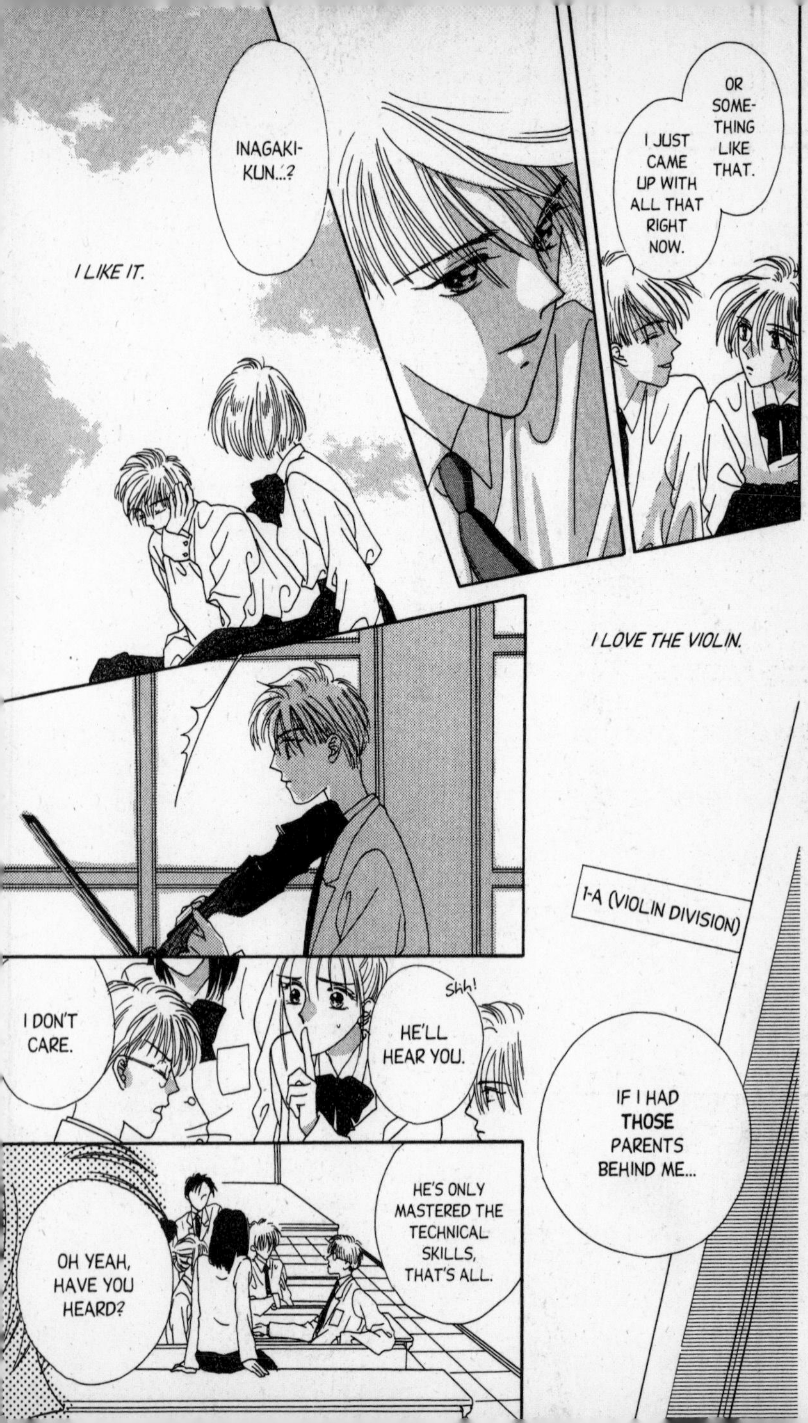
I JUST CAME UP WITH ALL THAT RIGHT NOW.
OR SOMETHING LIKE THAT.
INAGAKI-KUN...?
I LIKE IT.
I LOVE THE VIOLIN.
1-A (VIOLIN DIVISION)
IF I HAD THOSE PARENTS BEHIND ME...
Shh!
HE'LL HEAR YOU.
I DON'T CARE.
HE'S ONLY MASTERED THE TECHNICAL SKILLS, THAT'S ALL.
OH YEAH, HAVE YOU HEARD?

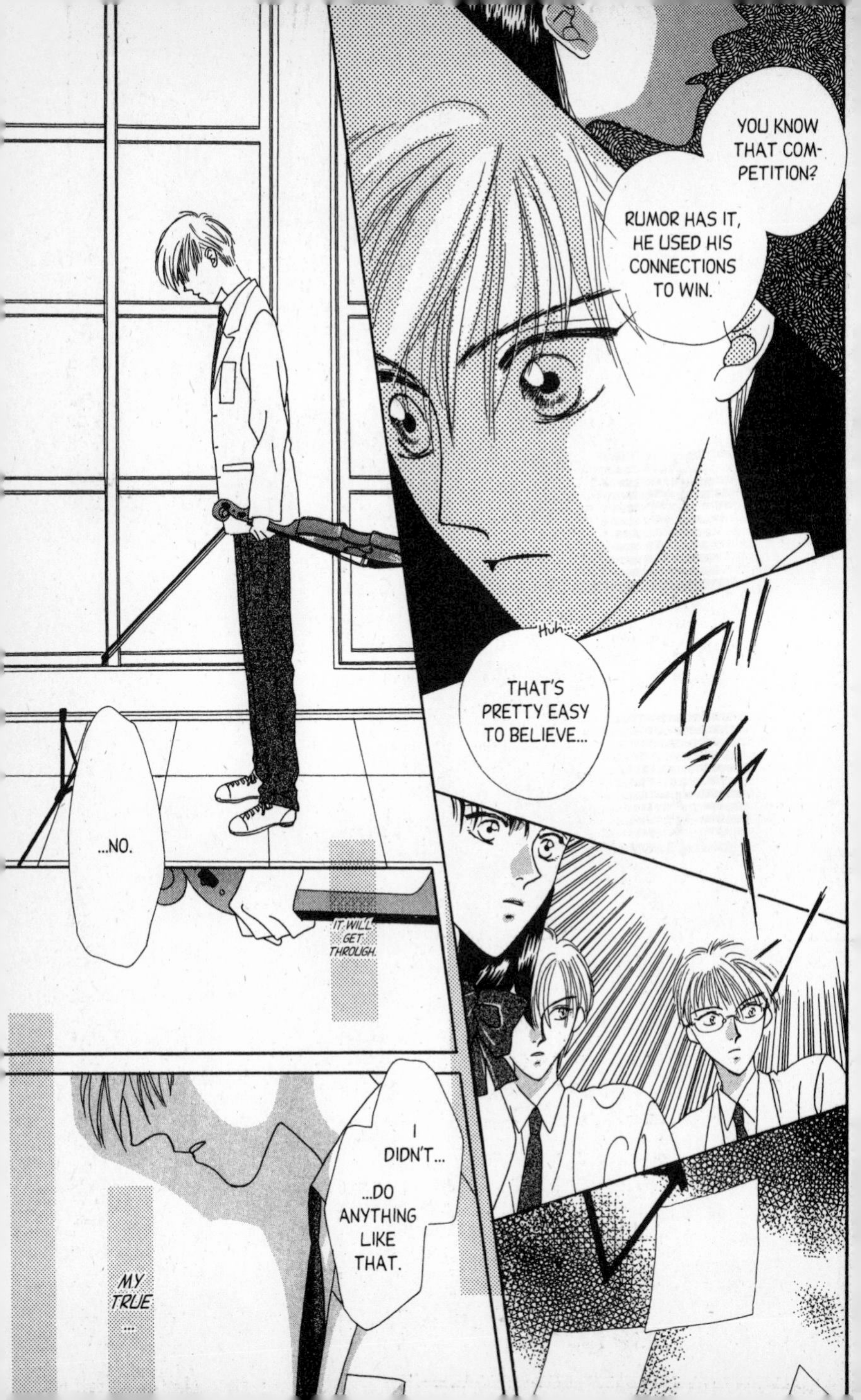
YOU KNOW THAT COM-PETITION?
RUMOR HAS IT, HE USED HIS CONNECTIONS TO WIN.
Huh
THAT'S PRETTY EASY TO BELIEVE...
...NO.
IT WILL GET THROUGH.
I DIDN'T...
...DO ANYTHING LIKE THAT.
MY TRUE ...

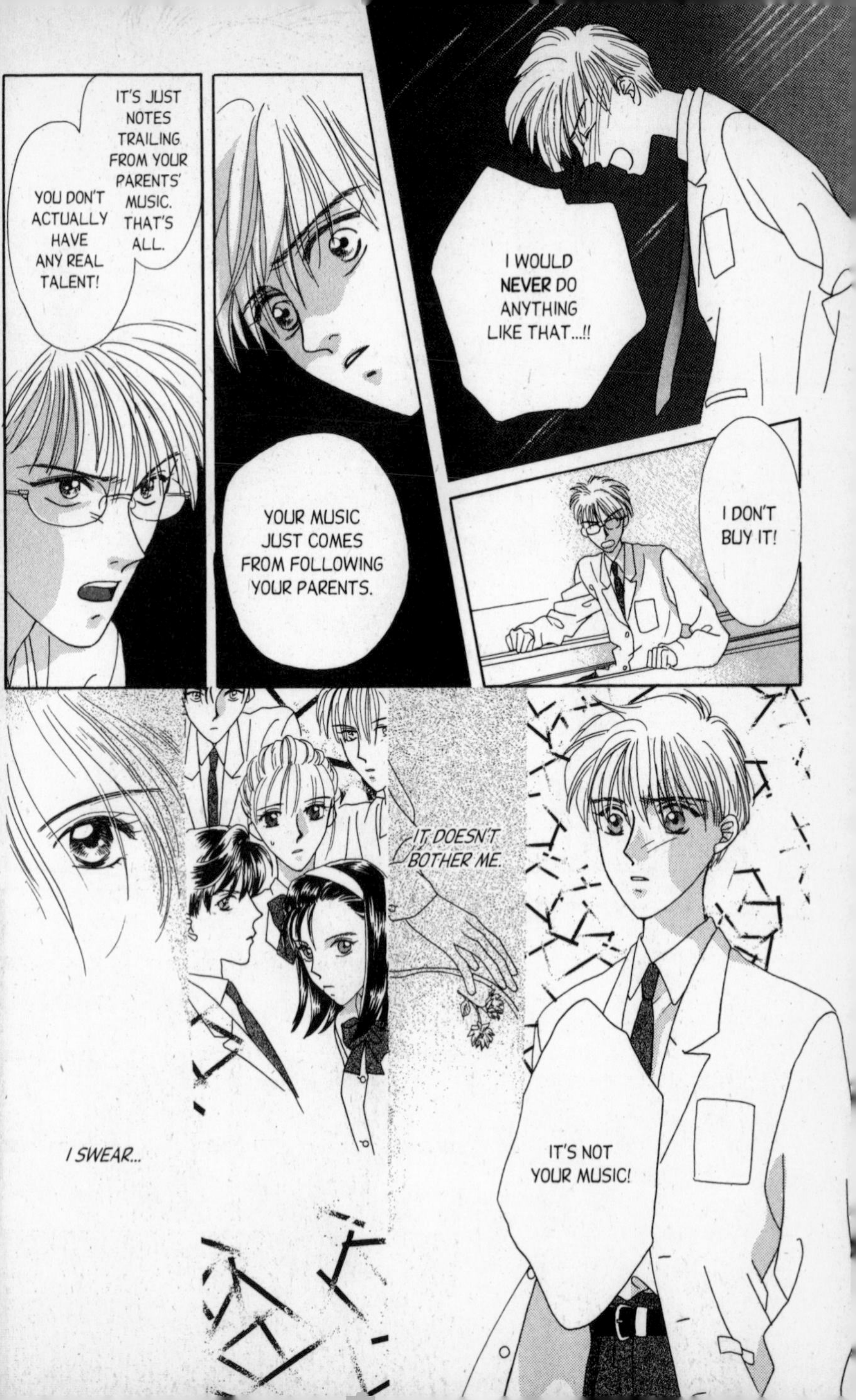
I WOULD **NEVER** DO ANYTHING LIKE THAT...!!
I DON'T BUY IT!
YOUR MUSIC JUST COMES FROM FOLLOWING YOUR PARENTS.
IT'S JUST NOTES TRAILING FROM YOUR PARENTS' MUSIC. THAT'S ALL.
YOU DON'T ACTUALLY HAVE ANY REAL TALENT!
IT'S NOT YOUR MUSIC!
IT DOESN'T BOTHER ME.
I SWEAR...

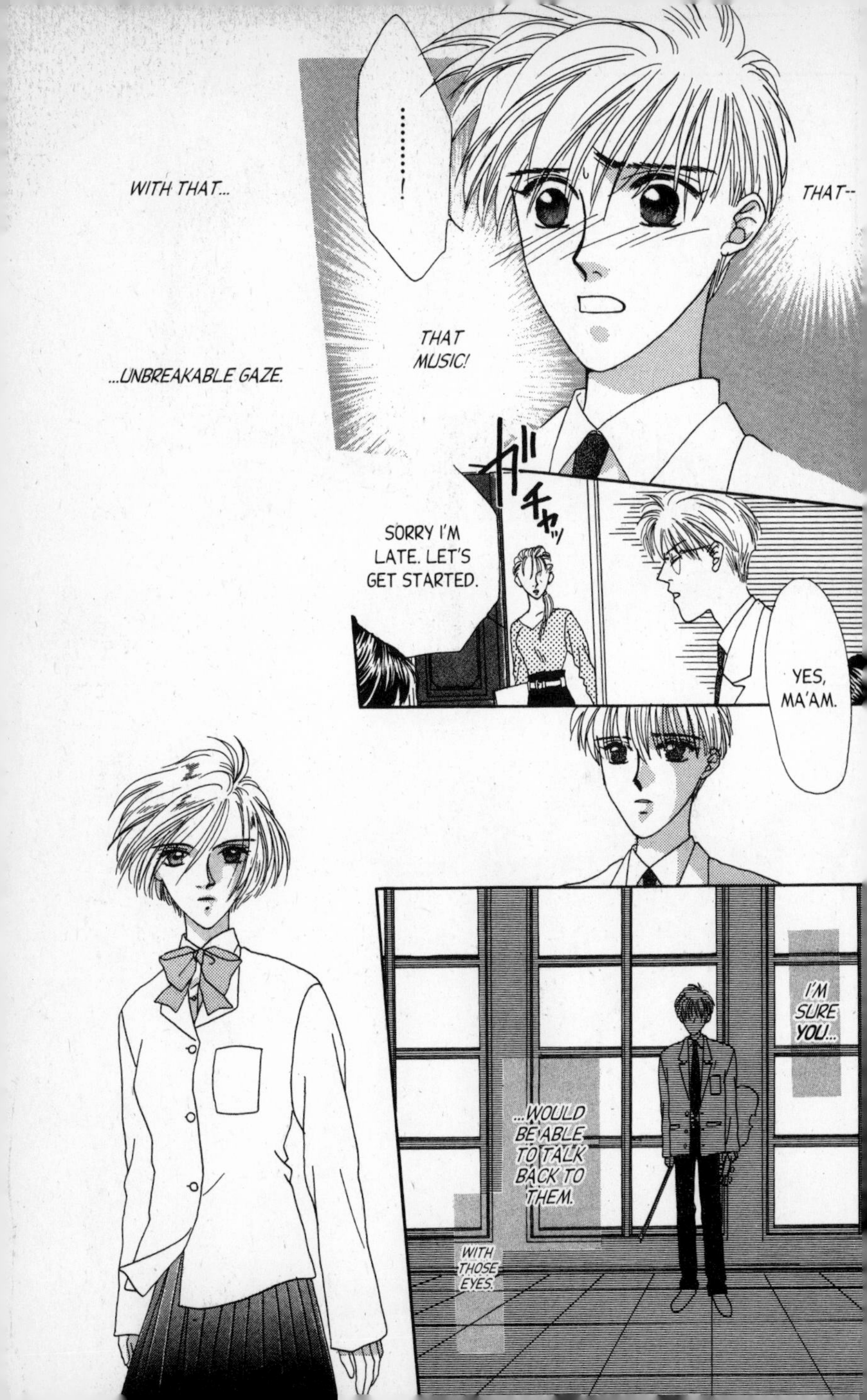
THAT--
……!
THAT MUSIC!
ガチャッ
SORRY I'M LATE. LET'S GET STARTED.
YES, MA'AM.
I'M SURE YOU...
...WOULD BE ABLE TO TALK BACK TO THEM.
WITH THOSE EYES.
WITH THAT...
...UNBREAKABLE GAZE.

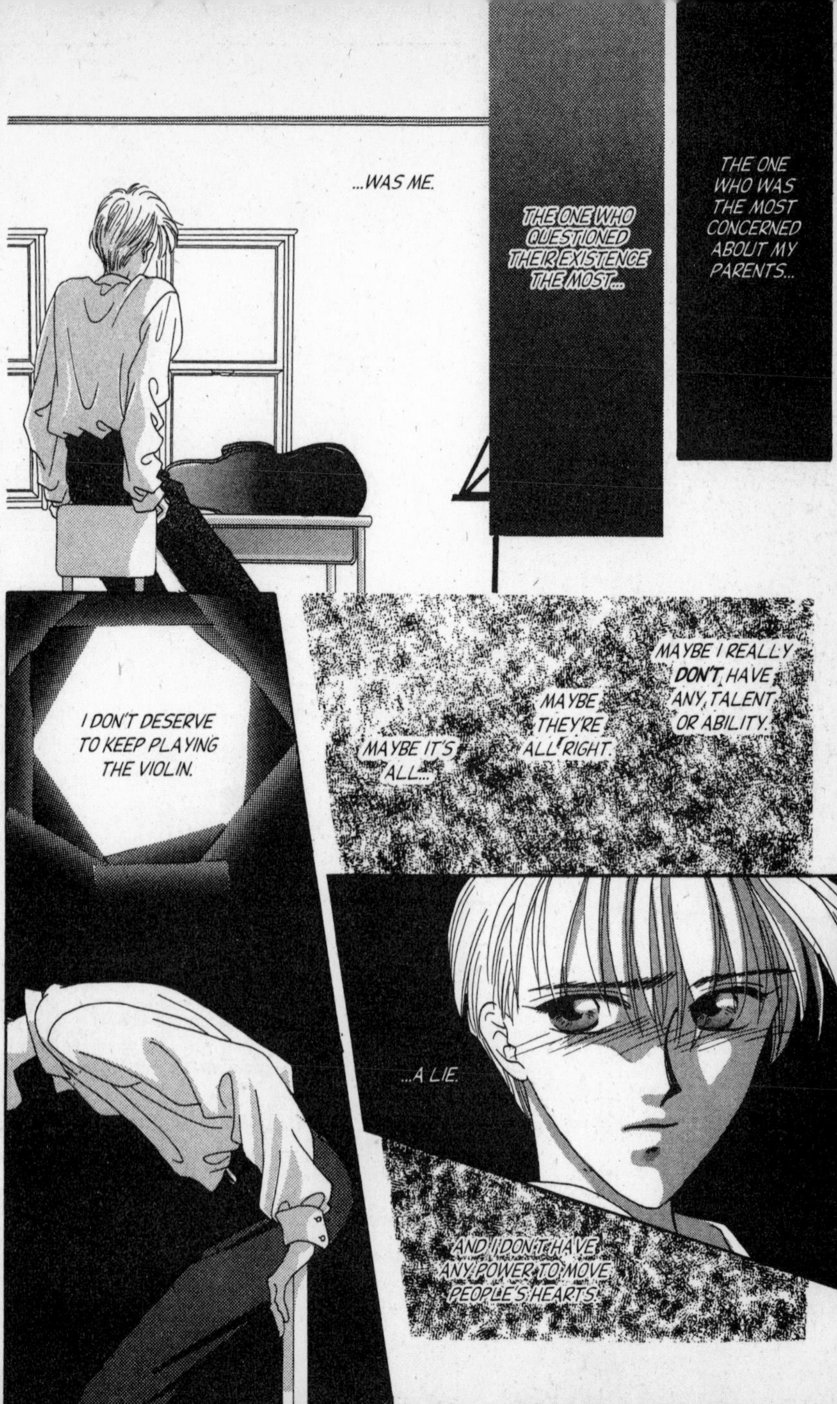
THE ONE WHO WAS THE MOST CONCERNED ABOUT MY PARENTS...
THE ONE WHO QUESTIONED THEIR EXISTENCE THE MOST...
...WAS ME.
MAYBE I REALLY DON'T HAVE ANY TALENT OR ABILITY.
MAYBE THEY'RE ALL RIGHT.
MAYBE IT'S ALL...
...A LIE.
AND I DON'T HAVE ANY POWER TO MOVE PEOPLE'S HEARTS.
I DON'T DESERVE TO KEEP PLAYING THE VIOLIN.

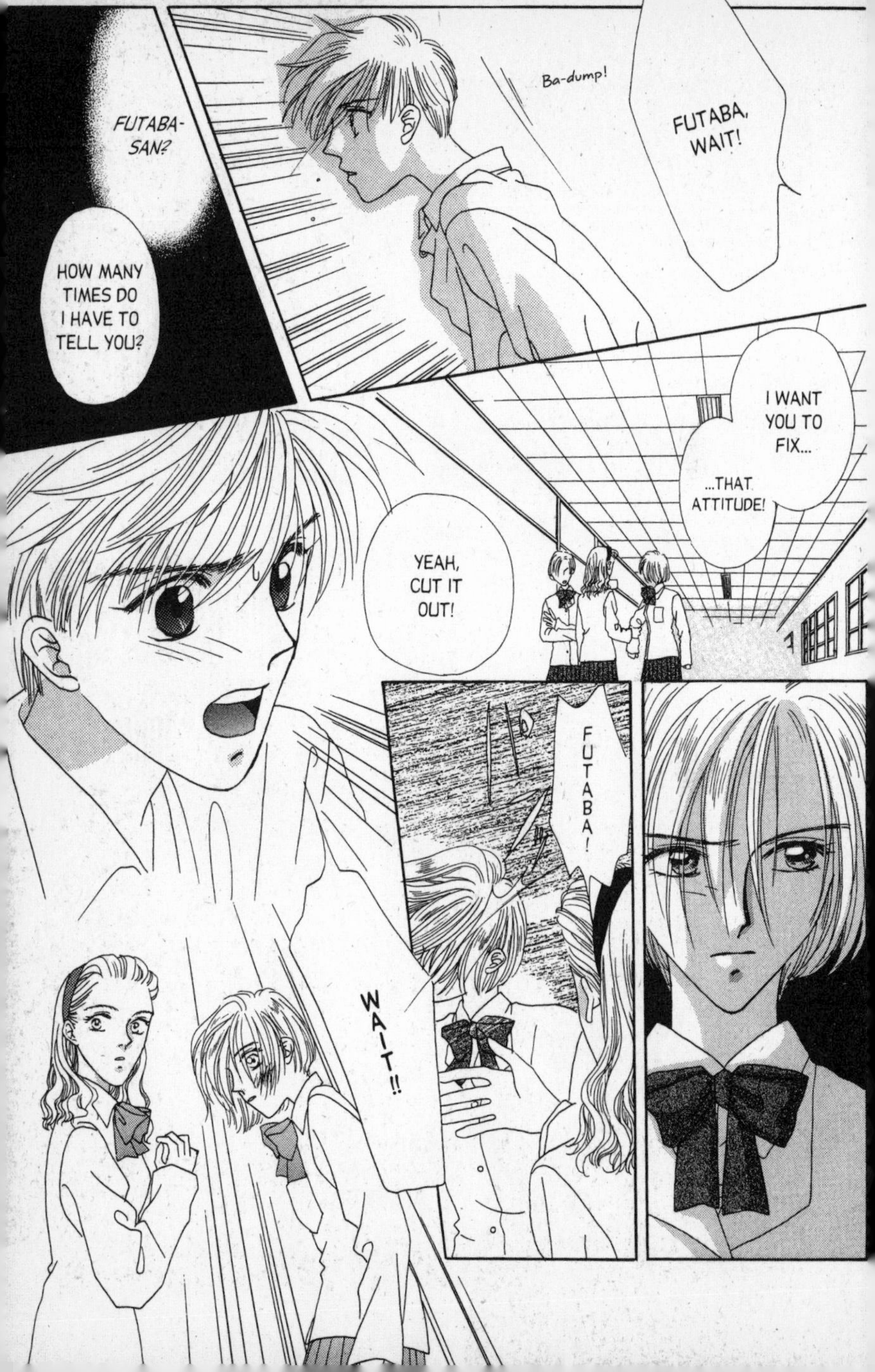
FUTABA, WAIT!
Ba-dump!
FUTABA-SAN?
HOW MANY TIMES DO I HAVE TO TELL YOU?
I WANT YOU TO FIX...
...THAT ATTITUDE!
YEAH, CUT IT OUT!
FUTABA!
WAIT!!

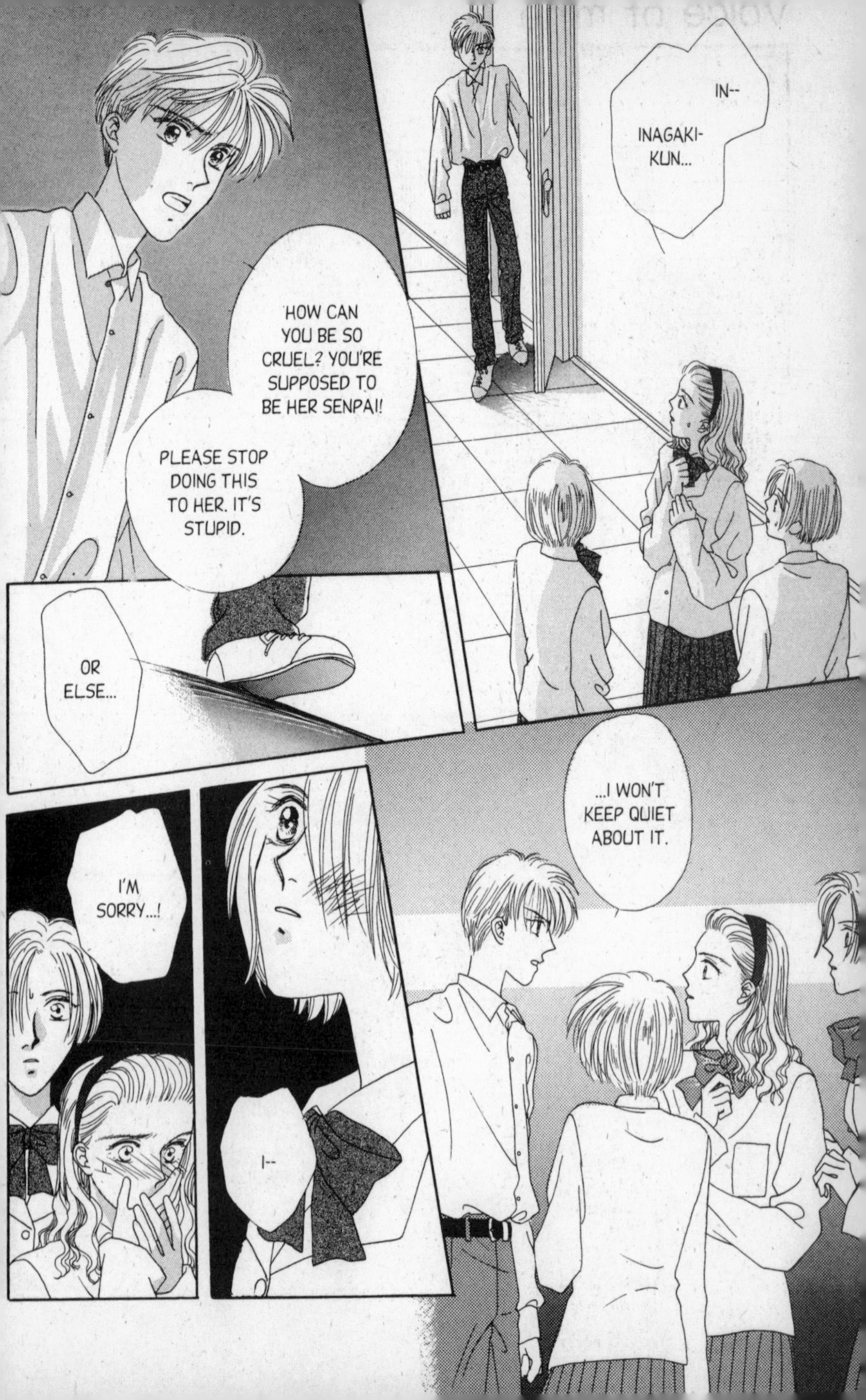
IN--
INAGAKI-KUN...
HOW CAN YOU BE SO CRUEL? YOU'RE SUPPOSED TO BE HER SENPAI!
PLEASE STOP DOING THIS TO HER. IT'S STUPID.
OR ELSE...
...I WON'T KEEP QUIET ABOUT IT.
I--
I'M SORRY...!

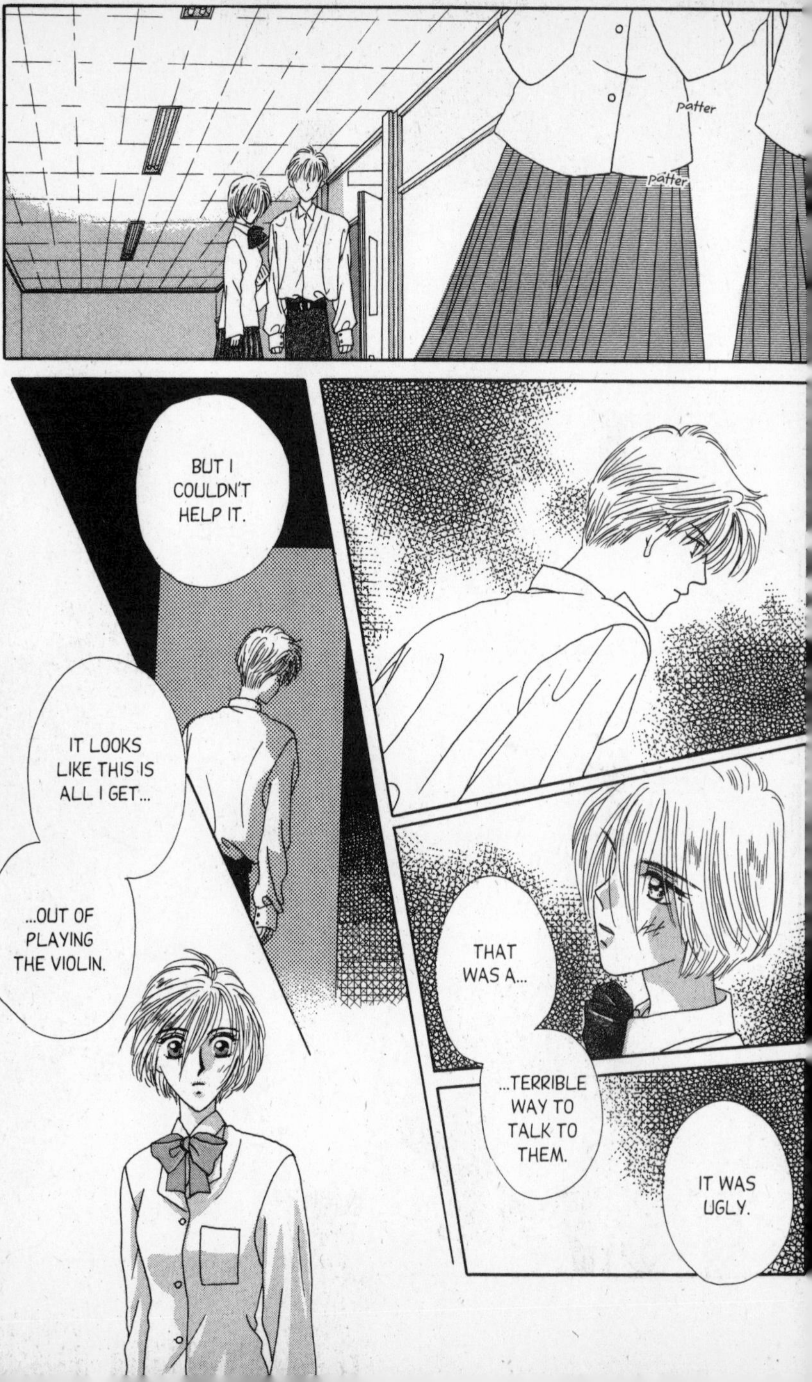
patter
patter
THAT WAS A...
...TERRIBLE WAY TO TALK TO THEM.
IT WAS UGLY.
BUT I COULDN'T HELP IT.
IT LOOKS LIKE THIS IS ALL I GET...
...OUT OF PLAYING THE VIOLIN.

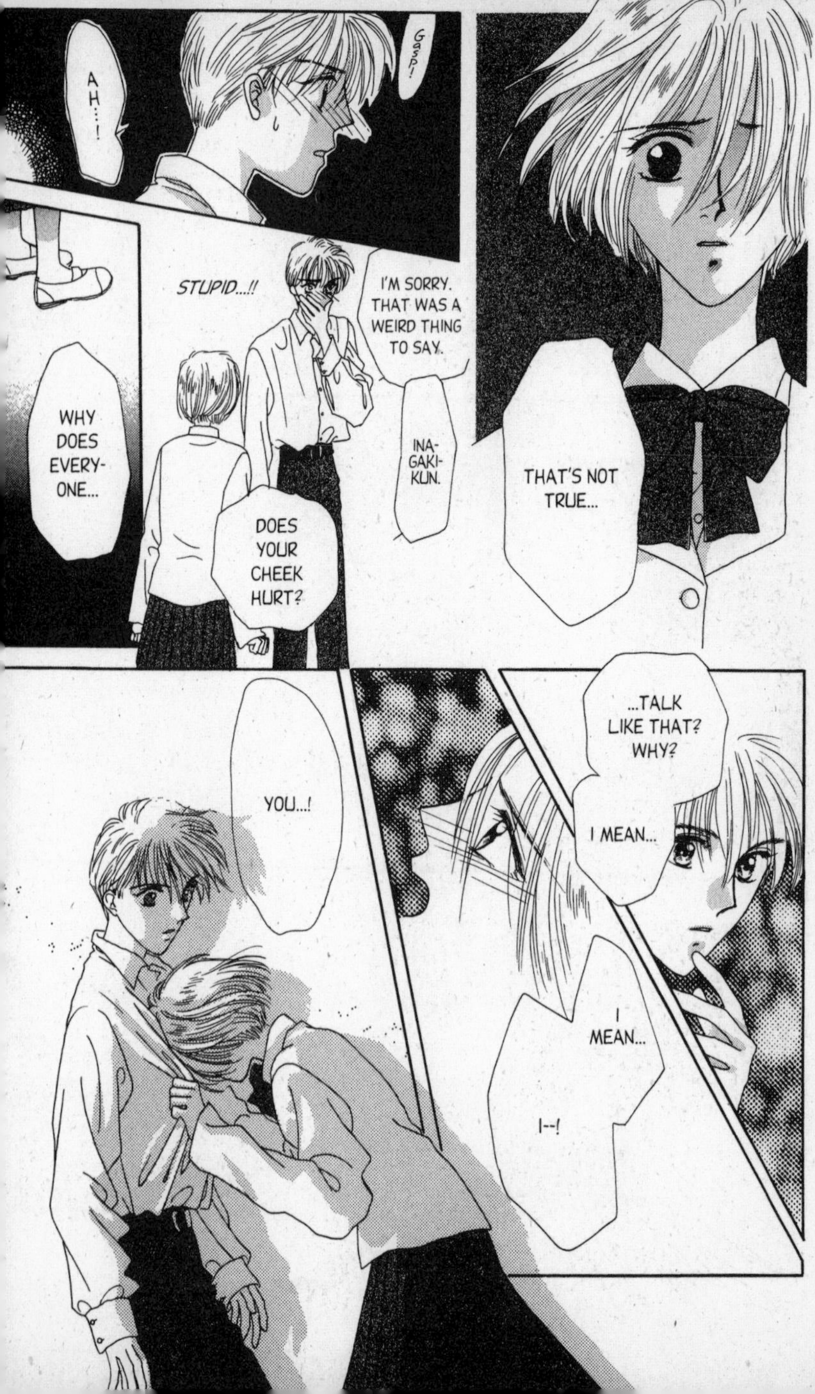
THAT'S NOT TRUE...
Gasp!
AH...!
I'M SORRY. THAT WAS A WEIRD THING TO SAY.
STUPID...!!
INA-GAKI-KUN.
DOES YOUR CHEEK HURT?
WHY DOES EVERY-ONE...
...TALK LIKE THAT? WHY?
I MEAN...
I MEAN...
I--!
YOU...!

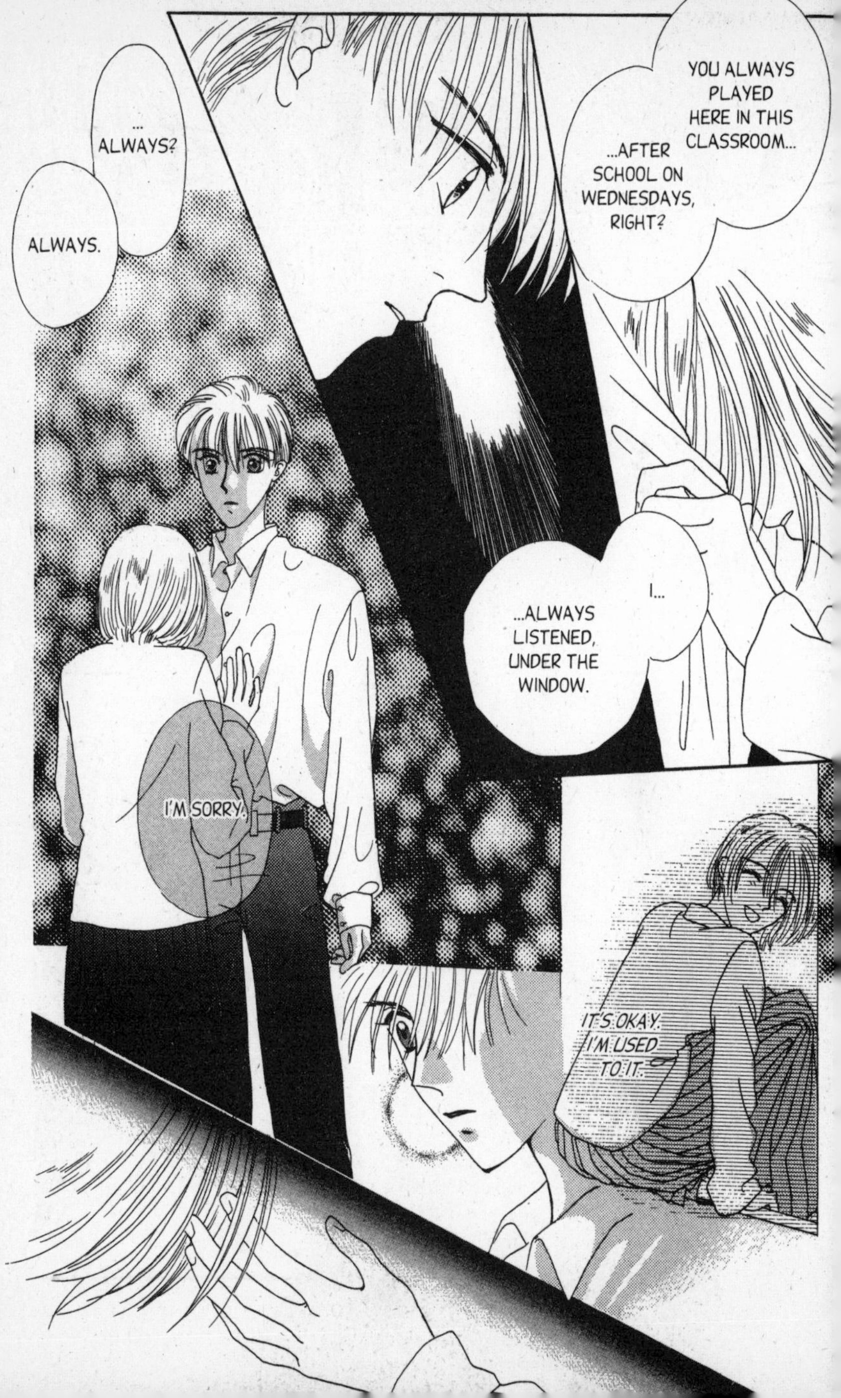
YOU ALWAYS PLAYED HERE IN THIS CLASSROOM...
...AFTER SCHOOL ON WEDNESDAYS, RIGHT?
I...
...ALWAYS LISTENED, UNDER THE WINDOW.
... ALWAYS?
ALWAYS.
I'M SORRY.
IT'S OKAY. I'M USED TO IT.

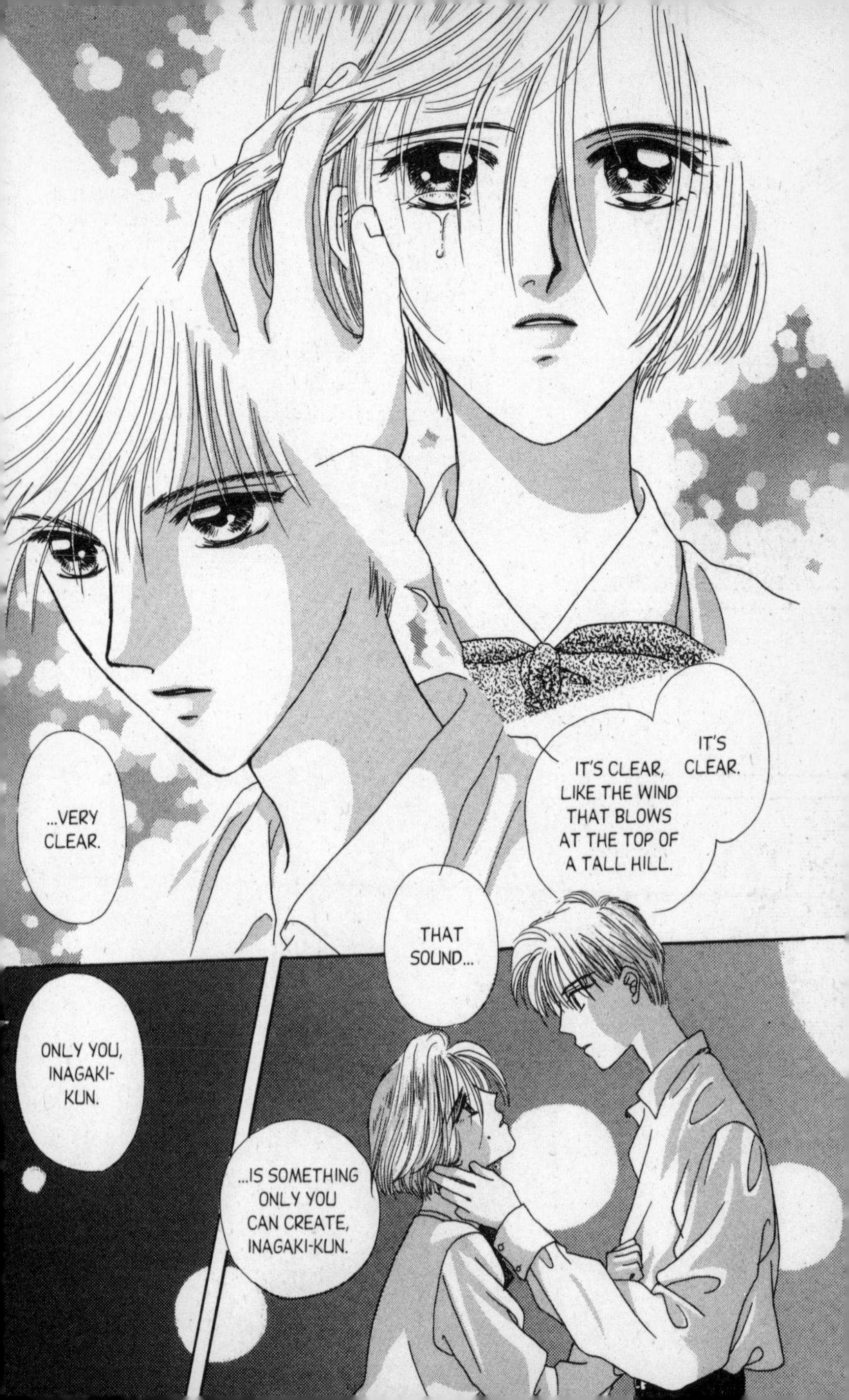
IT'S CLEAR.
IT'S CLEAR, LIKE THE WIND THAT BLOWS AT THE TOP OF A TALL HILL.
...VERY CLEAR.
THAT SOUND...
...IS SOMETHING ONLY YOU CAN CREATE, INAGAKI-KUN.
ONLY YOU, INAGAKI-KUN.

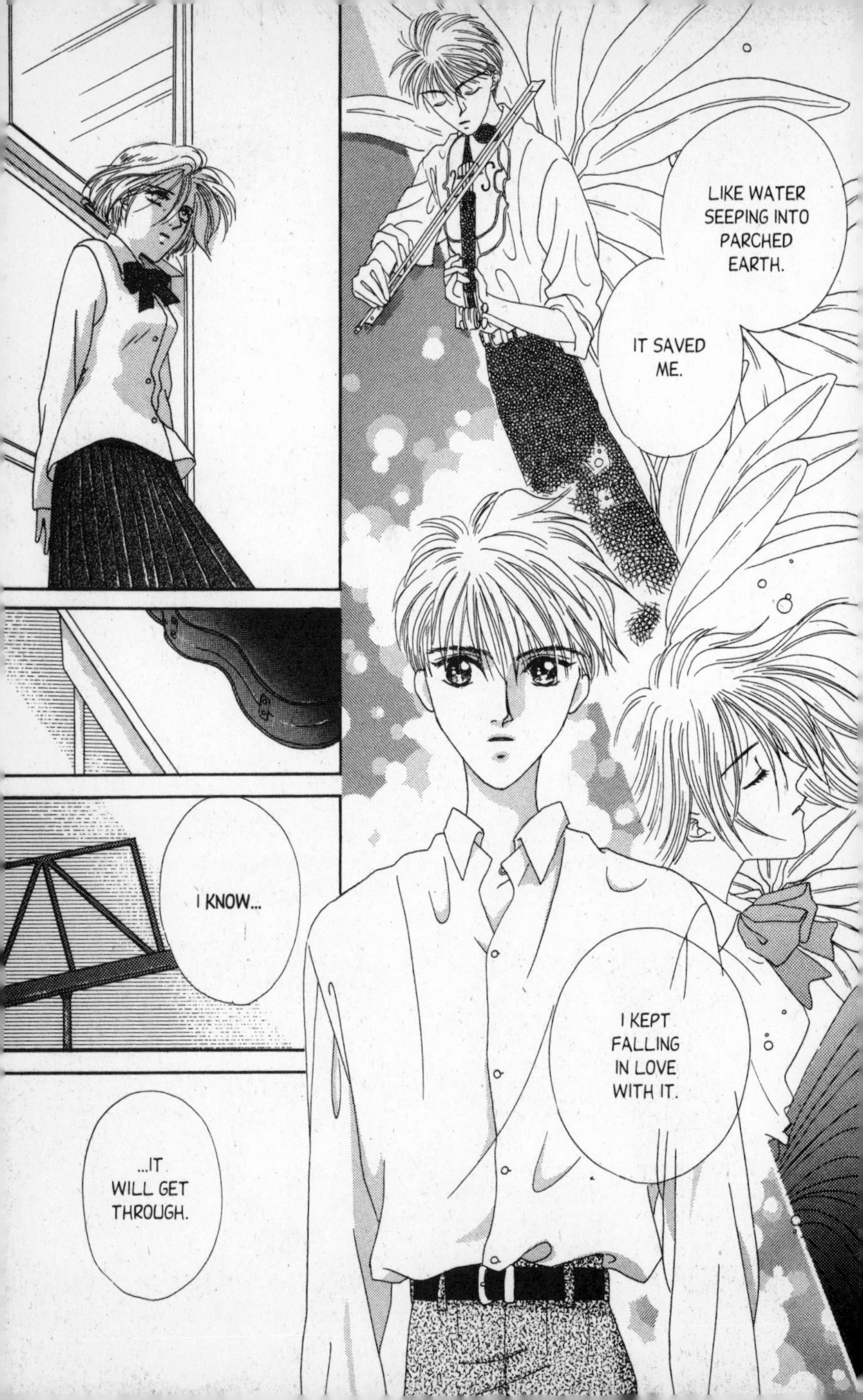
LIKE WATER SEEPING INTO PARCHED EARTH.
IT SAVED ME.
I KEPT FALLING IN LOVE WITH IT.
I KNOW...
...IT WILL GET THROUGH.

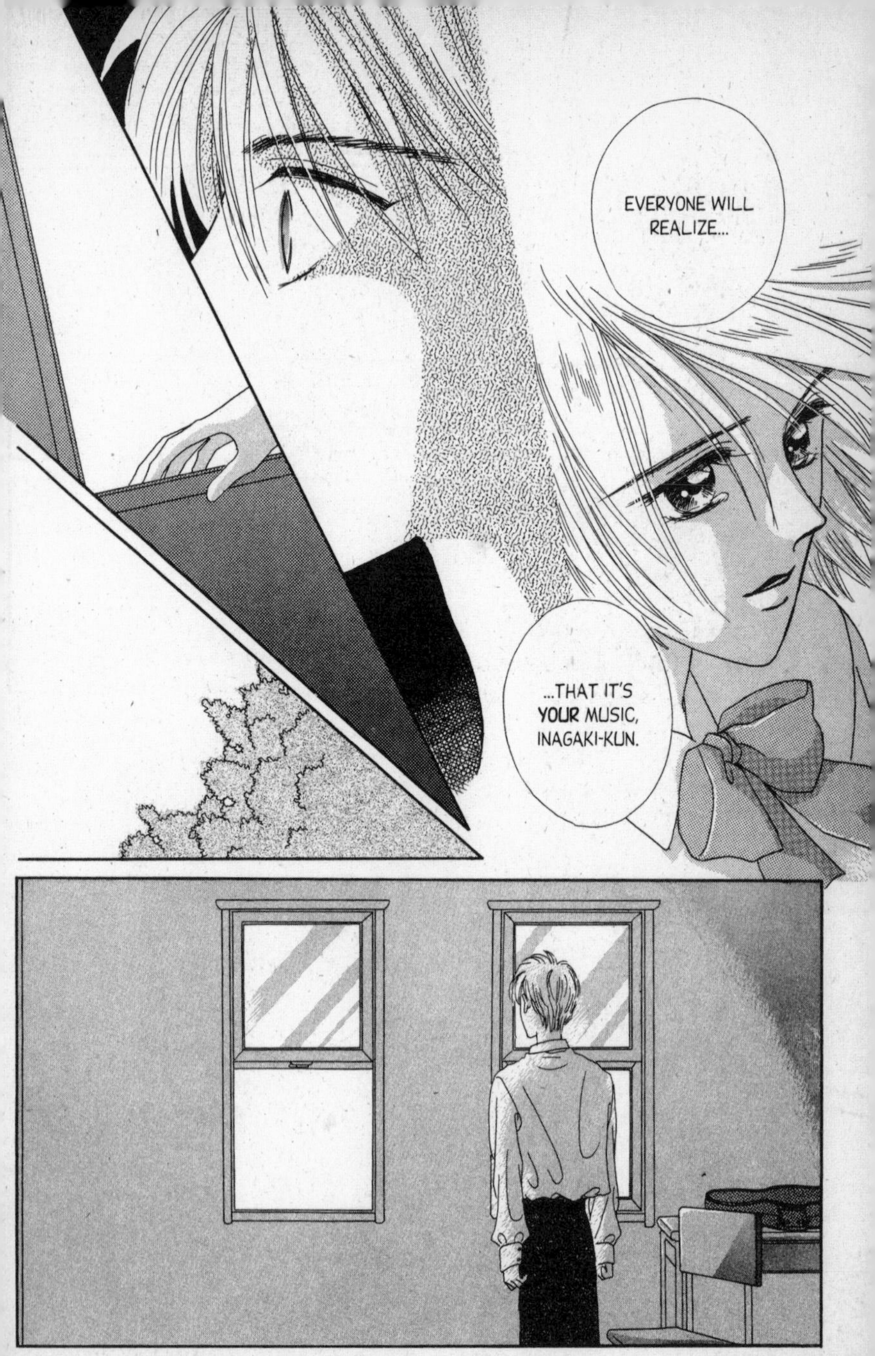
EVERYONE WILL REALIZE...
...THAT IT'S **YOUR** MUSIC, INAGAKI-KUN.

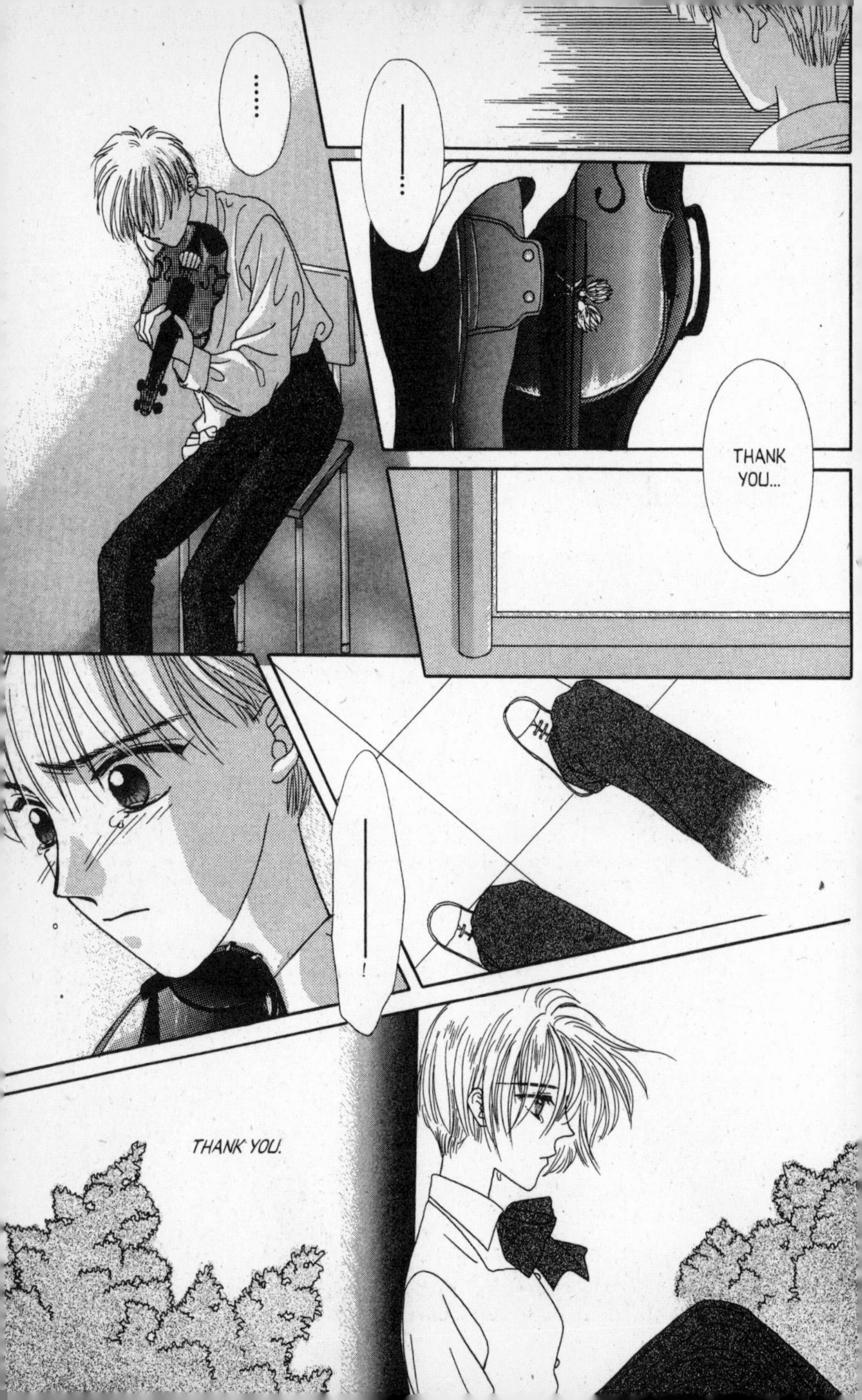
......
THANK YOU...
THANK YOU.

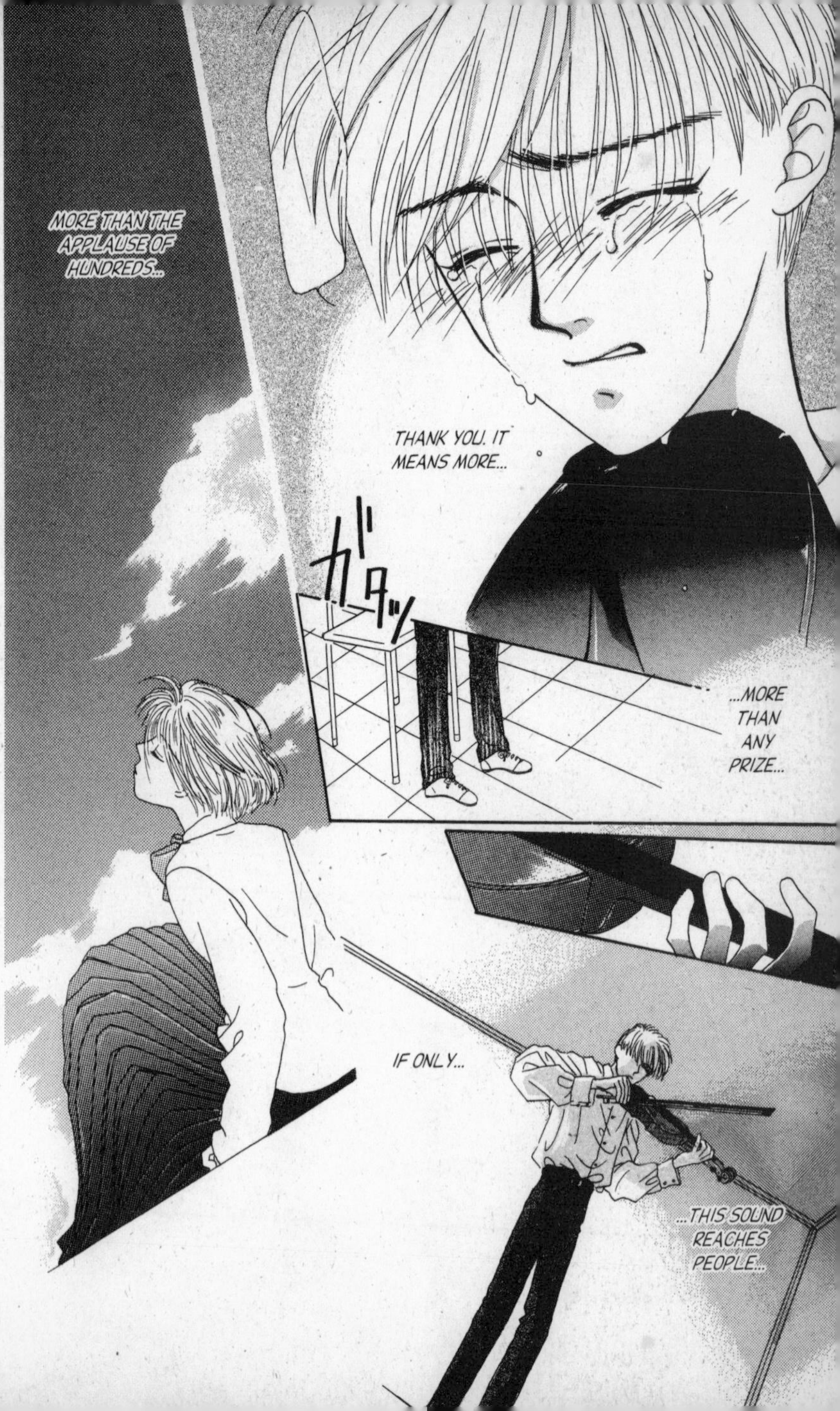
THANK YOU. IT MEANS MORE...
ガタッ
...MORE THAN ANY PRIZE...
IF ONLY...
...THIS SOUND REACHES PEOPLE...
MORE THAN THE APPLAUSE OF HUNDREDS...

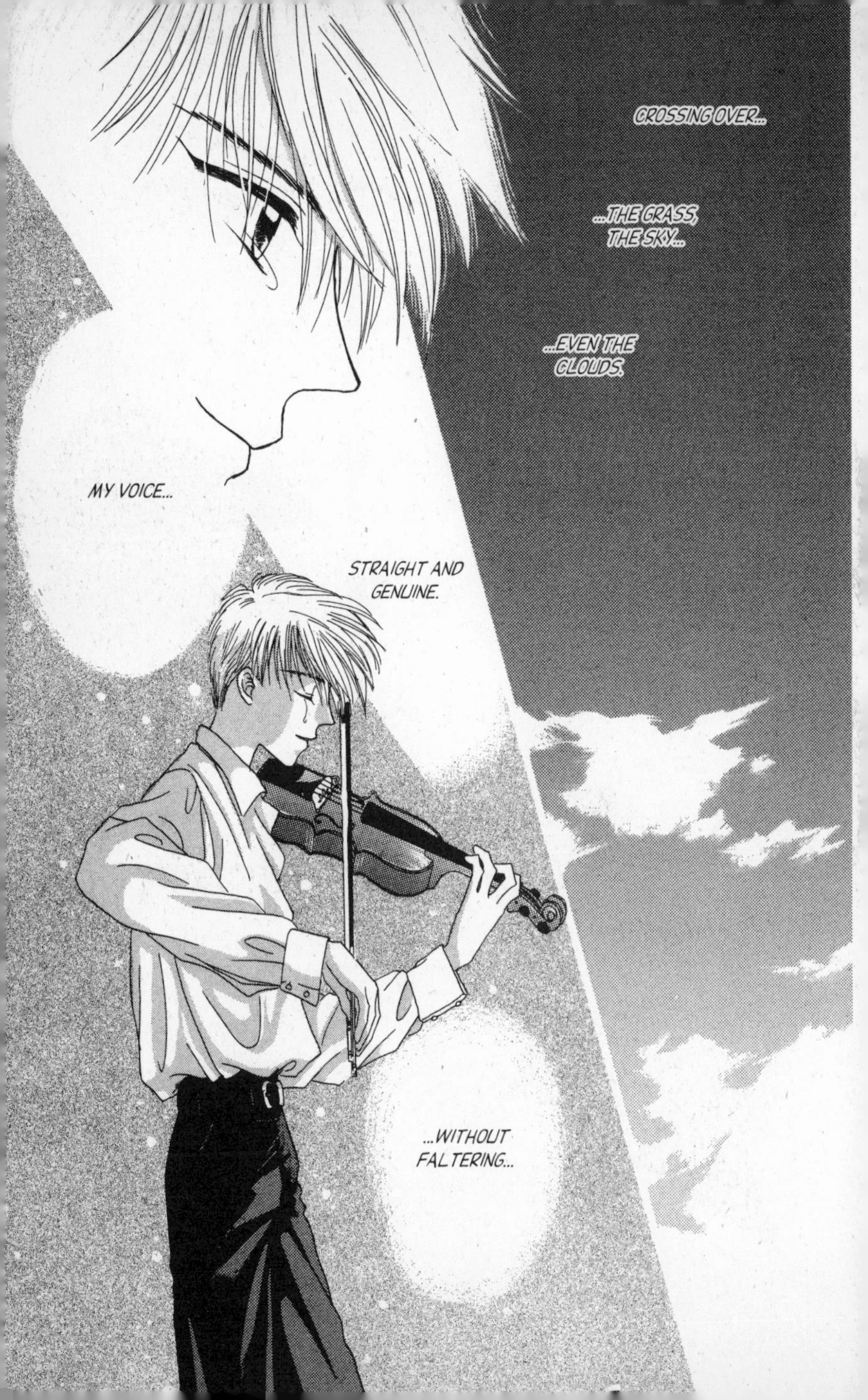
CROSSING OVER...
...THE GRASS, THE SKY...
...EVEN THE CLOUDS.
MY VOICE...
STRAIGHT AND GENUINE.
...WITHOUT FALTERING...

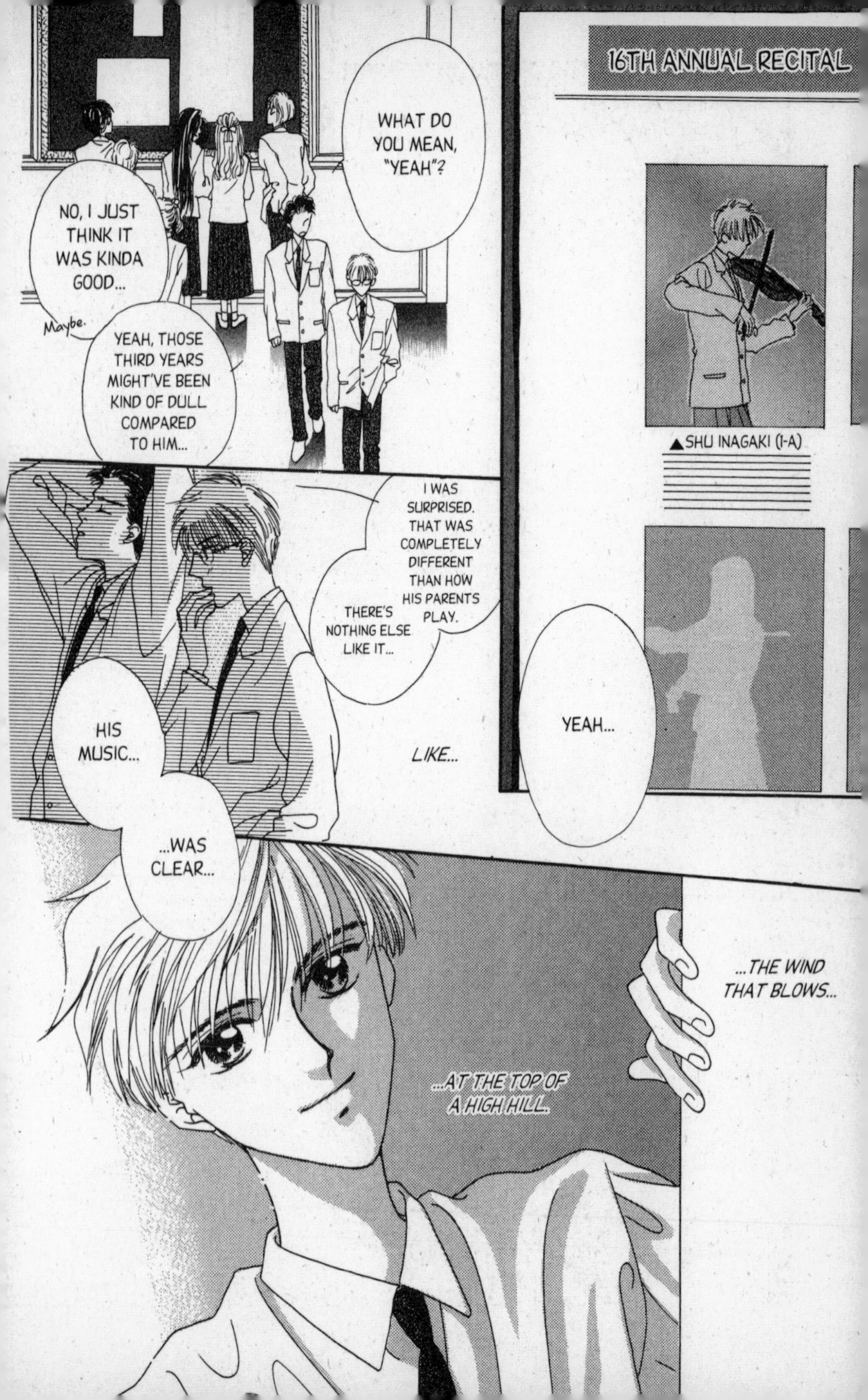
16TH ANNUAL RECITAL
▲SHU INAGAKI (1-A)
YEAH...
WHAT DO YOU MEAN, "YEAH"?
NO, I JUST THINK IT WAS KINDA GOOD...
Maybe.
YEAH, THOSE THIRD YEARS MIGHT'VE BEEN KIND OF DULL COMPARED TO HIM...
I WAS SURPRISED. THAT WAS COMPLETELY DIFFERENT THAN HOW HIS PARENTS PLAY.
THERE'S NOTHING ELSE LIKE IT...
LIKE...
HIS MUSIC...
...WAS CLEAR...
...THE WIND THAT BLOWS...
...AT THE TOP OF A HIGH HILL.

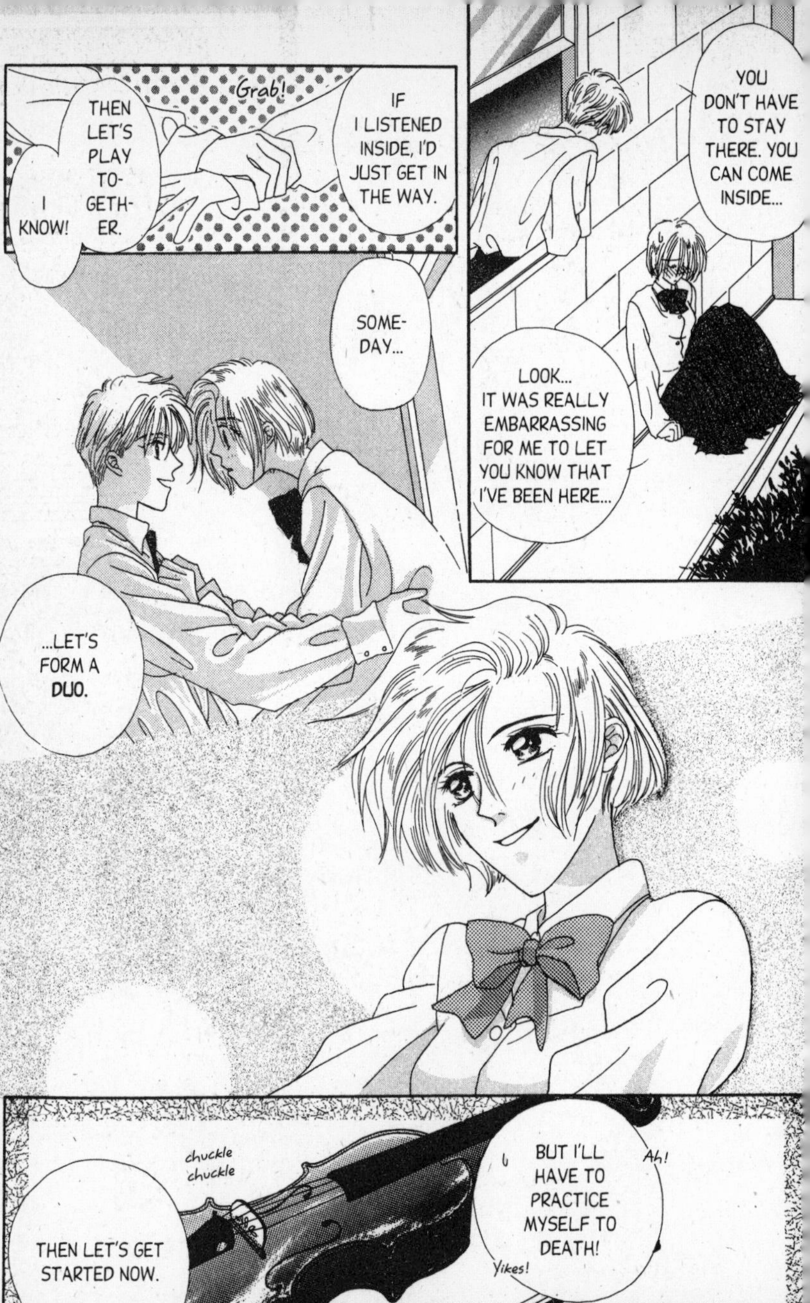
YOU DON'T HAVE TO STAY THERE. YOU CAN COME INSIDE...
LOOK... IT WAS REALLY EMBARRASSING FOR ME TO LET YOU KNOW THAT I'VE BEEN HERE...
IF I LISTENED INSIDE, I'D JUST GET IN THE WAY.
Grab!
I KNOW!
THEN LET'S PLAY TO-GETH-ER.
SOME-DAY...
...LET'S FORM A **DUO**.
Ah!
BUT I'LL HAVE TO PRACTICE MYSELF TO DEATH!
Yikes!
chuckle chuckle
THEN LET'S GET STARTED NOW.

Voice of Mine / End

I feel so grateful!

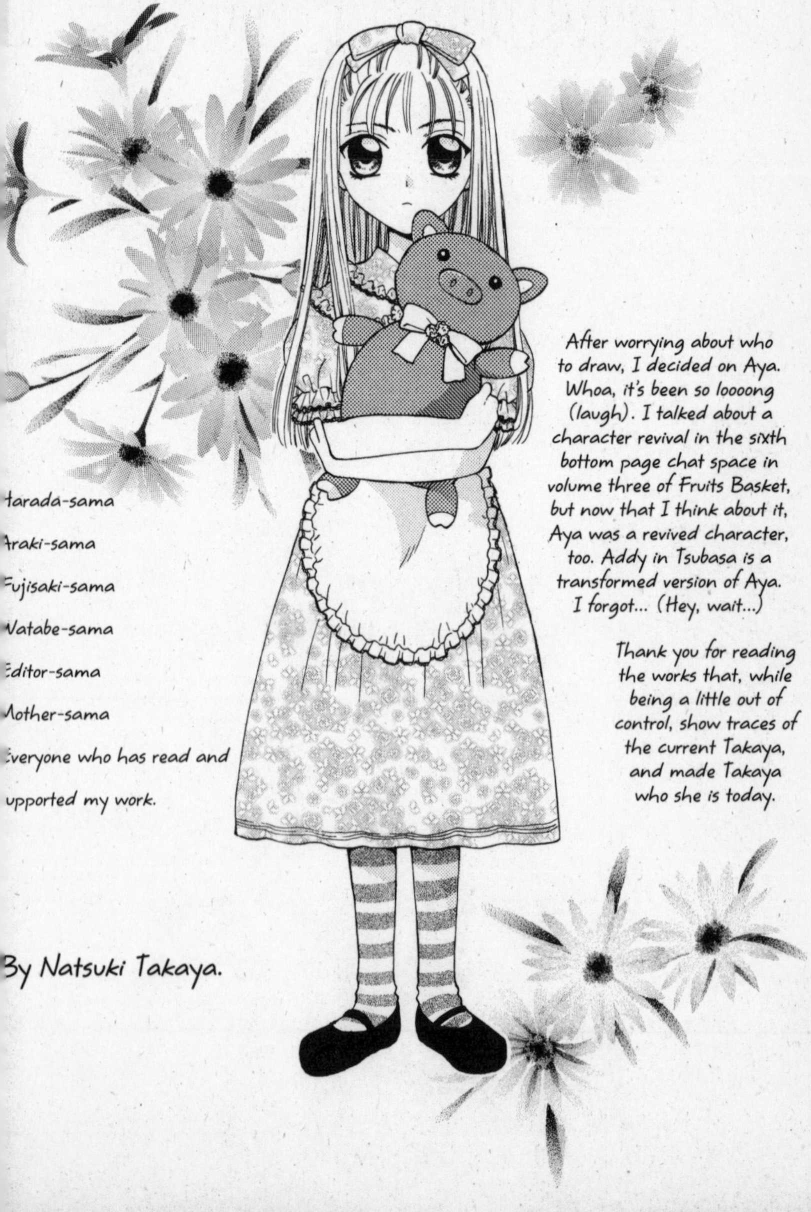

After worrying about who to draw, I decided on Aya. Whoa, it's been so loooong (laugh). I talked about a character revival in the sixth bottom page chat space in volume three of Fruits Basket, but now that I think about it, Aya was a revived character, too. Addy in Tsubasa is a transformed version of Aya. I forgot... (Hey, wait...)

Thank you for reading the works that, while being a little out of control, show traces of the current Takaya, and made Takaya who she is today.

Harada-sama

Araki-sama

Fujisaki-sama

Watabe-sama

Editor-sama

Mother-sama

Everyone who has read and supported my work.

By Natsuki Takaya.

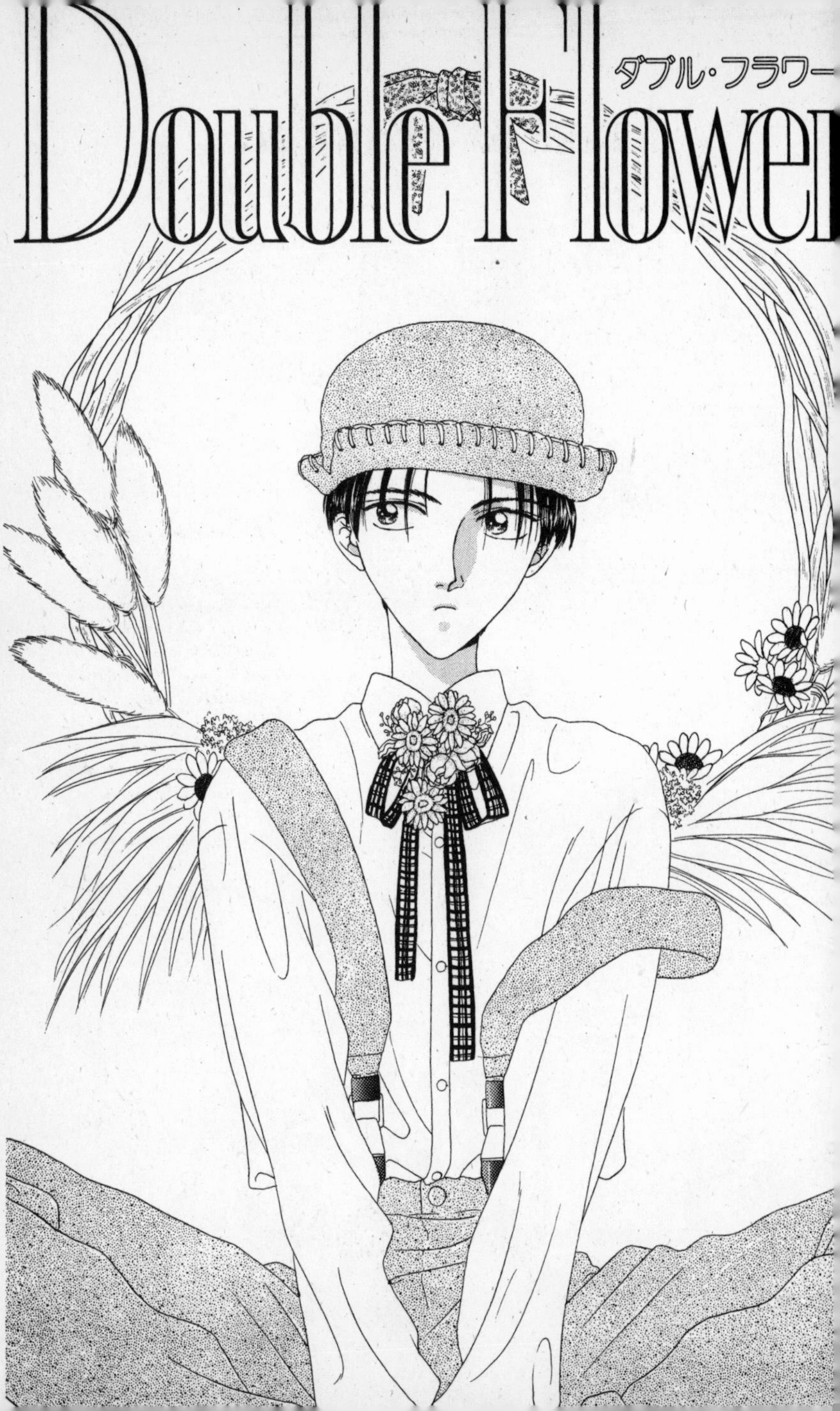
Double Flower
ダブル・フラワー

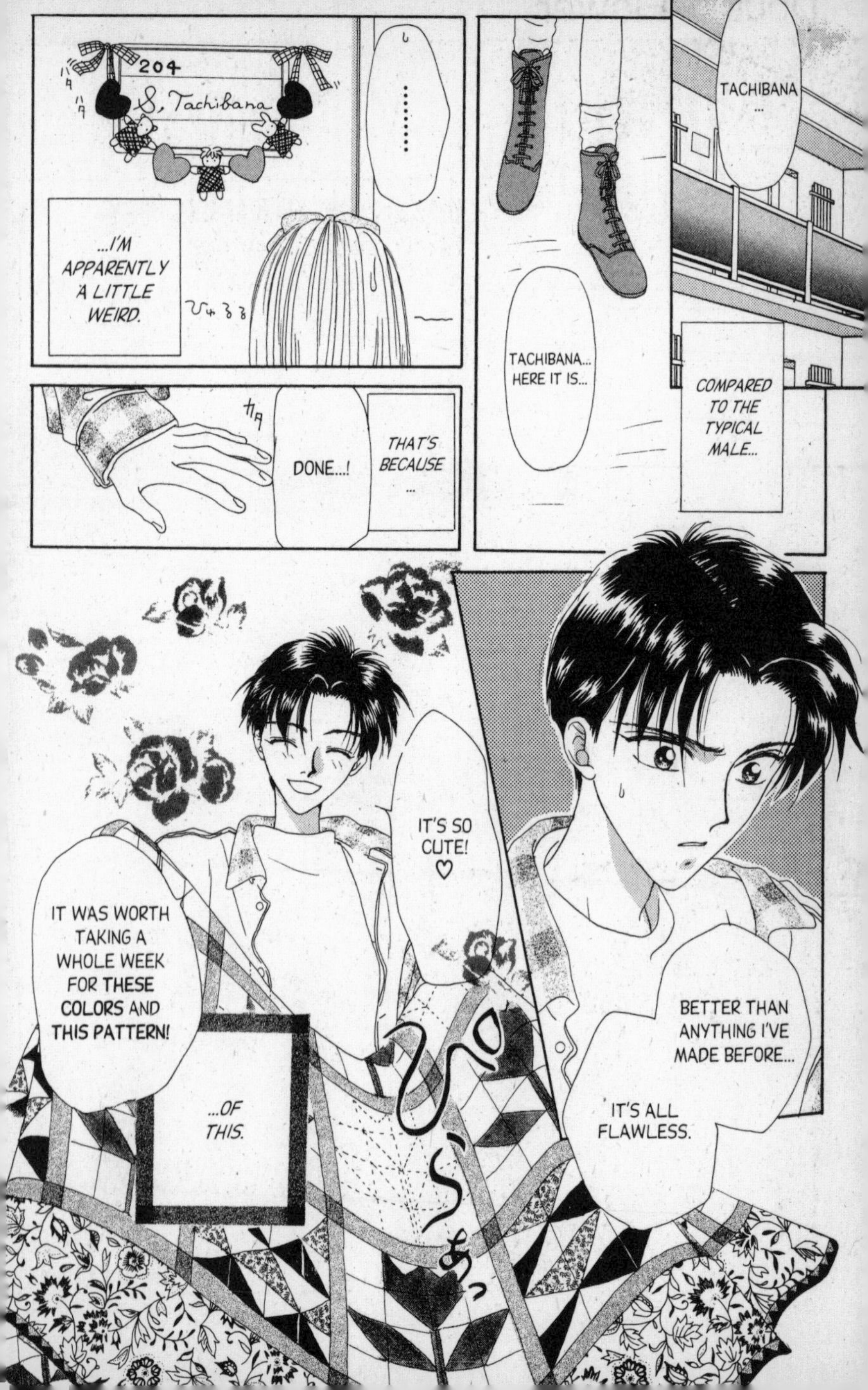

TACHIBANA ...
COMPARED TO THE TYPICAL MALE...
TACHIBANA... HERE IT IS...
......
204
S, Tachibana
...I'M APPARENTLY A LITTLE WEIRD.
THAT'S BECAUSE ...
DONE...!
BETTER THAN ANYTHING I'VE MADE BEFORE...
IT'S ALL FLAWLESS.
IT'S SO CUTE! ♡
IT WAS WORTH TAKING A WHOLE WEEK FOR THESE COLORS AND THIS PATTERN!
...OF THIS.

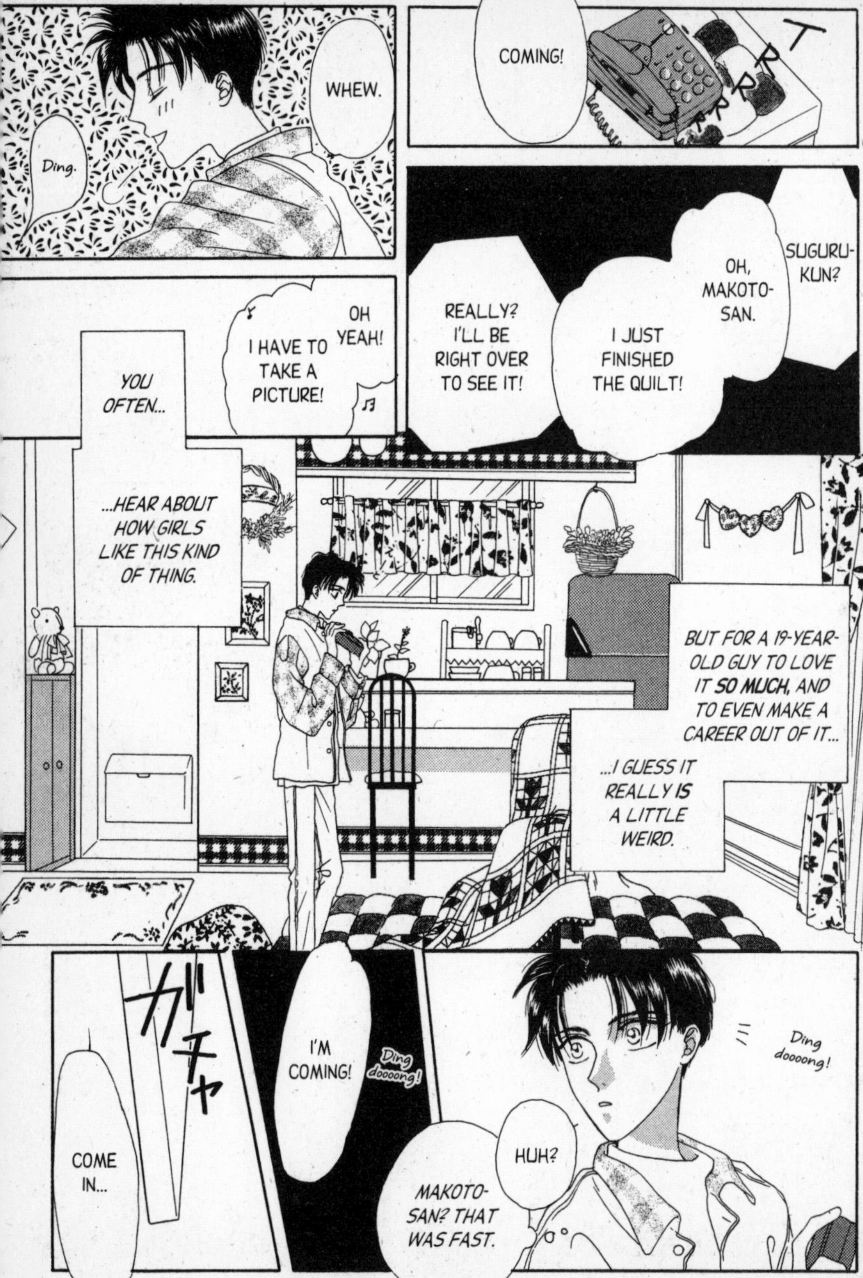
COMING!
WHEW.
Ding.
SUGURU-KUN?
OH, MAKOTO-SAN.
I JUST FINISHED THE QUILT!
REALLY? I'LL BE RIGHT OVER TO SEE IT!
OH YEAH! I HAVE TO TAKE A PICTURE!
YOU OFTEN...
...HEAR ABOUT HOW GIRLS LIKE THIS KIND OF THING.
BUT FOR A 19-YEAR-OLD GUY TO LOVE IT **SO MUCH**, AND TO EVEN MAKE A CAREER OUT OF IT...
...I GUESS IT REALLY **IS** A LITTLE WEIRD.
Ding dooong!
HUH?
MAKOTO-SAN? THAT WAS FAST.
Ding dooong!
I'M COMING!
ガチャ
COME IN...

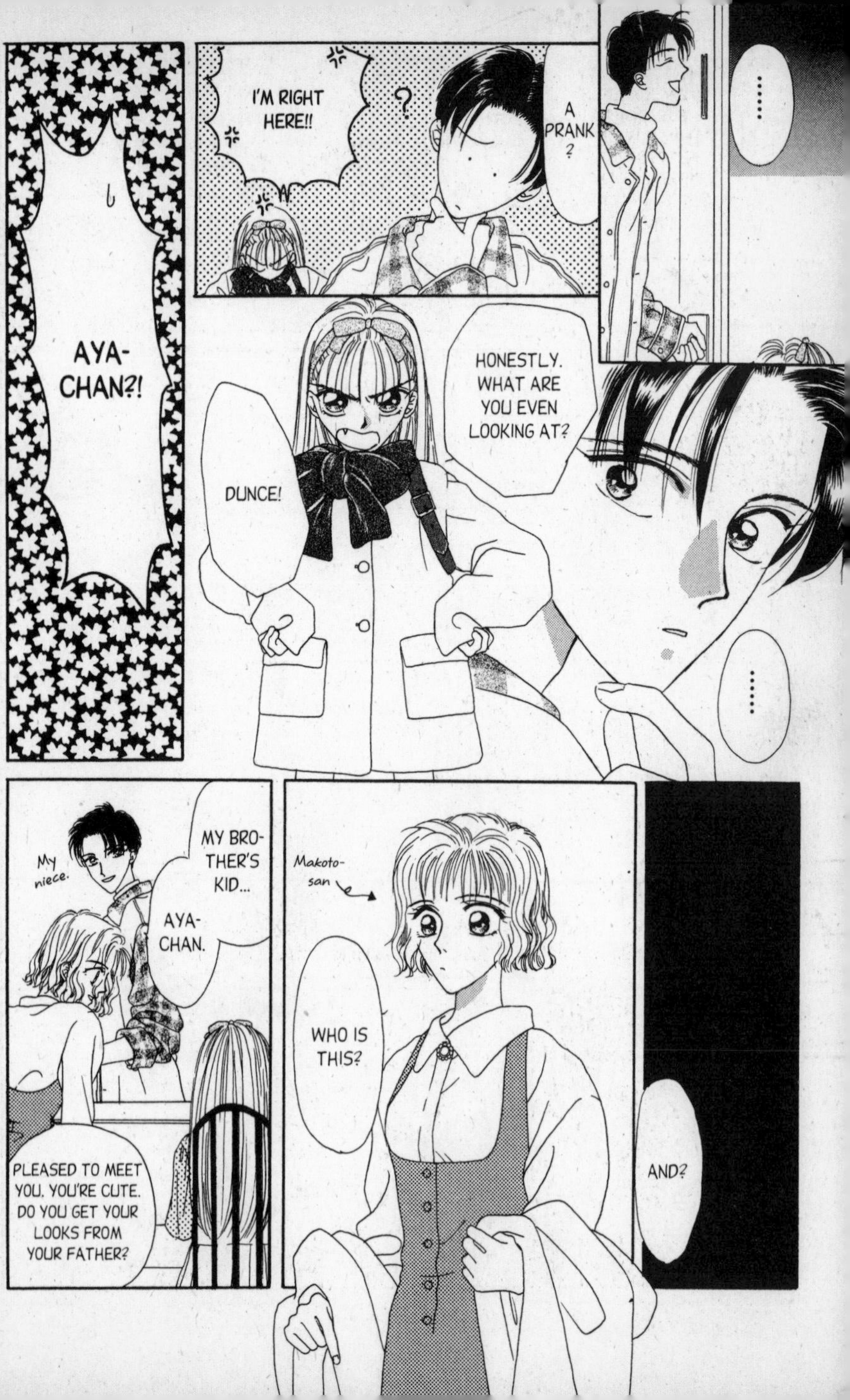
......
A PRANK?
?
I'M RIGHT HERE!!
......
HONESTLY. WHAT ARE YOU EVEN LOOKING AT?
DUNCE!
AYA-CHAN?!
AND?
Makoto-san
WHO IS THIS?
MY BROTHER'S KID...
AYA-CHAN.
My niece.
PLEASED TO MEET YOU. YOU'RE CUTE. DO YOU GET YOUR LOOKS FROM YOUR FATHER?

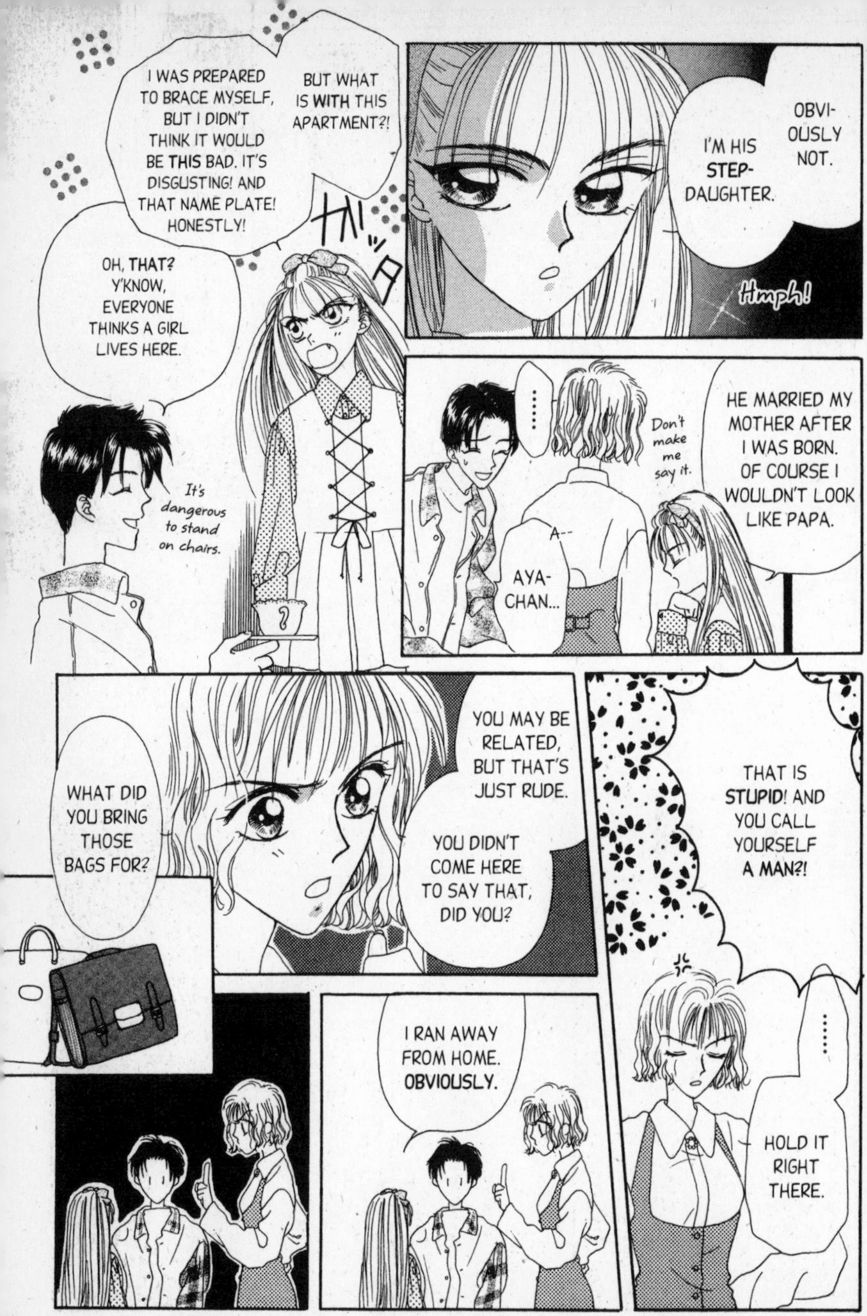
OBVIOUSLY NOT.
I'M HIS STEP-DAUGHTER.
Hmph!
HE MARRIED MY MOTHER AFTER I WAS BORN. OF COURSE I WOULDN'T LOOK LIKE PAPA.
Don't make me say it.
......
A--
AYA-CHAN...
BUT WHAT IS WITH THIS APARTMENT?!
I WAS PREPARED TO BRACE MYSELF, BUT I DIDN'T THINK IT WOULD BE THIS BAD. IT'S DISGUSTING! AND THAT NAME PLATE! HONESTLY!
OH, THAT? Y'KNOW, EVERYONE THINKS A GIRL LIVES HERE.
It's dangerous to stand on chairs.
THAT IS STUPID! AND YOU CALL YOURSELF A MAN?!
......
HOLD IT RIGHT THERE.
YOU MAY BE RELATED, BUT THAT'S JUST RUDE.
YOU DIDN'T COME HERE TO SAY THAT, DID YOU?
WHAT DID YOU BRING THOSE BAGS FOR?
I RAN AWAY FROM HOME. OBVIOUSLY.

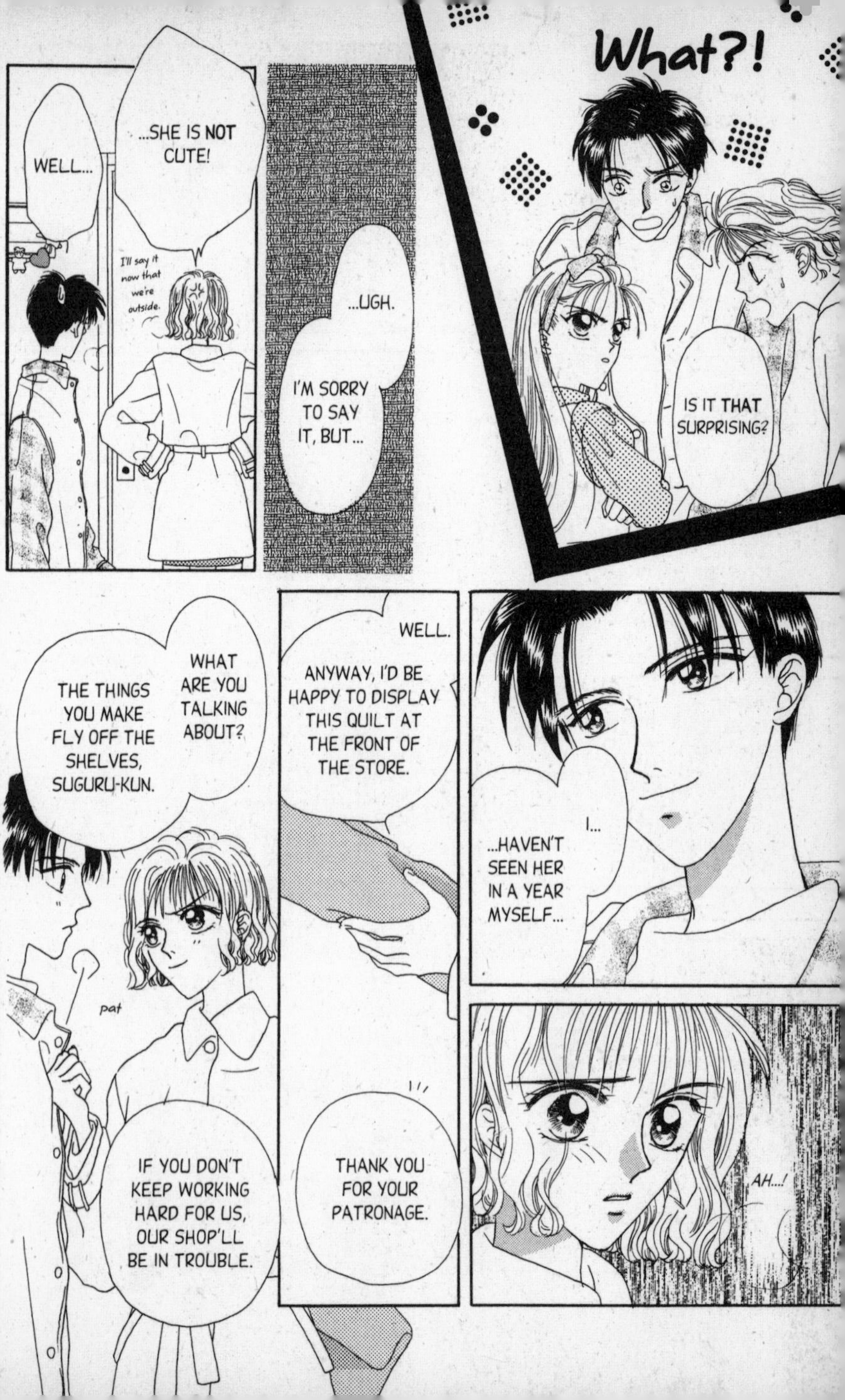
What?!
IS IT THAT SURPRISING?
...UGH.
I'M SORRY TO SAY IT, BUT...
...SHE IS NOT CUTE!
WELL...
I'll say it now that we're outside.
I...
...HAVEN'T SEEN HER IN A YEAR MYSELF...
AH...!
WELL.
ANYWAY, I'D BE HAPPY TO DISPLAY THIS QUILT AT THE FRONT OF THE STORE.
THANK YOU FOR YOUR PATRONAGE.
WHAT ARE YOU TALKING ABOUT?
THE THINGS YOU MAKE FLY OFF THE SHELVES, SUGURU-KUN.
pat
IF YOU DON'T KEEP WORKING HARD FOR US, OUR SHOP'LL BE IN TROUBLE.

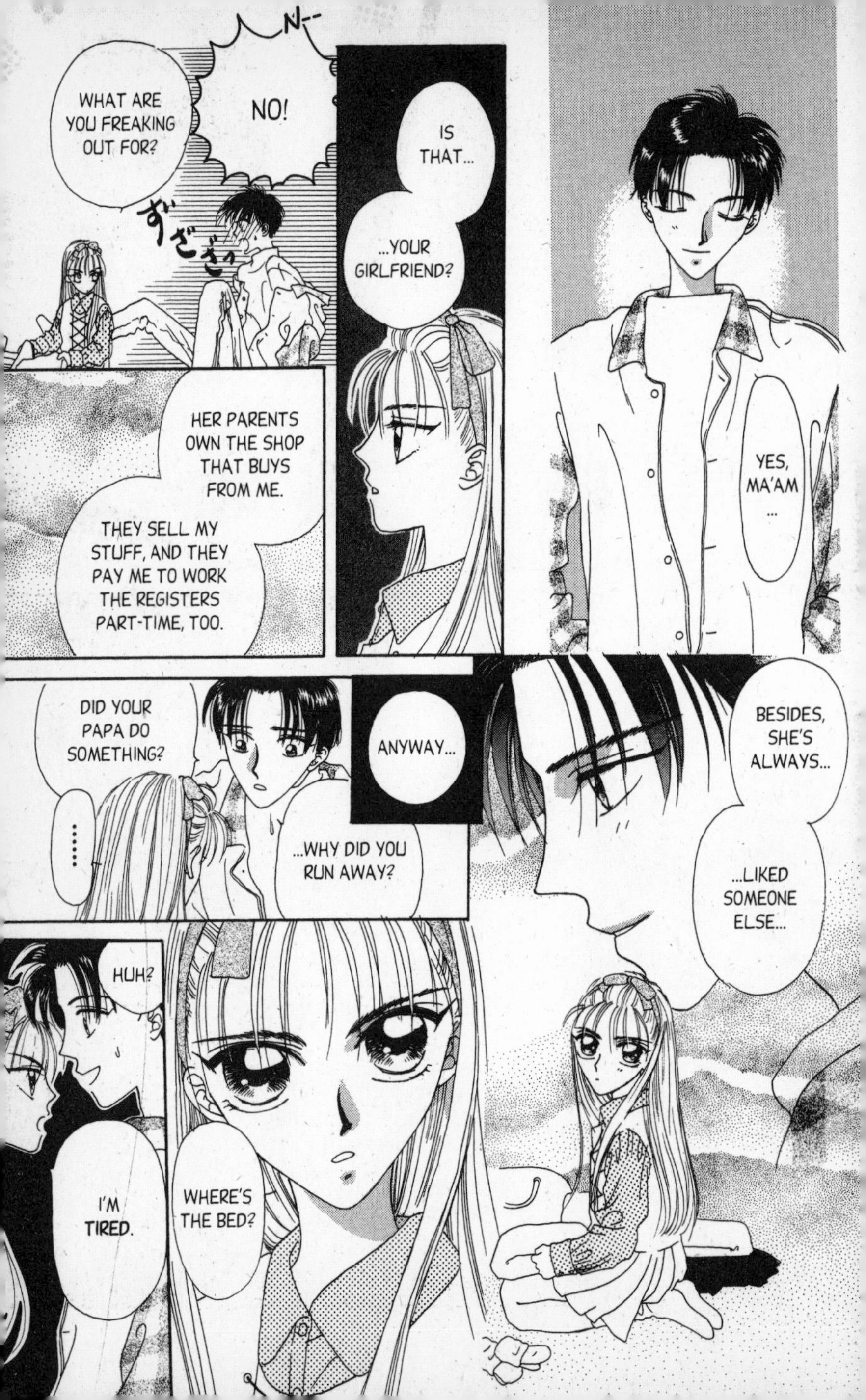
YES, MA'AM ...
IS THAT...
...YOUR GIRLFRIEND?
N--
NO!
WHAT ARE YOU FREAKING OUT FOR?
ずざざ
HER PARENTS OWN THE SHOP THAT BUYS FROM ME.
THEY SELL MY STUFF, AND THEY PAY ME TO WORK THE REGISTERS PART-TIME, TOO.
BESIDES, SHE'S ALWAYS...
...LIKED SOMEONE ELSE...
ANYWAY...
...WHY DID YOU RUN AWAY?
DID YOUR PAPA DO SOMETHING?
......
WHERE'S THE BED?
HUH?
I'M TIRED.

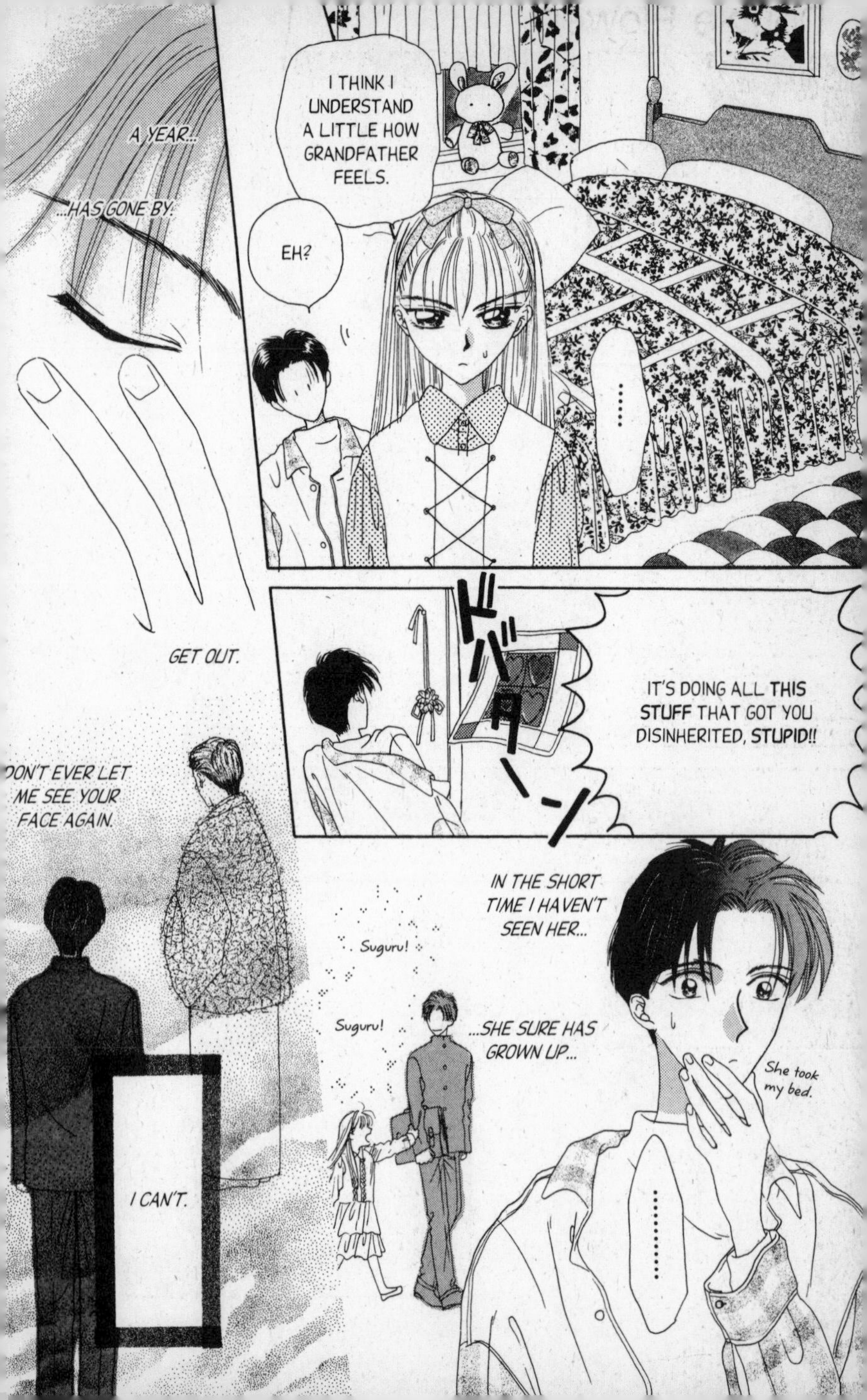
I THINK I UNDERSTAND A LITTLE HOW GRANDFATHER FEELS.
EH?
......
IT'S DOING ALL **THIS STUFF** THAT GOT YOU DISINHERITED, **STUPID!!**
IN THE SHORT TIME I HAVEN'T SEEN HER...
Suguru!
Suguru!
...SHE SURE HAS GROWN UP...
......
She took my bed.
A YEAR...
...HAS GONE BY.
GET OUT.
DON'T EVER LET ME SEE YOUR FACE AGAIN.
I CAN'T.

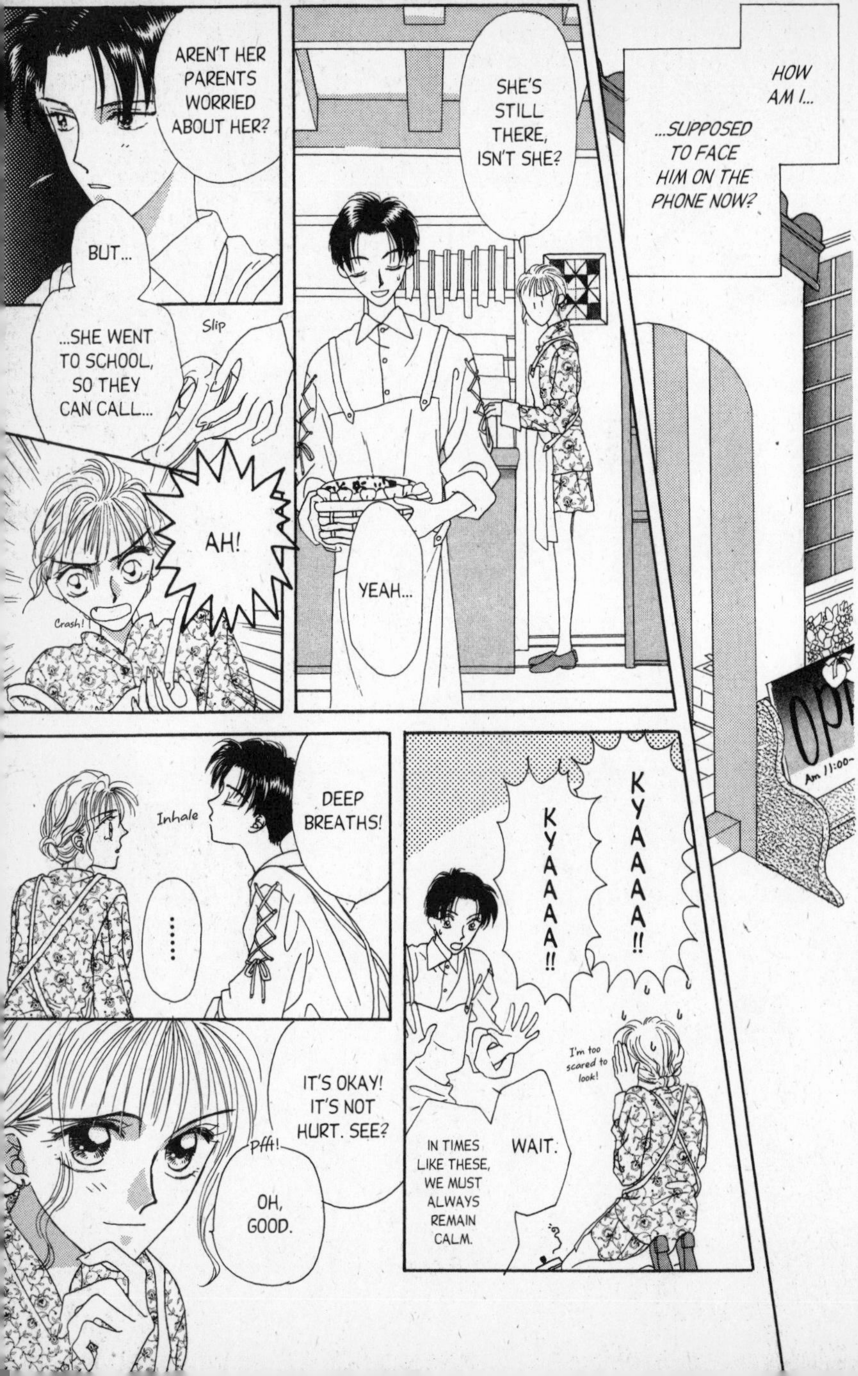
HOW AM I...
...SUPPOSED TO FACE HIM ON THE PHONE NOW?
SHE'S STILL THERE, ISN'T SHE?
YEAH...
AREN'T HER PARENTS WORRIED ABOUT HER?
BUT...
...SHE WENT TO SCHOOL, SO THEY CAN CALL...
Slip
AH!
Crash!
KYAAAAA!!
KYAAAA!!
I'm too scared to look!
WAIT.
IN TIMES LIKE THESE, WE MUST ALWAYS REMAIN CALM.
DEEP BREATHS!
Inhale
......
IT'S OKAY! IT'S NOT HURT. SEE?
Pff!
OH, GOOD.

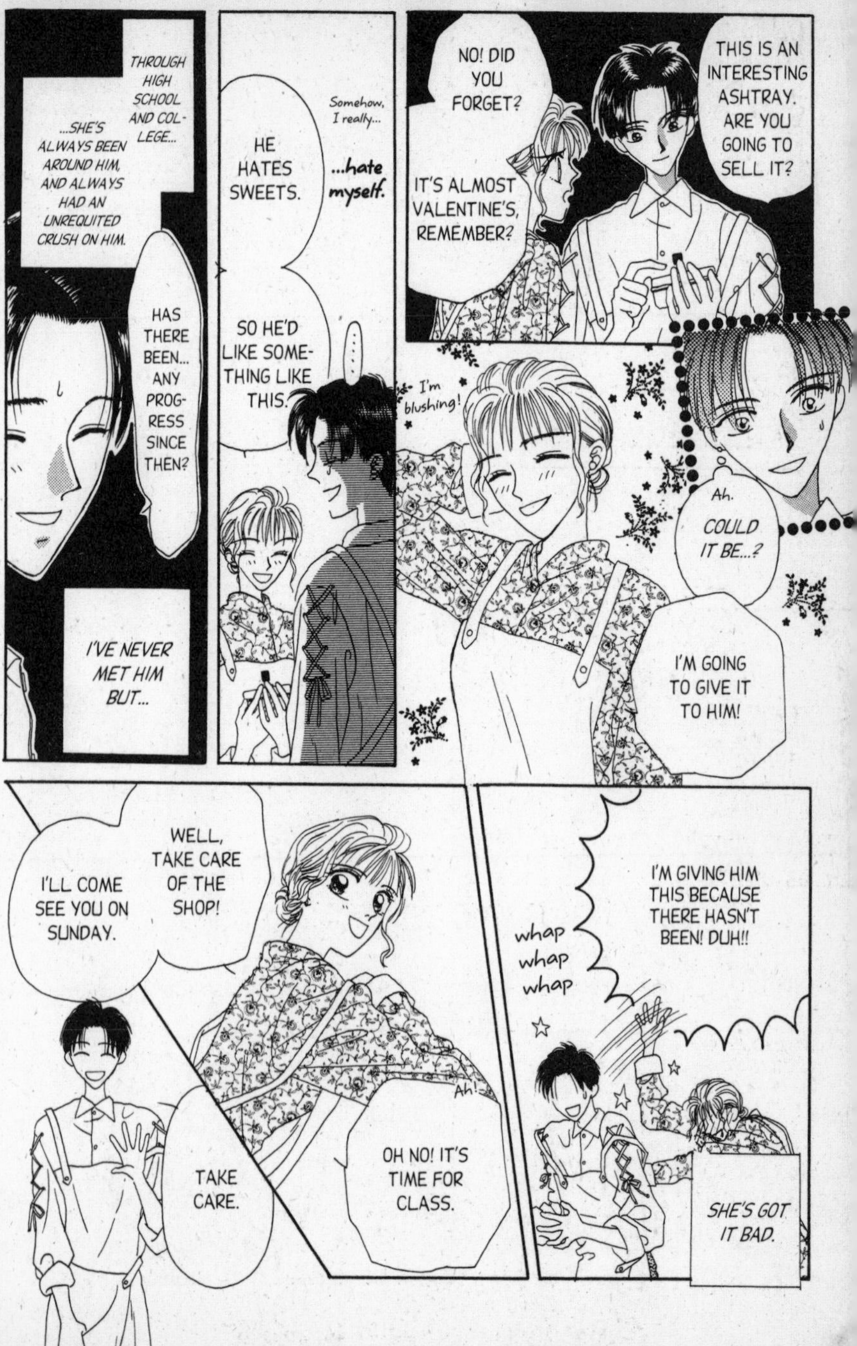

THIS IS AN INTERESTING ASHTRAY. ARE YOU GOING TO SELL IT?
NO! DID YOU FORGET?
IT'S ALMOST VALENTINE'S, REMEMBER?
Ah.
COULD IT BE...?
I'm blushing!
I'M GOING TO GIVE IT TO HIM!
HE HATES SWEETS.
SO HE'D LIKE SOMETHING LIKE THIS.
.....
Somehow, I really...
...hate myself.
THROUGH HIGH SCHOOL AND COLLEGE...
...SHE'S ALWAYS BEEN AROUND HIM, AND ALWAYS HAD AN UNREQUITED CRUSH ON HIM.
HAS THERE BEEN... ANY PROGRESS SINCE THEN?
I'VE NEVER MET HIM BUT...
I'M GIVING HIM THIS BECAUSE THERE HASN'T BEEN! DUH!!
whap whap whap
SHE'S GOT IT BAD.
Ah!
OH NO! IT'S TIME FOR CLASS.
WELL, TAKE CARE OF THE SHOP!
I'LL COME SEE YOU ON SUNDAY.
TAKE CARE.

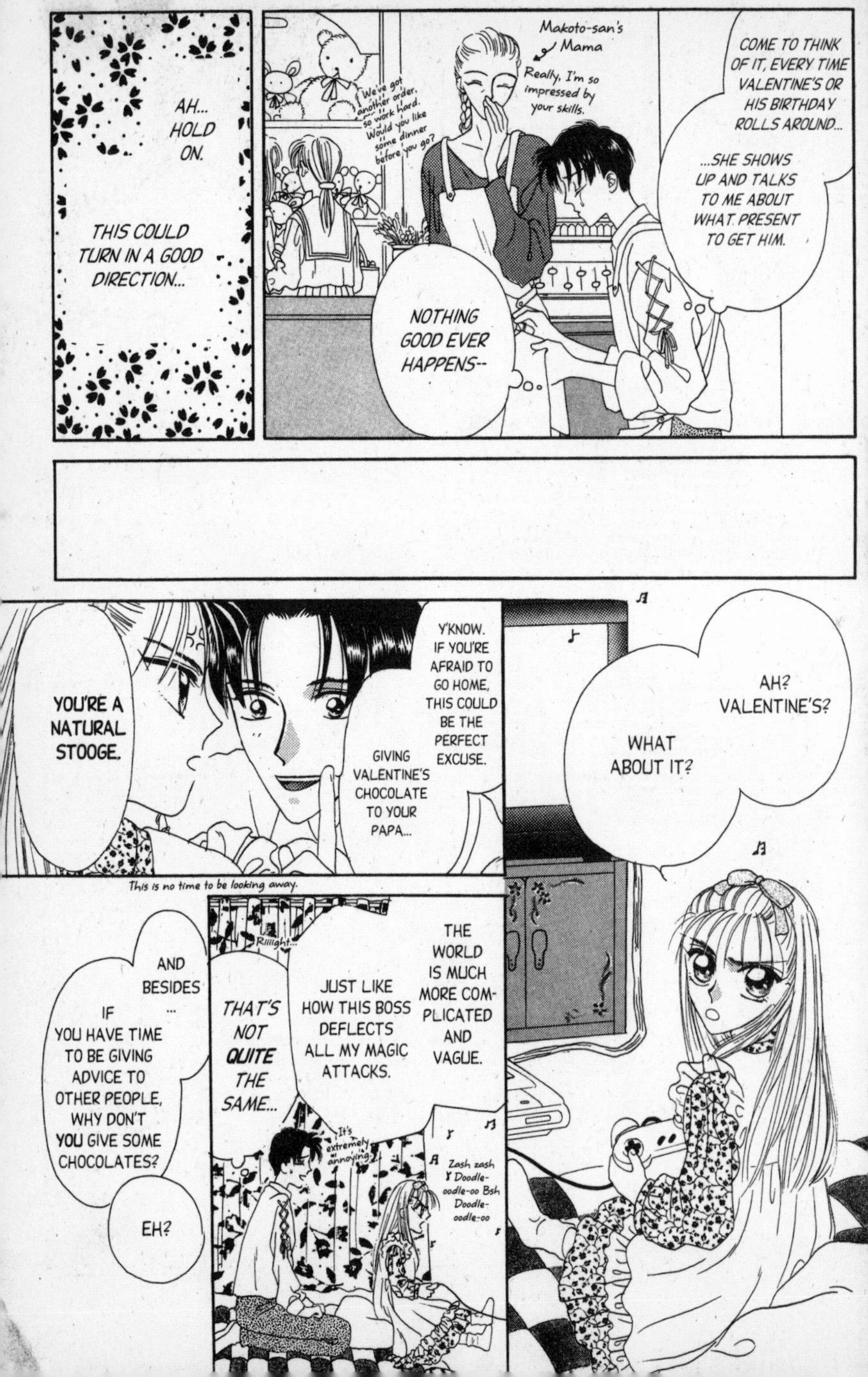
COME TO THINK OF IT, EVERY TIME VALENTINE'S OR HIS BIRTHDAY ROLLS AROUND...
...SHE SHOWS UP AND TALKS TO ME ABOUT WHAT PRESENT TO GET HIM.
Makoto-san's Mama
Really, I'm so impressed by your skills.
We've got another order, so work hard. Would you like some dinner before you go?
NOTHING GOOD EVER HAPPENS--
AH... HOLD ON.
THIS COULD TURN IN A GOOD DIRECTION...
AH? VALENTINE'S?
WHAT ABOUT IT?
Y'KNOW. IF YOU'RE AFRAID TO GO HOME, THIS COULD BE THE PERFECT EXCUSE.
GIVING VALENTINE'S CHOCOLATE TO YOUR PAPA...
YOU'RE A NATURAL STOOGE.
This is no time to be looking away.
THE WORLD IS MUCH MORE COMPLICATED AND VAGUE.
JUST LIKE HOW THIS BOSS DEFLECTS ALL MY MAGIC ATTACKS.
Riiiight...
THAT'S NOT QUITE THE SAME...
AND BESIDES...
IF YOU HAVE TIME TO BE GIVING ADVICE TO OTHER PEOPLE, WHY DON'T YOU GIVE SOME CHOCOLATES?
It's extremely annoying.
Zash zash Doodle-oodle-oo Bsh Doodle-oodle-oo
EH?

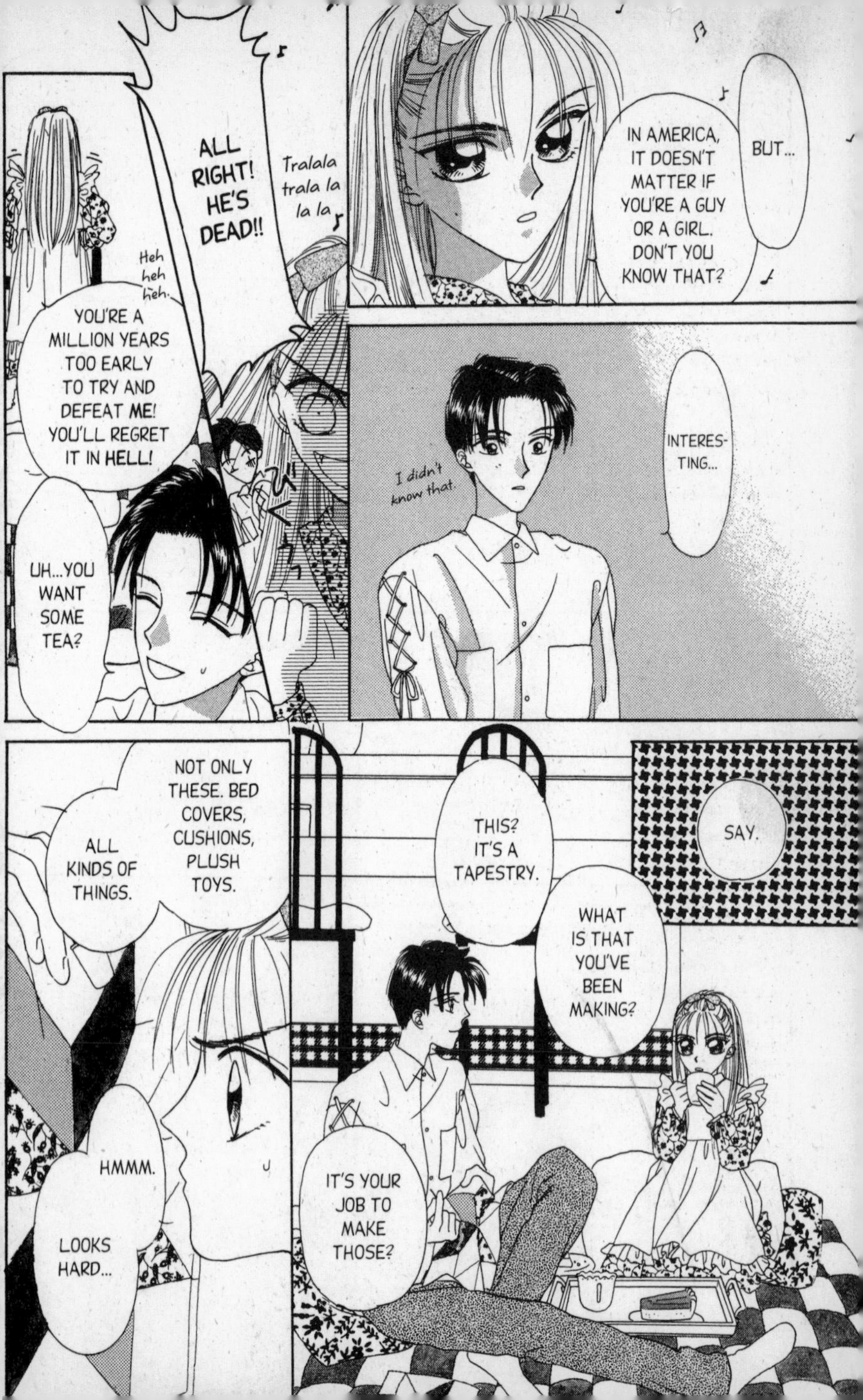

BUT...
IN AMERICA, IT DOESN'T MATTER IF YOU'RE A GUY OR A GIRL. DON'T YOU KNOW THAT?
INTERES-TING...
I didn't know that.
Tralala trala la la la
ALL RIGHT! HE'S DEAD!!
Heh heh heh.
YOU'RE A MILLION YEARS TOO EARLY TO TRY AND DEFEAT ME! YOU'LL REGRET IT IN HELL!
UH...YOU WANT SOME TEA?
SAY.
WHAT IS THAT YOU'VE BEEN MAKING?
THIS? IT'S A TAPESTRY.
IT'S YOUR JOB TO MAKE THOSE?
NOT ONLY THESE. BED COVERS, CUSHIONS, PLUSH TOYS.
ALL KINDS OF THINGS.
HMMM.
LOOKS HARD...

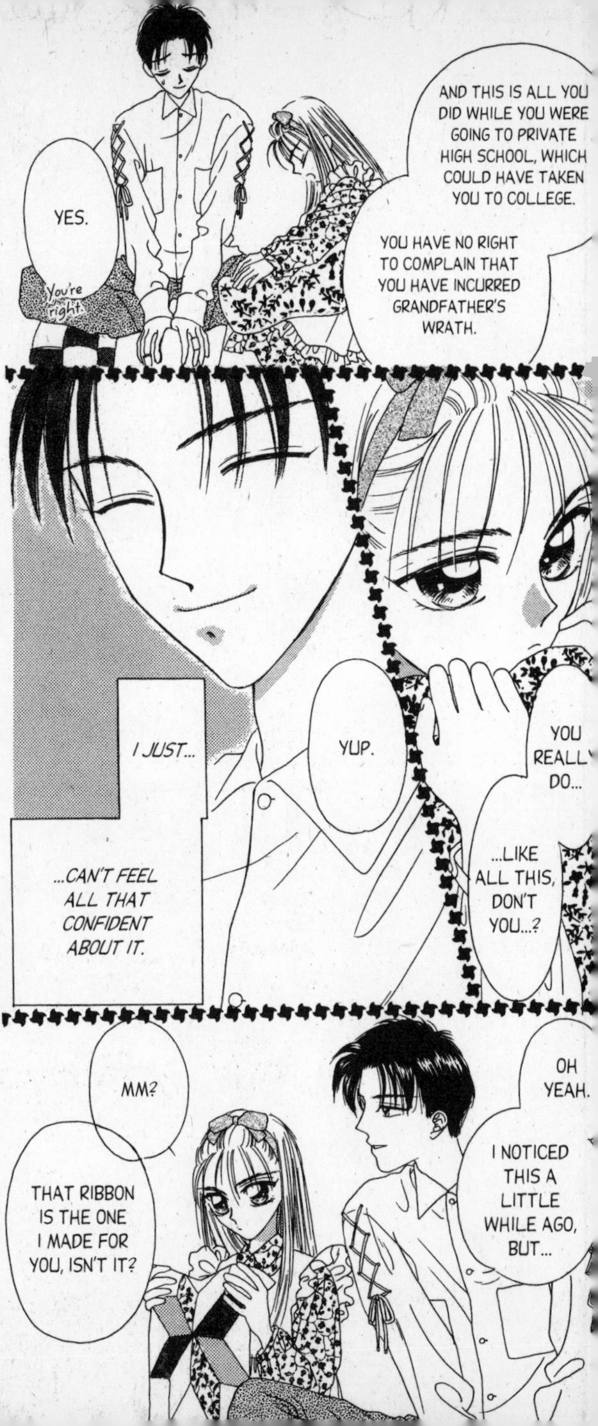
AND THIS IS ALL YOU DID WHILE YOU WERE GOING TO PRIVATE HIGH SCHOOL, WHICH COULD HAVE TAKEN YOU TO COLLEGE.
YOU HAVE NO RIGHT TO COMPLAIN THAT YOU HAVE INCURRED GRANDFATHER'S WRATH.
YES.
You're right.
YOU REALLY DO...
...LIKE ALL THIS, DON'T YOU...?
YUP.
I JUST...
...CAN'T FEEL ALL THAT CONFIDENT ABOUT IT.
OH YEAH.
I NOTICED THIS A LITTLE WHILE AGO, BUT...
MM?
THAT RIBBON IS THE ONE I MADE FOR YOU, ISN'T IT?

Part 3

Looking at my older works reminds me of the past. In those days, we all had some time, and I'd stay at friends' houses and get them to help. Like, "You want some (tone)...in this tiny place, too?" "If it's a pain, don't worry about it." "But you want me to put some there, right?" "Please do ♥" (This time, you can finally read it.) Or like how a giant scrap of tone got stuck in "Voice..." and we all got a big laugh out of it. (This time, we took it off...) Or how we'd have seven-hour long phone conversations. (My friend paid the phone bill. Ungrateful Takaya.) Or the bleeeep bleeeep, or the bleeeep bleeeep. (It was so bad I can't write it.) Or "It burns... it burns... it burns and burns..." (I can't forget that. I didn't know what I'd do when I had to listen to it on loop (laugh). This is all my personal business...

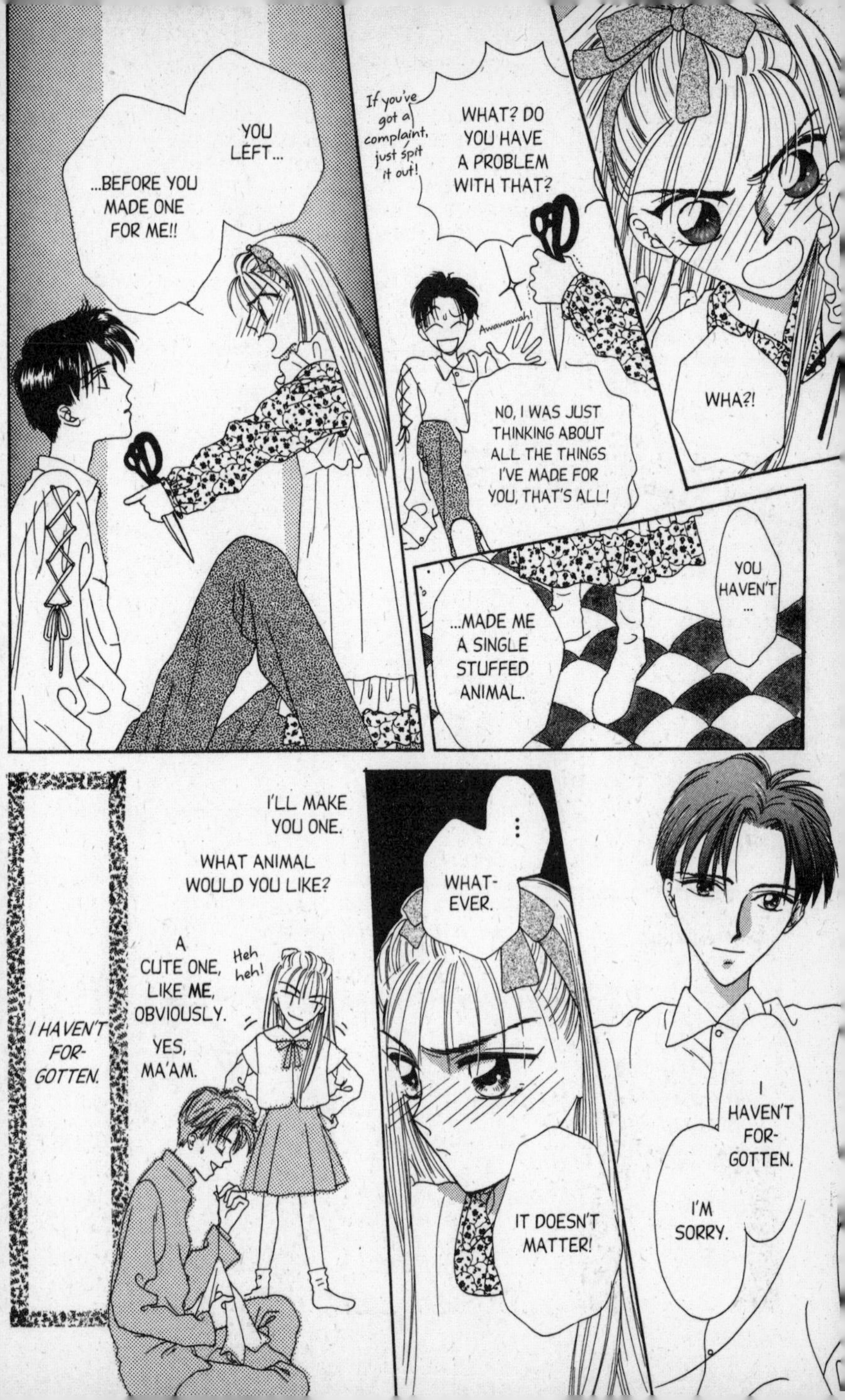

WHA?!
If you've got a complaint, just spit it out!
WHAT? DO YOU HAVE A PROBLEM WITH THAT?
Awawawah!
NO, I WAS JUST THINKING ABOUT ALL THE THINGS I'VE MADE FOR YOU, THAT'S ALL!
YOU HAVEN'T ...
...MADE ME A SINGLE STUFFED ANIMAL.
YOU LEFT...
...BEFORE YOU MADE ONE FOR ME!!
I HAVEN'T FORGOTTEN.
I'M SORRY.
...
WHATEVER.
IT DOESN'T MATTER!
I'LL MAKE YOU ONE.
WHAT ANIMAL WOULD YOU LIKE?
A CUTE ONE, LIKE ME, OBVIOUSLY.
Heh heh!
YES, MA'AM.
I HAVEN'T FORGOTTEN.

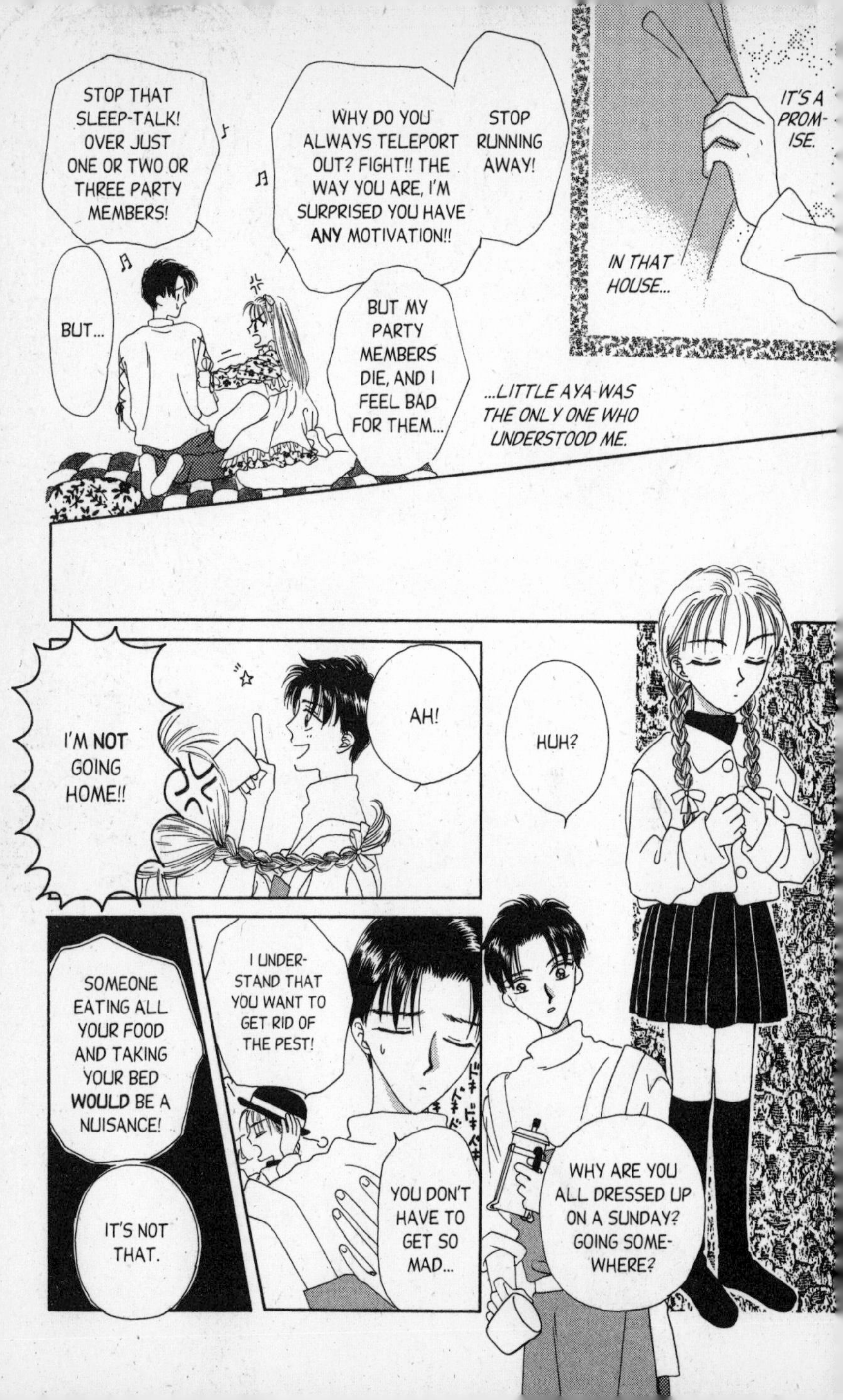
IT'S A PROMISE.
IN THAT HOUSE...
...LITTLE AYA WAS THE ONLY ONE WHO UNDERSTOOD ME.
STOP RUNNING AWAY!
WHY DO YOU ALWAYS TELEPORT OUT? FIGHT!! THE WAY YOU ARE, I'M SURPRISED YOU HAVE ANY MOTIVATION!!
STOP THAT SLEEP-TALK! OVER JUST ONE OR TWO OR THREE PARTY MEMBERS!
BUT MY PARTY MEMBERS DIE, AND I FEEL BAD FOR THEM...
BUT...
WHY ARE YOU ALL DRESSED UP ON A SUNDAY? GOING SOMEWHERE?
HUH?
AH!
I'M NOT GOING HOME!!
I UNDERSTAND THAT YOU WANT TO GET RID OF THE PEST!
YOU DON'T HAVE TO GET SO MAD...
SOMEONE EATING ALL YOUR FOOD AND TAKING YOUR BED WOULD BE A NUISANCE!
IT'S NOT THAT.

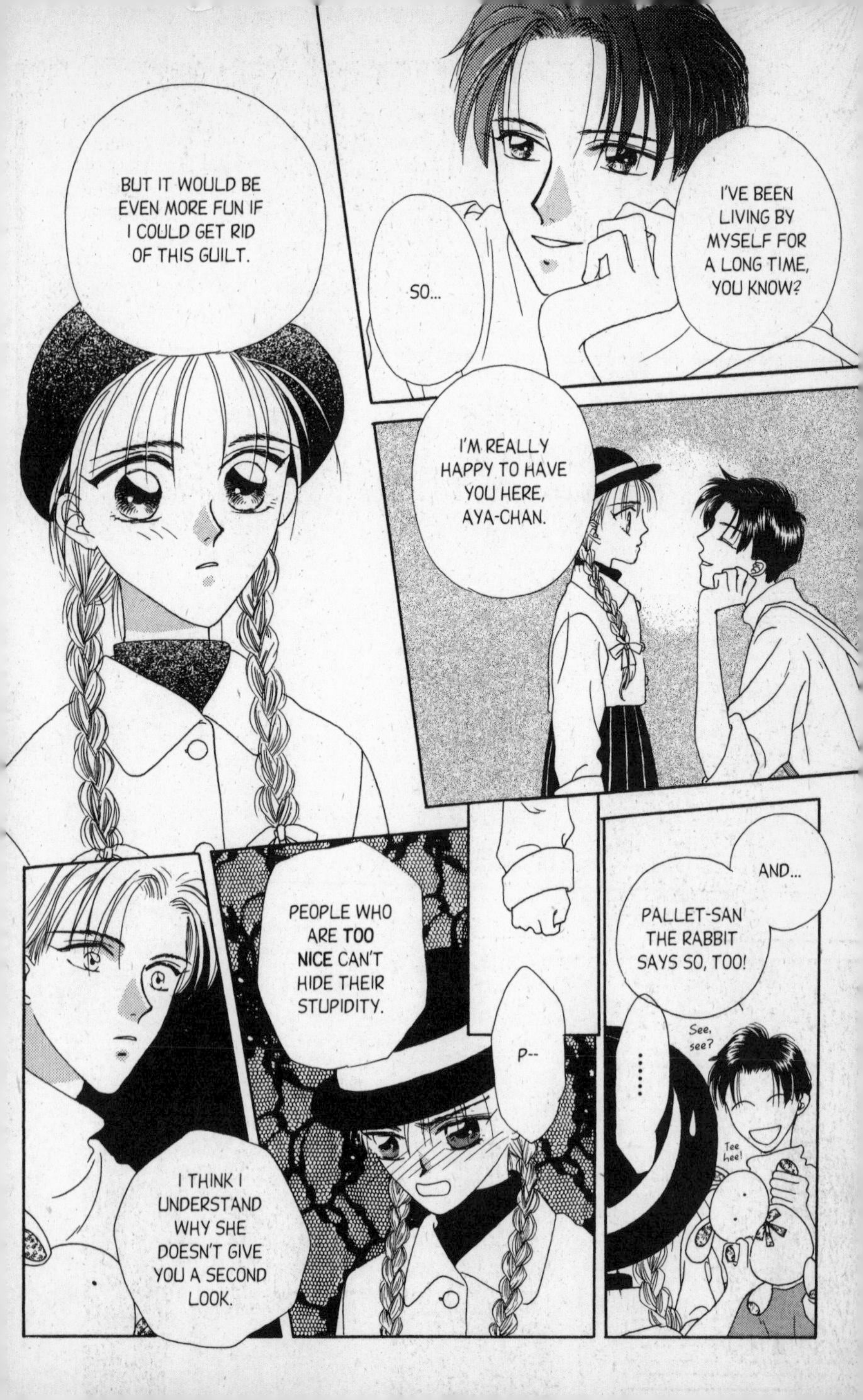
I'VE BEEN LIVING BY MYSELF FOR A LONG TIME, YOU KNOW?
SO...
I'M REALLY HAPPY TO HAVE YOU HERE, AYA-CHAN.
BUT IT WOULD BE EVEN MORE FUN IF I COULD GET RID OF THIS GUILT.
AND...
PALLET-SAN THE RABBIT SAYS SO, TOO!
See, see?
Tee hee!
......
P--
PEOPLE WHO ARE **TOO NICE** CAN'T HIDE THEIR STUPIDITY.
I THINK I UNDERSTAND WHY SHE DOESN'T GIVE YOU A SECOND LOOK.

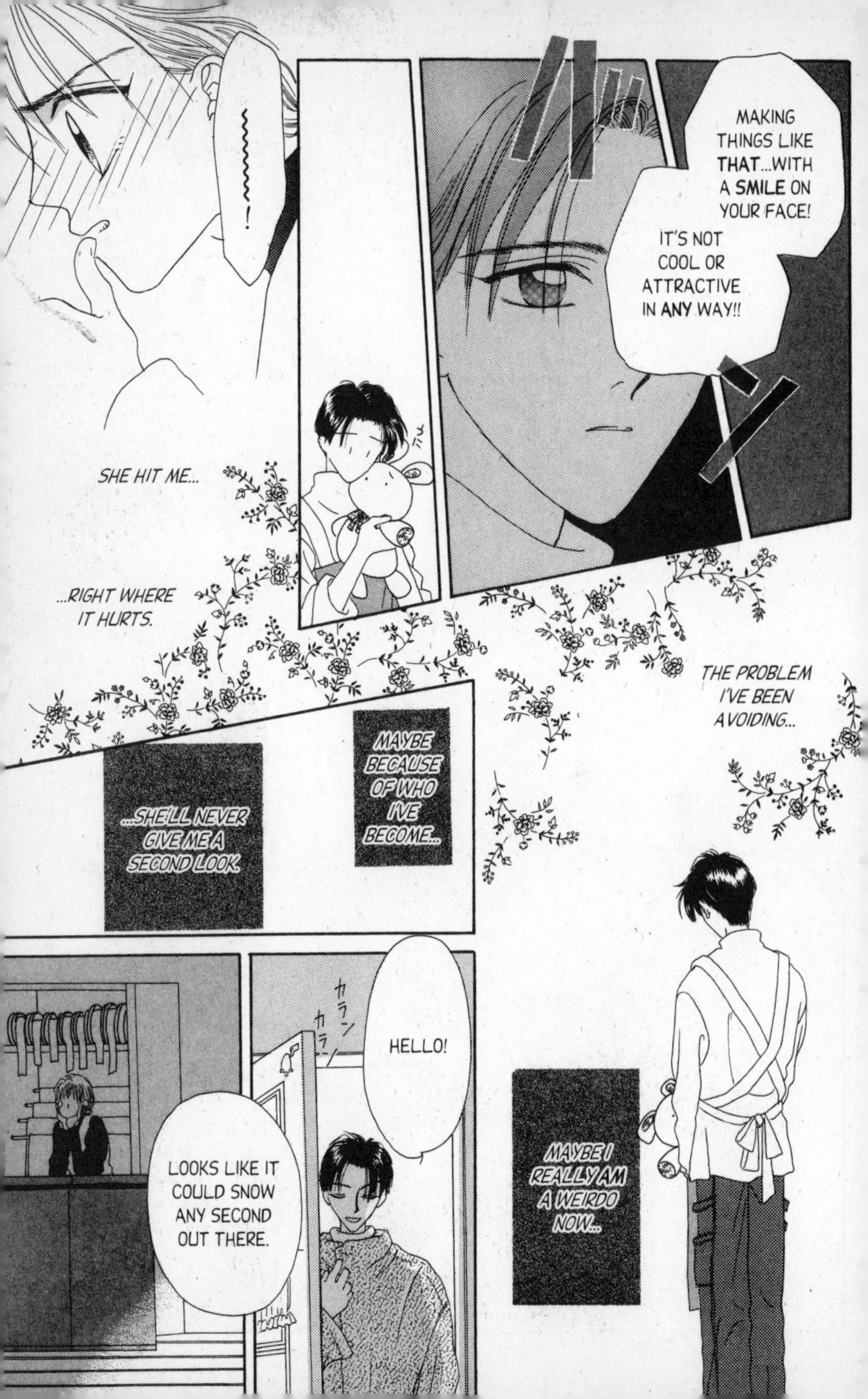
MAKING THINGS LIKE THAT...WITH A SMILE ON YOUR FACE!
IT'S NOT COOL OR ATTRACTIVE IN ANY WAY!!
SHE HIT ME...
...RIGHT WHERE IT HURTS.
THE PROBLEM I'VE BEEN AVOIDING...
MAYBE BECAUSE OF WHO I'VE BECOME...
...SHE'LL NEVER GIVE ME A SECOND LOOK.
MAYBE I REALLY AM A WEIRDO NOW...
カラン
カラン
HELLO!
LOOKS LIKE IT COULD SNOW ANY SECOND OUT THERE.

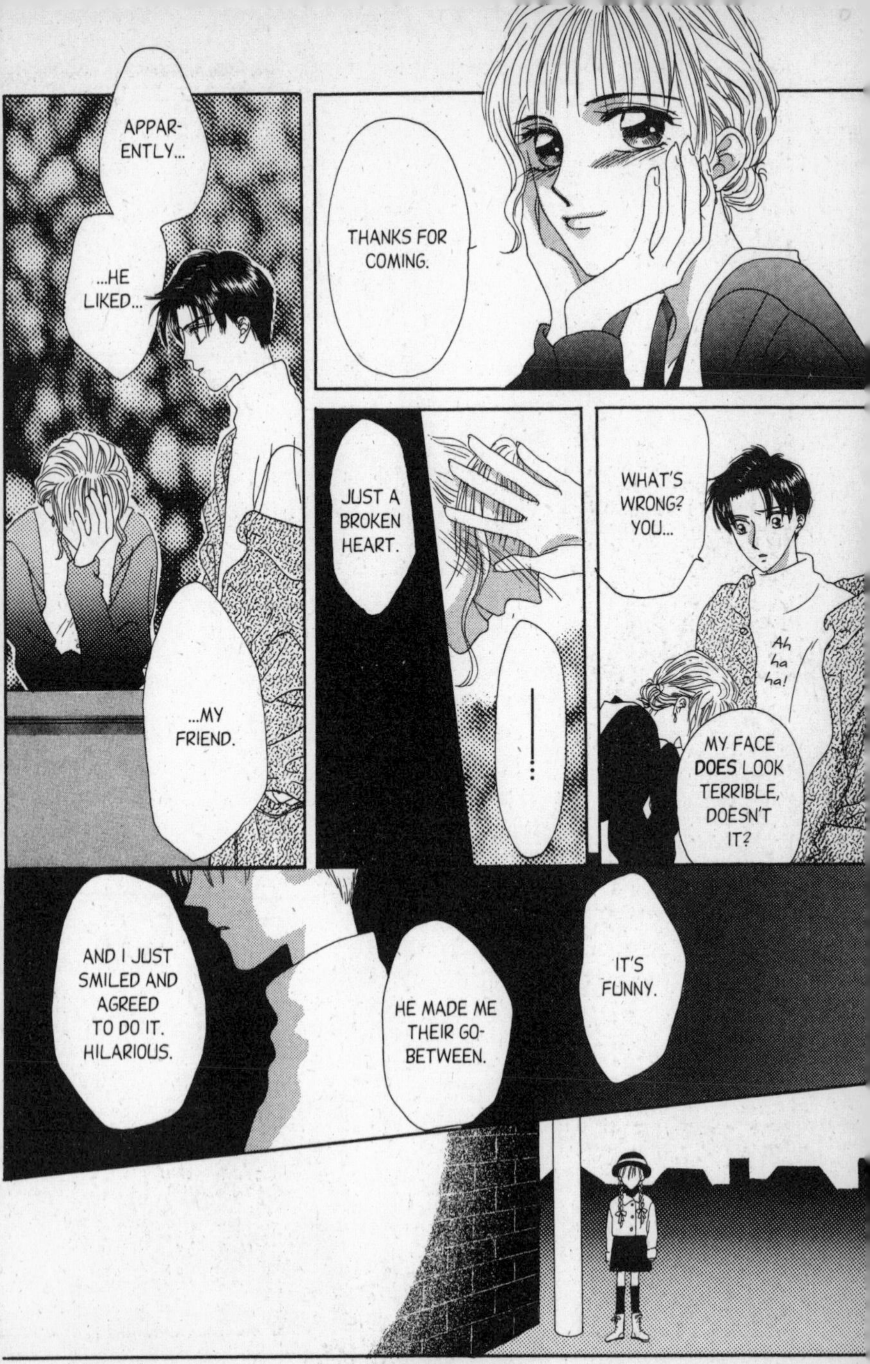
THANKS FOR COMING.
WHAT'S WRONG? YOU...
Ah ha ha!
MY FACE **DOES** LOOK TERRIBLE, DOESN'T IT?
JUST A BROKEN HEART.
...!
APPARENTLY...
...HE LIKED...
...MY FRIEND.
IT'S FUNNY.
HE MADE ME THEIR GO-BETWEEN.
AND I JUST SMILED AND AGREED TO DO IT. HILARIOUS.

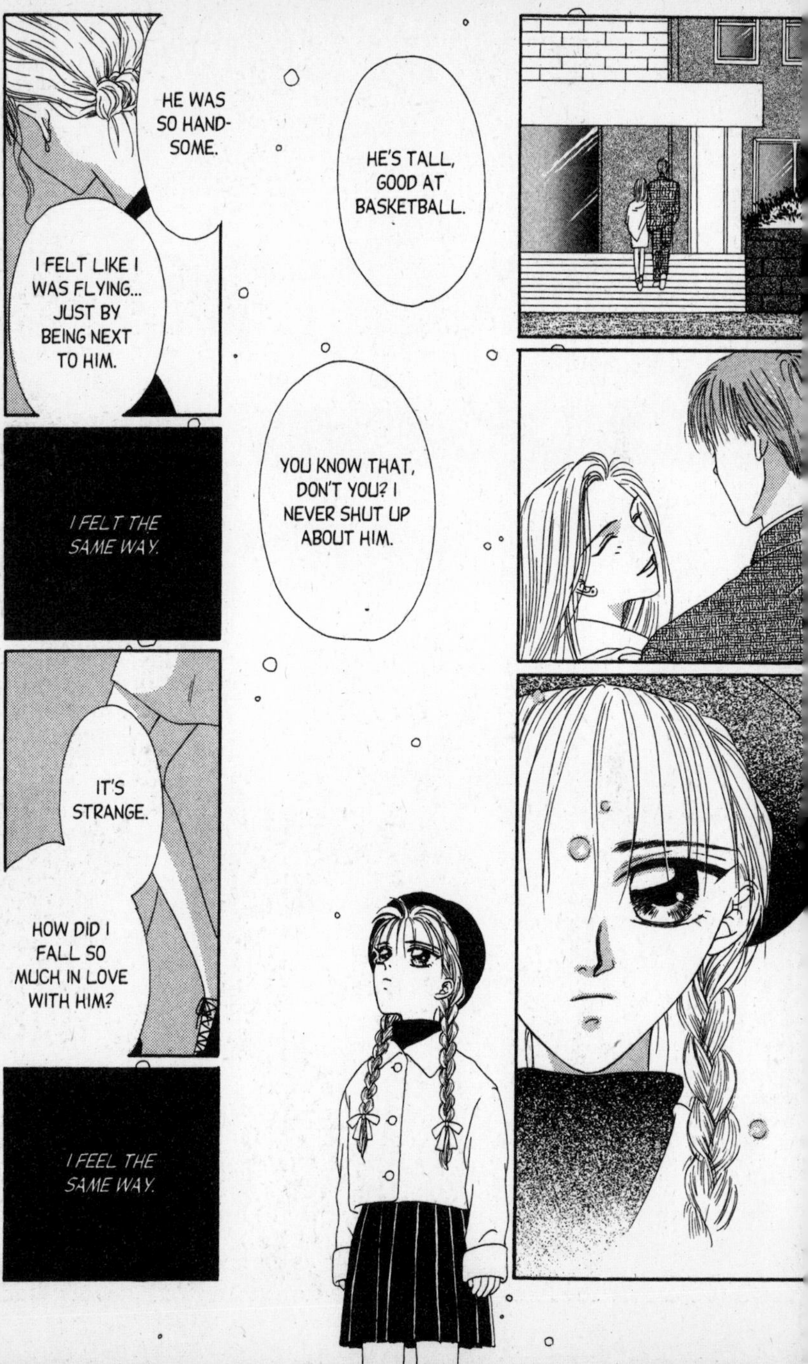
HE'S TALL, GOOD AT BASKETBALL.
YOU KNOW THAT, DON'T YOU? I NEVER SHUT UP ABOUT HIM.
HE WAS SO HAND-SOME.
I FELT LIKE I WAS FLYING... JUST BY BEING NEXT TO HIM.
I FELT THE SAME WAY.
IT'S STRANGE.
HOW DID I FALL SO MUCH IN LOVE WITH HIM?
I FEEL THE SAME WAY.

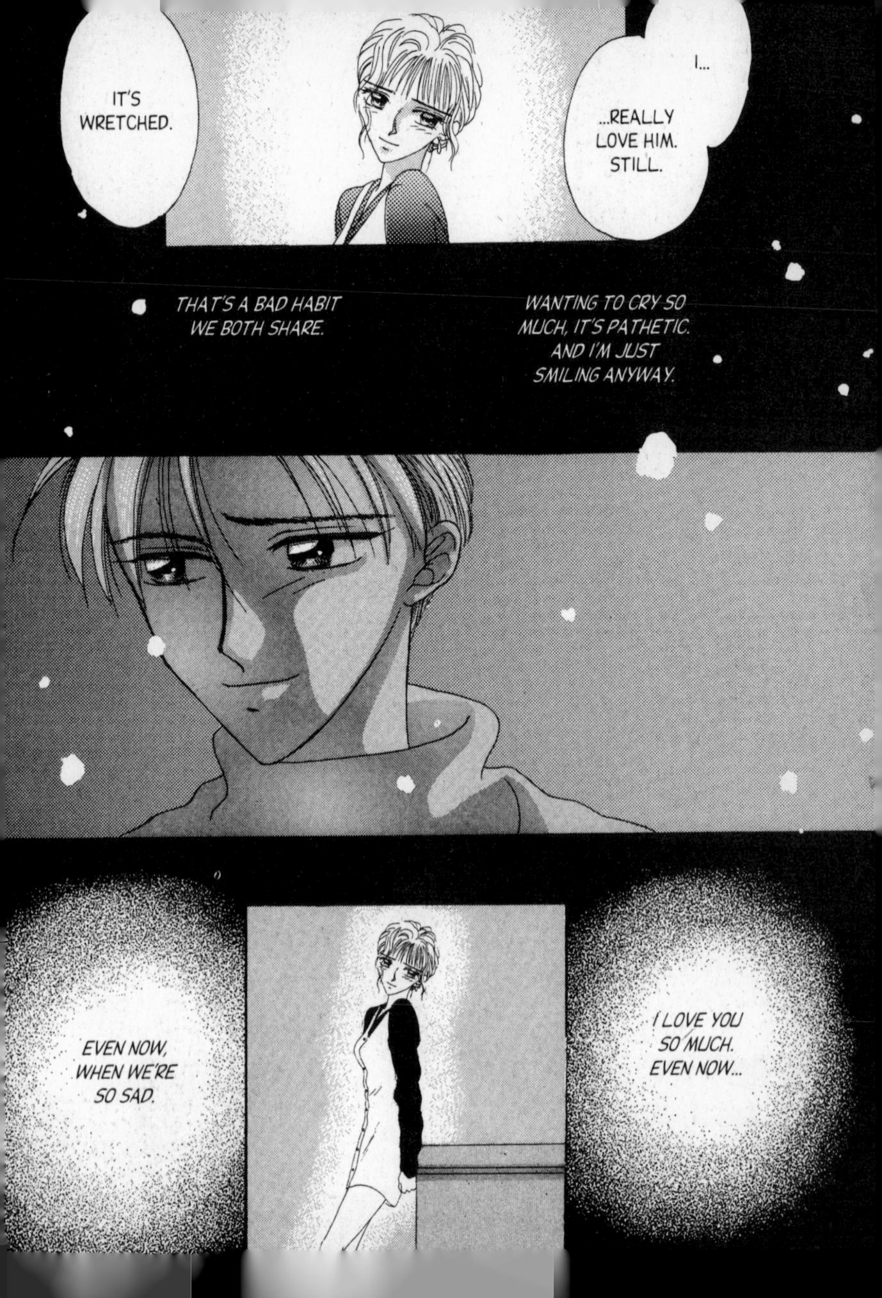
I...
...REALLY LOVE HIM. STILL.
IT'S WRETCHED.
WANTING TO CRY SO MUCH, IT'S PATHETIC. AND I'M JUST SMILING ANYWAY.
THAT'S A BAD HABIT WE BOTH SHARE.
I LOVE YOU SO MUCH. EVEN NOW...
EVEN NOW, WHEN WE'RE SO SAD.

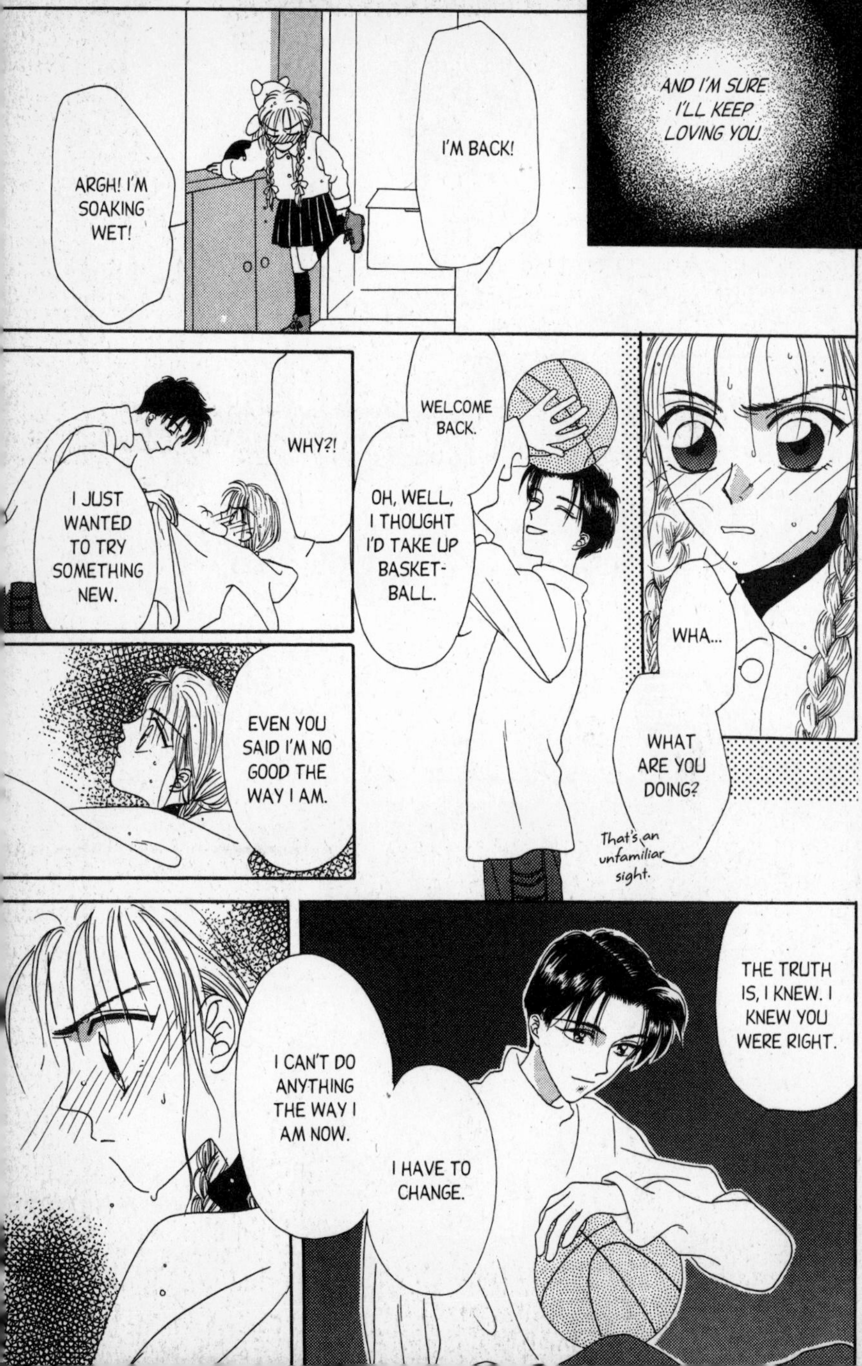
AND I'M SURE I'LL KEEP LOVING YOU.
I'M BACK!
ARGH! I'M SOAKING WET!
WHA...
WHAT ARE YOU DOING?
That's an unfamiliar sight.
WELCOME BACK.
OH, WELL, I THOUGHT I'D TAKE UP BASKET-BALL.
WHY?!
I JUST WANTED TO TRY SOMETHING NEW.
EVEN YOU SAID I'M NO GOOD THE WAY I AM.
THE TRUTH IS, I KNEW. I KNEW YOU WERE RIGHT.
I CAN'T DO ANYTHING THE WAY I AM NOW.
I HAVE TO CHANGE.

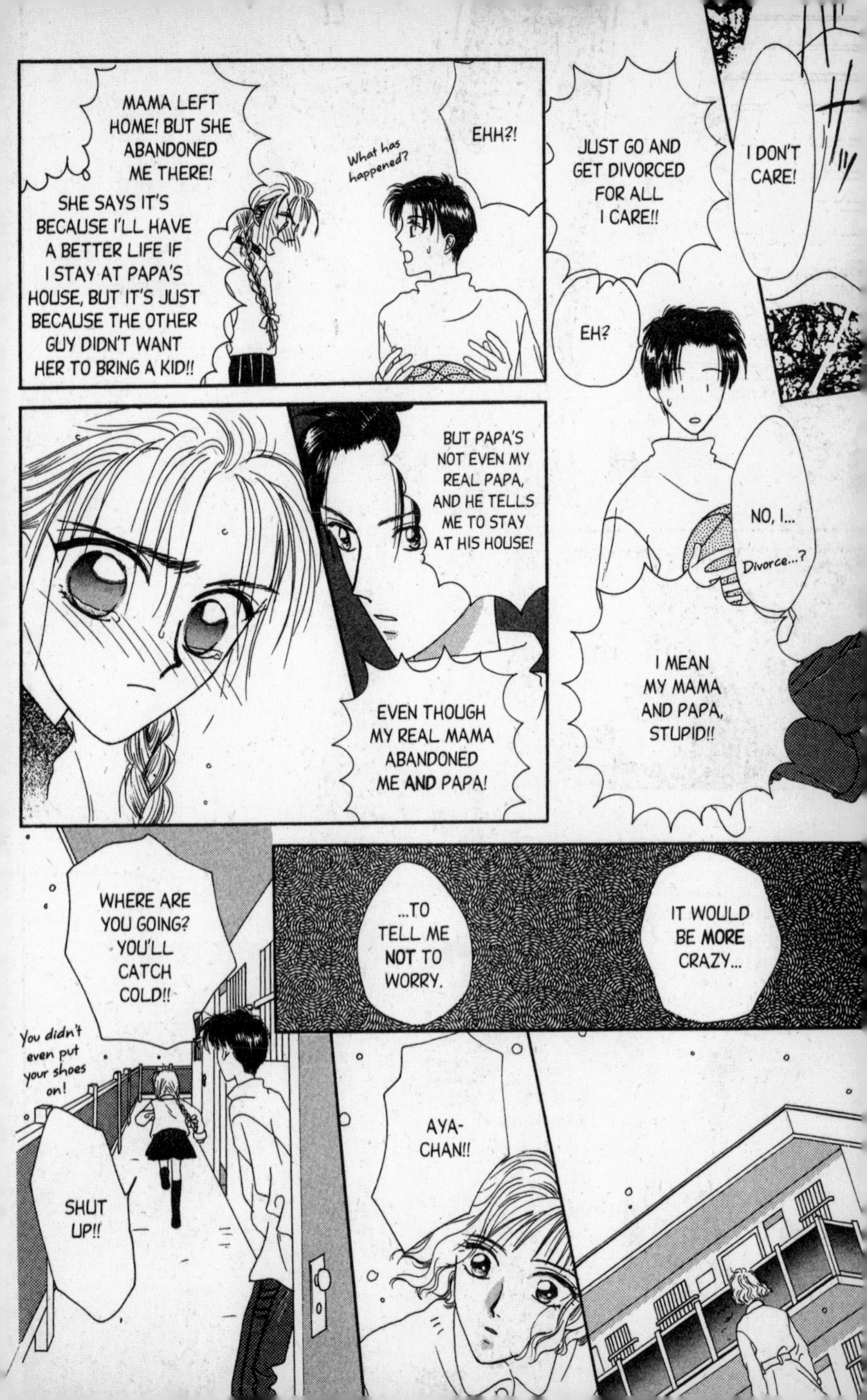
I DON'T CARE!
JUST GO AND GET DIVORCED FOR ALL I CARE!!
EH?
NO, I...
Divorce...?
I MEAN MY MAMA AND PAPA, STUPID!!
EHH?!
What has happened?
MAMA LEFT HOME! BUT SHE ABANDONED ME THERE!
SHE SAYS IT'S BECAUSE I'LL HAVE A BETTER LIFE IF I STAY AT PAPA'S HOUSE, BUT IT'S JUST BECAUSE THE OTHER GUY DIDN'T WANT HER TO BRING A KID!!
BUT PAPA'S NOT EVEN MY REAL PAPA, AND HE TELLS ME TO STAY AT HIS HOUSE!
EVEN THOUGH MY REAL MAMA ABANDONED ME AND PAPA!
IT WOULD BE MORE CRAZY...
...TO TELL ME NOT TO WORRY.
AYA-CHAN!!
WHERE ARE YOU GOING? YOU'LL CATCH COLD!!
You didn't even put your shoes on!
SHUT UP!!

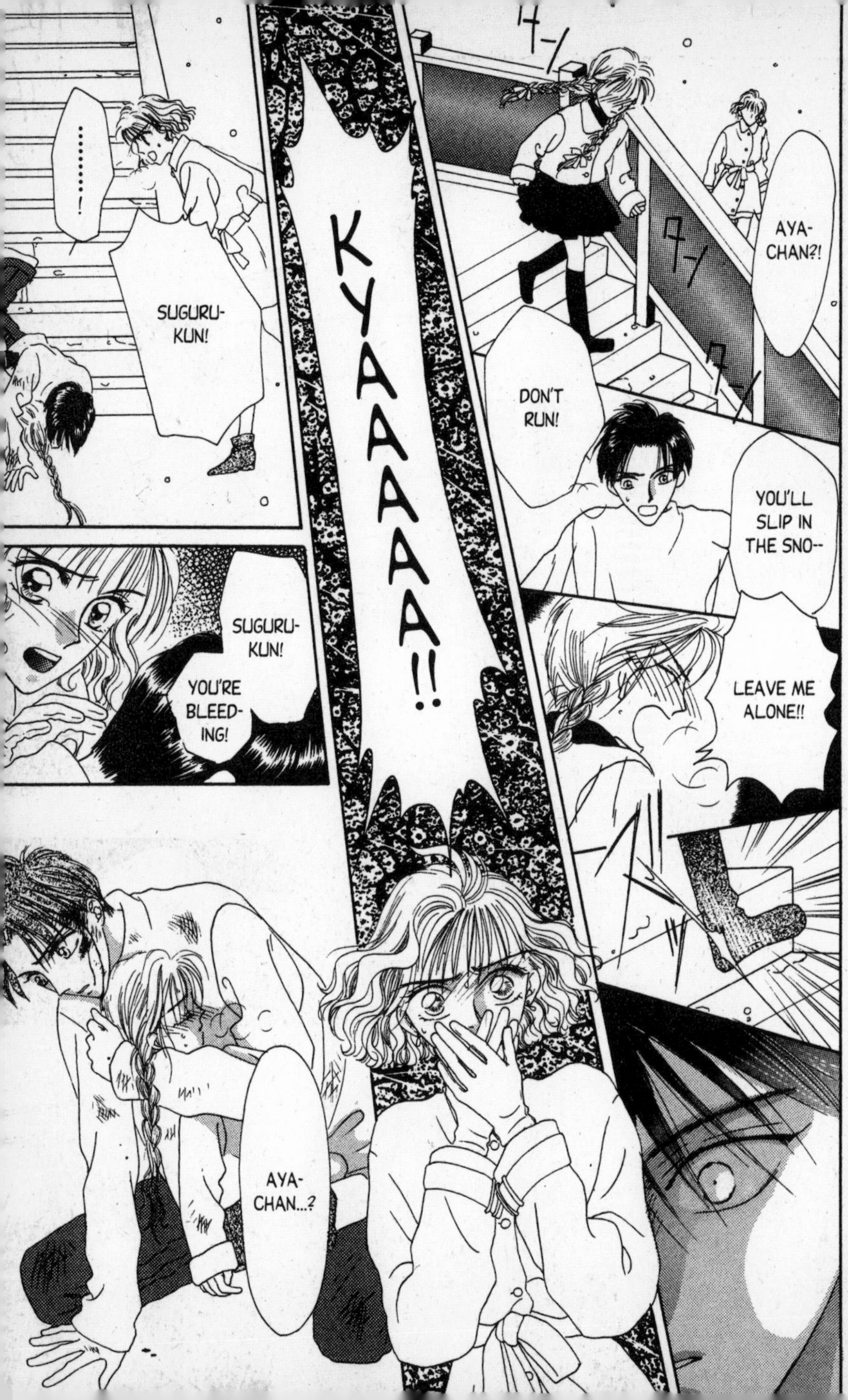
AYA-CHAN?!
DON'T RUN!
YOU'LL SLIP IN THE SNO--
LEAVE ME ALONE!!
KYAAAAA!!
......!
SUGURU-KUN!
SUGURU-KUN! YOU'RE BLEEDING!
AYA-CHAN...?

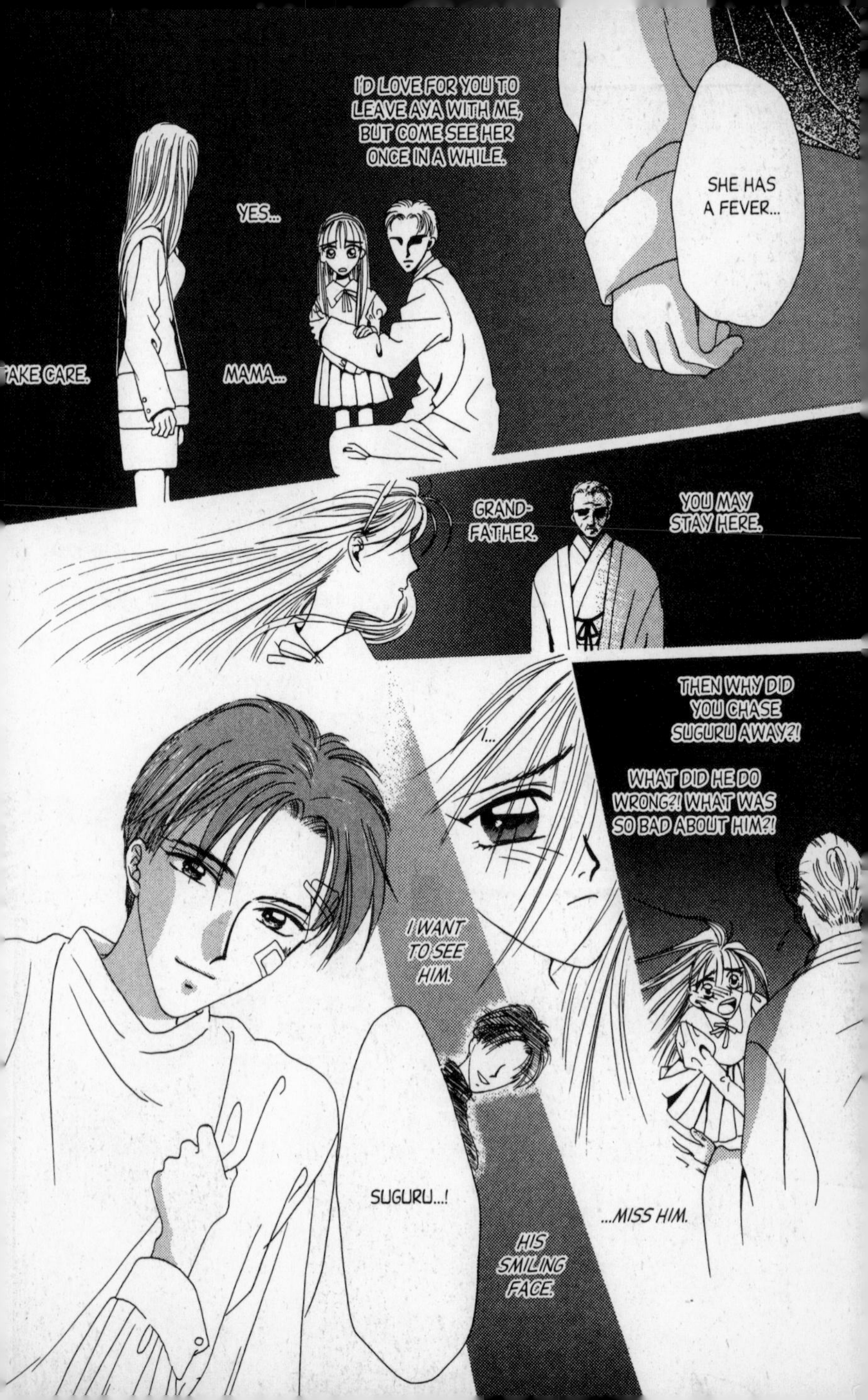
SHE HAS A FEVER...
I'D LOVE FOR YOU TO LEAVE AYA WITH ME, BUT COME SEE HER ONCE IN A WHILE.
YES...
MAMA...
TAKE CARE.
YOU MAY STAY HERE.
GRAND-FATHER.
THEN WHY DID YOU CHASE SUGURU AWAY?!
WHAT DID HE DO WRONG?! WHAT WAS SO BAD ABOUT HIM?!
I...
...MISS HIM.
I WANT TO SEE HIM.
HIS SMILING FACE.
SUGURU...!

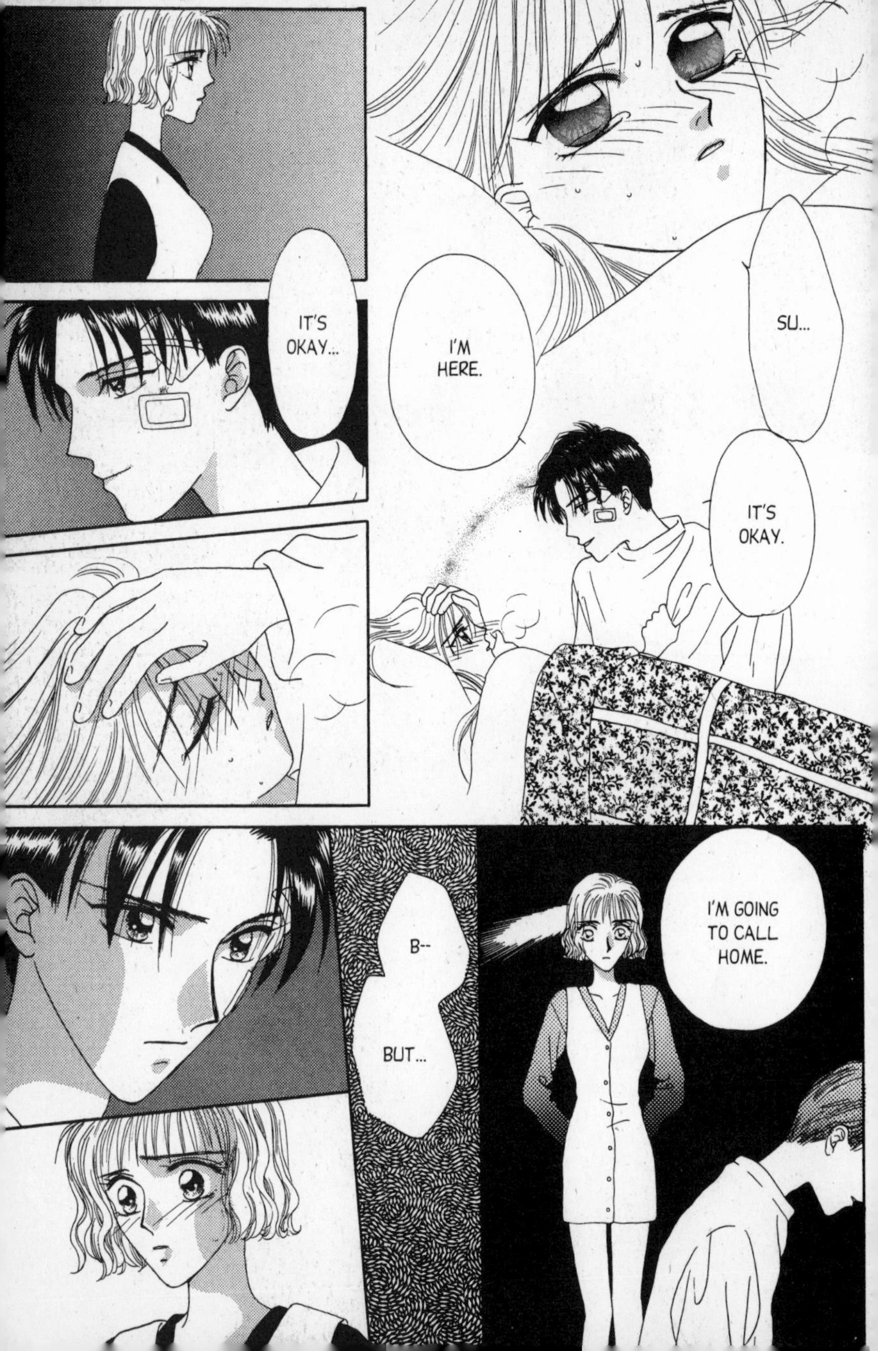
SU...
I'M HERE.
IT'S OKAY.
IT'S OKAY...
I'M GOING TO CALL HOME.
B--
BUT...

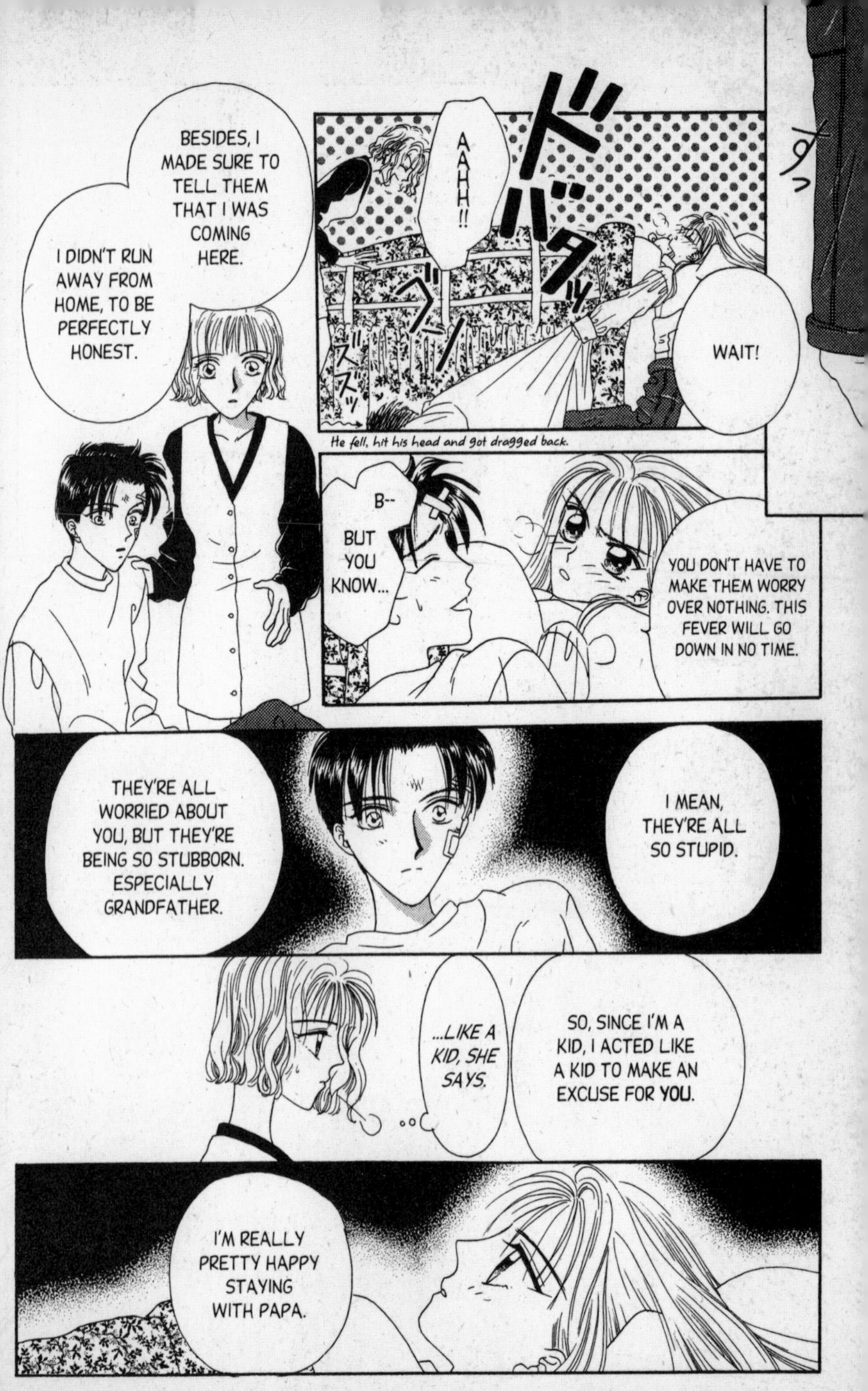
すっ
WAIT!
AAHH!!
ドバタッ
ゴン
ズズッ
He fell, hit his head and got dragged back.
YOU DON'T HAVE TO MAKE THEM WORRY OVER NOTHING. THIS FEVER WILL GO DOWN IN NO TIME.
B-- BUT YOU KNOW...
I DIDN'T RUN AWAY FROM HOME, TO BE PERFECTLY HONEST.
BESIDES, I MADE SURE TO TELL THEM THAT I WAS COMING HERE.
I MEAN, THEY'RE ALL SO STUPID.
THEY'RE ALL WORRIED ABOUT YOU, BUT THEY'RE BEING SO STUBBORN. ESPECIALLY GRANDFATHER.
SO, SINCE I'M A KID, I ACTED LIKE A KID TO MAKE AN EXCUSE FOR YOU.
...LIKE A KID, SHE SAYS.
I'M REALLY PRETTY HAPPY STAYING WITH PAPA.

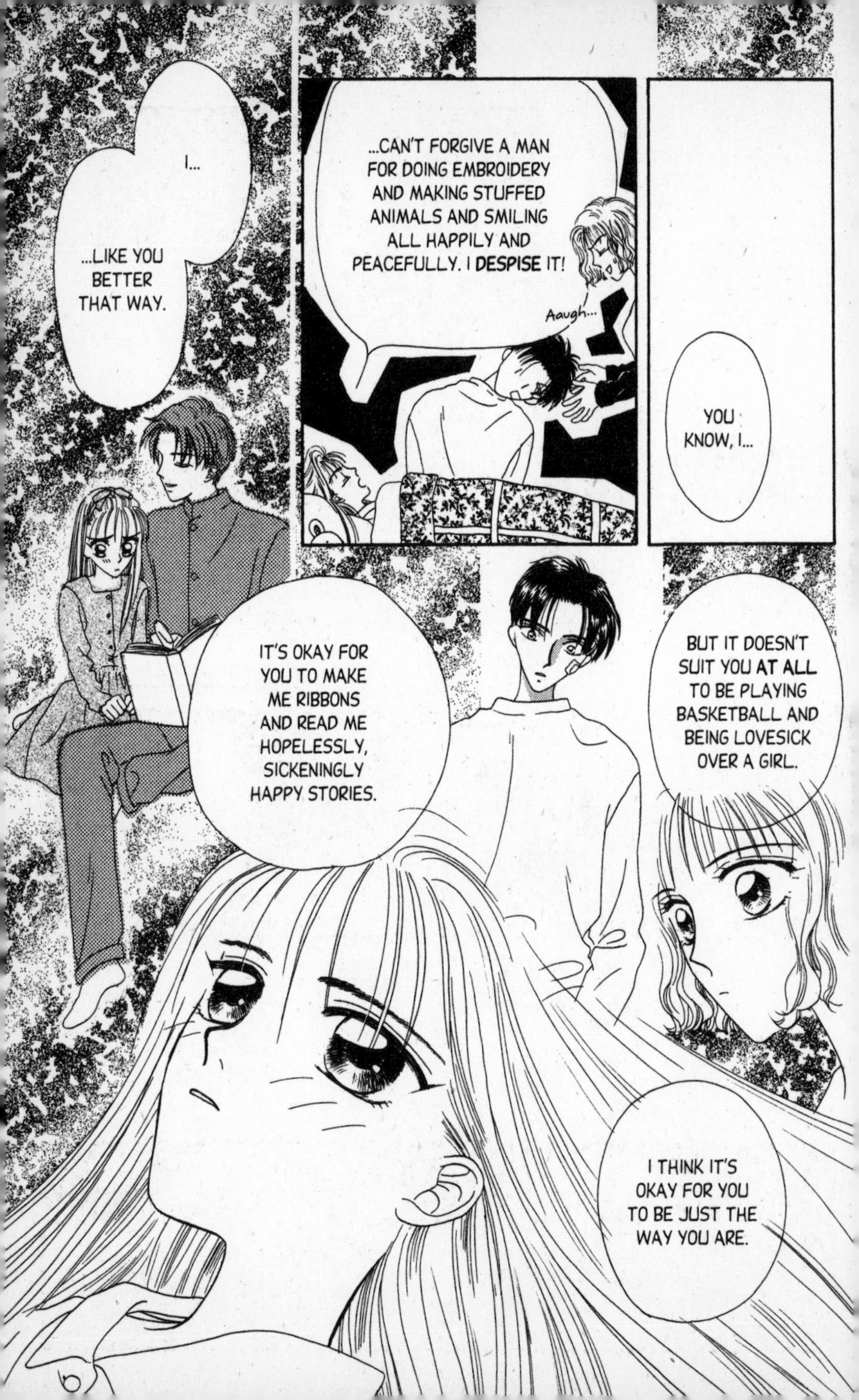
YOU KNOW, I...
...CAN'T FORGIVE A MAN FOR DOING EMBROIDERY AND MAKING STUFFED ANIMALS AND SMILING ALL HAPPILY AND PEACEFULLY. I DESPISE IT!
Aaugh...
BUT IT DOESN'T SUIT YOU AT ALL TO BE PLAYING BASKETBALL AND BEING LOVESICK OVER A GIRL.
IT'S OKAY FOR YOU TO MAKE ME RIBBONS AND READ ME HOPELESSLY, SICKENINGLY HAPPY STORIES.
I...
...LIKE YOU BETTER THAT WAY.
I THINK IT'S OKAY FOR YOU TO BE JUST THE WAY YOU ARE.

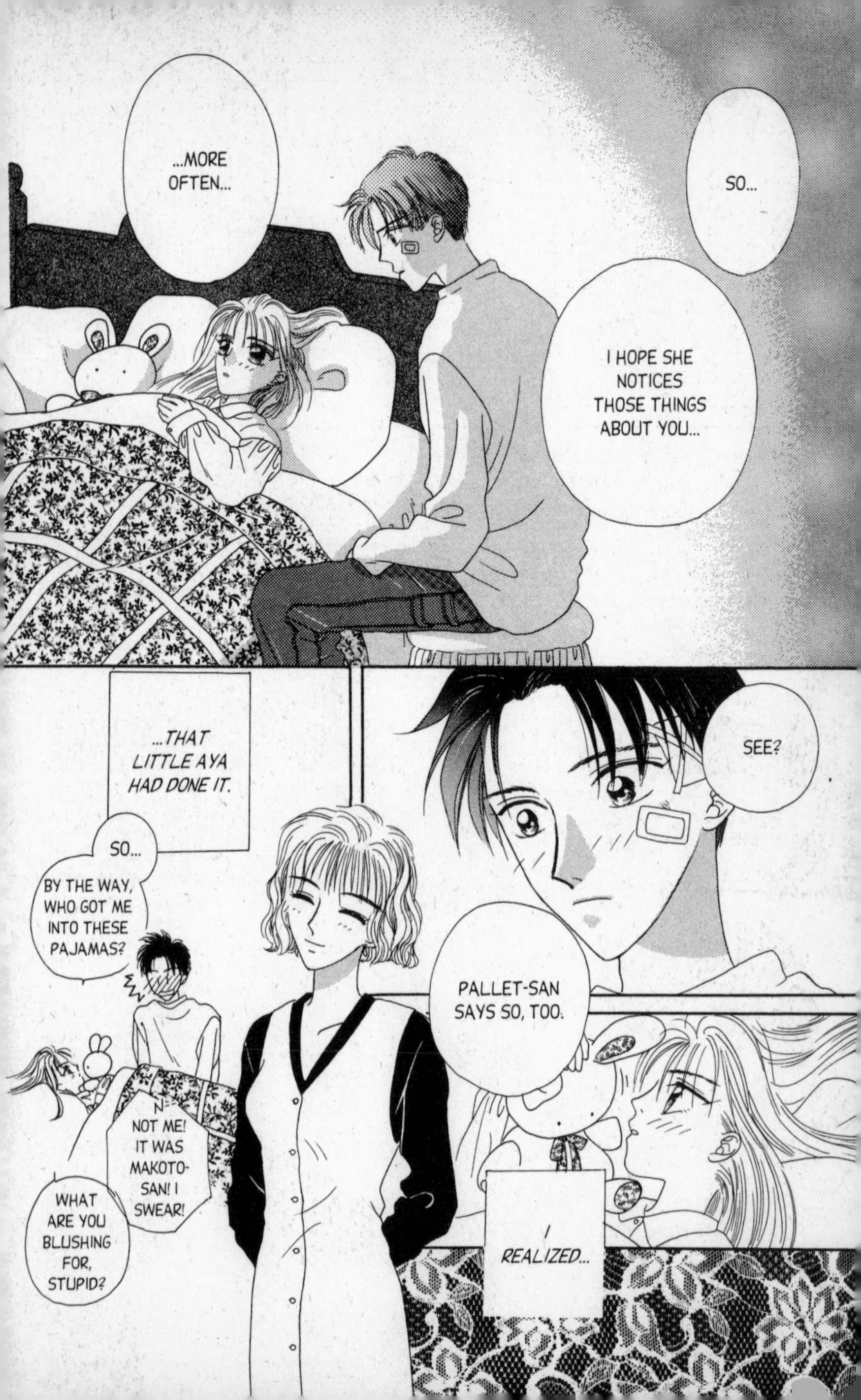
SO...
I HOPE SHE NOTICES THOSE THINGS ABOUT YOU...
...MORE OFTEN...
SEE?
PALLET-SAN SAYS SO, TOO.
I REALIZED...
...THAT LITTLE AYA HAD DONE IT.
SO...
BY THE WAY, WHO GOT ME INTO THESE PAJAMAS?
N- NOT ME! IT WAS MAKOTO-SAN! I SWEAR!
WHAT ARE YOU BLUSHING FOR, STUPID?

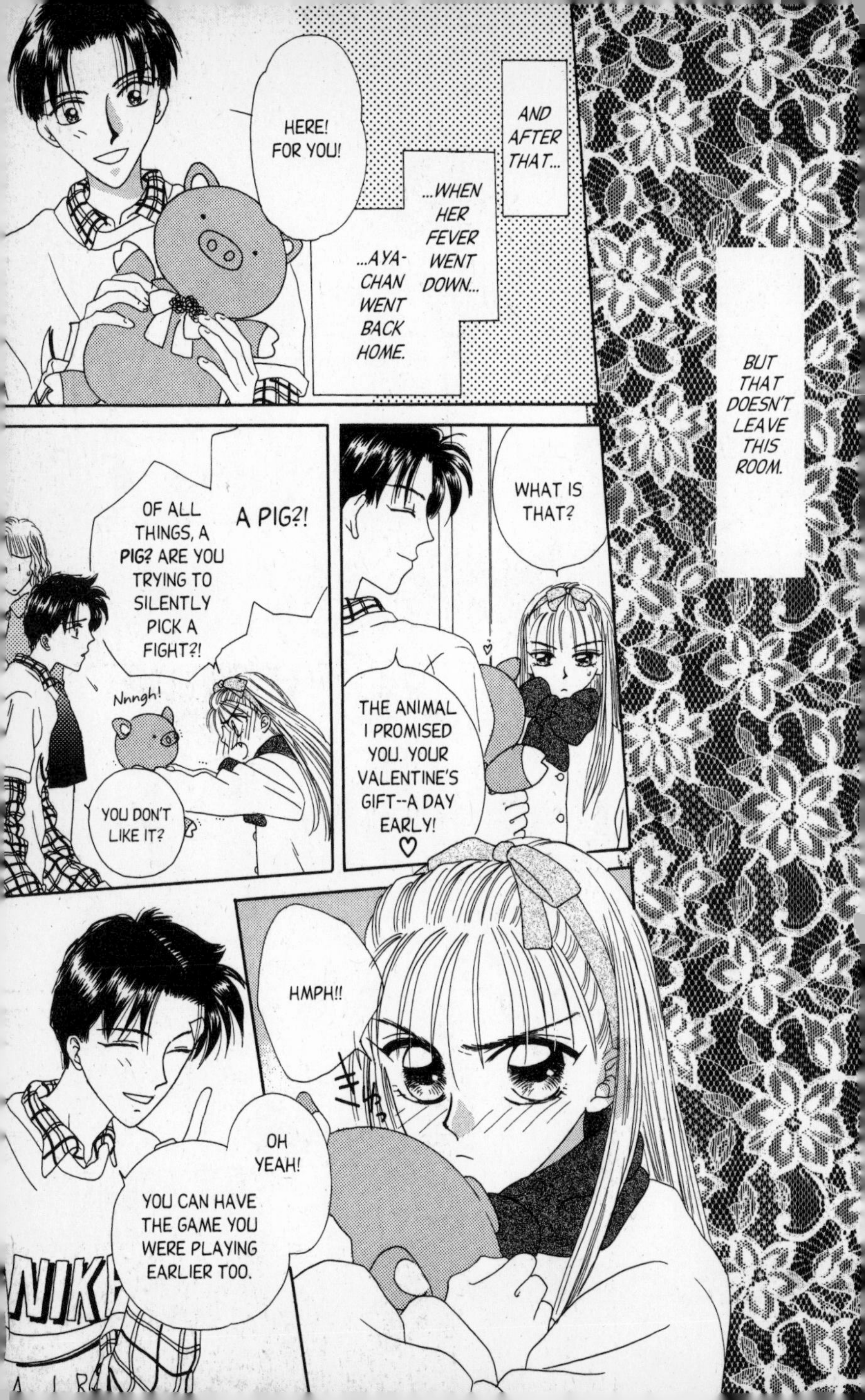
BUT THAT DOESN'T LEAVE THIS ROOM.
AND AFTER THAT...
...WHEN HER FEVER WENT DOWN...
...AYA-CHAN WENT BACK HOME.
HERE! FOR YOU!
WHAT IS THAT?
THE ANIMAL I PROMISED YOU. YOUR VALENTINE'S GIFT--A DAY EARLY! ♡
A PIG?!
OF ALL THINGS, A PIG? ARE YOU TRYING TO SILENTLY PICK A FIGHT?!
Nnngh!
YOU DON'T LIKE IT?
HMPH!!
OH YEAH!
YOU CAN HAVE THE GAME YOU WERE PLAYING EARLIER TOO.

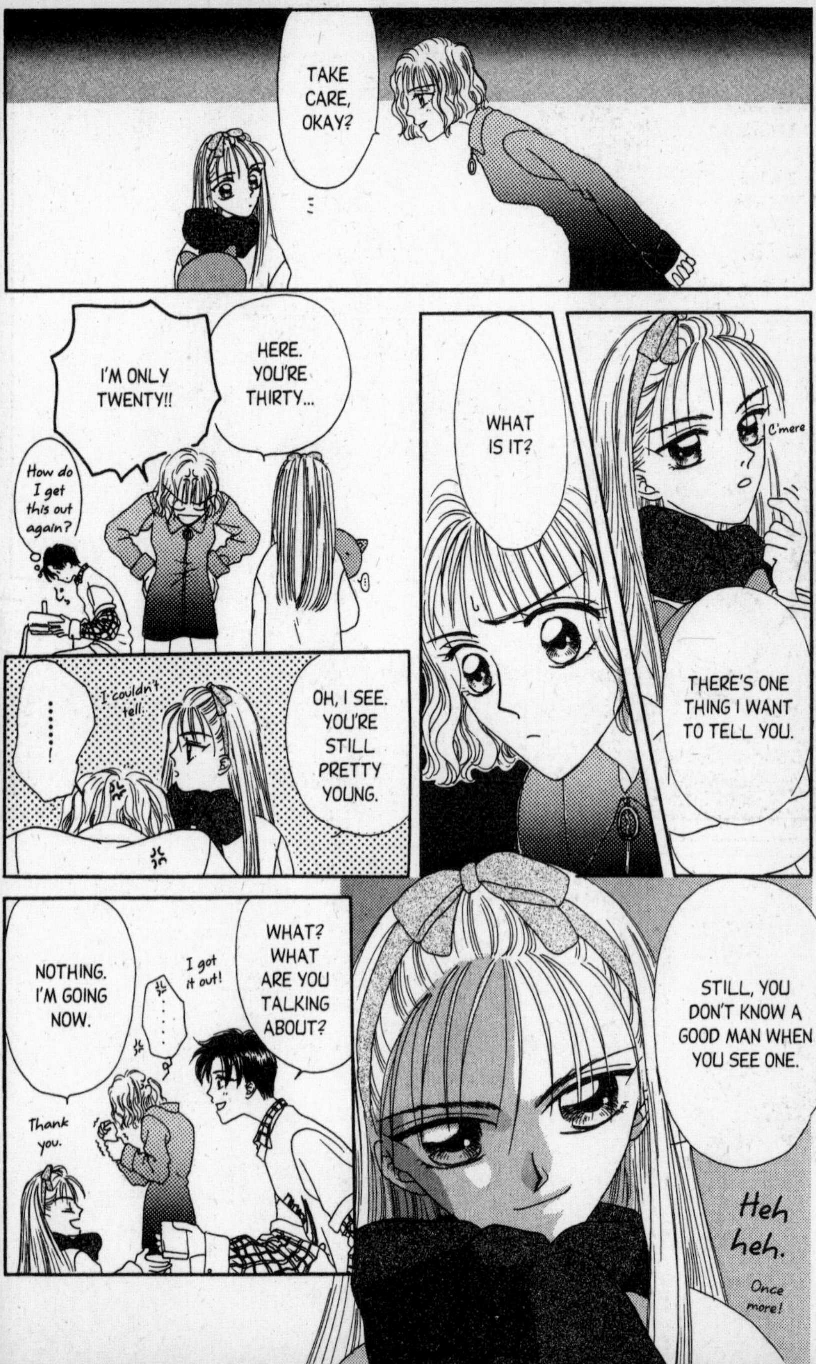

TAKE CARE, OKAY?
C'mere
THERE'S ONE THING I WANT TO TELL YOU.
WHAT IS IT?
HERE. YOU'RE THIRTY...
I'M ONLY TWENTY!!
How do I get this out again?
OH, I SEE. YOU'RE STILL PRETTY YOUNG.
I couldn't tell.
......!
STILL, YOU DON'T KNOW A GOOD MAN WHEN YOU SEE ONE.
Heh heh.
Once more!
WHAT? WHAT ARE YOU TALKING ABOUT?
I got it out!
NOTHING. I'M GOING NOW.
Thank you.

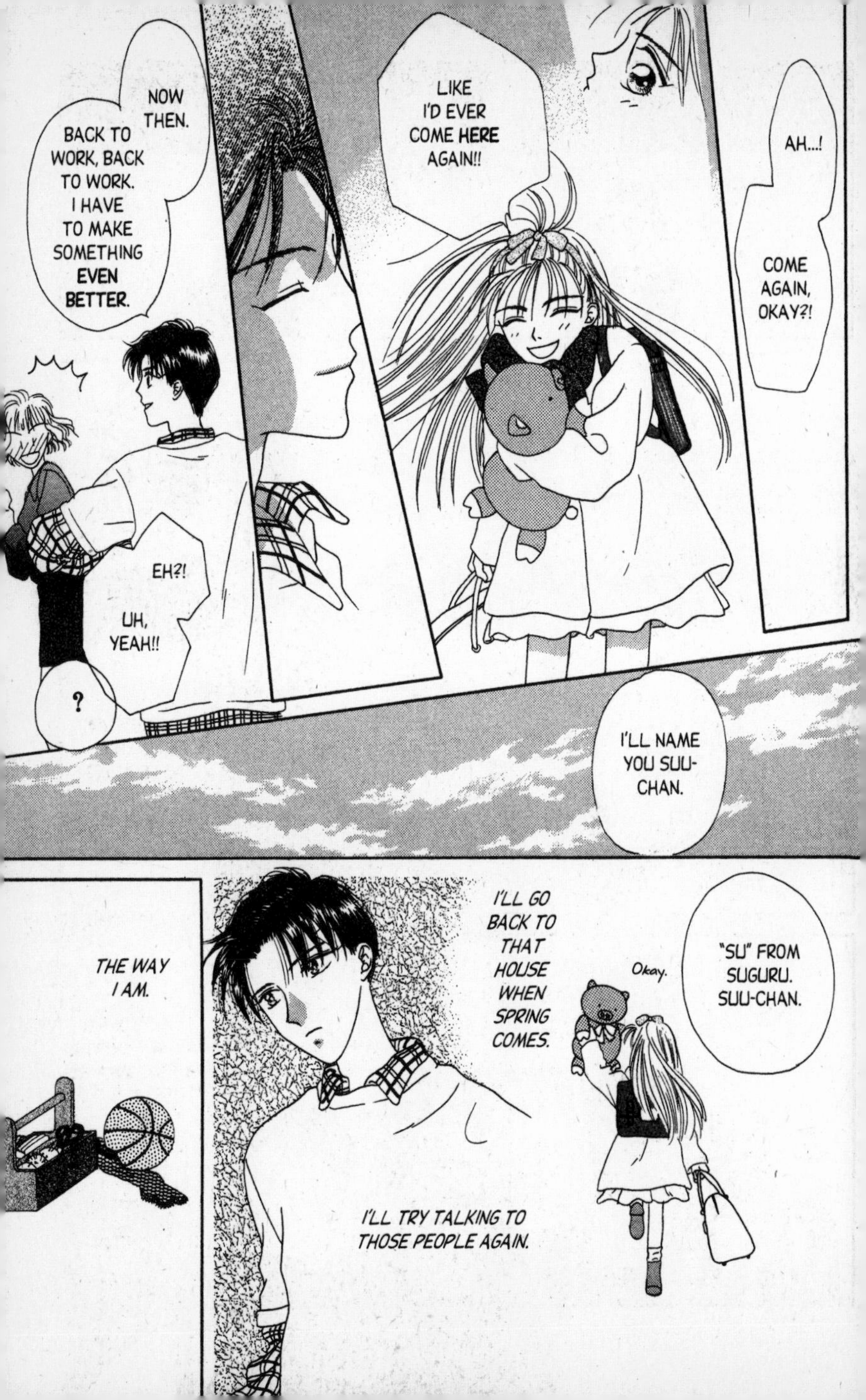
AH...!
COME AGAIN, OKAY?!
LIKE I'D EVER COME HERE AGAIN!!
NOW THEN.
BACK TO WORK, BACK TO WORK. I HAVE TO MAKE SOMETHING EVEN BETTER.
EH?!
UH, YEAH!!
?
I'LL NAME YOU SUU-CHAN.
"SU" FROM SUGURU. SUU-CHAN.
Okay.
I'LL GO BACK TO THAT HOUSE WHEN SPRING COMES.
I'LL TRY TALKING TO THOSE PEOPLE AGAIN.
THE WAY I AM.

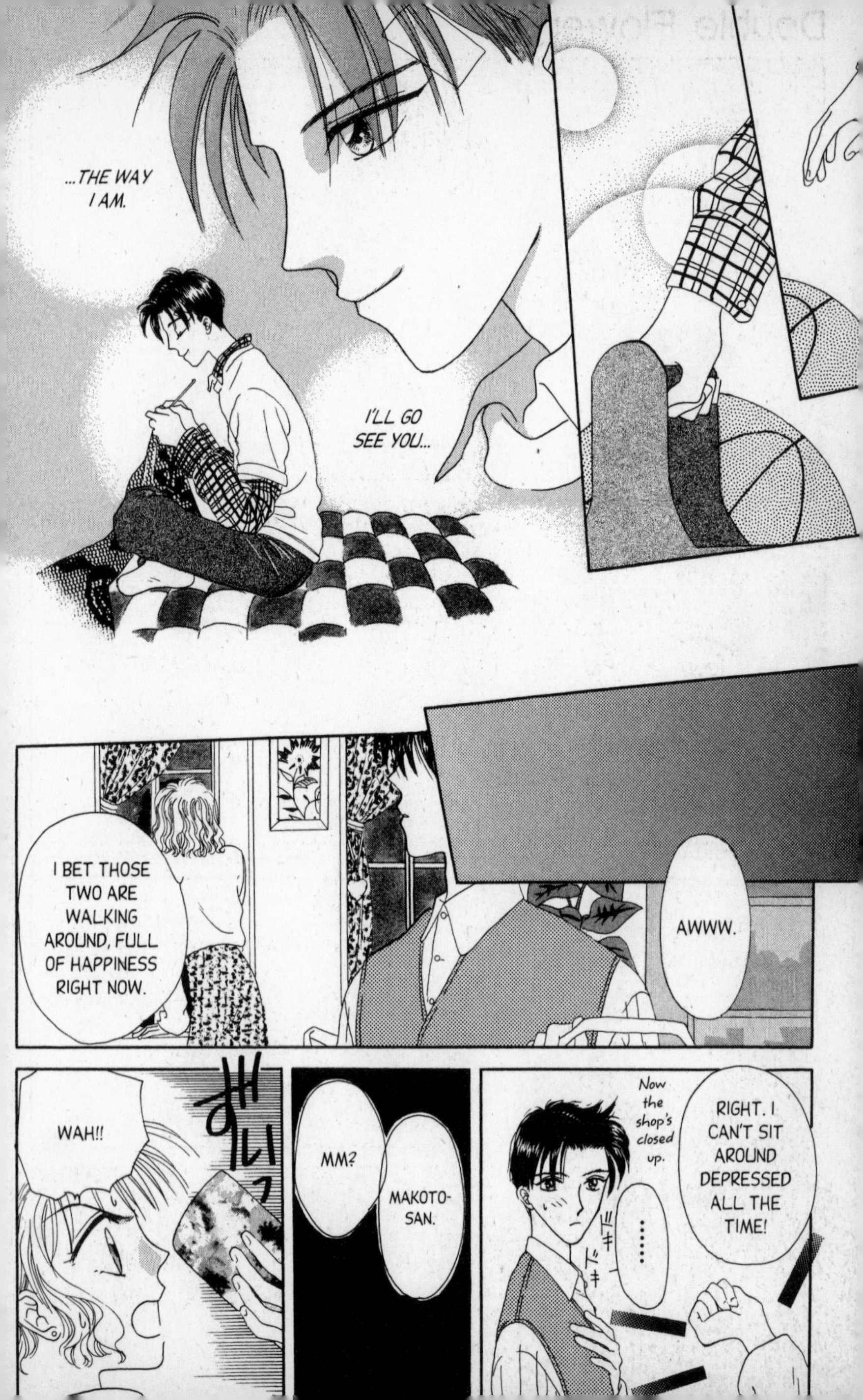
I'LL GO SEE YOU...
...THE WAY I AM.
AWWW.
I BET THOSE TWO ARE WALKING AROUND, FULL OF HAPPINESS RIGHT NOW.
RIGHT. I CAN'T SIT AROUND DEPRESSED ALL THE TIME!
Now the shop's closed up.
......
ドキドキ
MAKOTO-SAN.
MM?
WAH!!

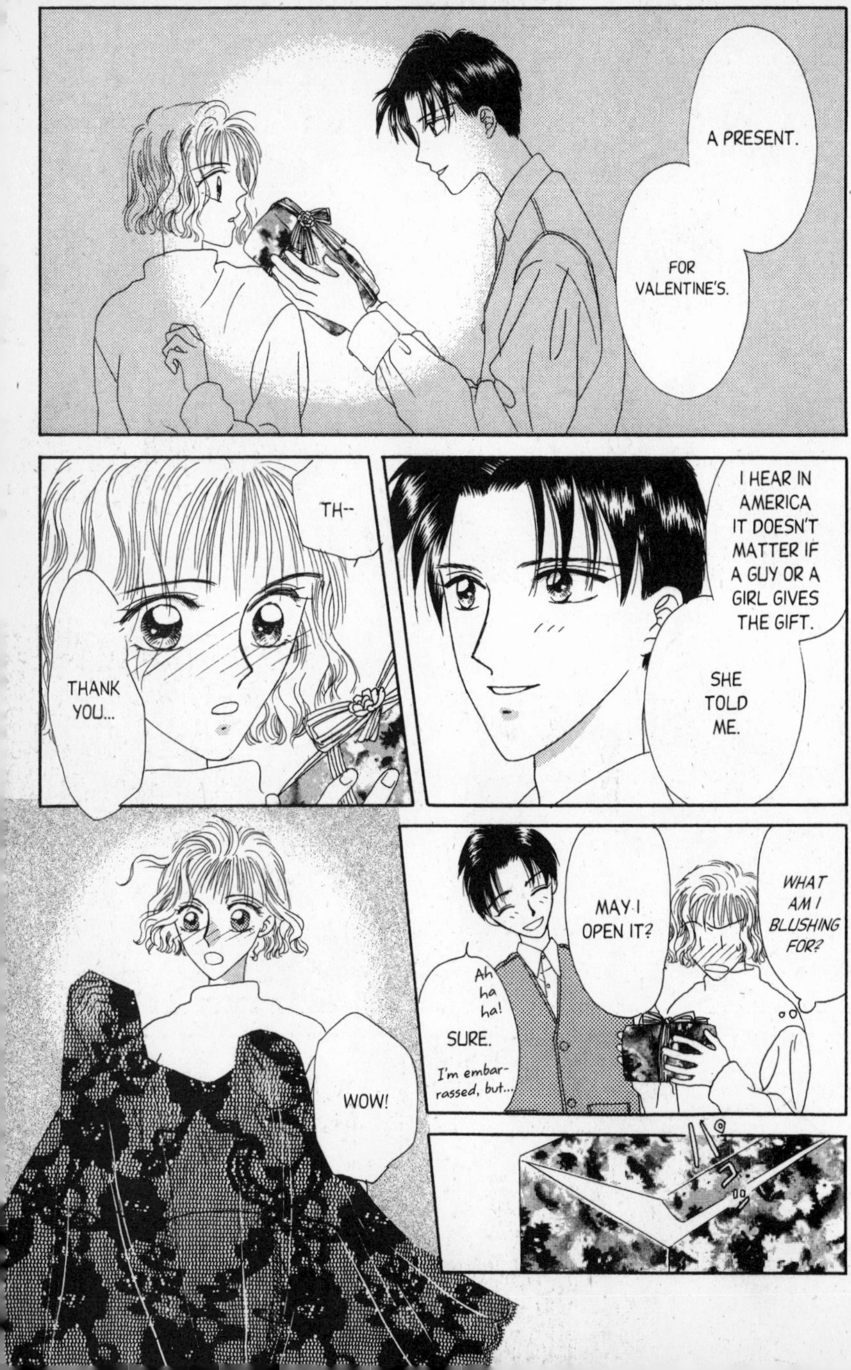
A PRESENT.
FOR VALENTINE'S.
I HEAR IN AMERICA IT DOESN'T MATTER IF A GUY OR A GIRL GIVES THE GIFT.
SHE TOLD ME.
TH--
THANK YOU...
WHAT AM I BLUSHING FOR?
MAY I OPEN IT?
Ah ha ha!
SURE.
I'm embarrassed, but...
WOW!

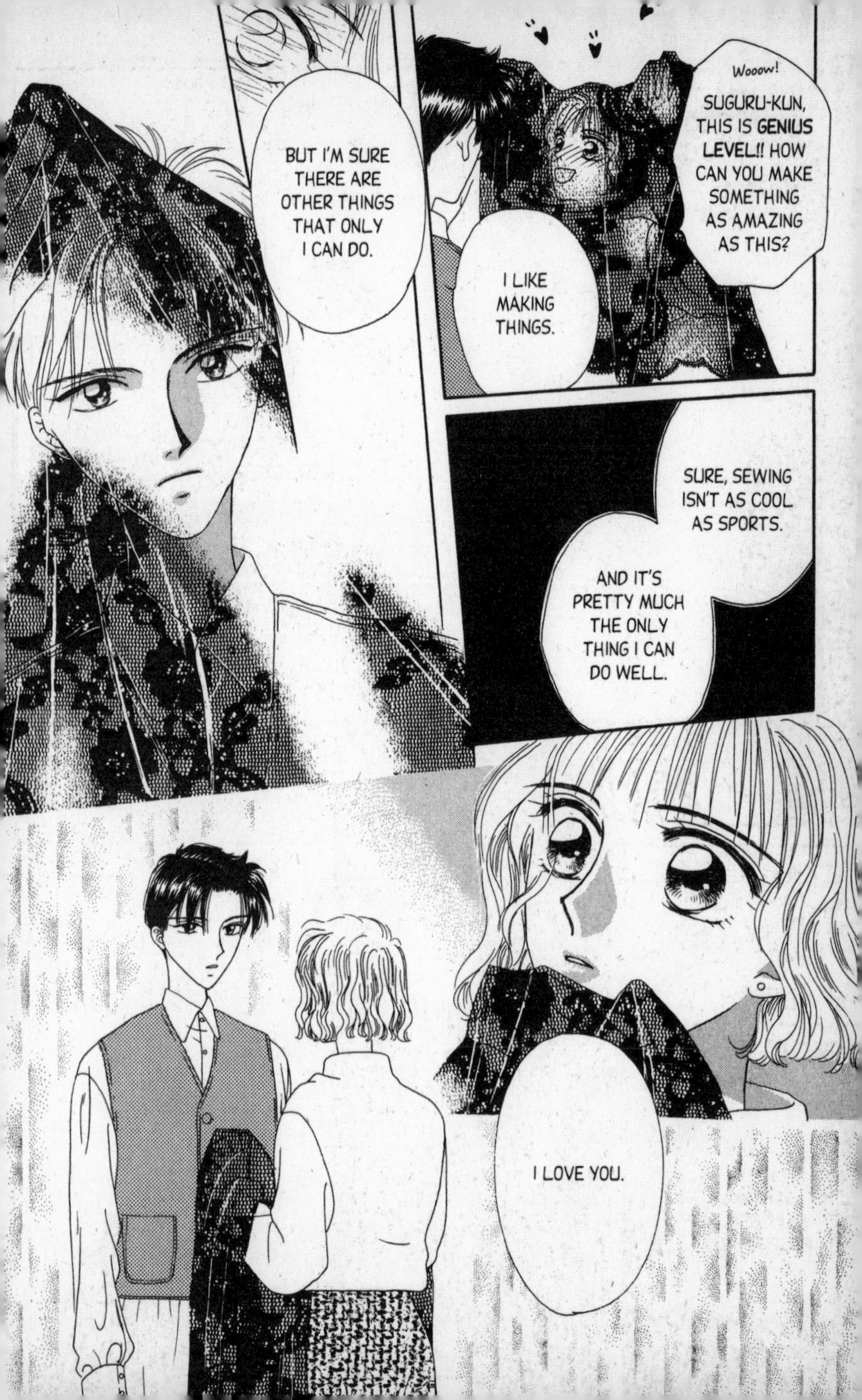
Wooow!
SUGURU-KUN, THIS IS GENIUS LEVEL!! HOW CAN YOU MAKE SOMETHING AS AMAZING AS THIS?
I LIKE MAKING THINGS.
SURE, SEWING ISN'T AS COOL AS SPORTS.
AND IT'S PRETTY MUCH THE ONLY THING I CAN DO WELL.
BUT I'M SURE THERE ARE OTHER THINGS THAT ONLY I CAN DO.
I LOVE YOU.

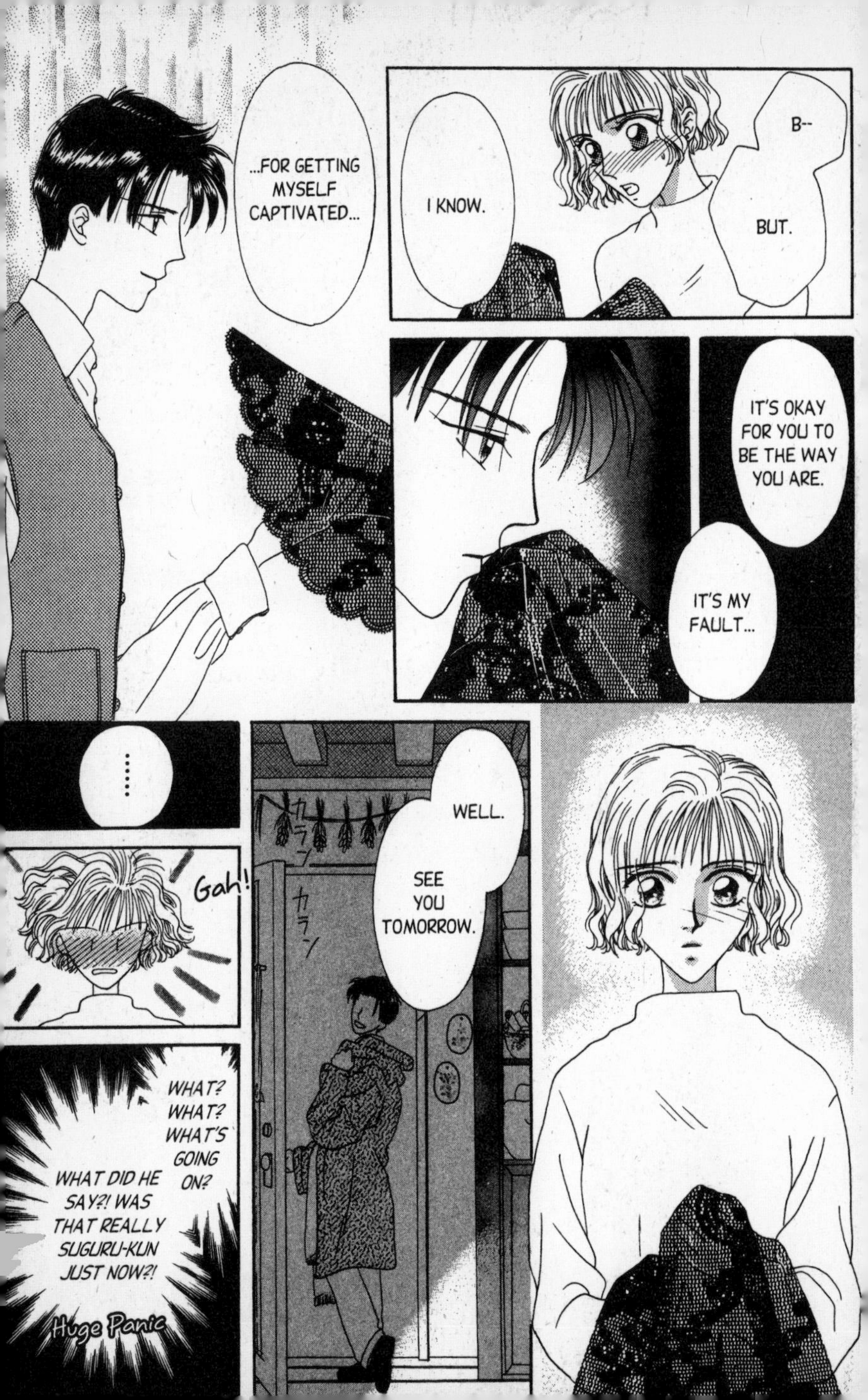
B--
BUT.
I KNOW.
IT'S OKAY FOR YOU TO BE THE WAY YOU ARE.
IT'S MY FAULT...
...FOR GETTING MYSELF CAPTIVATED...
WELL.
SEE YOU TOMORROW.
カラン
カラン
......
Gah!
WHAT? WHAT? WHAT'S GOING ON?
WHAT DID HE SAY?! WAS THAT REALLY SUGURU-KUN JUST NOW?!
Huge Panic

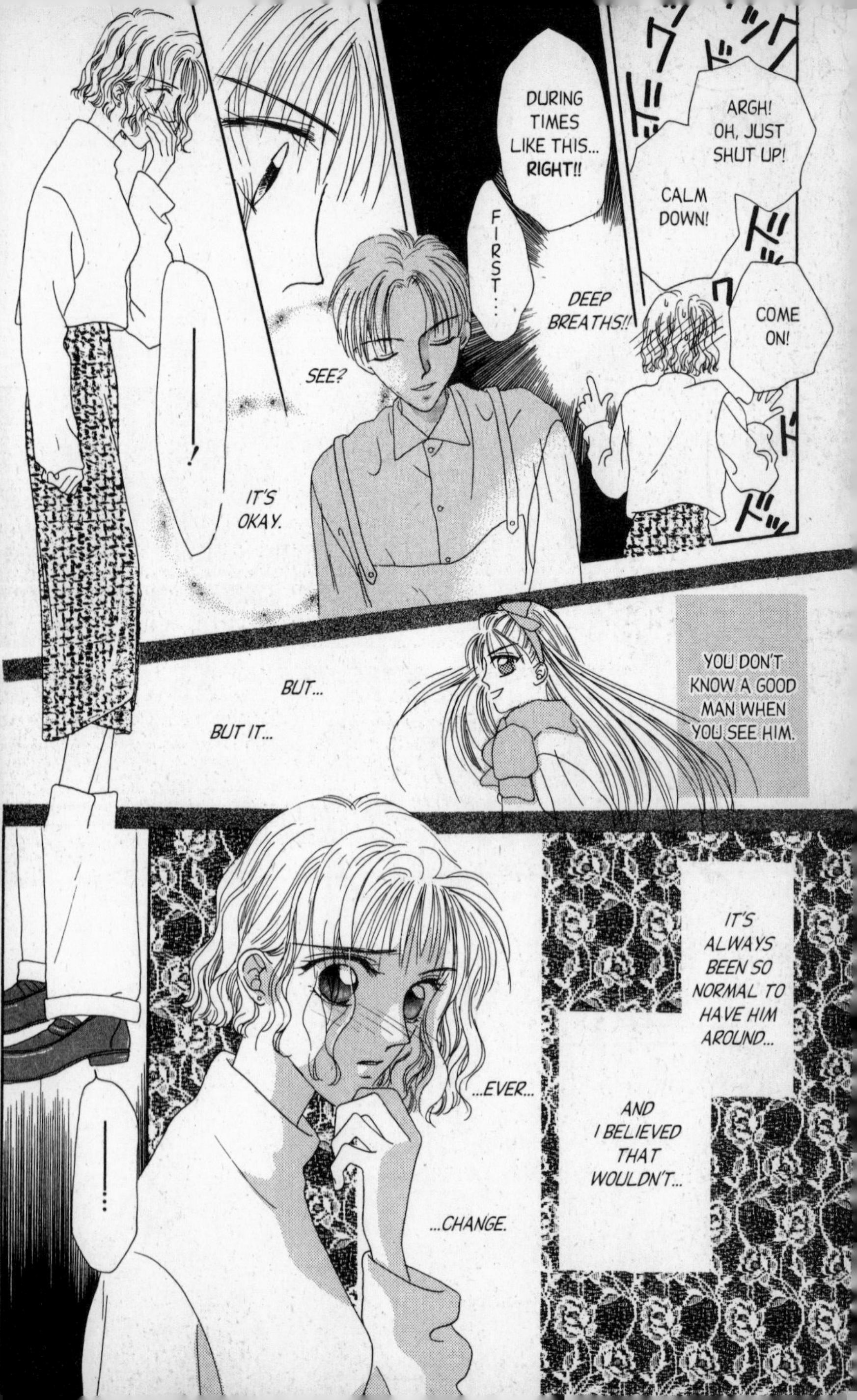

ARGH! OH, JUST SHUT UP!
CALM DOWN!
COME ON!
DEEP BREATHS!!
DURING TIMES LIKE THIS... RIGHT!!
FIRST...
SEE?
IT'S OKAY.
—!
YOU DON'T KNOW A GOOD MAN WHEN YOU SEE HIM.
BUT...
BUT IT...
IT'S ALWAYS BEEN SO NORMAL TO HAVE HIM AROUND...
AND I BELIEVED THAT WOULDN'T...
...EVER...
...CHANGE.
—....

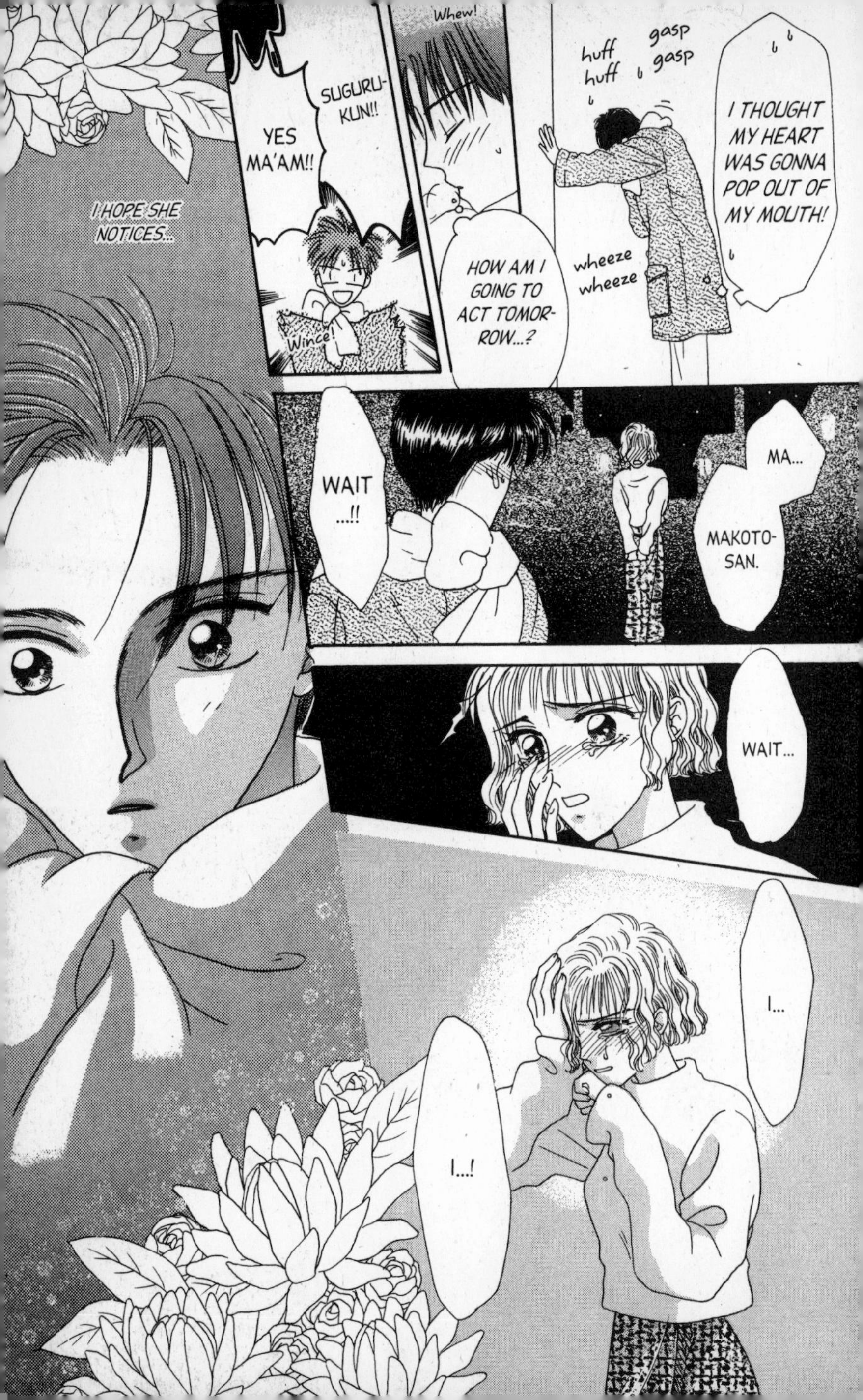
huff huff
gasp gasp
I THOUGHT MY HEART WAS GONNA POP OUT OF MY MOUTH!
wheeze wheeze
HOW AM I GOING TO ACT TOMORROW...?
Whew!
SUGURU-KUN!!
YES MA'AM!!
Wince!
MA... MAKOTO-SAN.
WAIT ...!!
WAIT...
I...
I...!
I HOPE SHE NOTICES...

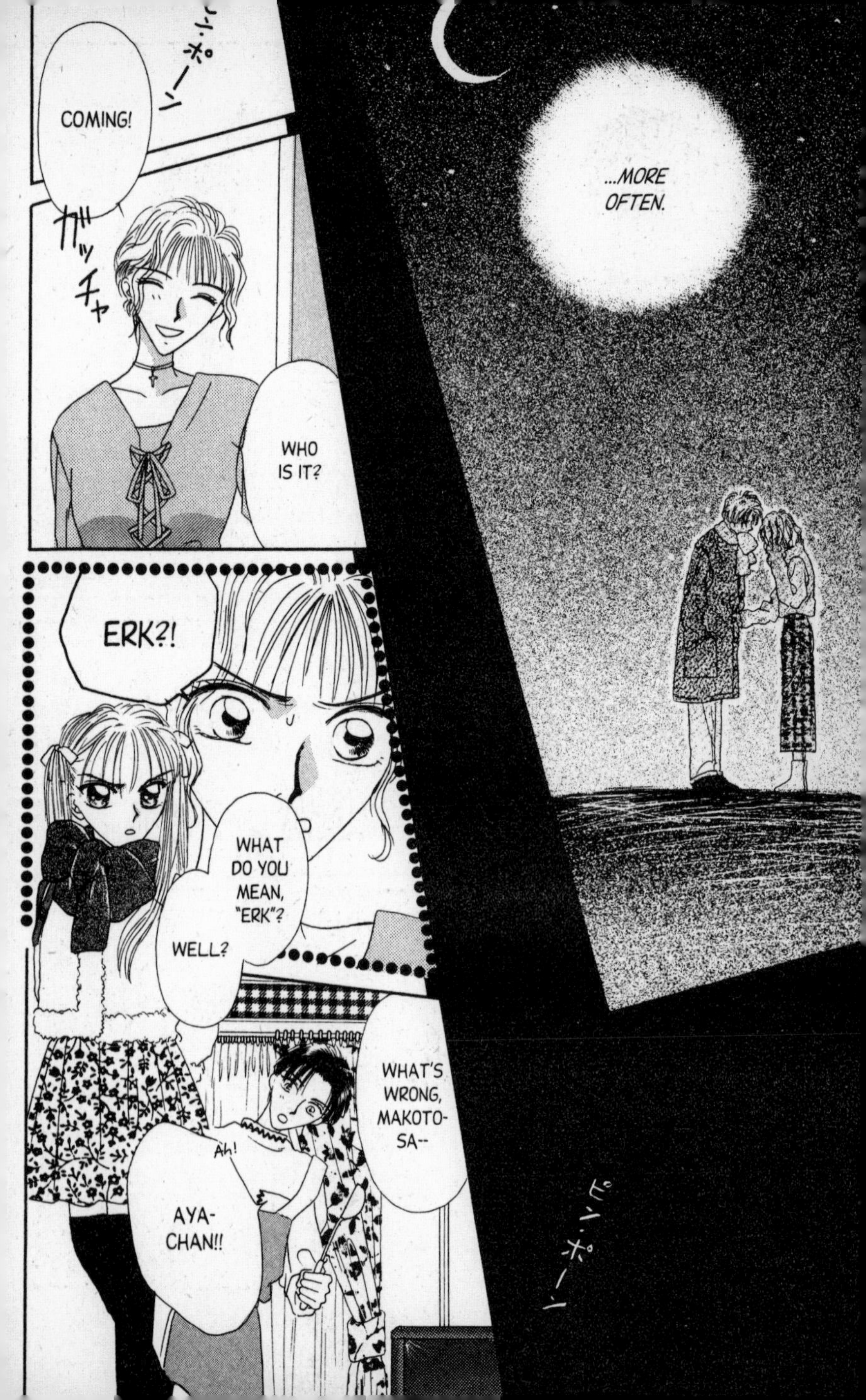
...MORE OFTEN.
ピン・ポーン
ン・ポーン
COMING!
ガッチャ
WHO IS IT?
ERK?!
WHAT DO YOU MEAN, "ERK"?
WELL?
WHAT'S WRONG, MAKOTO-SA--
Ah!
AYA-CHAN!!

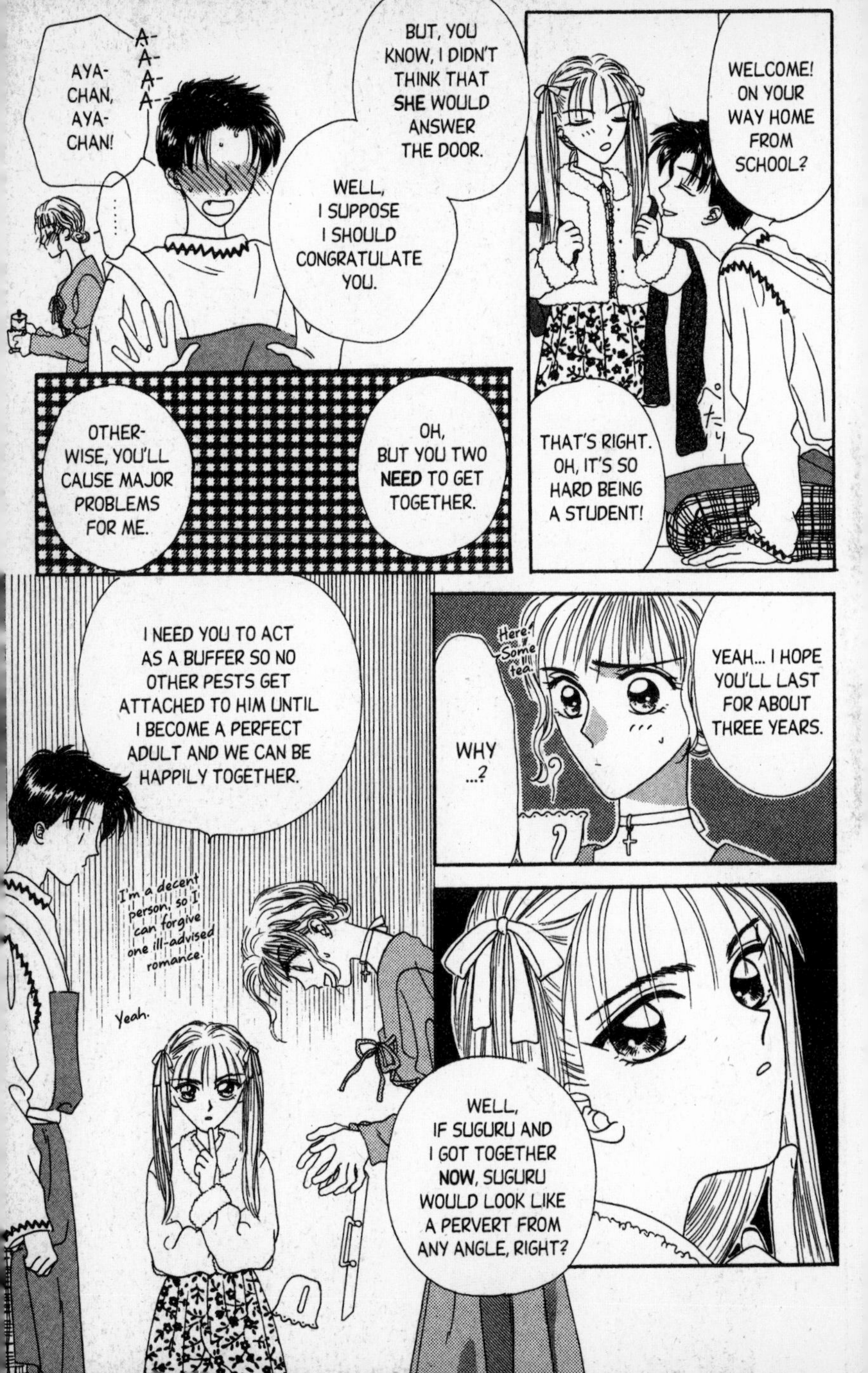

WELCOME! ON YOUR WAY HOME FROM SCHOOL?
THAT'S RIGHT. OH, IT'S SO HARD BEING A STUDENT!
BUT, YOU KNOW, I DIDN'T THINK THAT SHE WOULD ANSWER THE DOOR.
WELL, I SUPPOSE I SHOULD CONGRATULATE YOU.
A-A-A-A--
AYA-CHAN, AYA-CHAN!
......
OH, BUT YOU TWO NEED TO GET TOGETHER.
OTHER-WISE, YOU'LL CAUSE MAJOR PROBLEMS FOR ME.
YEAH... I HOPE YOU'LL LAST FOR ABOUT THREE YEARS.
Here. Some tea.
WHY ...?
WELL, IF SUGURU AND I GOT TOGETHER NOW, SUGURU WOULD LOOK LIKE A PERVERT FROM ANY ANGLE, RIGHT?
I NEED YOU TO ACT AS A BUFFER SO NO OTHER PESTS GET ATTACHED TO HIM UNTIL I BECOME A PERFECT ADULT AND WE CAN BE HAPPILY TOGETHER.
I'm a decent person, so I can forgive one ill-advised romance.
Yeah.

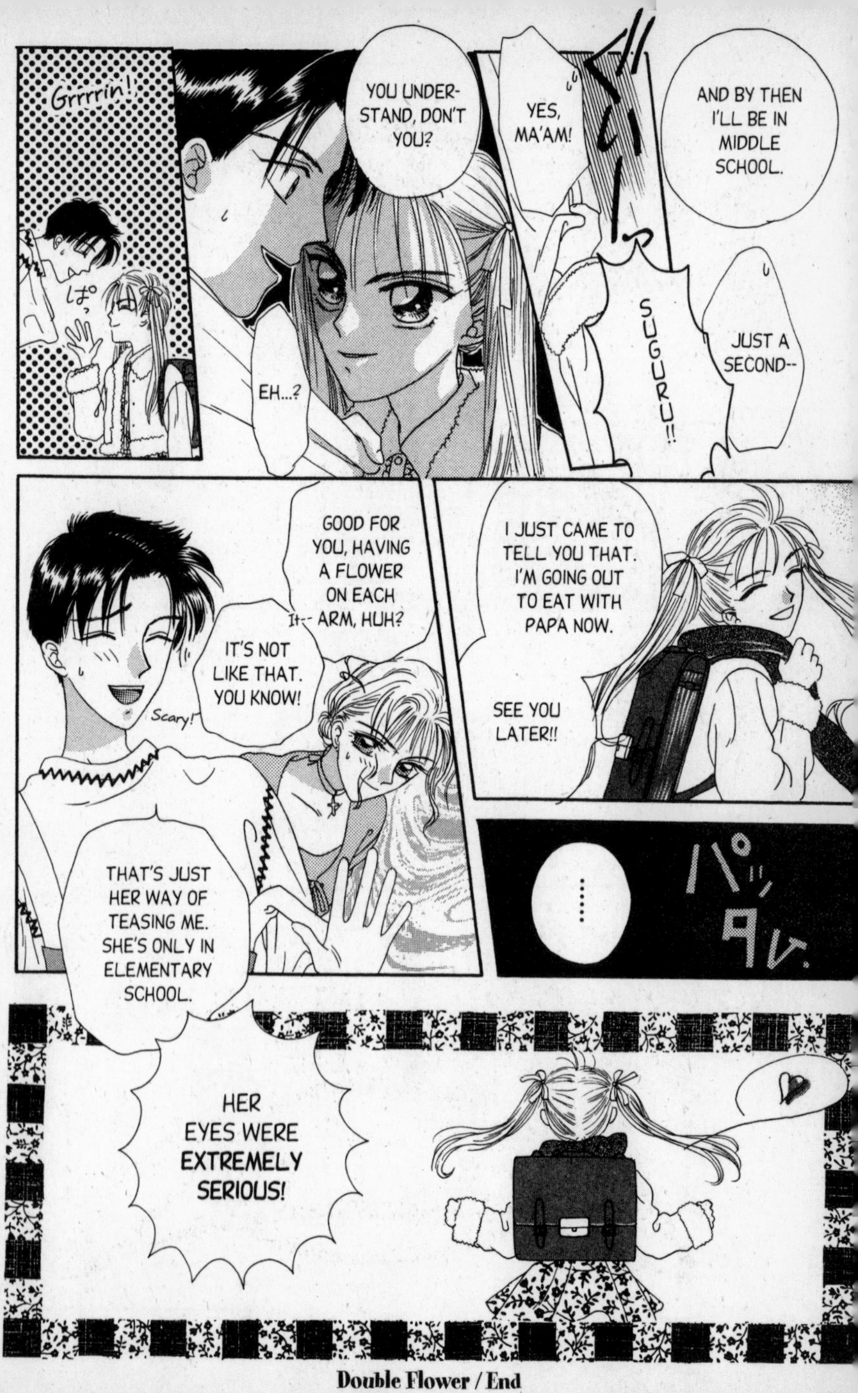
AND BY THEN I'LL BE IN MIDDLE SCHOOL.
JUST A SECOND--
SUGURU!!
YES, MA'AM!
YOU UNDER-STAND, DON'T YOU?
EH...?
Grrrrin!
ぱっ
I JUST CAME TO TELL YOU THAT. I'M GOING OUT TO EAT WITH PAPA NOW.
SEE YOU LATER!!
......
GOOD FOR YOU, HAVING A FLOWER ON EACH ARM, HUH?
It--
IT'S NOT LIKE THAT. YOU KNOW!
Scary!
THAT'S JUST HER WAY OF TEASING ME. SHE'S ONLY IN ELEMENTARY SCHOOL.
HER EYES WERE **EXTREMELY SERIOUS!**

Double Flower / End

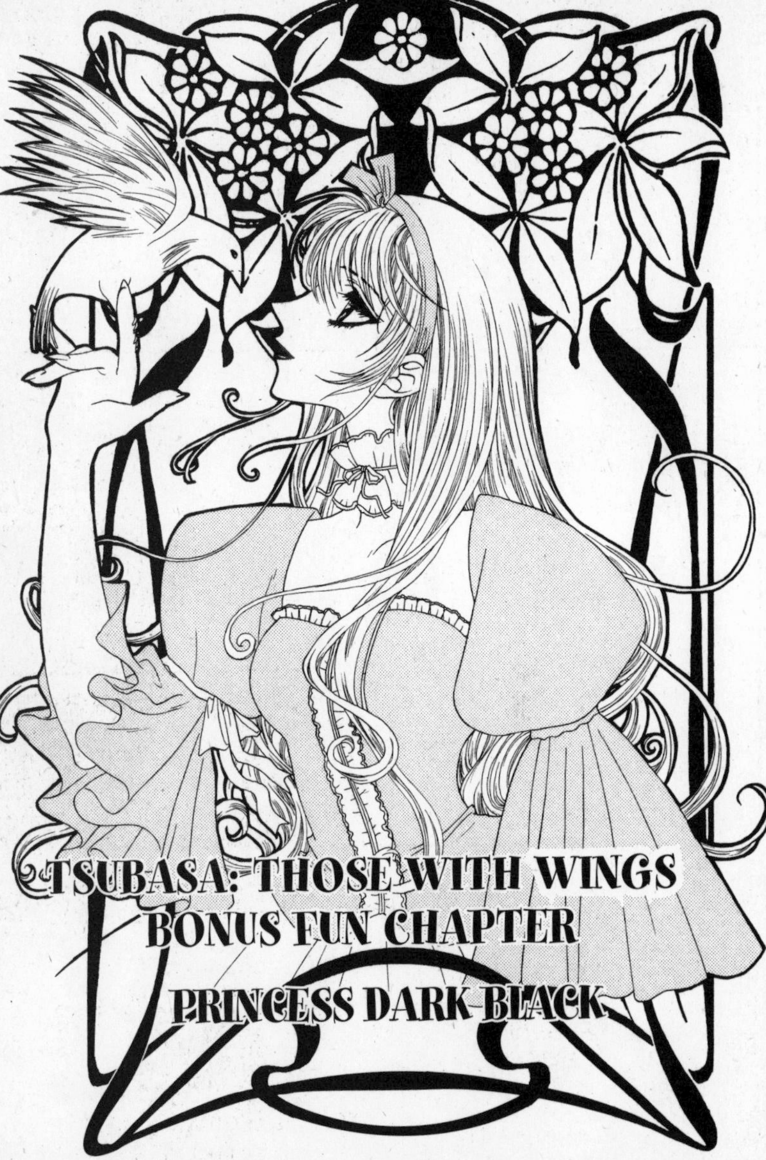
TSUBASA: THOSE WITH WINGS
BONUS FUN CHAPTER
PRINCESS DARK BLACK

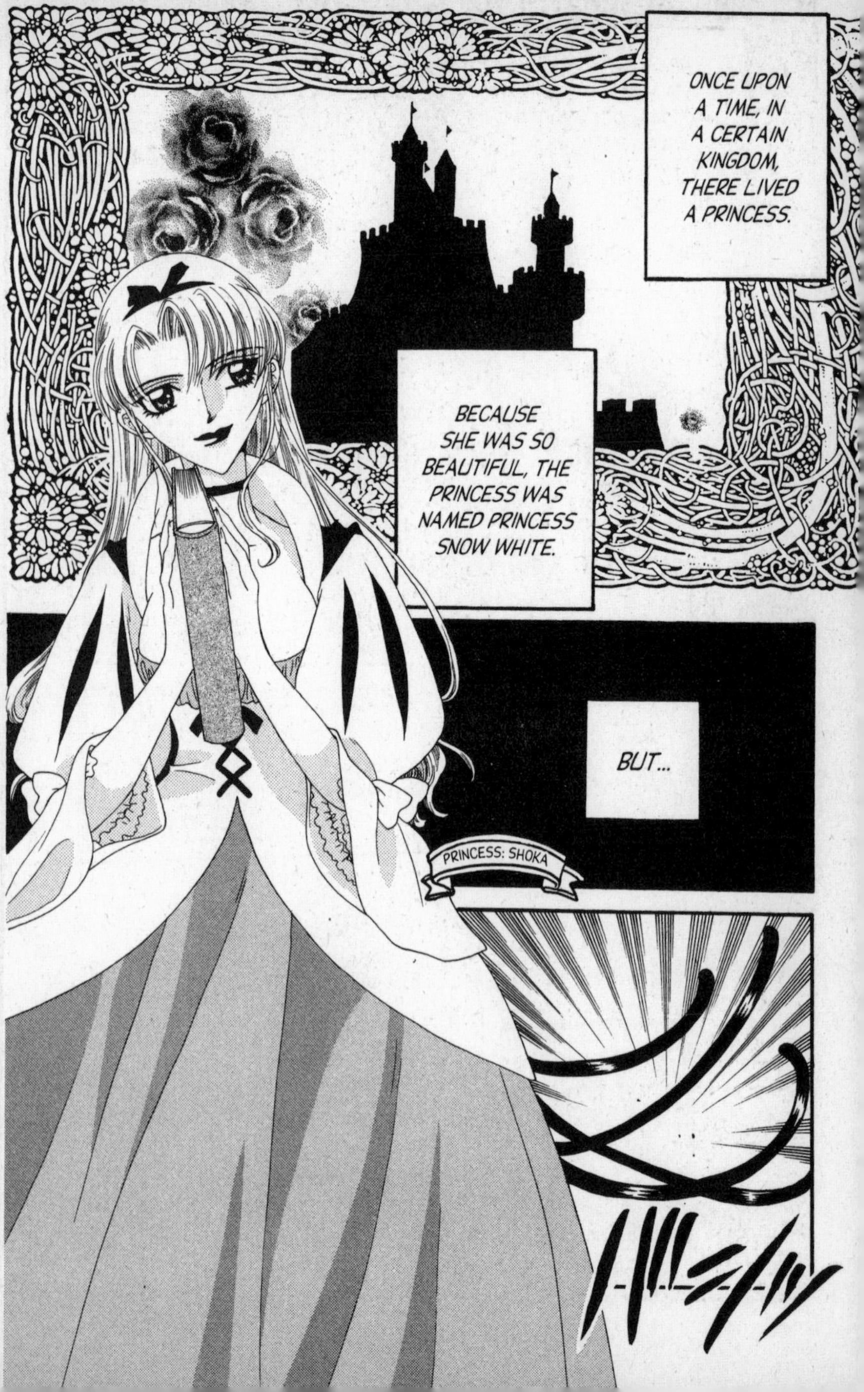
ONCE UPON A TIME, IN A CERTAIN KINGDOM, THERE LIVED A PRINCESS.
BECAUSE SHE WAS SO BEAUTIFUL, THE PRINCESS WAS NAMED PRINCESS SNOW WHITE.
BUT...
PRINCESS: SHOKA

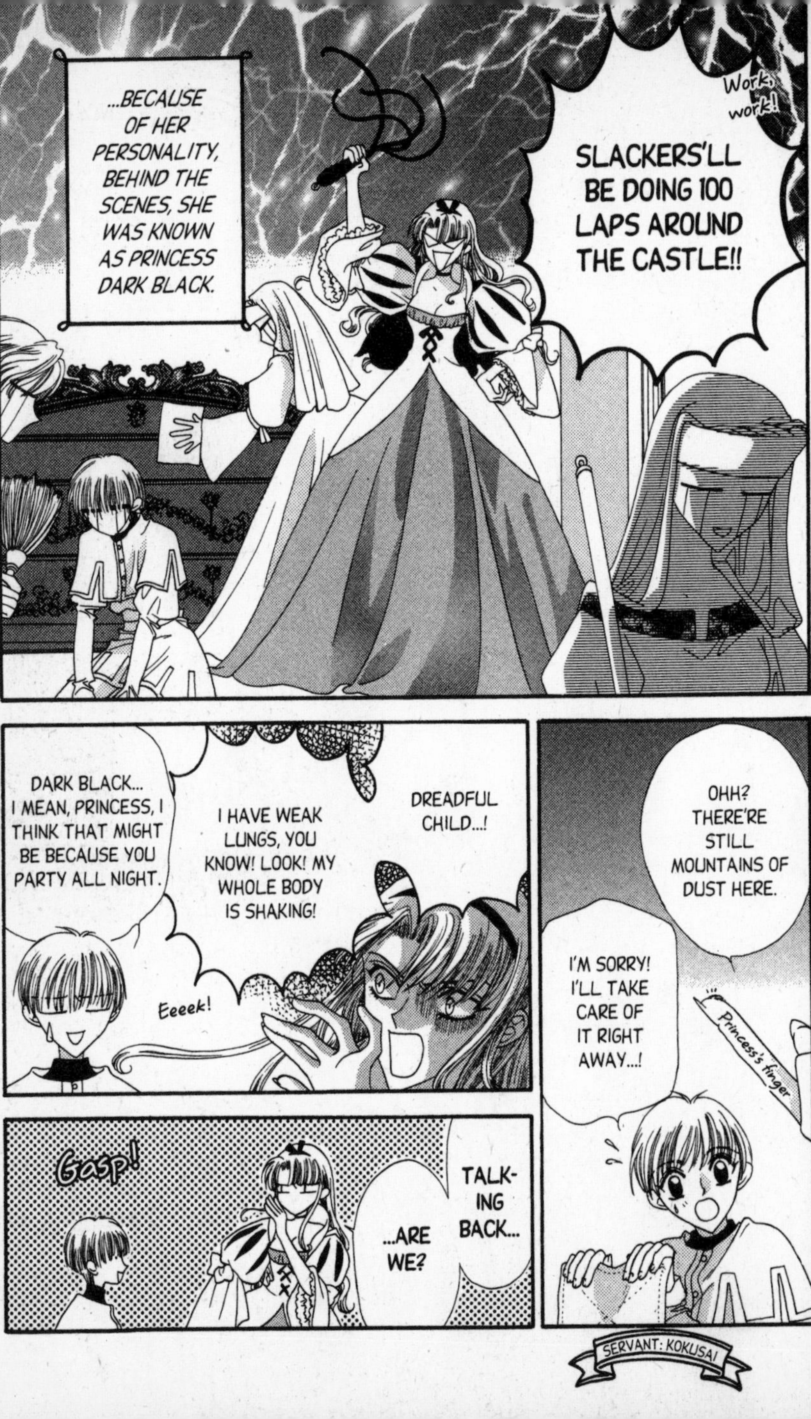
Work, work!
SLACKERS'LL BE DOING 100 LAPS AROUND THE CASTLE!!
...BECAUSE OF HER PERSONALITY, BEHIND THE SCENES, SHE WAS KNOWN AS PRINCESS DARK BLACK.
OHH? THERE'RE STILL MOUNTAINS OF DUST HERE.
Princess's finger
I'M SORRY! I'LL TAKE CARE OF IT RIGHT AWAY...!
DREADFUL CHILD...!
I HAVE WEAK LUNGS, YOU KNOW! LOOK! MY WHOLE BODY IS SHAKING!
DARK BLACK... I MEAN, PRINCESS, I THINK THAT MIGHT BE BECAUSE YOU PARTY ALL NIGHT.
Eeeek!
TALK-ING BACK...
...ARE WE?
Gasp!
SERVANT: KOKUSAI

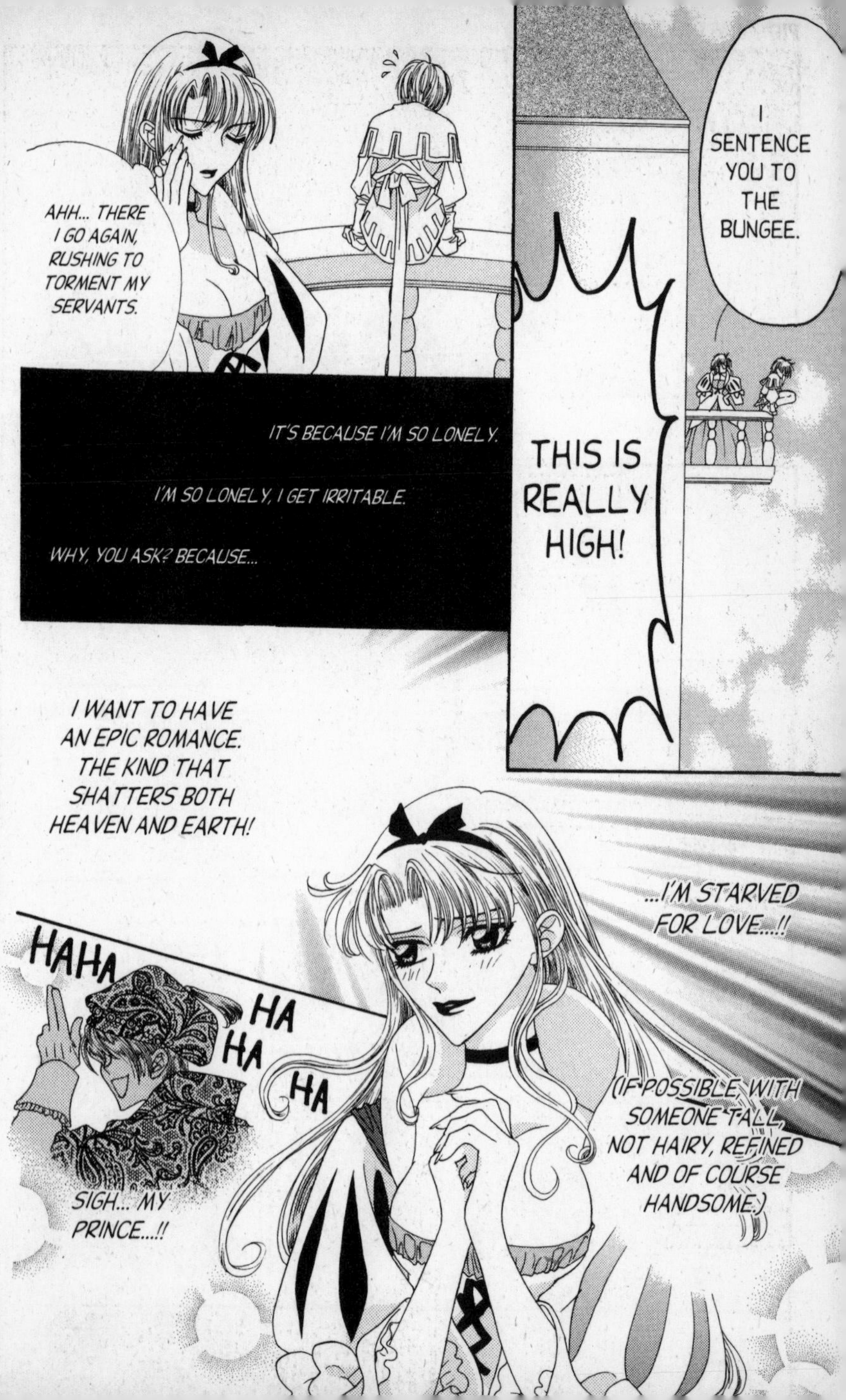
I SENTENCE YOU TO THE BUNGEE.
THIS IS REALLY HIGH!
AHH... THERE I GO AGAIN, RUSHING TO TORMENT MY SERVANTS.
IT'S BECAUSE I'M SO LONELY.
I'M SO LONELY, I GET IRRITABLE.
WHY, YOU ASK? BECAUSE...
I WANT TO HAVE AN EPIC ROMANCE. THE KIND THAT SHATTERS BOTH HEAVEN AND EARTH!
...I'M STARVED FOR LOVE...!!
(IF POSSIBLE, WITH SOMEONE TALL, NOT HAIRY, REFINED AND OF COURSE HANDSOME.)
HAHA
HA
HA
HA
SIGH... MY PRINCE...!!

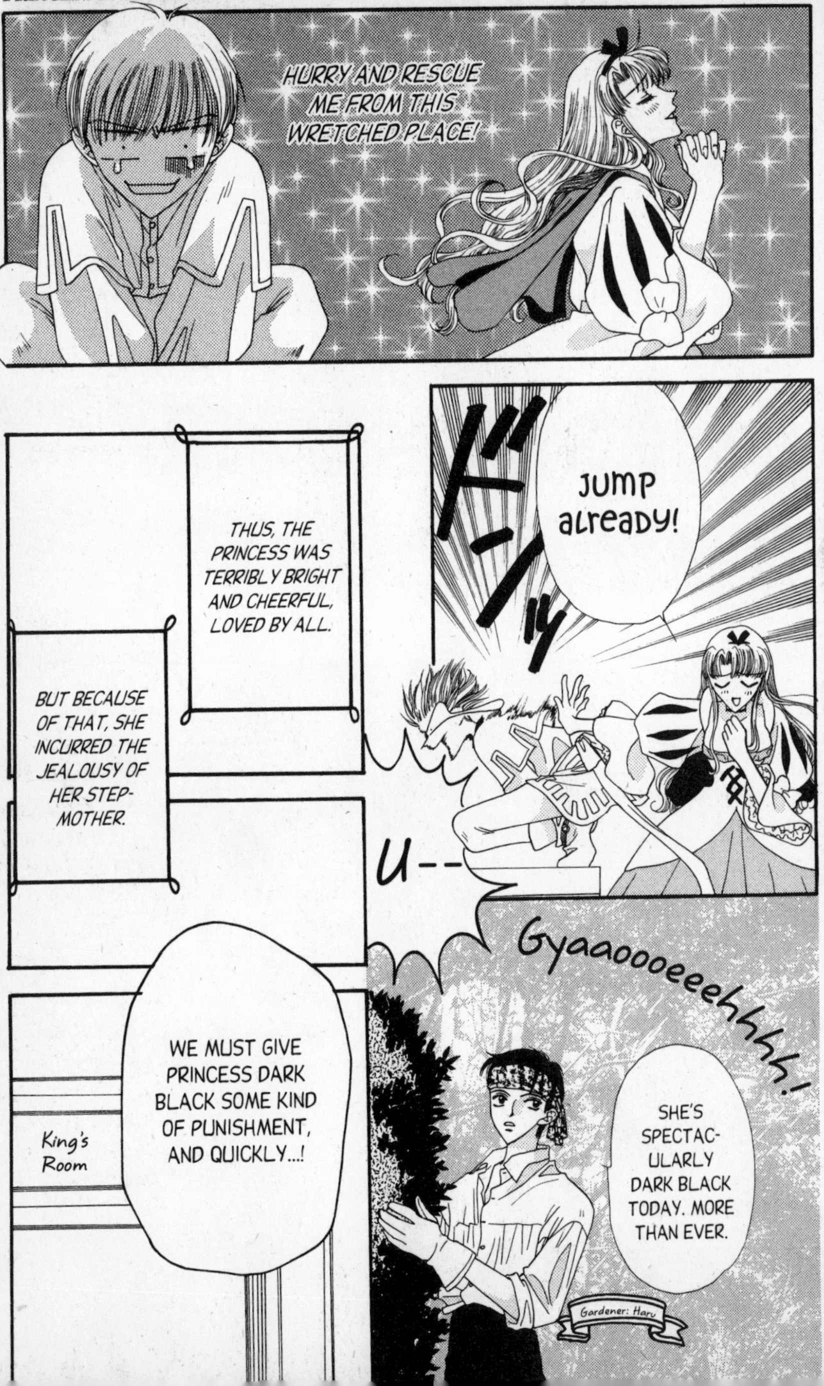
HURRY AND RESCUE ME FROM THIS WRETCHED PLACE!
ドンッ
JUMP already!
U--
Gyaaoooeeehhhh!
THUS, THE PRINCESS WAS TERRIBLY BRIGHT AND CHEERFUL, LOVED BY ALL.
BUT BECAUSE OF THAT, SHE INCURRED THE JEALOUSY OF HER STEP-MOTHER.
SHE'S SPECTAC-ULARLY DARK BLACK TODAY. MORE THAN EVER.
Gardener: Haru
King's Room
WE MUST GIVE PRINCESS DARK BLACK SOME KIND OF PUNISHMENT, AND QUICKLY...!

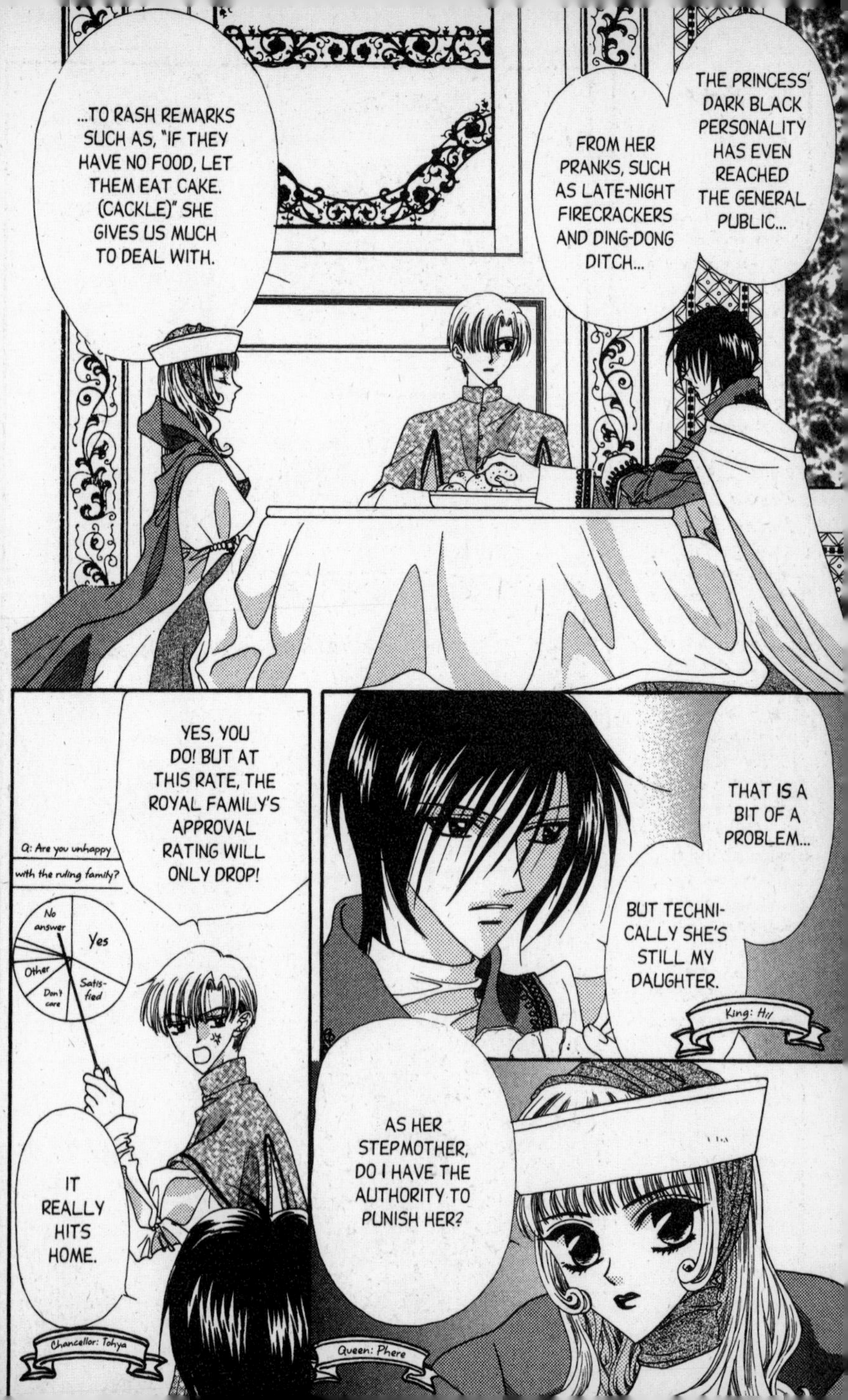
THE PRINCESS' DARK BLACK PERSONALITY HAS EVEN REACHED THE GENERAL PUBLIC...
FROM HER PRANKS, SUCH AS LATE-NIGHT FIRECRACKERS AND DING-DONG DITCH...
...TO RASH REMARKS SUCH AS, "IF THEY HAVE NO FOOD, LET THEM EAT CAKE. (CACKLE)" SHE GIVES US MUCH TO DEAL WITH.
THAT IS A BIT OF A PROBLEM...
BUT TECHNICALLY SHE'S STILL MY DAUGHTER.
King: Hil
AS HER STEPMOTHER, DO I HAVE THE AUTHORITY TO PUNISH HER?
Queen: Phere
YES, YOU DO! BUT AT THIS RATE, THE ROYAL FAMILY'S APPROVAL RATING WILL ONLY DROP!
Q: Are you unhappy with the ruling family?
No answer
Yes
Other
Don't care
Satis-fied
IT REALLY HITS HOME.
Chancellor: Tohya

Part 4

With one thing and another, next year, I will have known you for X years, so you know every bit of my shame and the harm I've done (laugh). Let's keep bleeeeep in a good way. (It's all blacked out writing.)

I just can't finish Persona 2. My Persona Cards aren't catching up. There's a whole ten levels between them and me. I mean, you want to use all the good Personas, right? Right now, I'm really looking forward to TokiMemo 2. It's not because I really like a particular character--
I love the TokiMemo system. And PS2 is coming out soon, too, so I hope there will be lots of interesting games for it. Ah, Resident Evil 3 is scary (laugh). Good luck, Jill (laugh).

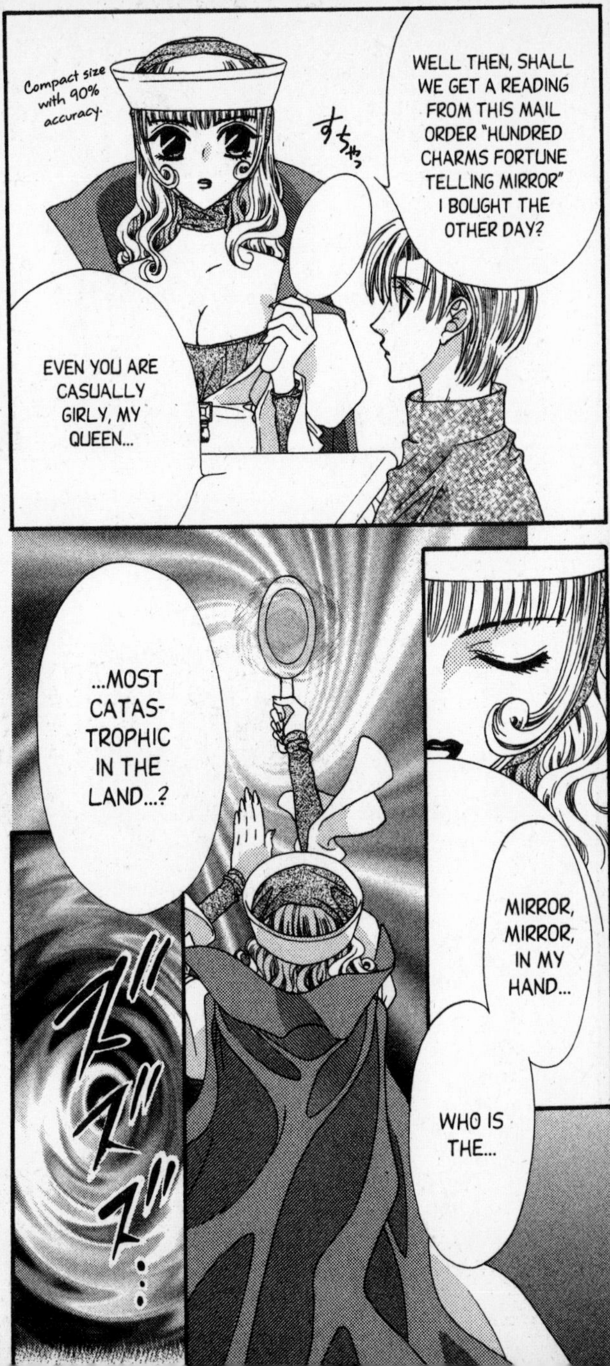
WELL THEN, SHALL WE GET A READING FROM THIS MAIL ORDER "HUNDRED CHARMS FORTUNE TELLING MIRROR" I BOUGHT THE OTHER DAY?
Compact size with 90% accuracy.
EVEN YOU ARE CASUALLY GIRLY, MY QUEEN...
MIRROR, MIRROR, IN MY HAND...
WHO IS THE...
...MOST CATAS-TROPHIC IN THE LAND...?

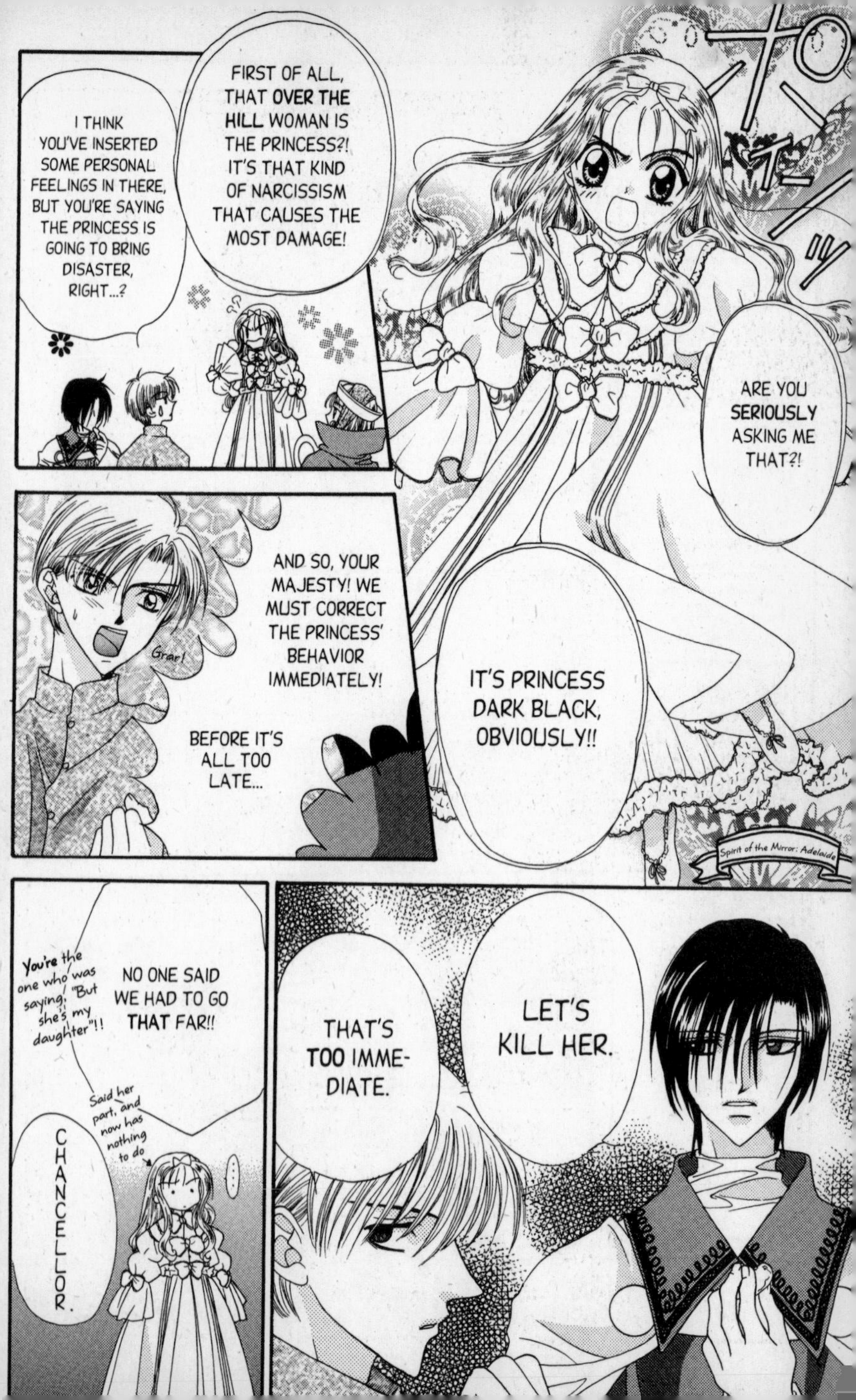
ARE YOU SERIOUSLY ASKING ME THAT?!
IT'S PRINCESS DARK BLACK, OBVIOUSLY!!
Spirit of the Mirror: Adelaide
FIRST OF ALL, THAT OVER THE HILL WOMAN IS THE PRINCESS?! IT'S THAT KIND OF NARCISSISM THAT CAUSES THE MOST DAMAGE!
I THINK YOU'VE INSERTED SOME PERSONAL FEELINGS IN THERE, BUT YOU'RE SAYING THE PRINCESS IS GOING TO BRING DISASTER, RIGHT...?
AND SO, YOUR MAJESTY! WE MUST CORRECT THE PRINCESS' BEHAVIOR IMMEDIATELY!
Grar!
BEFORE IT'S ALL TOO LATE...
LET'S KILL HER.
THAT'S TOO IMMEDIATE.
NO ONE SAID WE HAD TO GO THAT FAR!!
You're the one who was saying, "But she's my daughter"!!
CHANCELLOR.
Said her part, and now has nothing to do
...

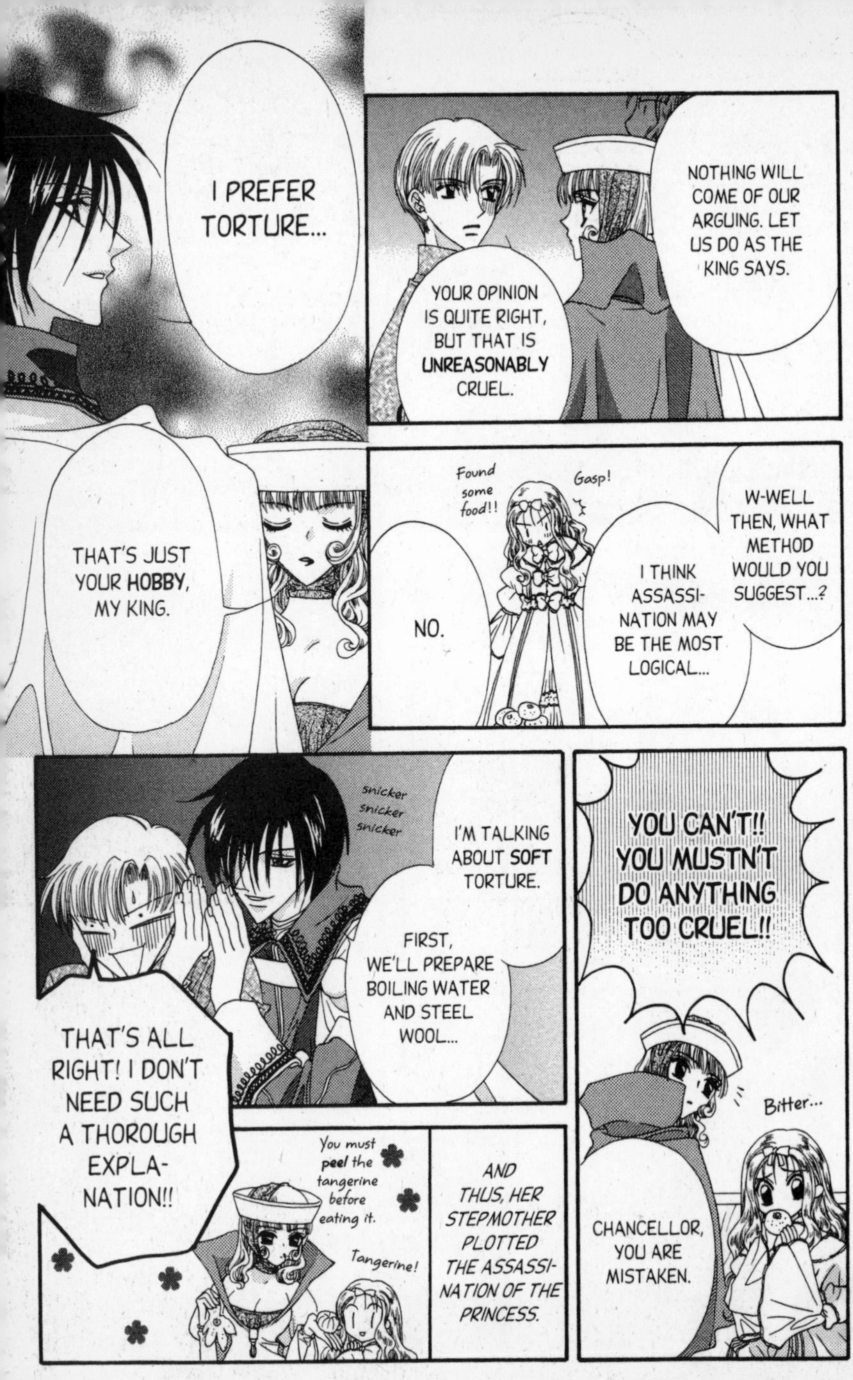
NOTHING WILL COME OF OUR ARGUING. LET US DO AS THE KING SAYS.
YOUR OPINION IS QUITE RIGHT, BUT THAT IS **UNREASONABLY** CRUEL.
W-WELL THEN, WHAT METHOD WOULD YOU SUGGEST...?
Gasp!
I THINK ASSASSINATION MAY BE THE MOST LOGICAL...
Found some food!!
NO.
I PREFER TORTURE...
THAT'S JUST YOUR **HOBBY**, MY KING.
YOU CAN'T!! YOU MUSTN'T DO ANYTHING TOO CRUEL!!
Bitter...
CHANCELLOR, YOU ARE MISTAKEN.
I'M TALKING ABOUT **SOFT** TORTURE.
snicker snicker snicker
FIRST, WE'LL PREPARE BOILING WATER AND STEEL WOOL...
THAT'S ALL RIGHT! I DON'T NEED SUCH A THOROUGH EXPLANATION!!
AND THUS, HER STEPMOTHER PLOTTED THE ASSASSINATION OF THE PRINCESS.
You must **peel** the tangerine before eating it.
Tangerine!

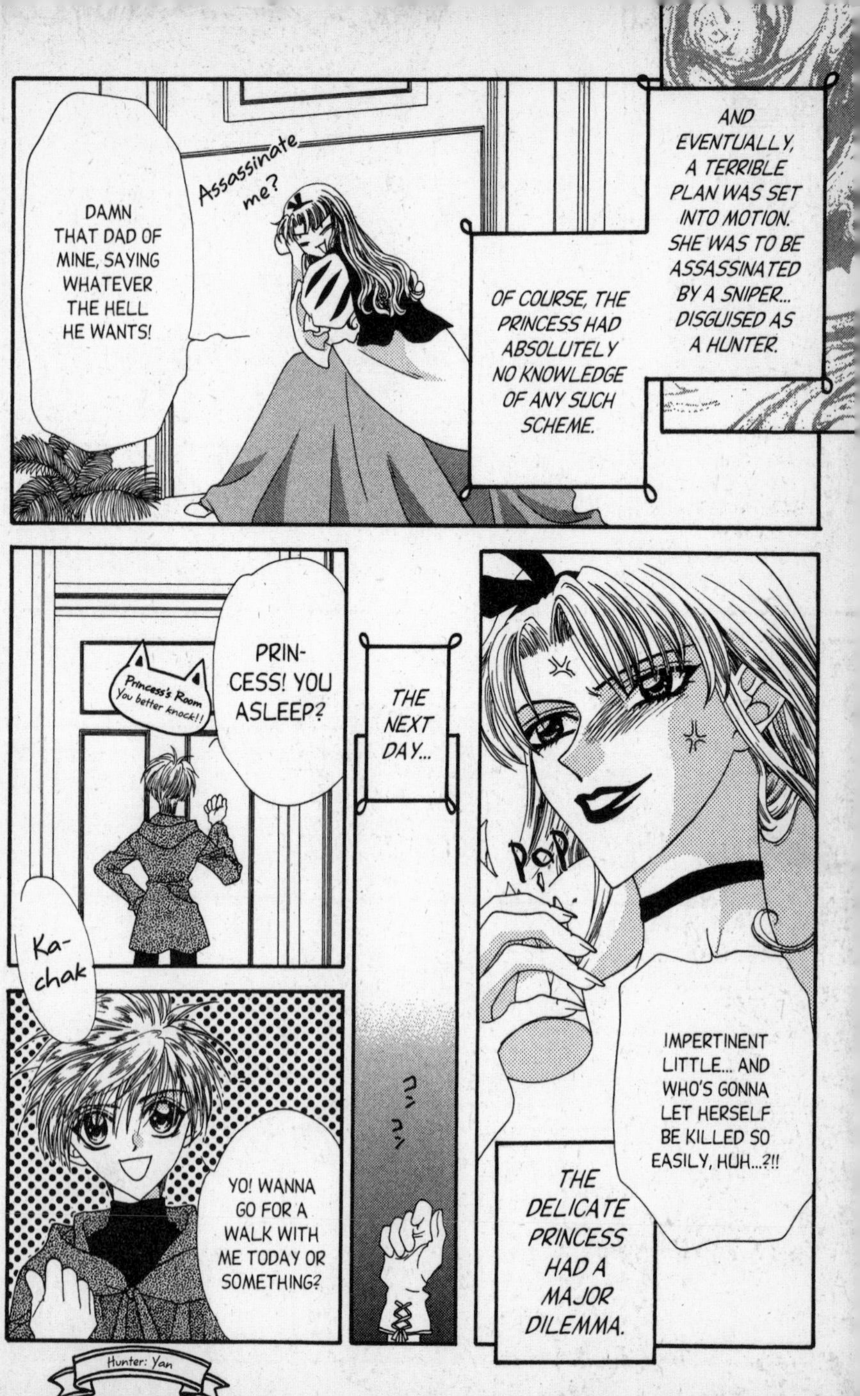
AND EVENTUALLY, A TERRIBLE PLAN WAS SET INTO MOTION. SHE WAS TO BE ASSASSINATED BY A SNIPER... DISGUISED AS A HUNTER.
OF COURSE, THE PRINCESS HAD ABSOLUTELY NO KNOWLEDGE OF ANY SUCH SCHEME.
Assassinate me?
DAMN THAT DAD OF MINE, SAYING WHATEVER THE HELL HE WANTS!
POP
IMPERTINENT LITTLE... AND WHO'S GONNA LET HERSELF BE KILLED SO EASILY, HUH...?!!
THE DELICATE PRINCESS HAD A MAJOR DILEMMA.
THE NEXT DAY...
PRIN-CESS! YOU ASLEEP?
Princess's Room You better knock!!
Ka-chak
YO! WANNA GO FOR A WALK WITH ME TODAY OR SOMETHING?
Hunter: Yan

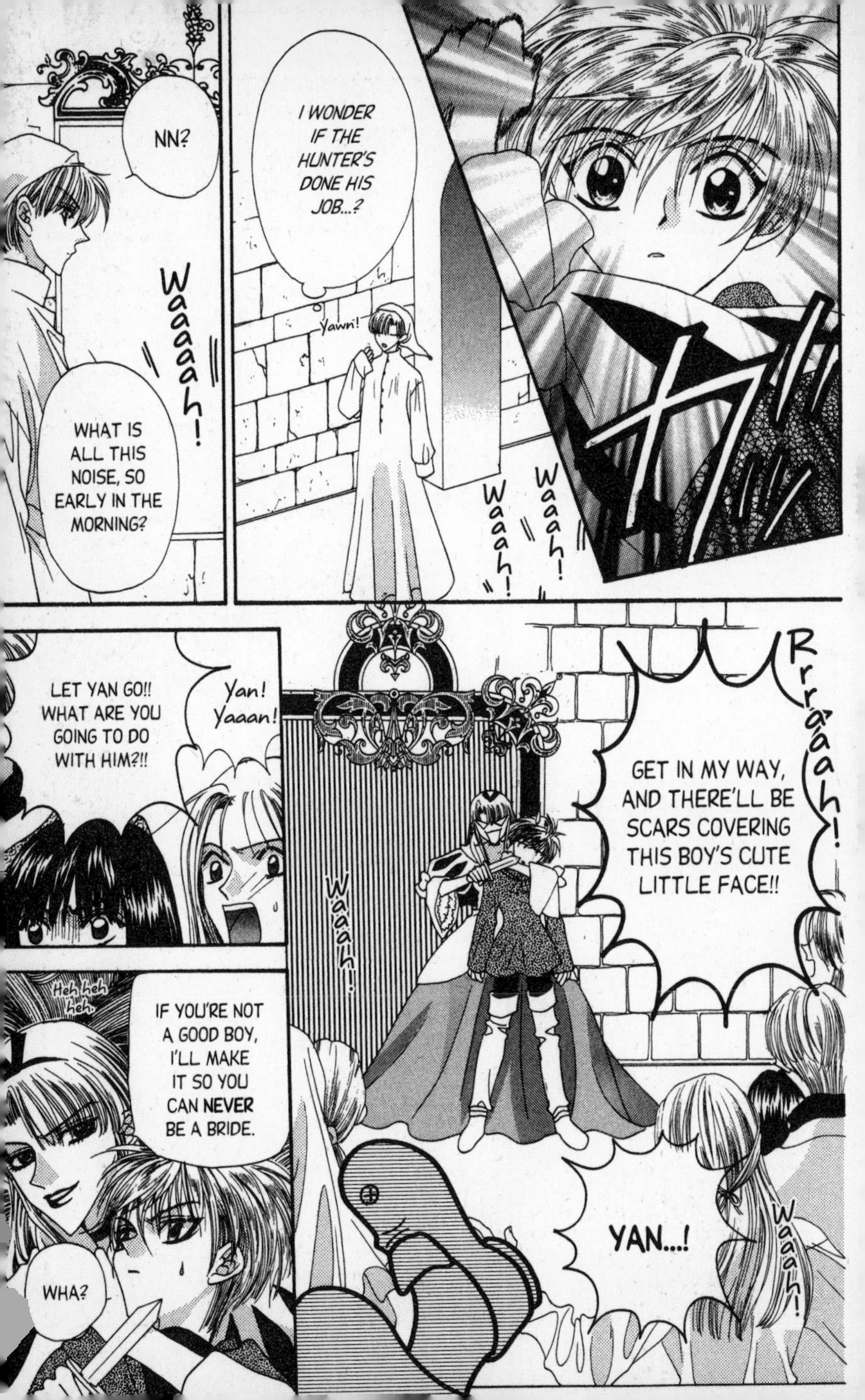

Waaaah!
Waaah!
I WONDER IF THE HUNTER'S DONE HIS JOB...?
Yawn!
NN?
Waaaaah!
WHAT IS ALL THIS NOISE, SO EARLY IN THE MORNING?
Rrraaah!
GET IN MY WAY, AND THERE'LL BE SCARS COVERING THIS BOY'S CUTE LITTLE FACE!!
Waaah!
Waaah!
YAN...!
Yan! Yaaan!
LET YAN GO!! WHAT ARE YOU GOING TO DO WITH HIM?!!
Heh heh heh.
IF YOU'RE NOT A GOOD BOY, I'LL MAKE IT SO YOU CAN **NEVER** BE A BRIDE.
WHA?

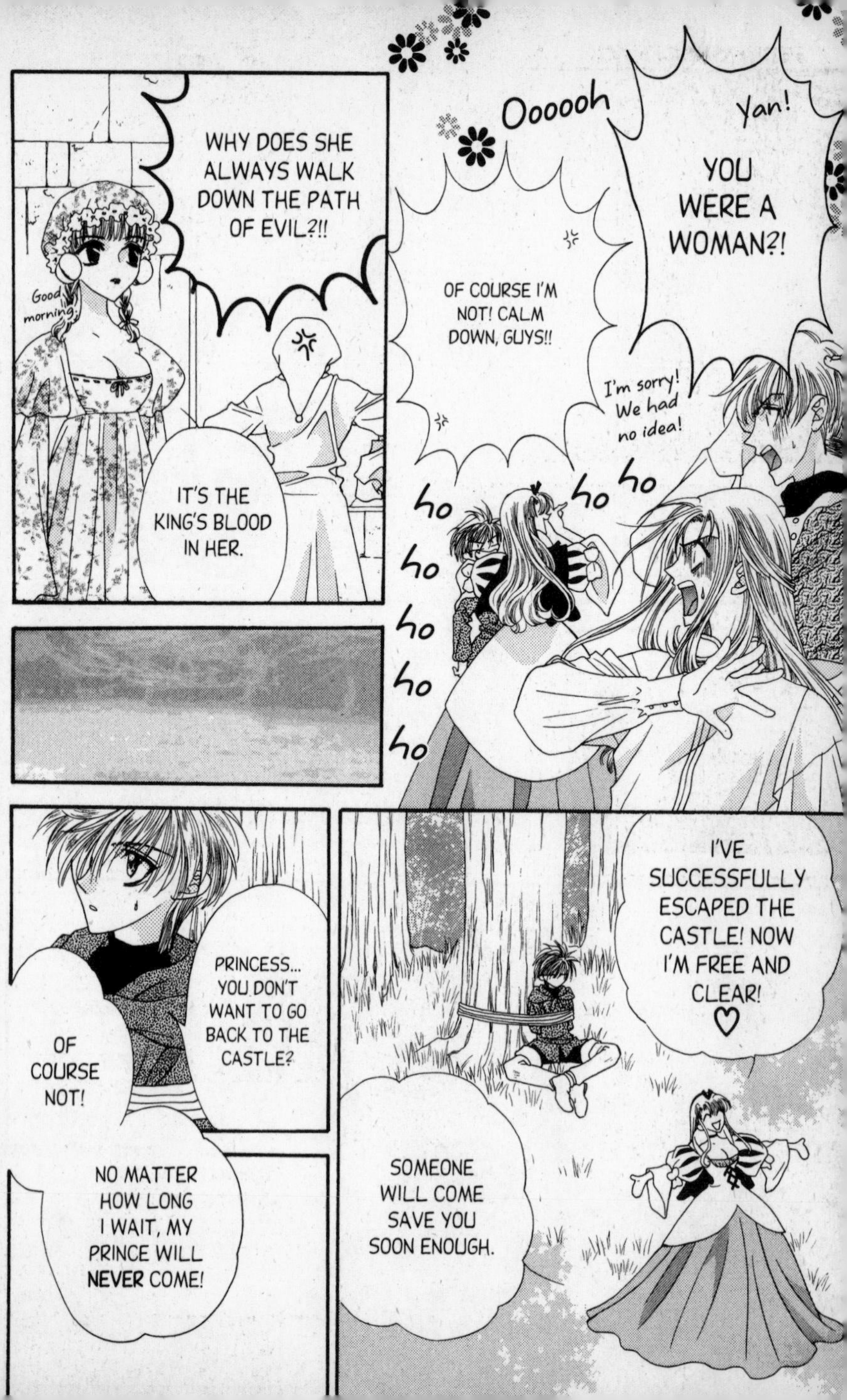
Yan!
YOU WERE A WOMAN?!
Ooooh
OF COURSE I'M NOT! CALM DOWN, GUYS!!
I'm sorry! We had no idea!
ho ho ho ho ho ho ho
WHY DOES SHE ALWAYS WALK DOWN THE PATH OF EVIL?!!
Good morning.
IT'S THE KING'S BLOOD IN HER.
I'VE SUCCESSFULLY ESCAPED THE CASTLE! NOW I'M FREE AND CLEAR! ♡
SOMEONE WILL COME SAVE YOU SOON ENOUGH.
PRINCESS... YOU DON'T WANT TO GO BACK TO THE CASTLE?
OF COURSE NOT!
NO MATTER HOW LONG I WAIT, MY PRINCE WILL **NEVER** COME!

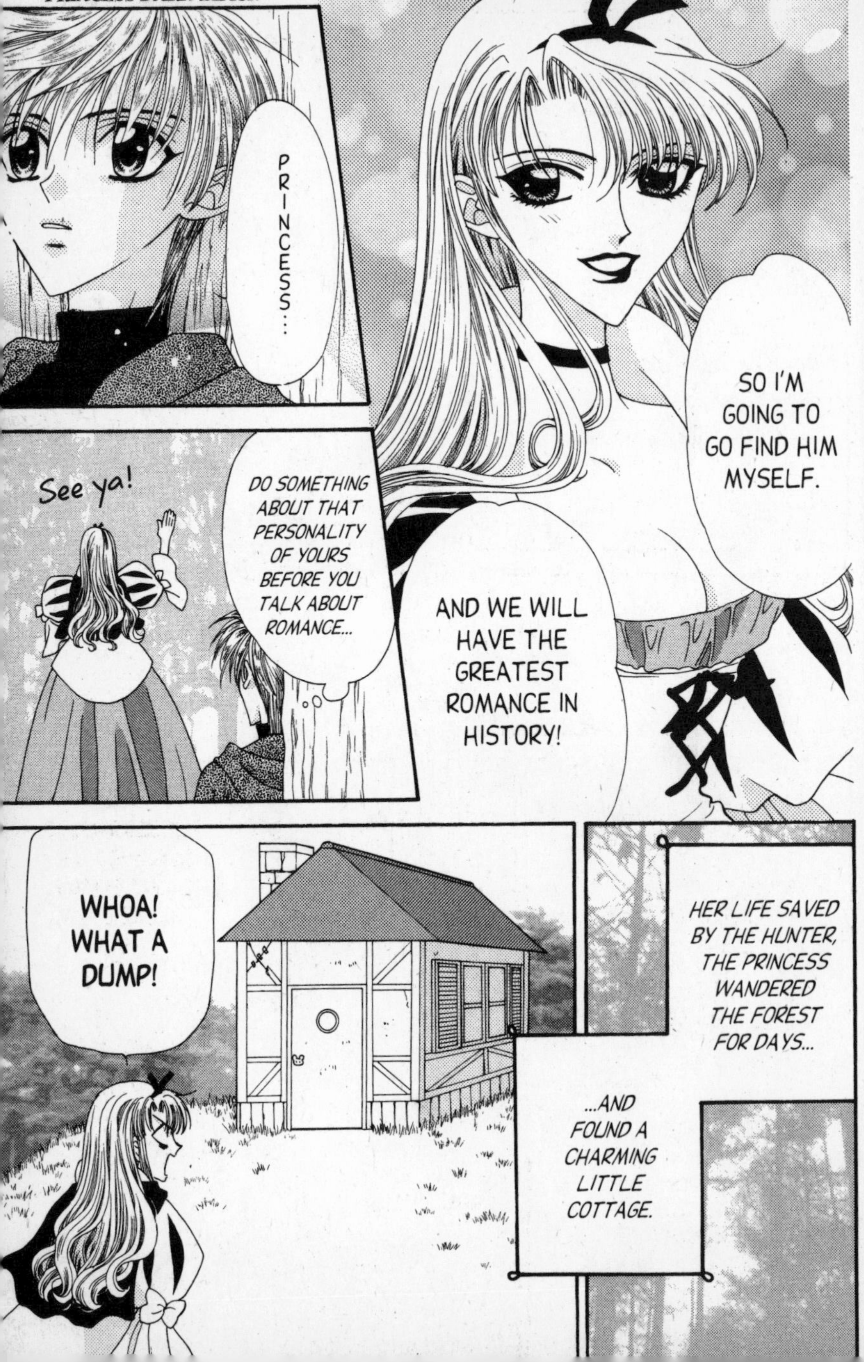
SO I'M GOING TO GO FIND HIM MYSELF.
AND WE WILL HAVE THE GREATEST ROMANCE IN HISTORY!
PRINCESS...
DO SOMETHING ABOUT THAT PERSONALITY OF YOURS BEFORE YOU TALK ABOUT ROMANCE...
See ya!
HER LIFE SAVED BY THE HUNTER, THE PRINCESS WANDERED THE FOREST FOR DAYS...
...AND FOUND A CHARMING LITTLE COTTAGE.
WHOA! WHAT A DUMP!

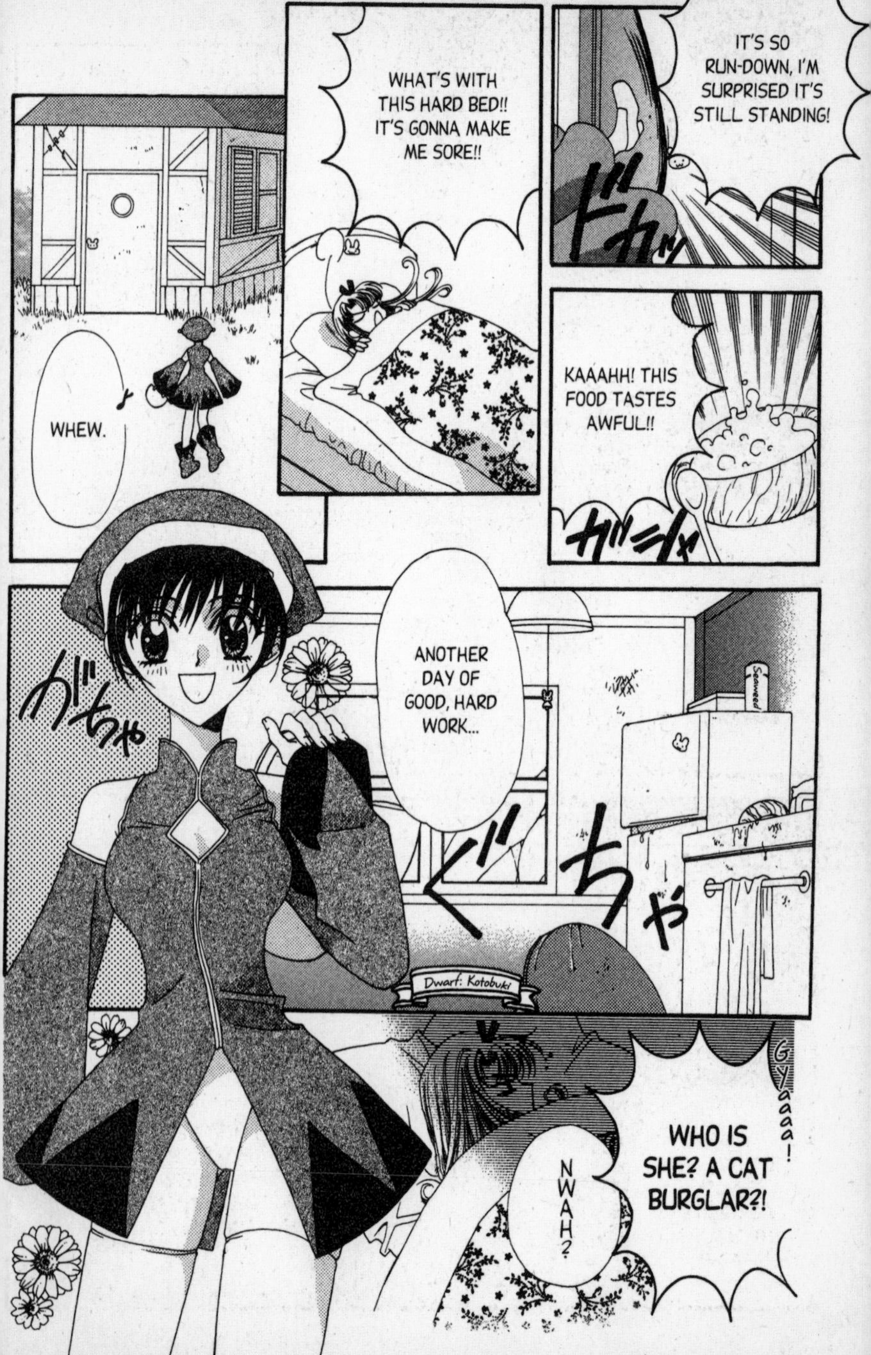

IT'S SO RUN-DOWN, I'M SURPRISED IT'S STILL STANDING!
KAAAHH! THIS FOOD TASTES AWFUL!!
WHAT'S WITH THIS HARD BED!! IT'S GONNA MAKE ME SORE!!
WHEW.
ANOTHER DAY OF GOOD, HARD WORK...
Seaweed
Dwarf: Kotobuki
GYaaaa!
WHO IS SHE? A CAT BURGLAR?!
NWAH?

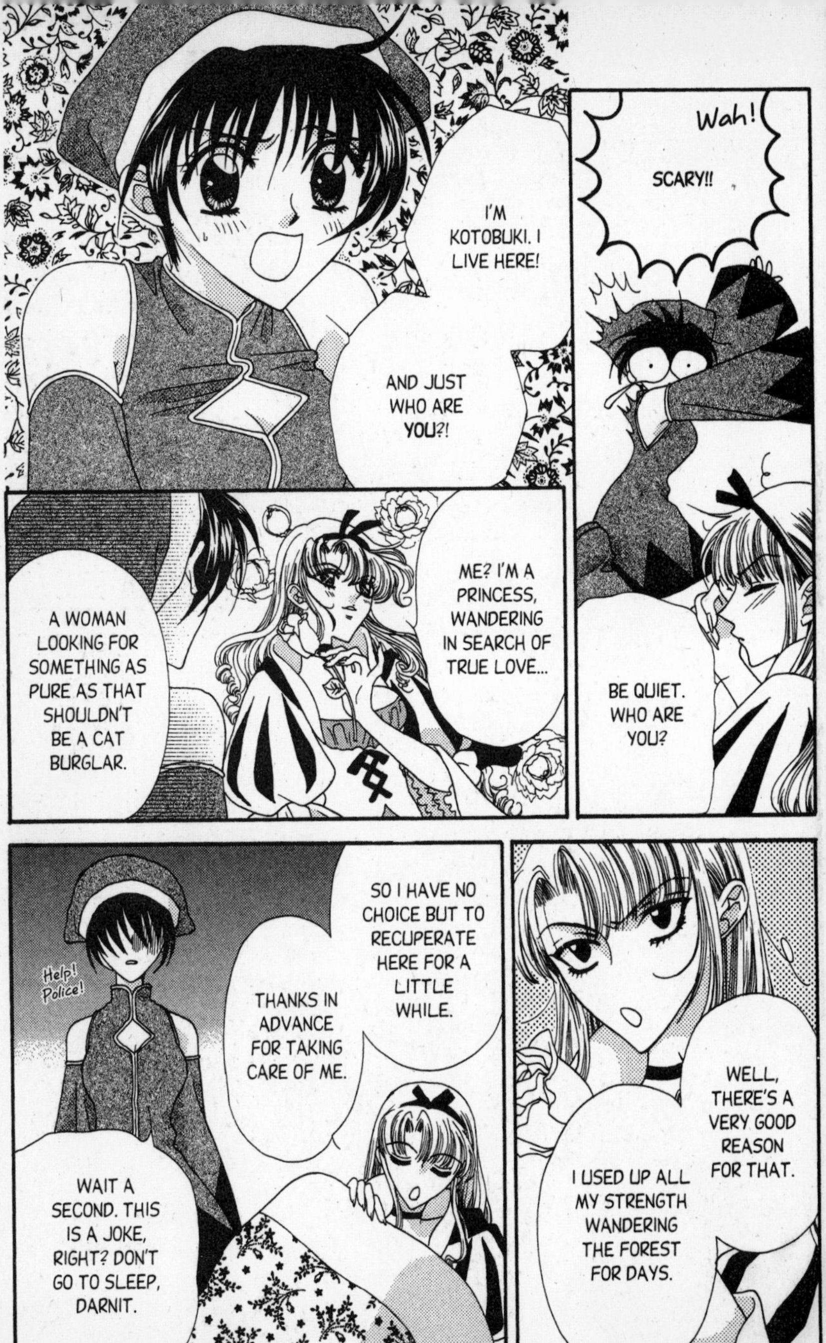
Wah!
SCARY!!
BE QUIET. WHO ARE YOU?
I'M KOTOBUKI. I LIVE HERE!
AND JUST WHO ARE YOU?!
ME? I'M A PRINCESS, WANDERING IN SEARCH OF TRUE LOVE...
A WOMAN LOOKING FOR SOMETHING AS PURE AS THAT SHOULDN'T BE A CAT BURGLAR.
WELL, THERE'S A VERY GOOD REASON FOR THAT.
I USED UP ALL MY STRENGTH WANDERING THE FOREST FOR DAYS.
SO I HAVE NO CHOICE BUT TO RECUPERATE HERE FOR A LITTLE WHILE.
THANKS IN ADVANCE FOR TAKING CARE OF ME.
Help! Police!
WAIT A SECOND. THIS IS A JOKE, RIGHT? DON'T GO TO SLEEP, DARNIT.

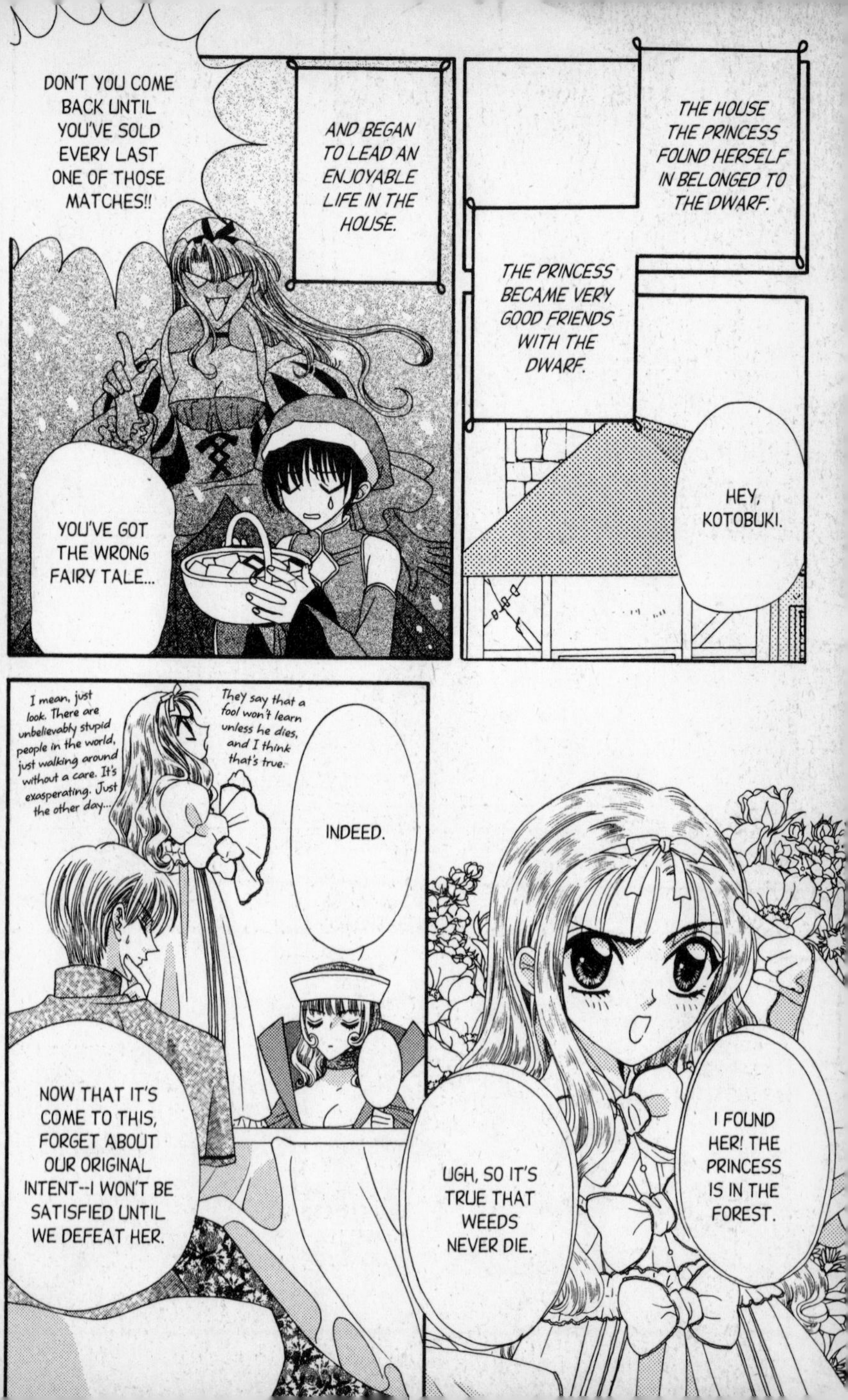
THE HOUSE THE PRINCESS FOUND HERSELF IN BELONGED TO THE DWARF.
THE PRINCESS BECAME VERY GOOD FRIENDS WITH THE DWARF.
HEY, KOTOBUKI.
AND BEGAN TO LEAD AN ENJOYABLE LIFE IN THE HOUSE.
DON'T YOU COME BACK UNTIL YOU'VE SOLD EVERY LAST ONE OF THOSE MATCHES!!
YOU'VE GOT THE WRONG FAIRY TALE...
I FOUND HER! THE PRINCESS IS IN THE FOREST.
UGH, SO IT'S TRUE THAT WEEDS NEVER DIE.
INDEED.
They say that a fool won't learn unless he dies, and I think that's true.
I mean, just look. There are unbelievably stupid people in the world, just walking around without a care. It's exasperating. Just the other day...
NOW THAT IT'S COME TO THIS, FORGET ABOUT OUR ORIGINAL INTENT--I WON'T BE SATISFIED UNTIL WE DEFEAT HER.

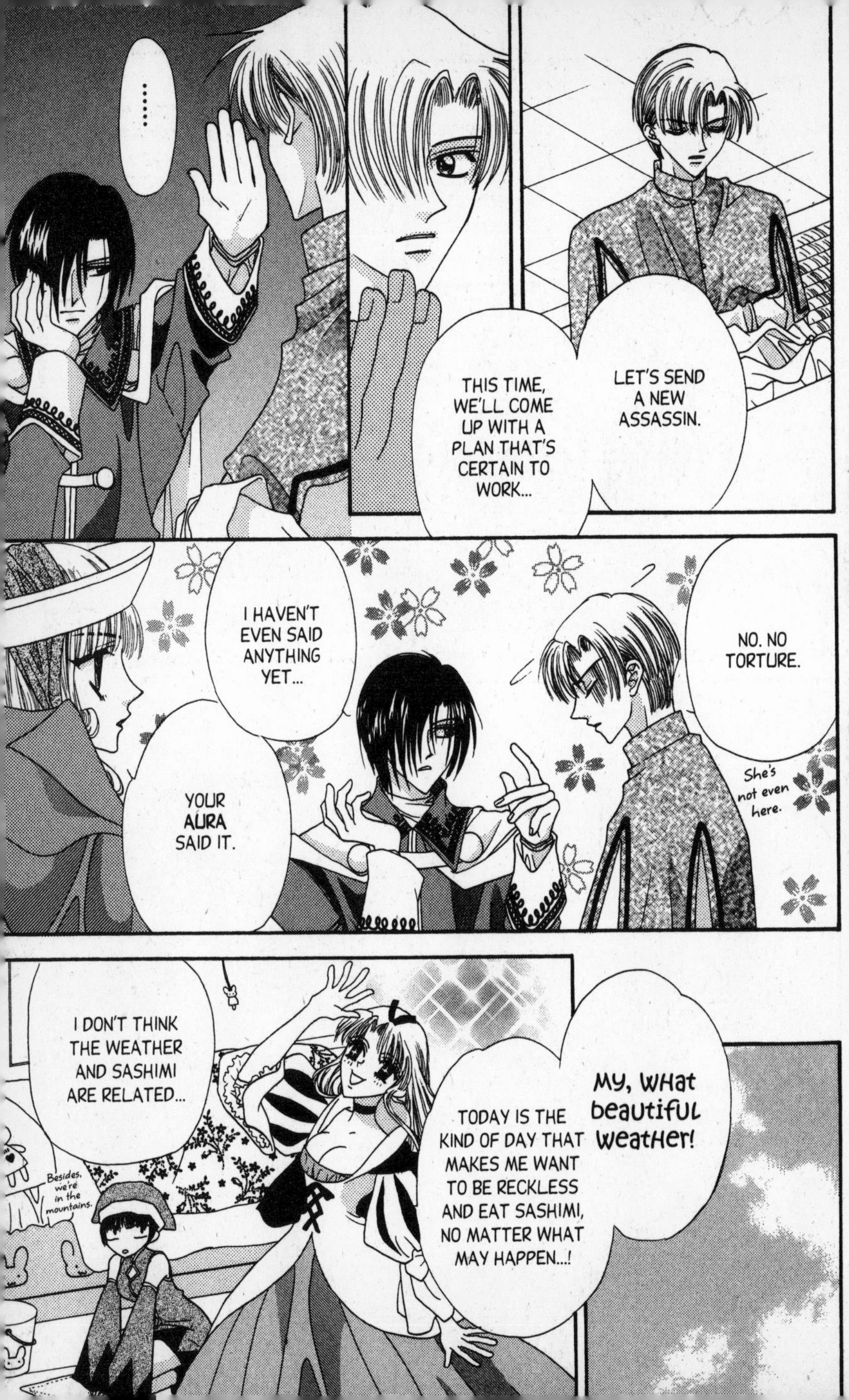
LET'S SEND A NEW ASSASSIN.
THIS TIME, WE'LL COME UP WITH A PLAN THAT'S CERTAIN TO WORK...
......
NO. NO TORTURE.
She's not even here.
I HAVEN'T EVEN SAID ANYTHING YET...
YOUR AURA SAID IT.
MY, WHAT beautiful weather!
TODAY IS THE KIND OF DAY THAT MAKES ME WANT TO BE RECKLESS AND EAT SASHIMI, NO MATTER WHAT MAY HAPPEN...!
I DON'T THINK THE WEATHER AND SASHIMI ARE RELATED...
Besides, we're in the mountains.

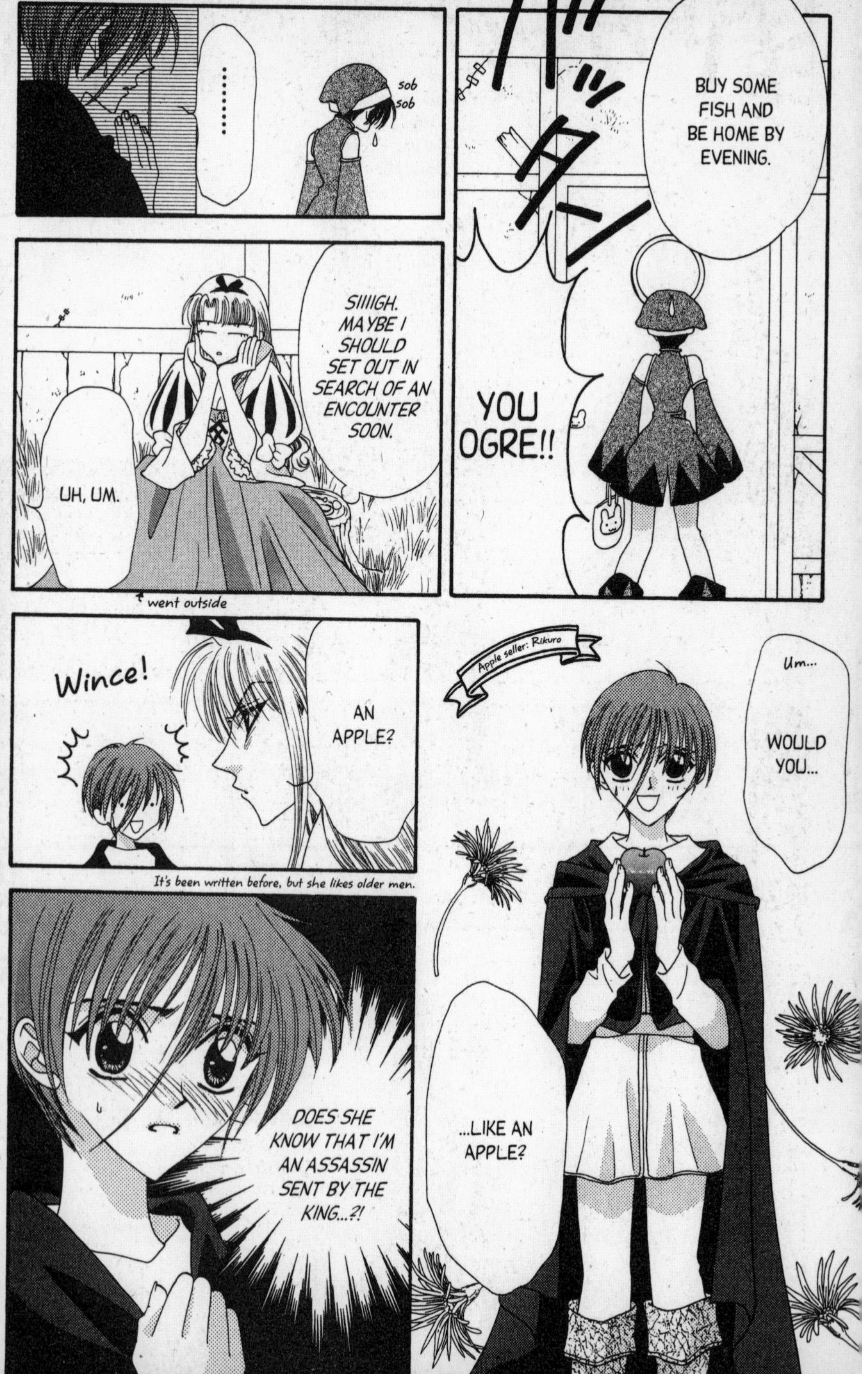
BUY SOME FISH AND BE HOME BY EVENING.
バッタン
YOU OGRE!!
......
sob sob
SIIIIGH. MAYBE I SHOULD SET OUT IN SEARCH OF AN ENCOUNTER SOON.
UH, UM.
went outside
Apple seller: Rikuro
Um... WOULD YOU...
...LIKE AN APPLE?
AN APPLE?
Wince!
It's been written before, but she likes older men.
DOES SHE KNOW THAT I'M AN ASSASSIN SENT BY THE KING...?!

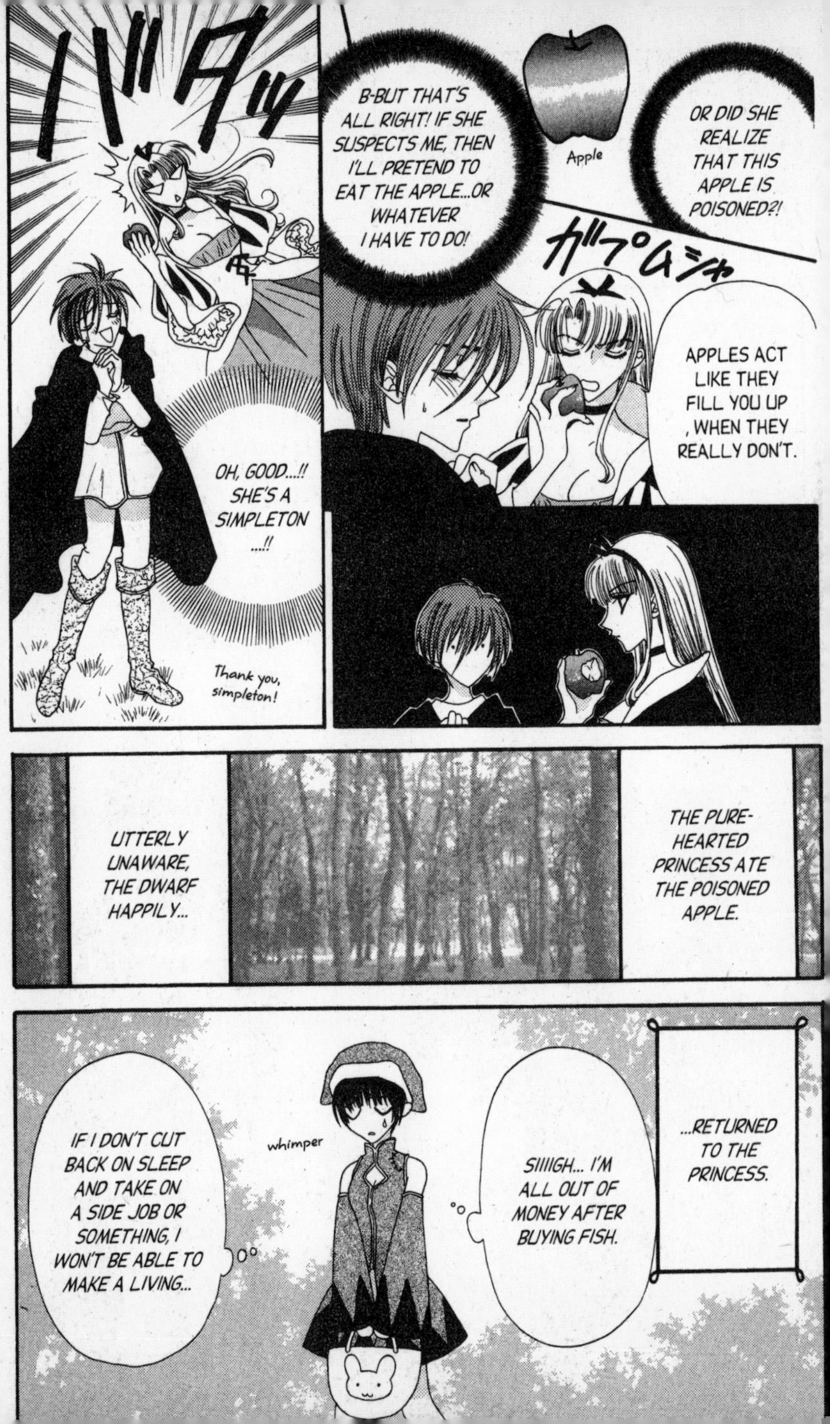
OR DID SHE REALIZE THAT THIS APPLE IS POISONED?!
Apple
B-BUT THAT'S ALL RIGHT! IF SHE SUSPECTS ME, THEN I'LL PRETEND TO EAT THE APPLE...OR WHATEVER I HAVE TO DO!
APPLES ACT LIKE THEY FILL YOU UP, WHEN THEY REALLY DON'T.
OH, GOOD...!! SHE'S A SIMPLETON ...!!
Thank you, simpleton!
THE PURE-HEARTED PRINCESS ATE THE POISONED APPLE.
UTTERLY UNAWARE, THE DWARF HAPPILY...
...RETURNED TO THE PRINCESS.
SIIIGH... I'M ALL OUT OF MONEY AFTER BUYING FISH.
whimper
IF I DON'T CUT BACK ON SLEEP AND TAKE ON A SIDE JOB OR SOMETHING, I WON'T BE ABLE TO MAKE A LIVING...

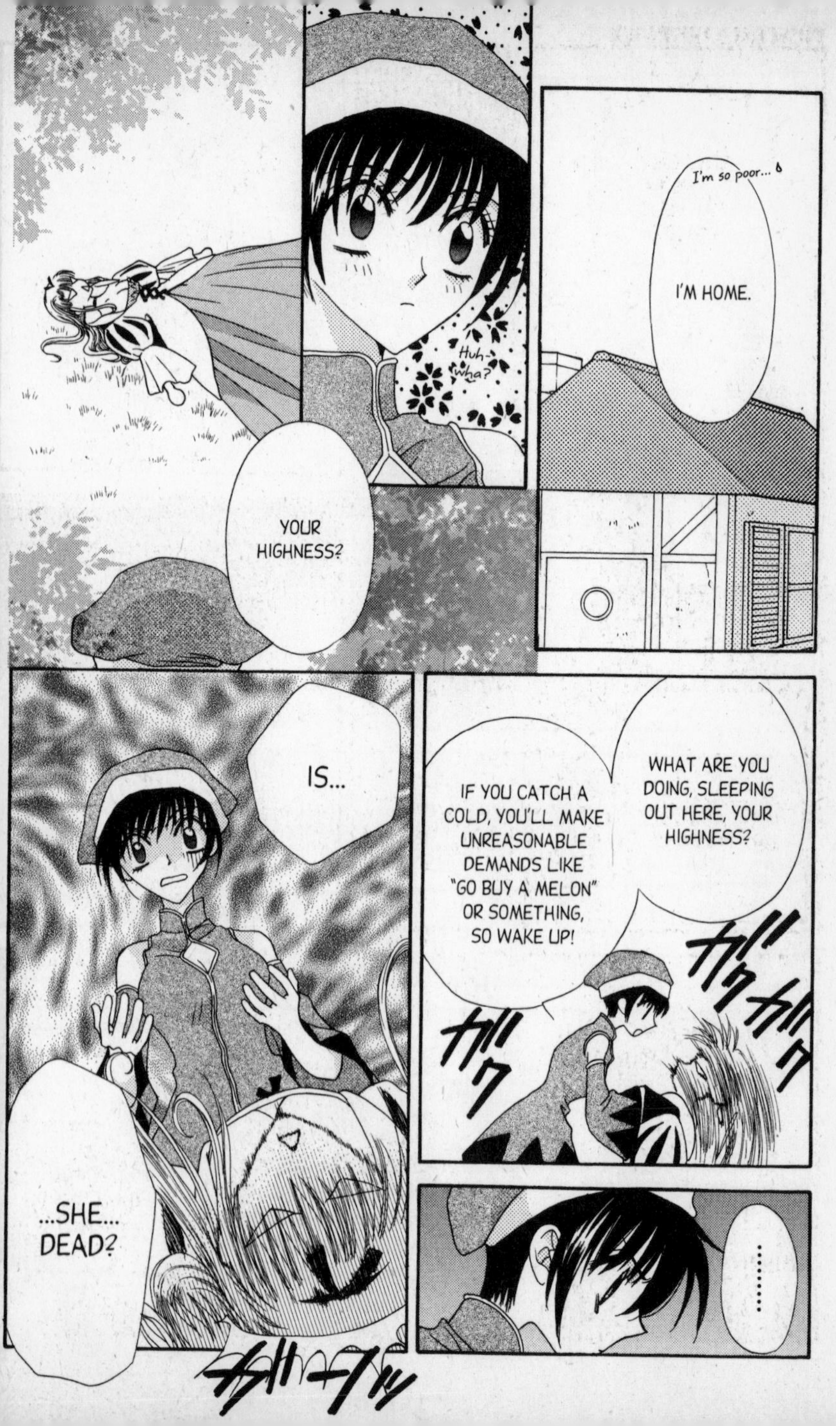
I'm so poor...
I'M HOME.
Huh-wha?
YOUR HIGHNESS?
WHAT ARE YOU DOING, SLEEPING OUT HERE, YOUR HIGHNESS?
IF YOU CATCH A COLD, YOU'LL MAKE UNREASONABLE DEMANDS LIKE "GO BUY A MELON" OR SOMETHING, SO WAKE UP!
....
IS...
...SHE... DEAD?

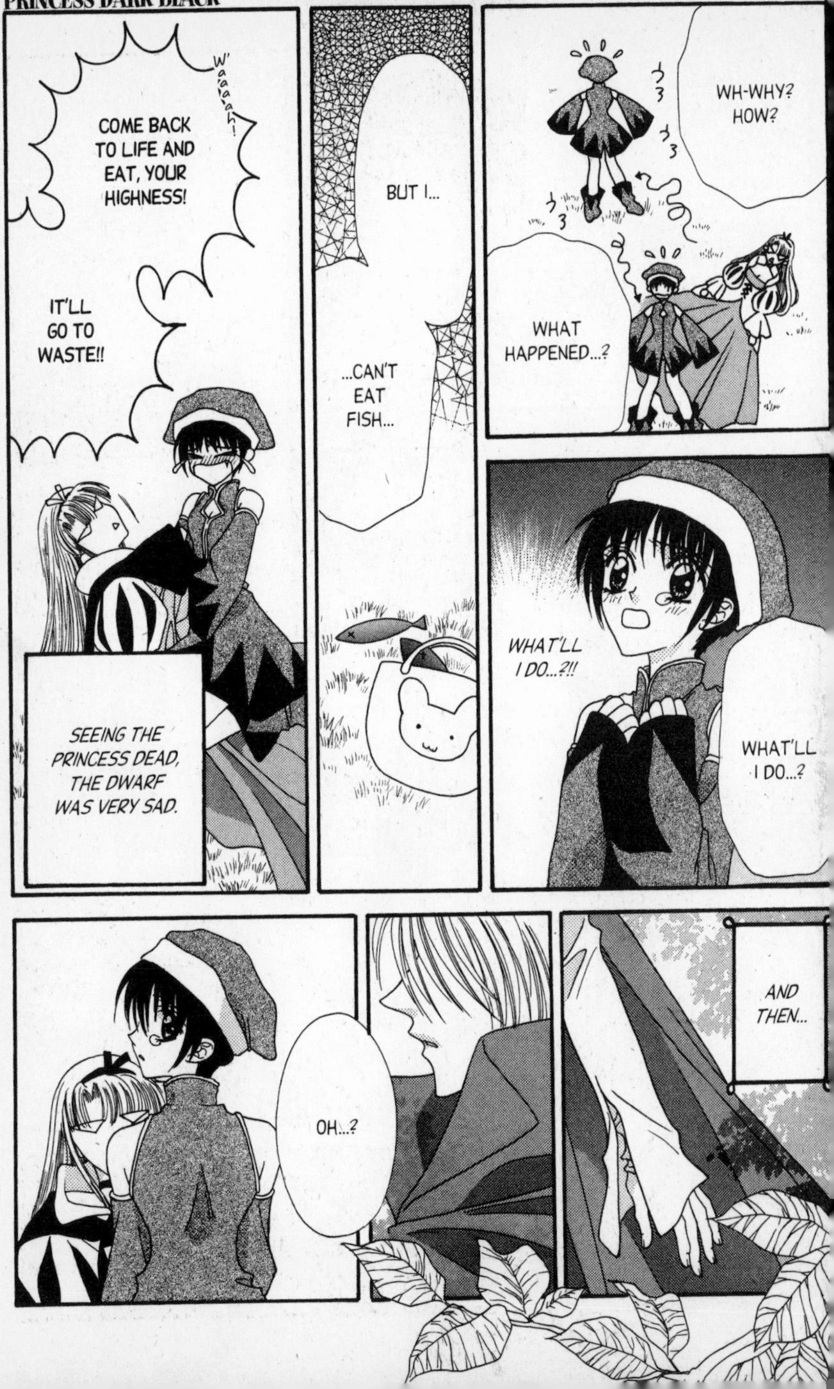
WH-WHY? HOW?
WHAT HAPPENED...?
WHAT'LL I DO...?
WHAT'LL I DO...?!!
BUT I...
...CAN'T EAT FISH...
W'aaaaah!
COME BACK TO LIFE AND EAT, YOUR HIGHNESS!
IT'LL GO TO WASTE!!
SEEING THE PRINCESS DEAD, THE DWARF WAS VERY SAD.
AND THEN...
OH...?

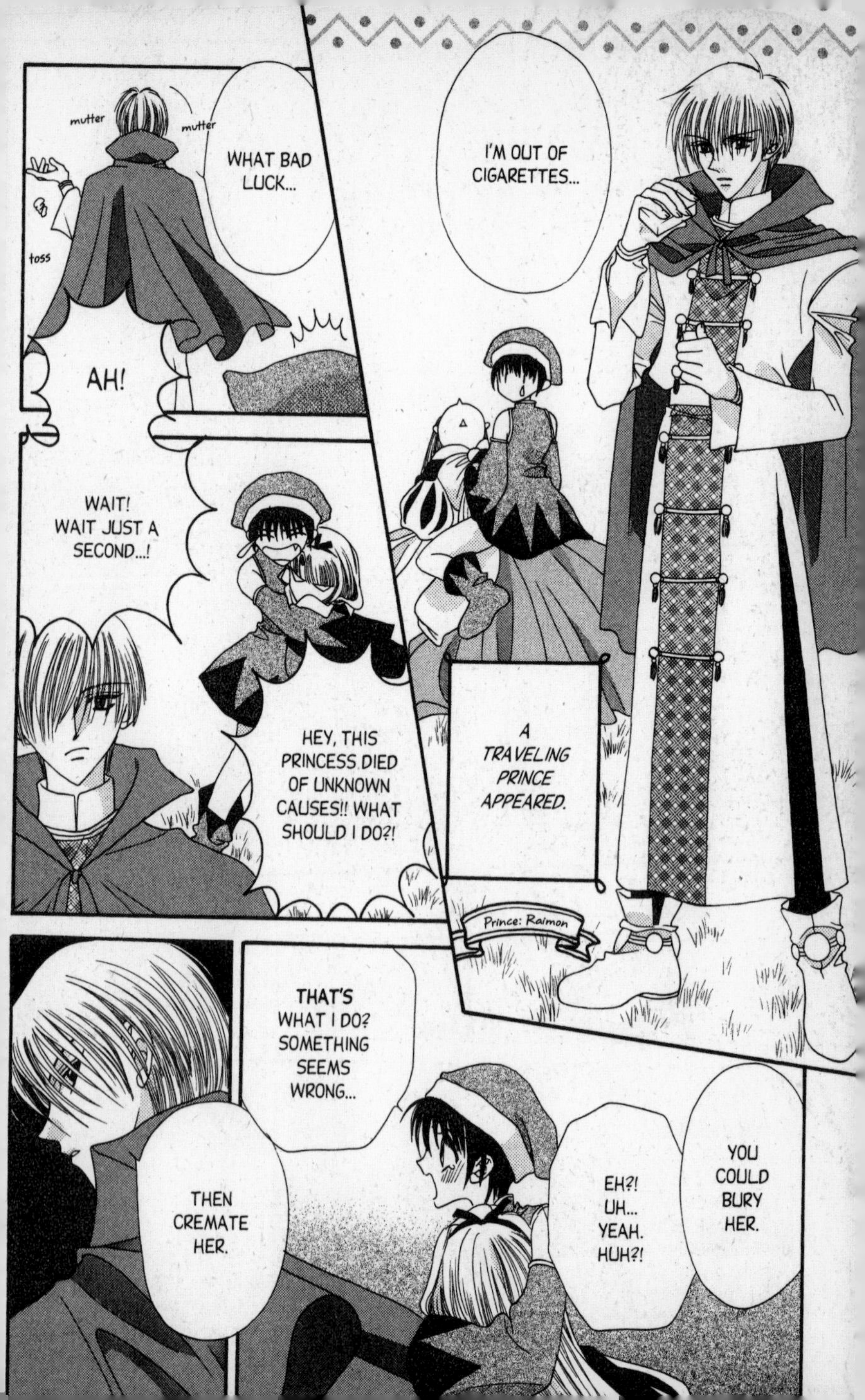
I'M OUT OF CIGARETTES...
A TRAVELING PRINCE APPEARED.
Prince: Raimon
mutter
mutter
WHAT BAD LUCK...
toss
AH!
WAIT! WAIT JUST A SECOND...!
HEY, THIS PRINCESS DIED OF UNKNOWN CAUSES!! WHAT SHOULD I DO?!
YOU COULD BURY HER.
EH?! UH... YEAH. HUH?!
THAT'S WHAT I DO? SOMETHING SEEMS WRONG...
THEN CREMATE HER.

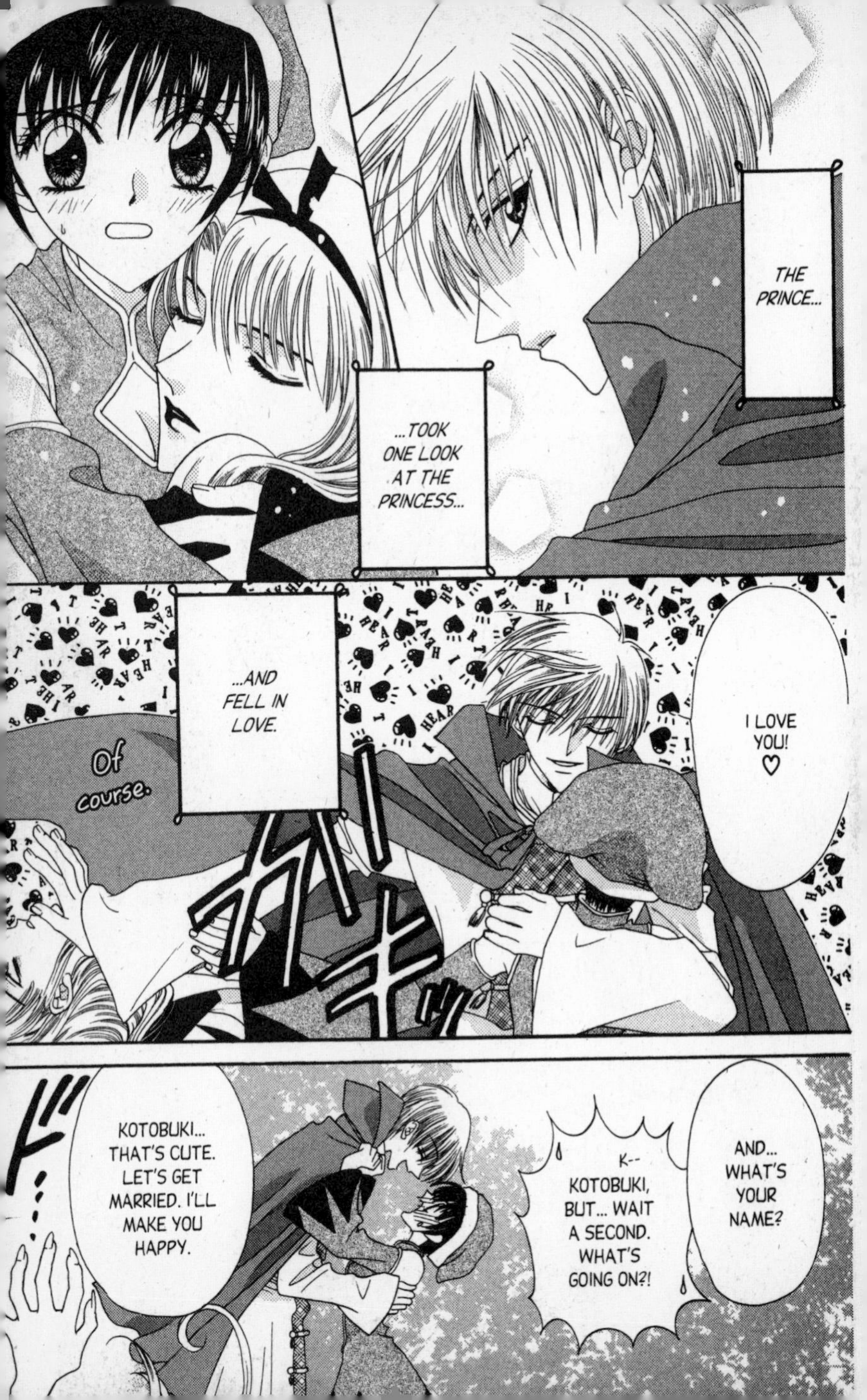
THE PRINCE...
...TOOK ONE LOOK AT THE PRINCESS...
I LOVE YOU! ♡
...AND FELL IN LOVE.
Of course.
AND... WHAT'S YOUR NAME?
K-- KOTOBUKI, BUT... WAIT A SECOND. WHAT'S GOING ON?!
KOTOBUKI... THAT'S CUTE. LET'S GET MARRIED. I'LL MAKE YOU HAPPY.

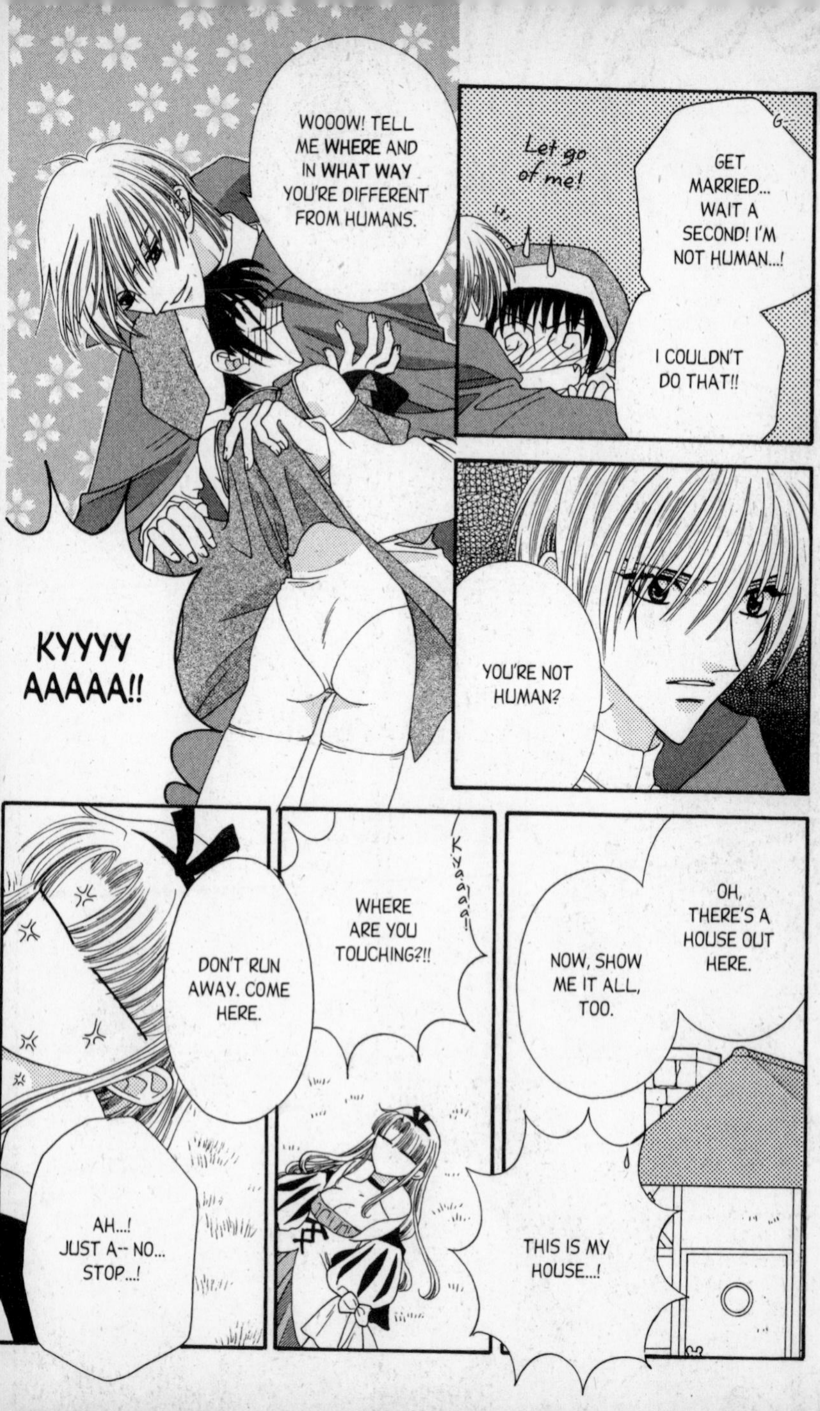
G--
GET MARRIED... WAIT A SECOND! I'M NOT HUMAN...!
Let go of me!
I COULDN'T DO THAT!!
YOU'RE NOT HUMAN?
WOOOW! TELL ME WHERE AND IN WHAT WAY YOU'RE DIFFERENT FROM HUMANS.
KYYYY AAAAA!!
OH, THERE'S A HOUSE OUT HERE.
NOW, SHOW ME IT ALL, TOO.
THIS IS MY HOUSE...!
Kyaaaa!
WHERE ARE YOU TOUCHING?!!
DON'T RUN AWAY. COME HERE.
AH...! JUST A-- NO... STOP...!

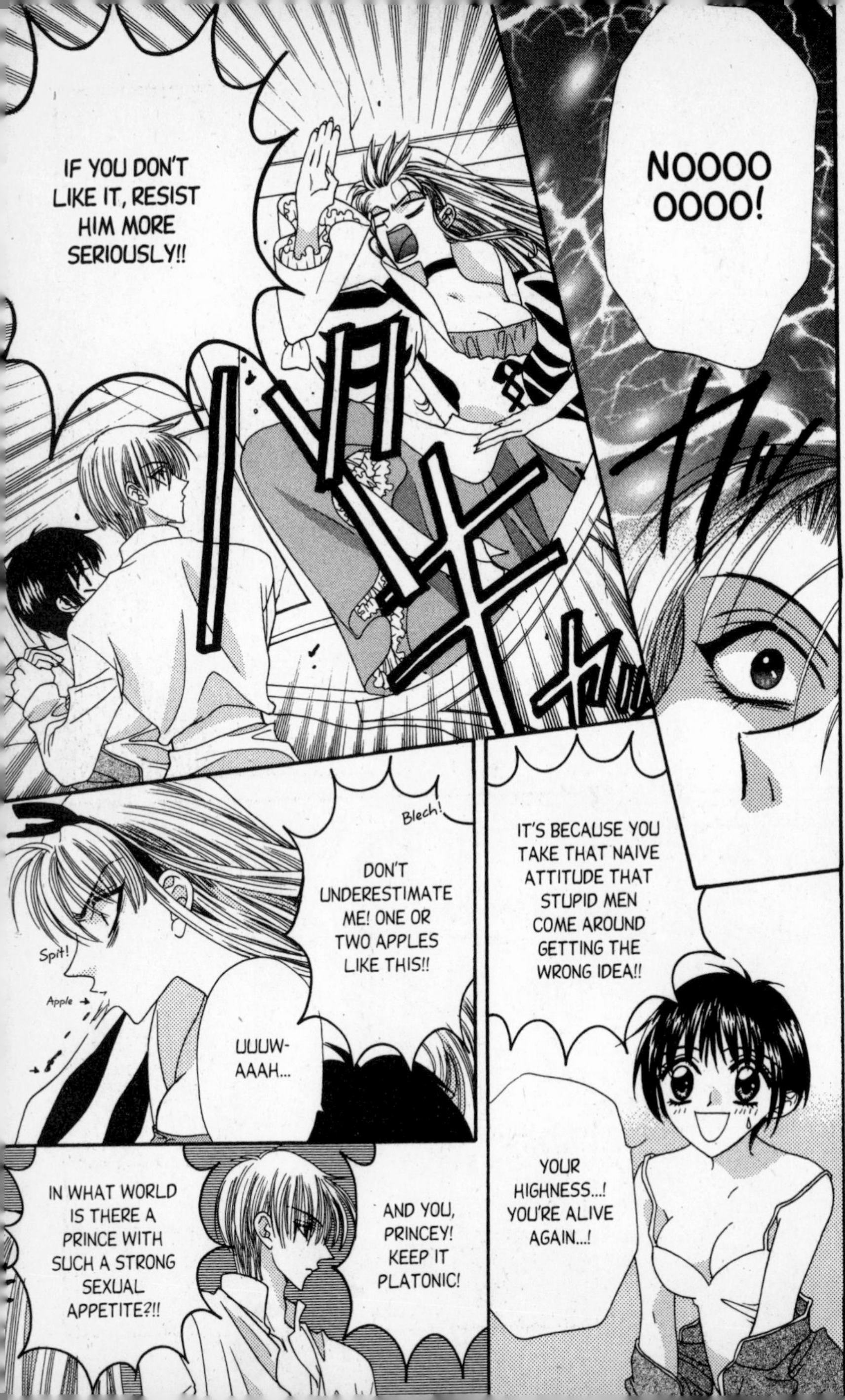
NOOOO OOOO!
IF YOU DON'T LIKE IT, RESIST HIM MORE SERIOUSLY!!
IT'S BECAUSE YOU TAKE THAT NAIVE ATTITUDE THAT STUPID MEN COME AROUND GETTING THE WRONG IDEA!!
YOUR HIGHNESS...! YOU'RE ALIVE AGAIN...!
Blech!
DON'T UNDERESTIMATE ME! ONE OR TWO APPLES LIKE THIS!!
UUUW-AAAH...
Spit!
Apple →
AND YOU, PRINCEY! KEEP IT PLATONIC!
IN WHAT WORLD IS THERE A PRINCE WITH SUCH A STRONG SEXUAL APPETITE?!!

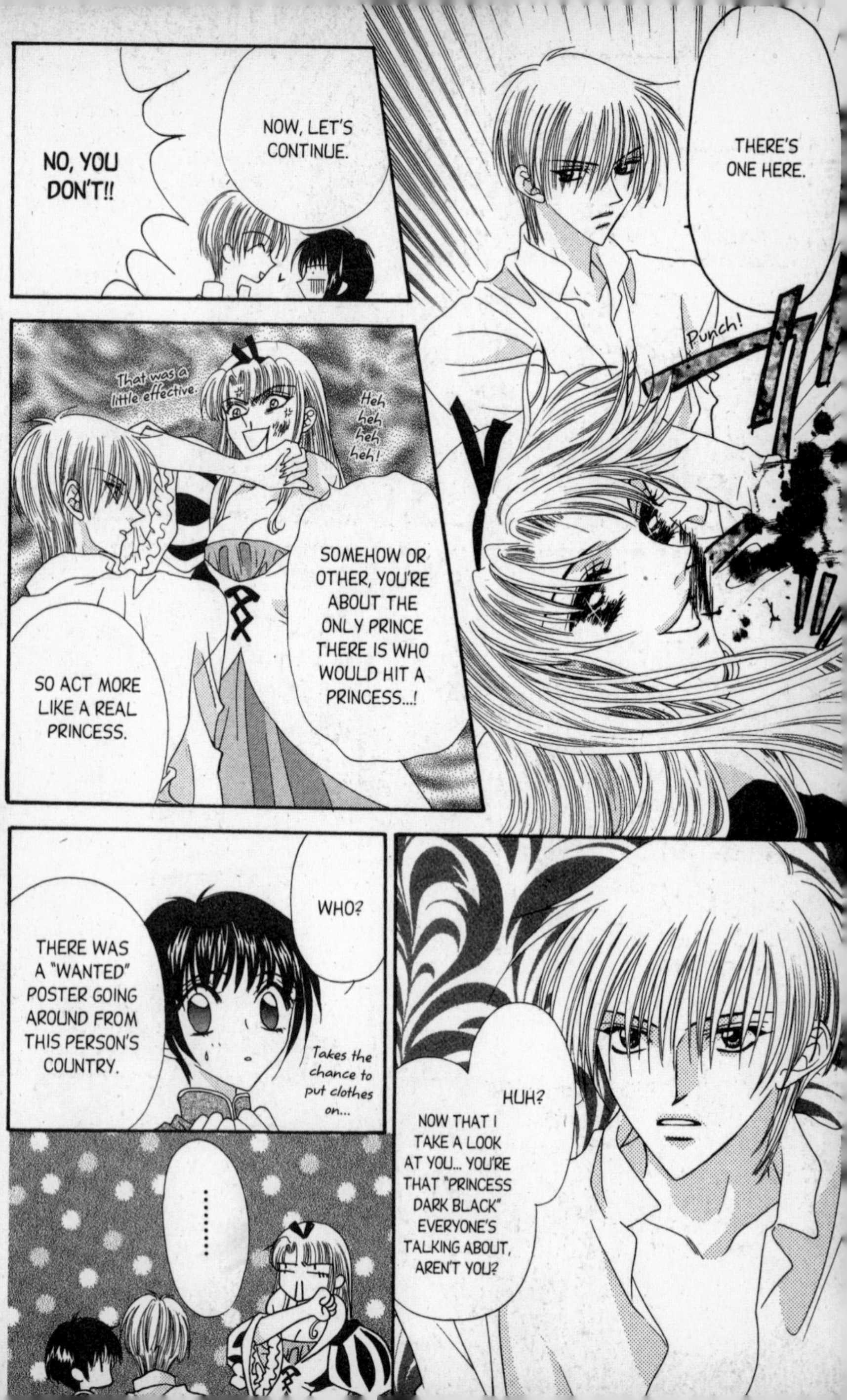
THERE'S ONE HERE.
Punch!
NOW, LET'S CONTINUE.
NO, YOU DON'T!!
That was a little effective.
Heh heh heh heh!
SOMEHOW OR OTHER, YOU'RE ABOUT THE ONLY PRINCE THERE IS WHO WOULD HIT A PRINCESS...!
SO ACT MORE LIKE A REAL PRINCESS.
HUH?
NOW THAT I TAKE A LOOK AT YOU... YOU'RE THAT "PRINCESS DARK BLACK" EVERYONE'S TALKING ABOUT, AREN'T YOU?
WHO?
THERE WAS A "WANTED" POSTER GOING AROUND FROM THIS PERSON'S COUNTRY.
Takes the chance to put clothes on...
....

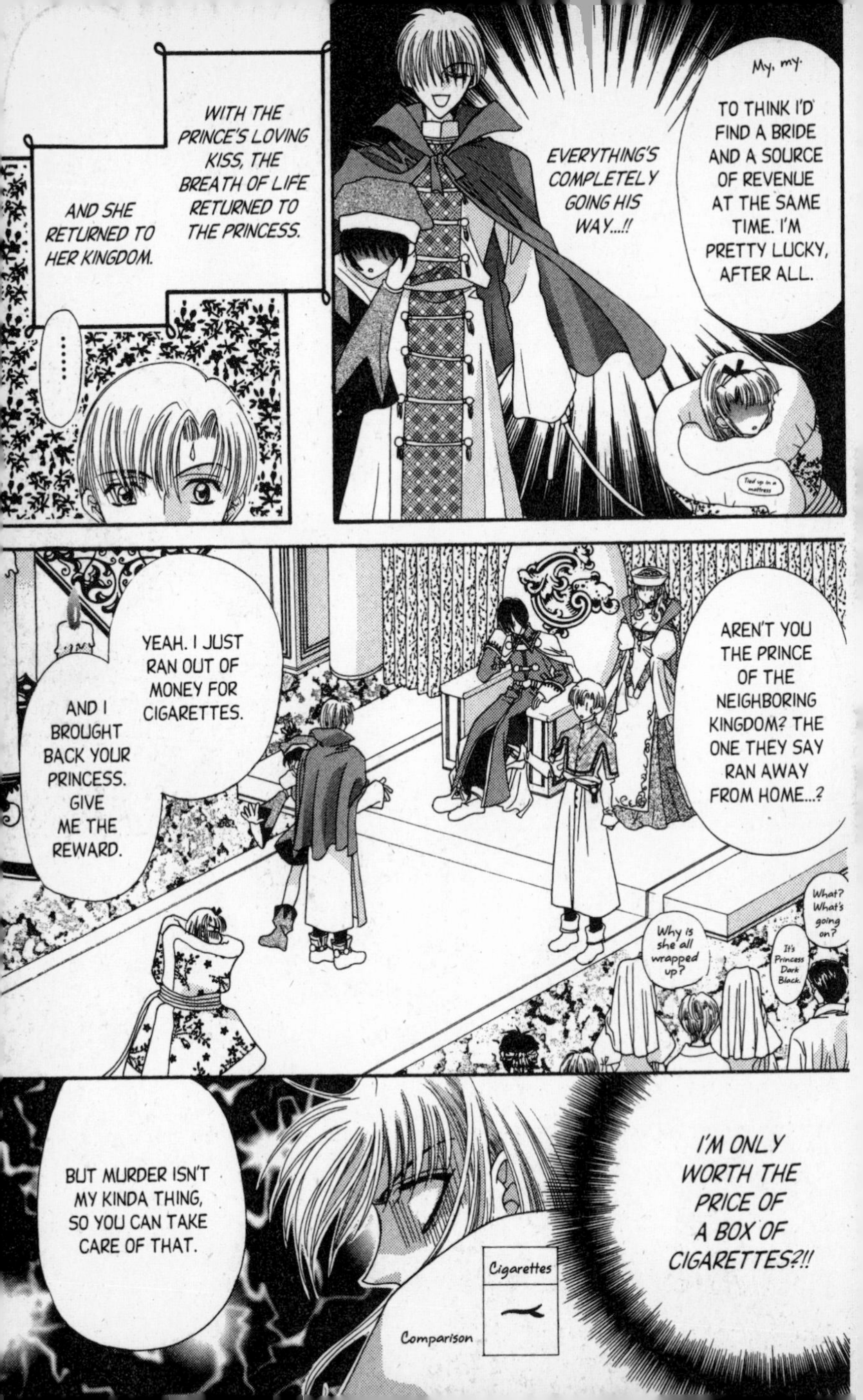
My, my.
TO THINK I'D FIND A BRIDE AND A SOURCE OF REVENUE AT THE SAME TIME. I'M PRETTY LUCKY, AFTER ALL.
EVERYTHING'S COMPLETELY GOING HIS WAY...!!
Tied up in a mattress
WITH THE PRINCE'S LOVING KISS, THE BREATH OF LIFE RETURNED TO THE PRINCESS.
AND SHE RETURNED TO HER KINGDOM.
......
AREN'T YOU THE PRINCE OF THE NEIGHBORING KINGDOM? THE ONE THEY SAY RAN AWAY FROM HOME...?
What? What's going on?
It's Princess Dark Black.
Why is she all wrapped up?
YEAH. I JUST RAN OUT OF MONEY FOR CIGARETTES.
AND I BROUGHT BACK YOUR PRINCESS. GIVE ME THE REWARD.
BUT MURDER ISN'T MY KINDA THING, SO YOU CAN TAKE CARE OF THAT.
I'M ONLY WORTH THE PRICE OF A BOX OF CIGARETTES?!!
Cigarettes
Comparison

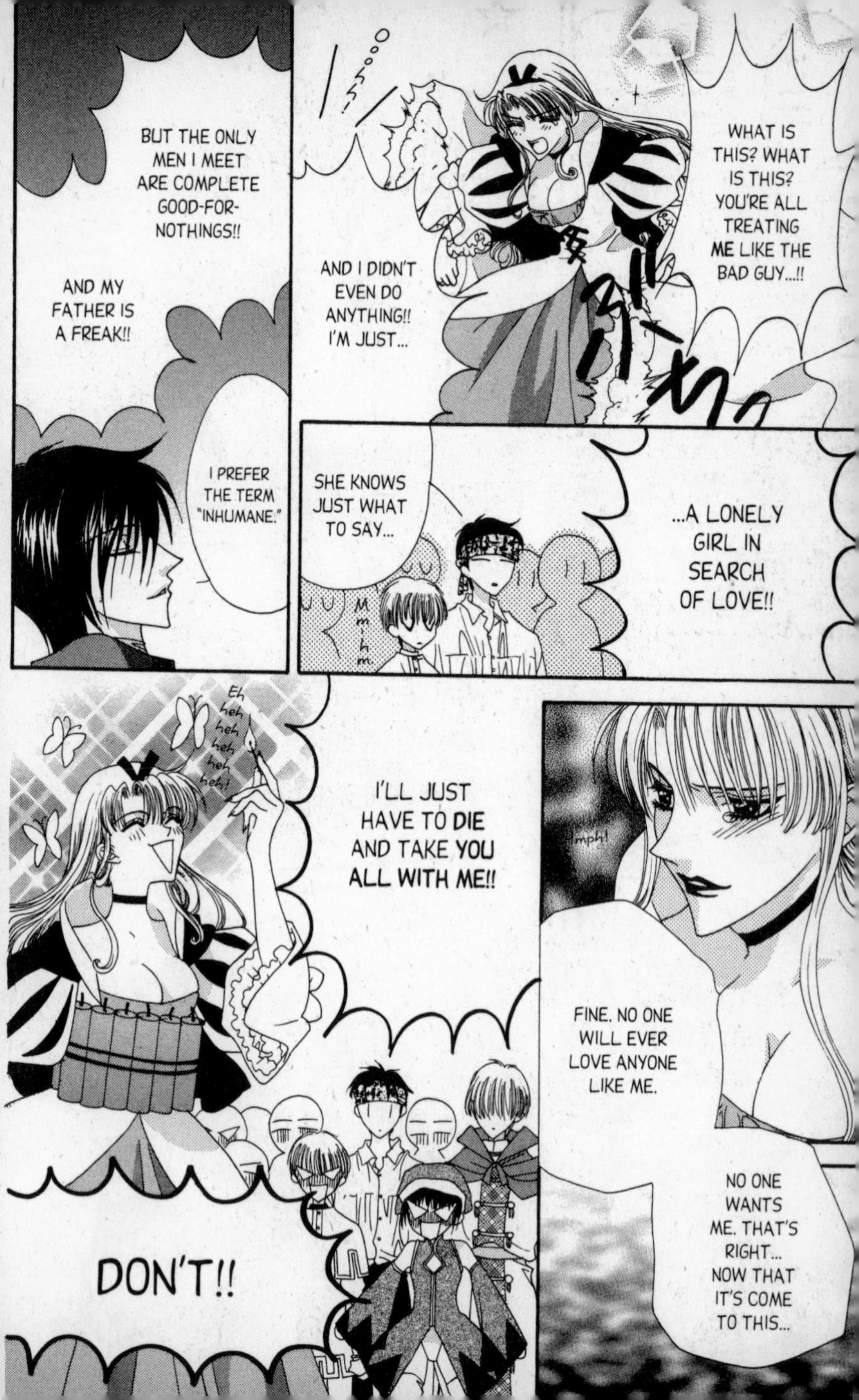
WHAT IS THIS? WHAT IS THIS? YOU'RE ALL TREATING ME LIKE THE BAD GUY...!!
AND I DIDN'T EVEN DO ANYTHING!! I'M JUST...
...A LONELY GIRL IN SEARCH OF LOVE!!
SHE KNOWS JUST WHAT TO SAY...
Mmhm
BUT THE ONLY MEN I MEET ARE COMPLETE GOOD-FOR-NOTHINGS!!
AND MY FATHER IS A FREAK!!
I PREFER THE TERM "INHUMANE."
Hmph!
FINE. NO ONE WILL EVER LOVE ANYONE LIKE ME.
NO ONE WANTS ME. THAT'S RIGHT... NOW THAT IT'S COME TO THIS...
Eh heh heh heh heh heh!
I'LL JUST HAVE TO DIE AND TAKE YOU ALL WITH ME!!
DON'T!!

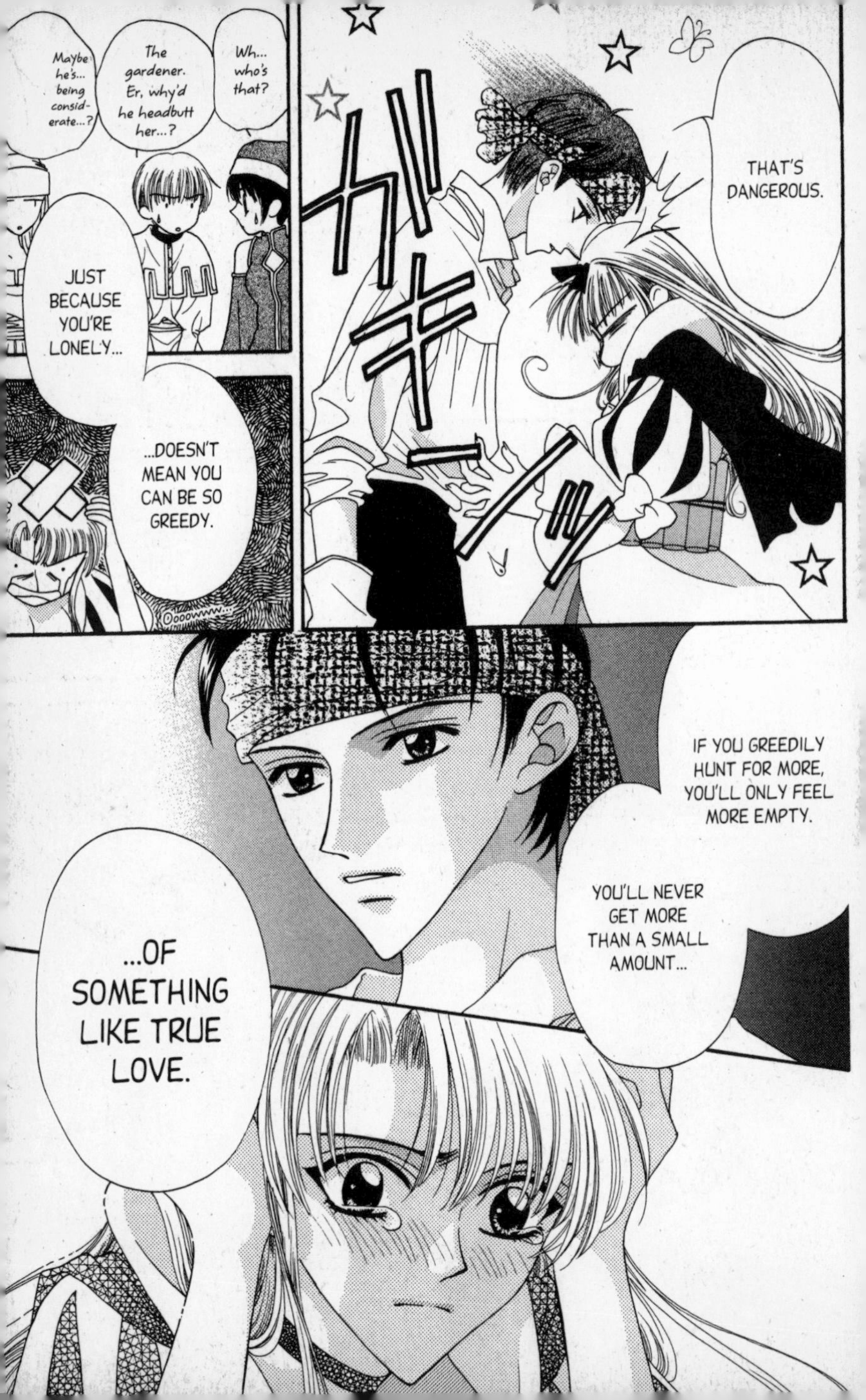
THAT'S DANGEROUS.
Wh... who's that?
The gardener. Er, why'd he headbutt her...?
Maybe he's... being consid-erate...?
JUST BECAUSE YOU'RE LONELY...
...DOESN'T MEAN YOU CAN BE SO GREEDY.
Oooowww...
IF YOU GREEDILY HUNT FOR MORE, YOU'LL ONLY FEEL MORE EMPTY.
YOU'LL NEVER GET MORE THAN A SMALL AMOUNT...
...OF SOMETHING LIKE TRUE LOVE.

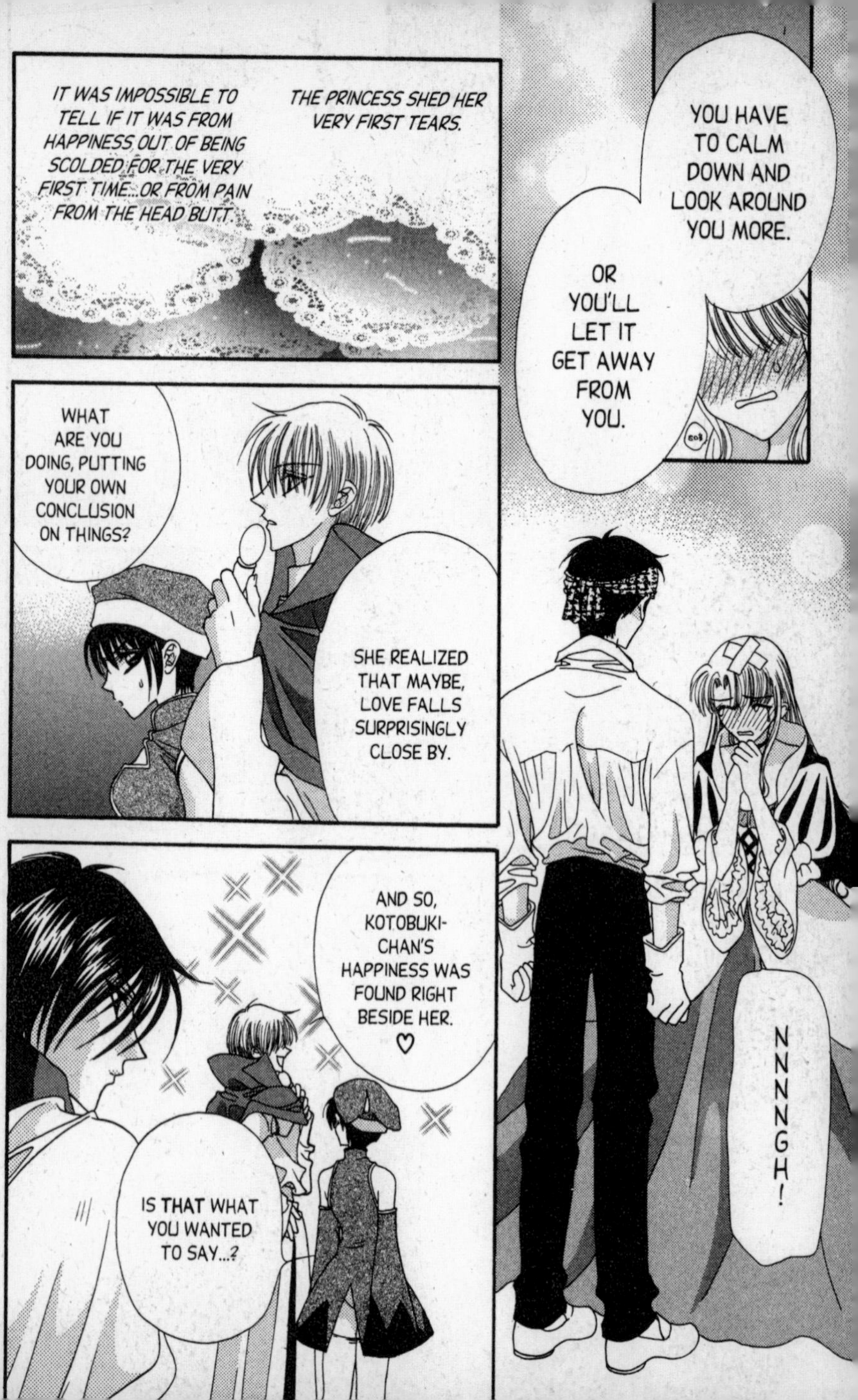
YOU HAVE TO CALM DOWN AND LOOK AROUND YOU MORE.
OR YOU'LL LET IT GET AWAY FROM YOU.
NNNNGH!
THE PRINCESS SHED HER VERY FIRST TEARS.
IT WAS IMPOSSIBLE TO TELL IF IT WAS FROM HAPPINESS OUT OF BEING SCOLDED FOR THE VERY FIRST TIME...OR FROM PAIN FROM THE HEAD BUTT.
SHE REALIZED THAT MAYBE, LOVE FALLS SURPRISINGLY CLOSE BY.
WHAT ARE YOU DOING, PUTTING YOUR OWN CONCLUSION ON THINGS?
AND SO, KOTOBUKI-CHAN'S HAPPINESS WAS FOUND RIGHT BESIDE HER. ♡
IS THAT WHAT YOU WANTED TO SAY...?

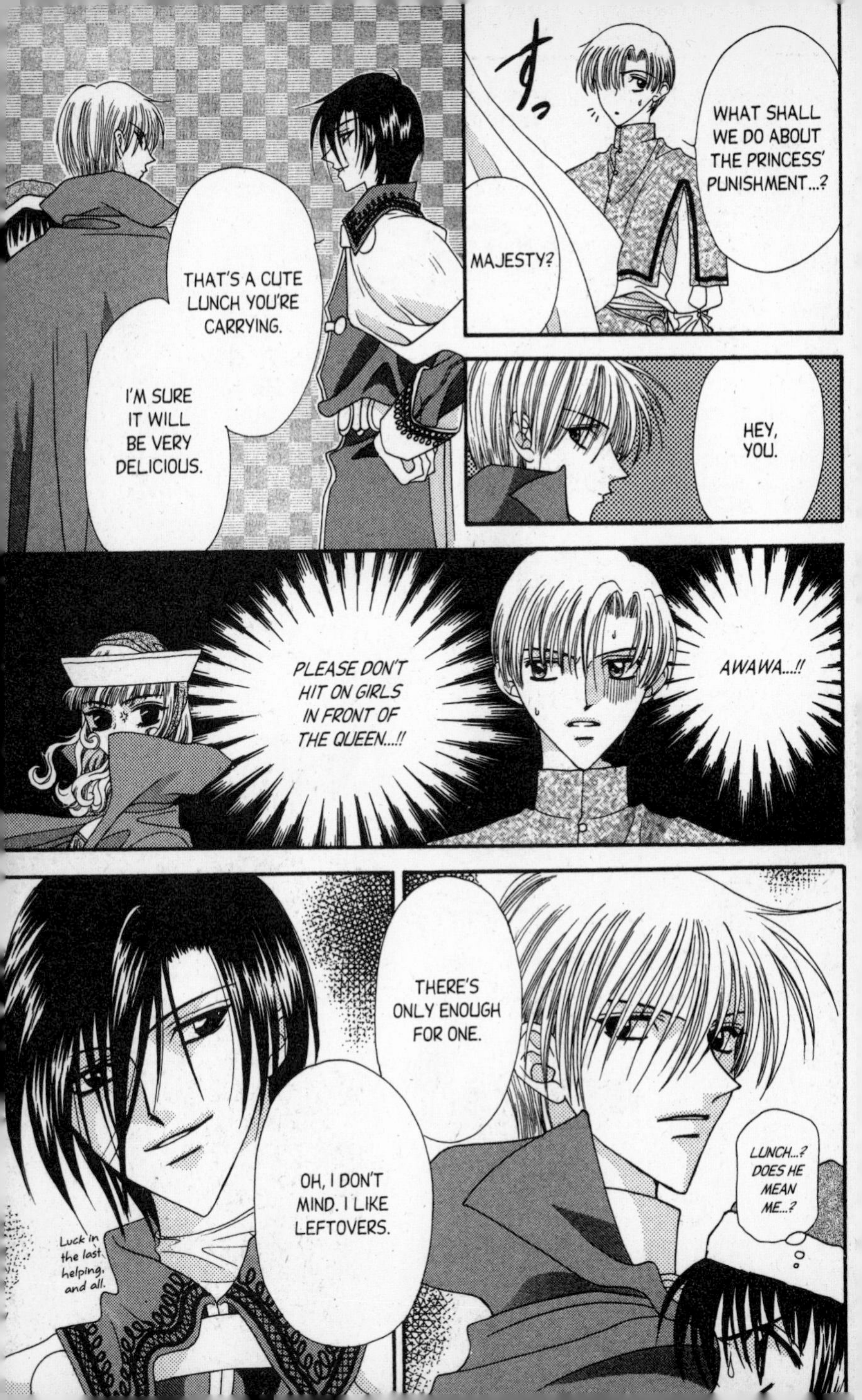
すっ
WHAT SHALL WE DO ABOUT THE PRINCESS' PUNISHMENT...?
MAJESTY?
HEY, YOU.
THAT'S A CUTE LUNCH YOU'RE CARRYING.
I'M SURE IT WILL BE VERY DELICIOUS.
AWAWA...!!
PLEASE DON'T HIT ON GIRLS IN FRONT OF THE QUEEN...!!
THERE'S ONLY ENOUGH FOR ONE.
LUNCH...? DOES HE MEAN ME...?
OH, I DON'T MIND. I LIKE LEFTOVERS.
Luck in the last helping, and all.

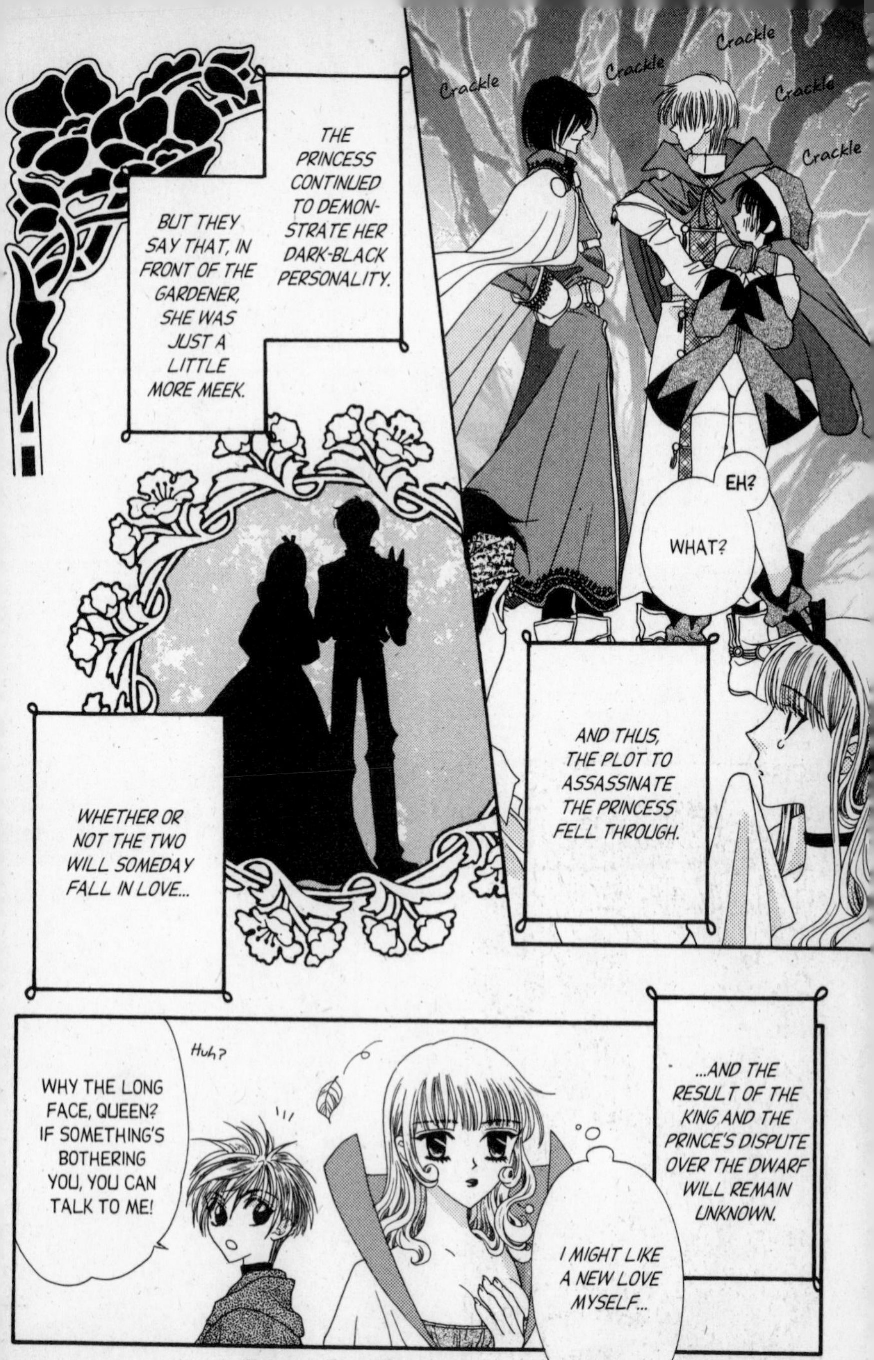
Crackle
Crackle
Crackle
Crackle
Crackle
EH?
WHAT?
THE PRINCESS CONTINUED TO DEMON-STRATE HER DARK-BLACK PERSONALITY.
BUT THEY SAY THAT, IN FRONT OF THE GARDENER, SHE WAS JUST A LITTLE MORE MEEK.
AND THUS, THE PLOT TO ASSASSINATE THE PRINCESS FELL THROUGH.
WHETHER OR NOT THE TWO WILL SOMEDAY FALL IN LOVE...
...AND THE RESULT OF THE KING AND THE PRINCE'S DISPUTE OVER THE DWARF WILL REMAIN UNKNOWN.
I MIGHT LIKE A NEW LOVE MYSELF...
Huh?
WHY THE LONG FACE, QUEEN? IF SOMETHING'S BOTHERING YOU, YOU CAN TALK TO ME!

Princess Dark Black / End

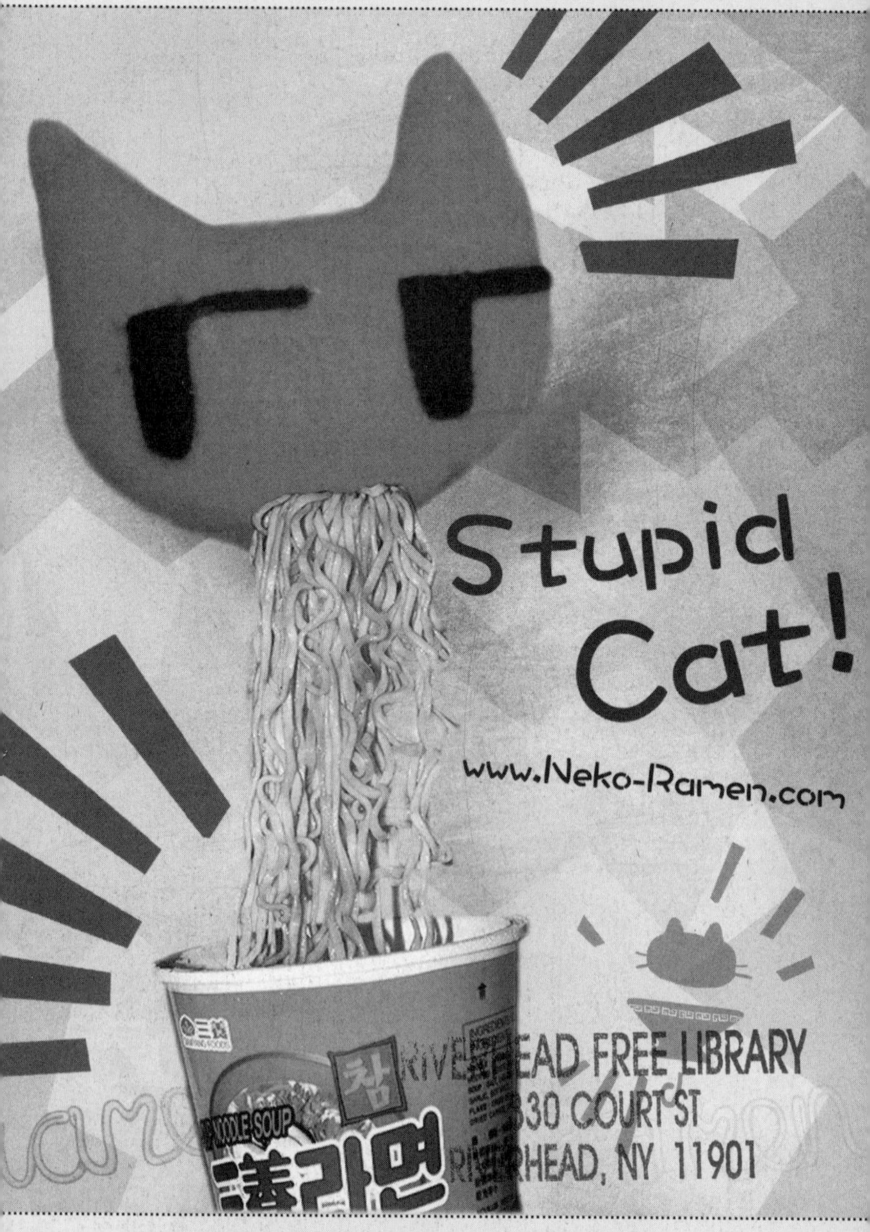
Stupid Cat!
www.Neko-Ramen.com

STOP!

This is the back of the book.
You wouldn't want to spoil a great ending!

This book is printed "manga-style," in the authentic Japanese right-to-left format. Since none of the artwork has been flipped or altered, readers get to experience the story just as the creator intended. You've been asking for it, so TOKYOPOP® delivered: authentic, hot-off-the-press, and far more fun!

1
2
3
4
5
6
7
8
9
10

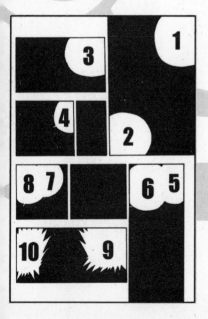

DIRECTIONS

If this is your first time reading manga-style, here's a quick guide to help you understand how it works.

It's easy... just start in the top right panel and follow the numbers. Have fun, and look for more 100% authentic manga from TOKYOPOP®!

THE MANGA REVOLUTION • LEADING THE MANGA REVOLUTION • LEADING
漫画革命

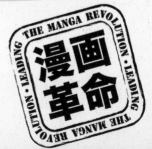

The second epic trilogy continues!

Princess Ai:
The Prism of Midnight Dawn

Ai fights to escape the clutches of her mysterious and malevolent captors, not knowing whether Kent, left behind on the Other Side, is even still alive. A frantic rescue mission commences, and in the end, even Ai's magical voice may not be enough to protect her from the trials of the Black Forest.

Dark secrets are revealed, and Ai must use all her strength and courage to face off against the new threat to Ai-Land. But will she ever see Kent again...?

"A very intriguing read that will satisfy old fans and create new fans, too."
– Bookloons